SKILLS & TRAINING directory

FOURTH EDITION

CONSULTANT EDITOR: **ADAM JOLLY**

The IM Skills and Training Handbook is based upon *The Training & Enterprise directory*, published in nine annual editions from 1989 – 1997.

First published in 1999
This edition (Fourth) 2003

120 Pentonville Road
London N1 9JN
www.kogan-page.co.uk

British Library Cataloguing-in-Publication Data
ISBN 0 7494 4052 X
ISSN 1478-694X

Typeset by Milan Associates Limited, London
Printed and bound in Great Britain by Cambrian Printers Ltd, Aberystwyth, Wales

Contents

Part One: Skills and Training

Part 1

1.1 Working with Business

Bryan Sanderson, Chairman of the Learning and Skills Council, highlights how the organisation is working with business to support skills development, organisational performance and productivity.

I have always been a great believer in putting the horse before the cart – listening to customers to find out what they want and what they need rather than taking a prescriptive route and delivering a product that does not fit the bill.

The prosperity of businesses across England, along with that of their existing and future employees, is why we are here. The Learning and Skills Council (LSC) was created to fund and plan education and training for everyone over the age of 16 years in this country, other than those in university. In the two years since we were set up by government to take over the work of the former Training and Enterprise Councils and the Further Education Funding Council, we have done a lot of listening in order to identify, plan and fund the types of learning and training that will be of most benefit to individuals and employers.

We have embarked on the largest research programme of its kind ever undertaken in this country to find out what people think about the education and training they receive within colleges and in the workplace. During the five years of this survey of learners we will listen to the views of more than 110,000 people, allowing us to identify areas for phased improvement.

That process has been extended into the business arena. In March 2003, we launched the country's biggest employer survey, talking to representatives from 70,000 companies to find out what types of skills they need in order to thrive. Businesses must have a voice in determining their destinies; by finding out where skills gaps exist, why, and what is being done by companies to develop their workforces, we will be able to offer the types of training that best meets their needs.

We have been aware from the outset that there will be no 'one size fits all' solution. That is why the LSC was created with a local and national structure, operating through a national office in Coventry and 47 local offices across England. This allows us to take fully into account local priorities when developing plans with partners to tailor teaching and training to the real needs of communities. After all, what's the point of training huge numbers of people in skills that are not required in an area while ignoring those where shortages are holding back the performance of local companies and the economies they help drive?

We were also acutely aware of the importance of involving business in what we do. That is why at least 40 per cent of all representatives on our national and local councils are drawn from companies of various sizes and from numerous sectors. Each of our local councils has now prepared, in consultation with partner organisations, strategic plans that map the way forward for the areas they serve – identifying skills needs and education and training priorities. These plans have been fed in to our national workforce development strategy to improve the country's skills, from the basics of reading, writing and counting to the higher level technical and managerial skills required to improve international competitiveness.

It is not all about listening though. We have launched many initiatives in recent months to test the best ways of improving performance by offering practical support, guidance and financial assistance to companies that recognise that the skills of their people are essential to success. Neither is it all about talking: we are driving forward in a climate of real national change, where government policies and increased levels of funding reinforce the determination to put quality education and training, matched to the needs of business, at the heart of what we do in this country.

Practical support

We have achieved much to be proud of in 2002. Participation in further education by people aged between 16 and 18 years rose by almost 3.8 per cent during the period and we exceeded our target of improving the basic skills of 240,000 adults by almost 9000 places.

The *Centres of Vocational Excellence* programme, which we began in our first year, moved forward at pace. Its aim is to establish specialist centres of excellence in colleges and training companies throughout the country in order to meet the needs of employers and address skills gaps. So far, approximately 200 colleges and work-based training providers are involved in the programme and we are well on track to increase that number to 400 by 2006.

It is estimated that of the 7 million adults in England who have difficulty with reading, writing and basic maths, around half are in work and that most of these are in low skilled, short-term employment. Latest figures indicate that a lack of basic skills in the workplace costs businesses in this country £4.8 billion a year. With this in mind, we have taken the lead in a £170 million employer training pilot project; this is operating in six areas of the country and is expected to cover around a quarter of LSC areas from September 2003. This encourages employers to give low skilled staff time off work to take free education and training courses.

The pilot schemes offer small firms and organisations between 110 per cent and 150 per cent of the average wage costs of the staff they allow time off to train. We aim to support around 3000 companies and up to 25,000 workers who lack basic skills or vocational qualifications at level 2 – roughly equivalent to a GCSE level. The effectiveness of these pilots will be evaluated before a decision is made on whether they should be rolled out across the country.

We also continued to promote modern apprenticeships. We are keen that more companies embrace the programme by employing young people who learn vocational skills while at work, ensuring they are given the specific training individual businesses require. The LSC is providing financial and training support to businesses employing modern apprenticeships in more than 80 industry sectors. By 2004, the government and LSC want approximately 175,000 people aged between 16 and 21 years to enter the modern apprenticeship programme each year.

The LSC and Business Link network is now delivering the £30 million Government Small Firms Initiative, which offers companies employing between five and 49 people up to £1,250 of free advice and support to allow them to work towards the Investors in People standard. Investors in People can help small companies recruit and retain skilled and motivated staff, increase customer satisfaction and improve their performance and competitiveness.

These are just a few of the headlines. Much more has been achieved both nationally and locally but we are acutely aware that we have only just scratched the surface. Much more still needs to be done as we embark on a long journey to fundamentally change attitudes to the importance of learning and training.

Priorities in 2003

The LSC's priorities this year centre on closing skills gaps and increasing participation in education and training. We want 80 per cent of all 16–18-year olds to be in some form of structured learning by 2004 and have a target of raising the literacy and numeracy standards of 750,000 adults during the same period.

We will continue to work with training and employers' organisations to address specific skills shortages and will help align the provision of further education with the needs of employers and the demand for skills in the future. We will also continue to listen, to learn and respond to the needs of companies both large and small and provide practical assistance to help improve their performance and that of the country as a whole.

Bryan Sanderson, Learning and Skills Council

The Learning and Skills Council (LSC) is responsible for all post-16 education and training outside of the university sector. This includes the planning and funding of further education colleges, school sixth forms, work-based training for young people, workforce development, adult and community learning, information, advice and guidance for adults and education business links. To find out more about the LSC and initiatives highlighted, visit www.lsc.gov.uk. For more information on the Small Firms Initiative and Investors in People, contact Business Link on 0845 5600 9006. To learn more about modern apprenticeships call the employer helpline on 0800 150 400.

1.2 The Approach of High Performance Work Organisations to Training

Investment Society of British Aerospace Companies (SBAC)

Investing in human capital is central to growth. Studies conducted by the manufacturing sectors in the UK and USA have found that establishments using a greater number of innovative HR practices had higher levels of value-added per employee, with the difference in productivity as high as 34 per cent.

> 'The right treatment of people – human capital – is a key driver for many businesses. A company, which loses its people, can lose its value overnight. Investors need to know this value, human capital, is secure – and is being maximised in the same way as its other assets – its plant and its machinery'
>
> —Right Honourable Patricia Hewitt, Secretary of State for Trade and Industry Speech to Cambridge Law Faculty, 5th July 2002.

Research in the UK aerospace industry has shown that enterprises that can be described as High Performing Work Organisations (HPWO) will tend to invest more heavily in the development of their human capital through training, exhibit the use of more innovative HR practices and out-perform others in the sector. (The SBAC Human Capital Audit 2002)

Similar studies in other manufacturing sectors such as steel, textiles and medical electronic instruments in the UK and USA have all found that establishments using a greater number of innovative HR practices had higher levels of value-added per employee, with the difference in productivity as high as 34 per cent.

These studies show that investing in human capital is central to successful organisational performance, and investment analysts and finance professionals increasingly recognise this. Government, too, is fully aware of the important role that people management plays and is considering making it a requirement that firms include the development of human assets in their annual reports.

What is a HPWO?

High Performance Work Organisations comprise complementary sets of work practices that create greater employee involvement and encourage the acquisition and deployment of skills. Typically they give workers much greater autonomy, thus transforming organisational routines and improving overall performance.

A HPWO consists of three distinct but inter-related groups of practices:

1 High involvement practices, which create greater opportunities for employee involvement, such as:
  - Semi-autonomous team working
  - Continuous improvement teams
  - Responsibility for own work quality

– Job rotation
– Information sharing programmes
– Briefing groups

2 Human resource practices, which help build skills levels, motivation and ability, such as:

– Appraisal
– Personal development plans
– Performance based rewards (skill and performance related pay)
– High levels of training on and off-the-job
– Sophisticated recruitment techniques
– Broad job grading structures

3 Employee relations practices, which can help build trust, loyalty and identity with the organisation, including:

– Harmonised terms and conditions of employment (pensions, leave etc)
– Formal grievance procedures (sex, race discrimination etc)
– Induction programmes
– Regular social gatherings for employees
– Same canteen and eating arrangements

The relationships between a HPWO, employee performance and organisational effectiveness are given in Figure 1.

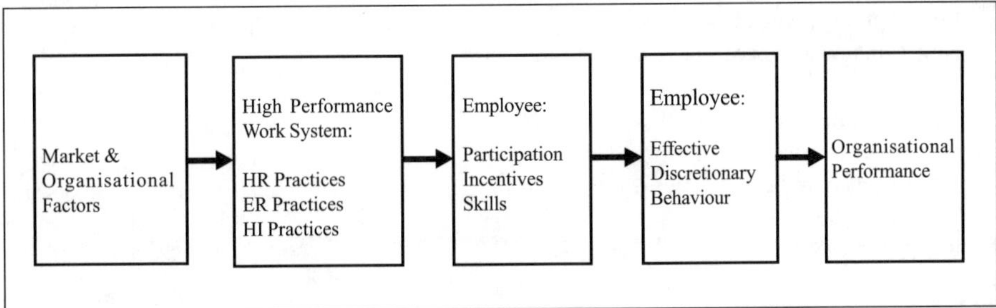

Figure 1: Model of a High Performance Work System

How widespread are HPWOs in aerospace?

Overall, the picture regarding high performance work practices in the aerospace industry is one of slow but steady diffusion.

However, there is still a long way to go before the full range of high performance work practices which make up a HPWO is comprehensively adopted by the UK aerospace industry. Taking all the high performance practices together for 2002 (a possible 34 practices in total), we found that only 11 per cent of establishments use at least two-thirds of them, and 45 per cent use less than half.

Does HPWO really make a difference?

There is an implicit belief that firms which adopt high performance work practices will as a matter of course experience improvements in organisational effectiveness. But what aspects of performance do these practices have an impact on, and how do we measure them? The SBAC Human Capital Audit used three types of performance measure:

- Measures to assess the *financial* performance, including profit, value-added and sales per employee.
- Measures of *operational* efficiency, including on-time delivery rates, rework rates and the total number of stock turns over a year.
- *Employee* measures from labour costs as a percentage of total operating costs to absence and employee turnover rates.

Industry mean and median performance against these measures for 2002 are shown in the table below:

Table 1: Performance Measure 2002

Measures	**2002**	
	Mean	**Median**
Financial:		
Value-added per employee (£)	55,442	50,000
Profit per employee (£)	9,040	5,882
New capital equipment spend as % of turnover(%)	6	4
Operational:		
On-time delivery (%)	84	90
Stock turns (number)	8	5
Scrap rate (%)	4	2
Rework rate (%)	5	2
Labour:		
Employee turnover (%)	6	5
Employee absence (%)	4	3
Labour costs as % of total *operating* costs(%)	44	41

Do certain practices have more impact on performance than others? This is an important question for firms considering investing in new workplace practices. Certainly, giving people a stake in the business was particularly effective. Use of profit sharing and of share ownership schemes in 1997 correlated respectively with higher sales per employee and higher value-added per employee in 2002. But we also found that greater provision of information to employees - through, for example, briefing groups - was associated with higher levels of profit per employee. And lastly, employee turnover was lower where firms gave employees more responsibility for the quality of their own work.

However, while these individual practices are important to focus on it needs to be emphasised that they should be seen as part of a wider, more integrated set of practices that constitute a HPWO.

Investing in Human Capital: Training

In a knowledge-intensive and increasingly global industry such as aerospace, investment in training and development is crucial in developing specialist skills and absorbing new knowledge and perspectives.

The SBAC Human Capital Audit 2002 revealed a not entirely encouraging picture. It used two measures to assess off-the-job training – expenditure and days per employee (see Table 2). The number of days devoted to training has only increased slightly over the last 5 years. Expenditure on training per employee has increased on average - from £220 in 1997 to £337 in 2002. The increase in average expenditure compared with the median expenditures suggests that some firms are spending considerably more on training than others.

Table 2: Investment in non-management training

	1997		1999		2002	
	Mean	Median	Mean	Median	Mean	Median
Expenditure per non-mgmt employee (£)	220	132	286	179	337	161
Days training (off-the-job)	4	2	5	3	4	3

Source: Templeton College

Training and the HPWO

Through greater use of high performance work practices such as team-working, multi-skilling and information sharing, the workplace itself has become an important place of learning. The distinction between technical knowledge and production skill is breaking down as workers use their knowledge to solve production problems. Instead of narrowly focusing on the job-in-hand, workers in high performance organisations are more aware of, and take responsibility for, the bigger picture.

This use of high performance practices is institutionalising learning in the workplace and potentially blurring the distinction between on- and off-the-job training. Significantly, our interviews in a number of aerospace firms revealed that an increasing amount of off-the-job training is actually now workplace-based, with organisations bringing in specialist training consultants to provide on-site learning and support.

But does more use of high performance practices therefore mean less investment in off-the-job training and development of front-line workers? Definitely not, according to our findings. Companies that use a greater number of high performance work practices are also investing more in off-the-job training. This is shown in Table 3, which provides expenditure on off-the-job training per employee from the three surveys, and, for 2002, gives training spend as a proportion of the wage bill.

Table 3: Training Expenditure for Non-Management Employees

High Performance Work Organisation	1997 Training spend per non-mgmt emp (£)	1999 Training spend per non-mgmt emp (£)	2002 Training spend per non-mgmt emp (£)	2002 Training spend as % of non-mgmt wage bill %
First quartile	169	231	167	0.9
Second quartile	220	241	225	1.9
Third quartile	226	308	583	2.5
Fourth quartile	250	369	432	2.3

We also found clear evidence that a worrying gap in investment in training is opening up between companies according to whether they are high or low use on the HPWO index. The gap in training expenditure between these two groups widened from 48 per cent in 1997 to 159 per cent in 2002. Those companies high on the index in 2002 devoted 2.6 times more of their total wage bill to training than the rest.

Our analysis has already shown that the greater use of high performance work practices pays off in terms of higher value-added and sales per employee. These additional findings suggest that an important factor in the HPWO is good provision of training and development.

Investors in People (IiP)

The number of aerospace companies that were accredited as Investors in People grew steadily over the three surveys. 37 per cent of firms were IiP accredited in 2002 compared to 26 per cent in 1999 and 19 per cent in 1997. In line with wider surveys of IiP, we found larger aerospace companies were more likely to be accredited: the median number of employees in IiP accredited firms was 200 in 2002, compared to 78 among the rest.

But how much more do IiP organisations actually invest in training and development? Table 4 compares training expenditure per employee in IiP and non-IiP aerospace organisations. Across the three surveys IiP companies spent much more on off-the-job training. In 2002, for example, IiP firms spent an average of £433 per head, compared to £278 for the rest. It is also illuminating to compare growth in expenditure on training among the two groups. In IiP companies, spending on training outstripped inflation between 1997 and 2002, growing by 72 per cent. For the remainder, it barely kept ahead at 31 per cent. Clearly, IiP accredited organisations, being generally bigger, have greater resources to spend on training. However, even after size was taken into account, Investors in People accreditation correlated significantly with greater spending on training. It is unclear whether there is a causal relationship between IiP accreditation and higher levels of expenditure.

Table 4: Investors in People and Training Expenditure for Non-Management Employees

IiP accredited	1997 Training spend per non-mgmt emp (£)	1999 Training spend per non-mgmt emp (£)	2002 Training spend per non-mgmt emp (£)
Yes	252	408	433
No	213	245	278

Investor in People organisations are also more likely to use high performance work practices, as shown in Table 5. In 2002, 60 per cent of the companies that made most use of HPWPs were members of Investors in People, compared to only 9 per cent of firms which made least use. A broadly similar pattern was evident in 1997 and 1999.

Table 5: Investors in People and High Performance Work Systems

High Performance Work Organisation	Percentage of firms with IiP		
	1997	1999	2002
First quartile	6	18	9
Second quartile	9	20	26
Third quartile	27	17	50
Fourth quartile	39	39	60

High investment in training does not, on its own, make an enterprise a High Performing Work Organisation but those enterprises that make greater use of the High Performing Work Practices and which exhibit superior business performance are likely to cite a high investment in human capital development through training as an important element of their success.

This is an abridged extract from High Performance Work Organisation in UK Aerospace, published by the Society of British Aerospace Companies (SBAC), 2002.

The SBAC is the UK's national aerospace trade association. Member companies have world-class capabilities and lead Europe in the breadth and depth of aerospace products, from airframes and engines to equipment and satellites. SBAC also organises the Farnborough International Exhibition & Flying Display.

For further information contact Jon Cook by e-mail at jon.cook@sbac.co.uk

1.3 The Adult Learning Inspectorate, Setting the Scene

For the first time in this country we have a single framework which brings together all elements of post-16 inspection.

The Adult Learning Inspectorate (ALI) was created on 1 April 2001 under the provisions of the Learning and Skills Act. The ALI's chief inspector is supported by 4 directors, 13 inspection managers, 140 full-time inspectors and 87 support staff. In addition, some 650 associate inspectors have been recruited. About half the ALI's full-time inspectors were recruited from the inspectorates of the former Training Standards Council (TSC) and the Further Education Funding Council (FEFC). The chief inspector, directors and support staff are based at a new, purpose-built centre in Coventry and inspection managers and inspectors carry out their administrative work from their homes.

The ALI is playing a pivotal role in the quality assurance of the new post-16 learning sector. Its remit covers government-funded provision for well over five million learners. The ALI is responsible for inspecting an extensive range of government-funded learning, including work-based learning for people over 16, learning for those over 19 in further education colleges, learndirect provision, adult and community learning and Jobcentre Plus programmes such as the New Deal. The ALI shares responsibility for inspecting further education colleges with the Office for Standards in Education (OFSTED). A joint inspection programme, involving teams of inspectors drawn from the ALI and OFSTED, has been launched successfully. OFSTED has responsibility for the overall programme. The ALI and OFSTED share responsibility for providing lead inspectors for individual inspections. The ALI often leads on inspections of institutions in which adult learners are in the majority.

The Learning and Skills Act places the ALI, as well as OFSTED, under an obligation to carry out area inspections of learning for 16-19 year olds. The area inspection programme was started in late 1999. Increasingly, local Learning and Skills Councils (LSCs) and local education authorities take the findings from area inspections into account in their planning of post-16 education and training. The ALI inspects education and training in prisons and young offender institutions. This work is undertaken in collaboration with Her Majesty's Inspectorate of Prisons (HMIP) and, on occasion, with OFSTED.

It is also within the ALI's remit to accept commissions to inspect provision overseas and training in this country funded wholly from private sources. The Secretary of State requires the ALI to offer inspection services in support of the British Council's work to promote training abroad leading to British qualifications. The ALI has successfully carried out a commission from the government of Oman to inspect programmes in the sultanate, which lead to national vocational qualifications (NVQs). Although government spending on work-based learning in this country is considerable, it is dwarfed by the amount of money employers invest collectively in education and training, by drawing on their own resources. It has been recognised that if the ALI is to maximise its effectiveness in improving the skills of our national workforce, it must also inspect learning that is privately funded and disseminate good practice to as wide an audience as possible. To do this effectively will be a major challenge in the months and years ahead.

All inspection under the provisions of the Learning and Skills Act is carried out in accordance with the *Common Inspection Framework*. This sets out general principles of inspection and specifies evaluation requirements which apply to individual providers. The framework focuses on the learner, and on evaluating the effectiveness of education and training in meeting all learners' needs. For the first time in this country we have a single framework which brings together all elements of post-16 inspection, thereby enabling an overall assessment of the quality of post-16 education and training to be made, and valid comparisons between constituent parts of the sector to be drawn.

David Sherlock, Chief Inspector of Adult Learning

The ALI is a government body responsible for raising the standards of education and training for young people and adults in England by inspecting and reporting on the quality of learning provision they receive.

To find out more visit: www.ali.gov.uk
Adult Learning Inspectorate
Spring Place
Coventry Business Park
Herald Avenue
Coventry CV5 6UD

Tel: 0870 240 7744
Fax: 0870 242 1444
E-mail: enquiries @ali.gov.uk

1.4 Training in Small Firms

Contrary to Government assumptions, small businesses provide extensive training, says Samantha Gemmell, Managing Director of Creative Media Matrix and member of the Small Business Council's 'Workforce Development Interest Group'. Policymakers need to show much greater understanding of the variety and extent of training practices within small businesses.

Since the Small Business Council was formed in May 2000, its Workforce Development Interest Group has been working to identify the factors that assist in the development of the skills base existing in small companies and which leads to growth in small and medium-sized enterprises. It has also been considering how the education system can lay the foundations for a skilled workforce.

Underlying the Council's study has been the need to overturn the assumption of many policymakers that small businesses don't train. For many years, this notion has driven Whitehall policy and has led to the poor design of Government training support structures for the small business sector. The Council believes that Government must accept and support all forms of training within small firms rather than trying to impose its own prescriptive training provisions upon them.

Low skill levels are often cited as a reason for Britain's relatively poor labour productivity and low economic performance. As a result, raising employers' and employees' demand for training has become a major policy objective. Of particular importance within small business is informal training – learning that takes place at the workplace on- or off-the-job. However, many studies have ignored this reality and have concluded that small firms provide less training than larger businesses. On top of this misplaced assumption, policymakers have extended the argument to suggest that small employers provide insufficient training.

Last year, in order to measure levels of training in small firms, the Council commissioned Kingston University to research the issue. The resulting 'Measuring Training in Small Firms' report (published in March 2003) offers a more relevant definition of training in the context of small business and suggests ways in which Government can work with, rather than against, small businesses to increase productivity and the demand for skills in the economy.

For a small business, the ability of staff to do their job is more important than paper qualifications because these are neither a guarantee of quality nor a reflection of actual skills. When recruiting, employers place more emphasis on experience, employer references and worker's attitude.

The report shows that small businesses do train, but they provide training that is directly relevant to their own business needs. Businesses need to, in order to survive. Skills are a means to an end, rather than an end in themselves and formal qualifications are often an incidental result of developing workforce skills, rather than a primary motivation for training.

The report reveals a range of reasons why in-house, informal training is generally of more value to small businesses than formal, external training. Such reasons include the financial cost of providing training, the time cost involved in releasing employees and the quality and relevance of external training.

Informal training can be difficult to quantify, but the report suggests several techniques that the Government could implement to do this. Such methods could be carefully piloted and then refined to enable the superior measurement of informal training. The proposed techniques include:

- Measuring the time involved in undertaking and providing training and learning activities.
- Calculating the cost of training, derived by multiplying time spent by an inputted hourly pay rate.
- Measuring increases in an employees' remuneration as they gain more skills.

Employability and productivity are sometimes erroneously regarded as separate contradictory drivers to training: productivity being achieved through skills-driven informal training and employability through qualification driven formal training. However, the Council believes that these two drivers don't require different Government strategies, as all forms of training have a positive impact on employability and productivity. DfES policy should be clear on what it is aiming to achieve and needs to recognise the link between employability and job performance.

All successful organisations are sales-driven and market-led. This means that the most appropriate starting place for a skills strategy is listen to what employers say they need and then develop the supply-side to meet the demand. The Council makes the following suggestions for taking this forward:

- Skills Passport – a record of informal and formal training which would be a permanent record of competencies attained by individuals.
- Skills Audit – small businesses should be encouraged to undertake a skills audit as part of short and long term business objectives.
- Intermediaries – the Government should recognise that entrepreneurs learn best from other entrepreneurs. Therefore, relevant public funding should support professional intermediaries. The Council suggests a 'light touch' standard for such intermediaries so that qualifying for the standard is a simple, non-bureaucratic exercise.
- Training providers should work with small businesses to design formal courses with employer-recognised skill outputs rather than just content or qualification outputs.
- Vocational courses should be redesigned with an emphasis on work-based skills rather than paper and exams.

Small firms are big business and the success of the small business sector, which provides 45 per cent of private sector economic activity, is critical for the UK economy. Training is often distinguished by its formality, but most types of informal training – those often more suited to the needs and demands of small businesses – are equally valid. The Council calls for policymakers to recognise and support all forms of learning within small businesses and encourage them to enhance their training in a way that works for them. It is hoped that this new report will encourage fresh, informed debate of the training issue within the Government.

The Small Business Council, formed in May 2000, is an independent, non-departmental public body which advises the Secretary of State for Trade and Industry and the Chief Executive of the Small Business Service on issues relating to small businesses. The Council is made up of 22 members, who are owners and managers of small businesses, from all parts of the UK and representing different business sectors. The Council meets regularly, with sub-groups liaising at other times on individual topics including Finance, Environment and Rural Affairs, Regulation, Skills and Small Business and Government.

For further information about the Council, please write to: Small Business Council, 6th Floor, Kingsgate House, 66 - 74 Victoria Street, London, SW1E 6SW. An electronic version of the full Kingston University report is available at: www.sbs.gov.uk/organisation/sbc.asp.

1.5 Skills Action: Putting Forward the Economic Development Case

By improving skill levels, regional development agencies also contribute to the economic regeneration of their regions of responsibility.

Putting regional development agencies in context

Regional development agencies (RDAs) were established for eight of the nine English regions on 1 April 1999 to promote economic development and regeneration. They operate as non-departmental public bodies and so are managed by their own chief executive and have their own staff; each remains responsive to regional views and accountable to ministers, from whom they receive their funding, via parliament.

The position is different in London where an RDA was created on 3 July 2000. Although its functions are the same as for the other RDAs and its funding is received from central government, it is accountable to the Mayor of London rather than government ministers.

RDAs are the lead regional bodies for coordinating activities concerned with upskilling the workforce, inward investment, improving business competition and social, physical and economic regeneration. They can also provide funding towards regional regeneration activities in conjunction with other regional partners. The nine English RDAs are:

- Advantage West Midlands (AWM);
- East of England Development Agency (EEDA);
- East Midlands Development Agency (EMDA);
- London Development Agency (LDA);
- Northwest Development Agency (NWDA);
- One North East (ONE);
- South East England Development Agency (SEEDA);
- South West of England Regional Development Agency (SWERDA);
- Yorkshire Forward.

The regional approach to improving skills

Skills and employment issues are complex and differ widely across the regions. However, there is one common thread across all the regions – skills issues are an absolute priority for improving economic prosperity in all parts of England. RDAs are playing a leading role in linking public sector support and working with business leaders to ensure that today's and tomorrow's workforce is better equipped with skills that businesses need.

Each of the nine English RDAs have created strong regional partnerships for employment and skills which have led to the development of a framework for regional employment and skills action (FRESA) in each of the regions. Each FRESA pulls together, for the first time, the breadth of current employment and skills issues across each region, along with accurate information about skills shortages, skills gaps, employment opportunities and threats.

Although led by RDAs, each FRESA partnership brings together business and public sector partners, creating a single voice and delivery vehicle to tackle skills priorities in the regions. Members usually include learning and skills councils, further and higher education colleges and universities, Job Centre Plus, Connexions, the Small Business Service, national training organisations and business organisations such as the Confederation of British Industry (CBI).

FRESAs design and development has engendered an unprecedented level of partnership working in all the regions. A huge amount of work has gone into mapping skills issues and setting priorities – now attention can be turned to addressing the most urgent priorities.

FRESAs are also unique because three government departments – the Department of Trade and Industry (DTI), the Department for Education and Skills and the Department for Work and Pensions, were instrumental in their inception. This level of 'joined-up' working is a major breakthrough for RDAs, and their partners. The role of RDAs cuts across government departments, national bodies, agencies, public and private providers, employers and customers, which has been helpful in this respect.

All regions have areas of prosperity and areas of deprivation and poverty; skills issues vary accordingly. In the east of England, for example, the phenomenal growth of the high-tech and bio-tech clusters around Cambridge have resulted in significant skills shortages, which will damage the future growth of these world-renowned clusters. In contrast, employees of Vauxhall, Luton, required retraining for new skills to gain employment when the company closed its car production facility in the town last year.

Accurate labour market intelligence gathered over recent years enables RDAs and their partners to target specific training and skills activities on areas and groups of people in greatest need. By addressing the disparities of development and prosperity within our regions, we begin to address the national needs of the UK.

The FRESA

Each FRESA document 'does what it says on the label'. It is a framework, designed to be the starting point for action. Since they were published, each RDA and its wide range of partners has been busy putting implementation plans into place. Within each FRESA there are top, high, medium and low priorities.

Each region has a small number of top priorities. These are issues that are seen as critical to the region; for example, in the north-east the top priorities are to:

- create a step change in content, delivery, support and performance of young people at Key Stage 3 (age 10–14) and beyond;
- accelerate demand for high level skills supported by a new talent fund;
- improve the delivery of basic skills to the current workforce.

These contrast with three of the top priorities in the east of England, which are to:

- increase participation in higher education;
- ensure more in-work learning so that there is workforce progression;
- improve skills for employability, through for example, an adult learning pilot scheme.

These priorities go deep into the roots of regional and national needs for a better educated, motivated and skilled workforce. By going back to Key Stage 3, this top priority aims to meet a long-term need to improve the overall education and training of the future workforce. Such an approach feeds into the longer-term aim of creating a world class economy based on high skill and high value.

In other regions there are different priorities; as an example, in the east of England, one of the top priorities is to manage and mitigate the effects of redundancy on the rural economy. Although the effect of large scale redundancies can be seen in the immediate workforce in urban areas, there is clearly a corresponding but more complex ripple effect across all areas and through the supply chains, with changes in the rural economy.

Across each region, the framework helps the right groups of agencies, organisations and individuals to work together to minimise the effects of redundancy with appropriate interventions. It's not just about getting people off the unemployment register – the additional knowledge now available means that training for redundant employees can be aimed at skills gaps and skills shortages within the local area.

What does the FRESA mean for people working in the skills arena?

Through FRESAs, RDAs and their partners have devised strategies for tackling skills and employment issues that are directly affecting both employers and individuals. The action plans tackle many issues, from increasing the level of basic skills attainment to responding to government targets for increased participation in higher education, helping existing industries to survive or developing new ones and revitalising market towns.

The FRESAs and their supporting labour market intelligence help regions to pinpoint opportunities where there are skills gaps or skills shortages. Further information is available on each RDA's website (Figure 1).

Case study: EEDA's support for skills development in the east of England

Skills shortages in construction

Significant research with the Construction Industry Training Board (CITB), construction businesses and local Learning and Skills Councils (LSCs), helped develop understanding of the needs of the construction sector, and why the sector is failing to attract sufficient entrants into its workforce at many levels. There is now a regional business-led forum, and over the past 18 - months the local LSCs have led the development, with businesses, of a number of centres of vocational excellence within several of the region's further education colleges.

The new government announcements about infrastructure development in housing, roads and airport expansion compounds the need for a significant increase in construction workers at all levels. This effective partnership will now explore new and innovative ways of delivering the appropriate skills training, packaged to suit the sector and its current and future workforce.

Supporting the agricultural sector

A wide partnership was brought together through EEDA to address the skills and diversification needs of farmers and their workforce across the region. This is a unique project that covers all

Figure 1 : RDA websites

Advantage West Midlands (AWM)
www.advantagewm.co.uk

East of England Development Agency (EEDA)
www.eeda.org.uk

East Midlands Development Agency (EMDA)
www.emda.org.uk

London Development Agency (LDA)
www.lda.gov.uk

Northwest Development Agency (NWDA)
www.nwda.co.uk

One North East (ONE)
www.onenortheast.co.uk

South East England Development Agency (SEEDA)
www.seeda.co.uk

South West of England Regional Development Agency (SWERDA)
www.southwestrda.org.uk

Yorkshire Forward
www.yorkshire-forward.com

For all RDAs
www.rdauk.org

In addition, EEDA has a specific website about skills activities and its FRESA – for further information visit www.skillsforum.org.uk.

six counties of the east of England. It brings together further and higher education providers of land-based courses with the National Farmers Union, the sector skills council for the environmental and land-based sector (LANTRA), the Department of Environment, Food and Rural Affairs (Defra), Business Links and others, to provide a single, farmer-friendly approach to their needs.

Throughout the severe problems resulting from BSE, swine fever and foot and mouth, the project supplied training and diversification support to over 2500 farmers and farm-workers. This project continues to develop and expand the training and business skills support offered to our farming community.

Supporting a regional response to a major redundancy

When the Vauxhall closure was announced in Luton, EEDA led a partnership to address the economic and social consequences of the closure. Over 2000 people were made redundant, and there was significant impact on the local economy, the wider supply chain and the population.

As well as rigorous and speedy economic and social impact studies, EEDA supported Jobcentre Plus and the local LSC in leveraging significant European funding to deliver all the training and retraining needed to minimise the impact of redundancy on the workforce and their families. Some 2000 people received support before the closure. EEDA remains involved in the partnership, which is now addressing appropriate regeneration of the Vauxhall site to ensure that new opportunities are available to incoming companies.

Vincent Watts is chair of the East of England Development Agency (EEDA) the driving force behind economic regeneration in Bedfordshire, Cambridgeshire, Essex, Hertfordshire, Norfolk and Suffolk. On behalf of the nine English RDAs, Mr Watts leads the work to prioritise skills nationally. He was Vice Chancellor of the University of East Anglia from 1997 until 2002. Previously a partner at an international management consultancy (1976–97), he led the firm's worldwide government work in human resources, financial management, procurement and supply management. He has also been seconded to the Home Office, Department of Health, the Treasury and Cabinet Office.
Mr Watts is a fellow and past member of Council of the Institute of Chartered Accountants in England and Wales where he was chairman of the Examination Committee and a member of the Education and Training Directorate. He is a fellow of the Institute of Management Consultants and has been a member of Council of the Operational Research Society.

1.6 Skills, Productivity and SMEs

While most companies agree that training should be an integral part of the business, the structures presently in place too often do not fulfil the particular needs of SMEs.

Improving skills, boosting productivity and achieving sustainable employment are key national priorities, uniquely shared by government and business. Workforce development is a national priority, evidenced by employers seeking better skilled staff, and the Learning and Skills Council as a major government agent.

But while there is a belief that training brings direct benefit to business, hard evidence to prove this is illusive. Although many of the large blue chip companies have a long track record in training and developing the skills of their staff, work in this area is somewhat patchy within small and medium-size enterprises (SMEs).

The need for more knowledge on the extent of training and development within SMEs, combined with the negative attitudes of employers and employees, prompted the Learning and Skills Development Agency (LSDA) to conduct a research project. The aim was to discover the types of learning that are taking place in SMEs, to assess their effectiveness, to gauge the extent and effectiveness of workforce development and establish how companies select their priorities. Based on a survey of managers in firms employing between two and 250 people, plus focus group sessions with employees, it presented a snap-shot picture of attitudes to training and development within small firms in the 21st century.

The findings were published in August 2002 as *Working Towards Skills: Perspectives on Workforce Development in SMEs*. Predictably, almost all employers who responded to the postal survey agreed that training and development was necessary for business growth and that it led to greater productivity. Only 12 per cent felt that it was not necessary in the present circumstances. Although there is a commonly held perception that employers in small firms are not interested in the development of their staff, research shows otherwise; many of the employers questioned agreed that training and development was necessary for individuals' personal growth. Over 85 per cent said that it led to better-motivated staff and only 20 per cent felt that it disrupted work. Although concerns that training staff would lead to staff being poached, only 15 per cent agreed that developing their workforce would lead to increased turnover.

But whilst attitudes towards training and development were positive, the findings of the National Skills Task Force (2000) show that this does not always extend into practice. Less than half of firms employing fewer than 25 people provided any off-the-job training for their employees, compared to more than 90 per cent of those employing 200 or more. With ever-increasing pressure on businesses to perform in a highly competitive market, setting aside time for such activities is often seen as secondary to meeting business objectives.

One of the key messages emerging from the research is that any initiative designed to support workforce development in SMEs must take into account the particular needs of these kind of organisations. Many of the recent initiatives designed to encourage take-up of training have failed to do this by not being able to demonstrate how learning can support business objectives or adapt to the way SMEs operate. Training and development must be informal, flexible and embedded into the context of the workplace, as SMEs frequently have difficulty releasing staff for off-the-job training at fixed times. Moreover, it is often troublesome for learning providers such as colleges or training companies to provide training for a handful of staff, at a time and place that suits the employer and at an affordable cost.

Overcoming Barriers

Language

Small firms require a different approach from that favoured by the bigger companies. One of the barriers, identified by the LSDA research, is that of language. There is a negative reaction to terms like 'training' and 'skills' , which are often associated with the government training schemes of the 1980s. Words like 'personal development' and 'learning' provoked more positive responses. One employer said, 'I would use the word 'learning' to say that I learn something new every day. If someone says 'training' it sounds more proper and official'.

Informal learning

Delivering learning to SMEs requires a less formal approach, using managers, supervisors and peers, rather than specialists in training and development. Learning should be seen as something on-going, rather than an activity that happens at a set time. The approach of one graphics and design company in the survey to get staff together in small, informal groups to learn about new software. The firm also uses its website to share problems and present learning solutions. But a more formal approach can work just as well. LSDA's research identifies examples of small firms employing less than 20 people who have a highly structured approach to training using annual reviews, often within the framework of Investors in People.

Cascading training

There is a need to encourage staff who have some responsibility for learning in their companies to become trainers, learning facilitators, coaches, mentors or 'skills champions'. To make training and development work for SMEs the emphasis has to be on informal, time-efficient training which is linked to business performance, not a rigid one-size-fits-all approach.

Selling learning

Selling the concept of learning to employees means demonstrating the benefits to them as well as the organisation. Many staff, particularly the low-paid, have low aspirations and need to be persuaded to engage in learning. Employers' perceptions of the training needs of their staff are often narrow and highly specific. These perceptions may not coincide with the desire of some employees for accredited, transferable skills. Some employees said their employers did not make any attempt to assess their training needs and few had been asked by their employer for their views about staff development.

LSDA's research on basic skills in the workplace highlights the need to market learning in positive ways using a 'rough guide' approach that demonstrates their direct application.

The way ahead

The UK still has one third fewer people qualified to NVQ Level 2 than either France or Germany and only half as many people qualified to Level 3 than Germany. There is a clear case for more investment in vocational education and training, particularly within SMEs. The lack of investment in vocational skills training and an absence of deep learning at initial experience levels has undoubtedly resulted in a legacy of an unskilled workforce without the capacity to develop their skills further or transfer learning to new contexts.

Raising our game plan means making skill building attractive. Many SMEs see the benefits it can bring, not only to the bottom line, but also to the motivation of employees. Attitudes to training are clearly changing.

LSDA is now engaged in more detailed research into the nature of learning that is taking place in small firms. This has revealed a range of practices across different types of firms and in different sectors. Emerging issues include:

- That the effectiveness of prior formal learning has an impact on the manager's belief in training and capacity to promote informal learning;
- That perceptions of what 'learning' means in relationship to the business requires awareness raising and time for reflection;
- People are still relying heavily on reading trade magazines, books and technical manuals to find about new techniques;
- There needs to be a distinction between acquiring knowledge on a course and using it in practice;
- There are examples of 'bespoke' learning packages, some of which carry accreditation, being purchased by small companies;
- Some formal needs, such as basic IT, are easy to source. But as small firms increasingly diversify and occupy niche markets, their training needs become more specialised and harder to meet cost effectively. Providers of support need to fine-tune their offer to be useful to particular circumstances, and this will have a knock-on effect on economies of scale;
- There is a need for a wide range of credible experts and mentors, who can work with business on a 1-to-1 basis.

SMEs need to:

- Develop the capacity of staff to become learning champions, cascading training throughout the organisation;
- Demonstrate the benefits of learning to employees as well as the employer;
- View learning as something ongoing that happens throughout the working week;
- Assess the training needs of staff and respond flexibly in ways that suit them;
- Provide opportunities for staff to develop and grow.

Learning providers need to:

- Offer flexible solutions to SMEs;
- Work in partnership with other organisations to provide training for a number of similar organisations cost-effectively;
- Use technology to help people access training;
- Understand the particular needs of SMEs – and respond to them.

The Learning and Skills Development Agency (LSDA) is a strategic national resource for the development of policy and practice in post-16 education and training. It was previously known as the Further Education Development Agency. The work of the LSDA covers research, policy advice, professional and organisational development, and curriculum support for all learning providers involved in post-16 education and training. These include those working in further education and sixth form colleges, school sixth forms, adult and community education, and work-based education and training. The work of LSDA is supported by a grant from the Learning and Skills Council. For further information visit www.lsda.org.uk.

'Working Towards Skills: Perspectives on Workforce Development in Small and Medium Sized Enterprises' by *Maria Hughes, Vince Keddie, Peter Webb and Mark Corney is available free of charge from Information Services, LSDA, Regent Arcade House, 19-25 Argyll Street, London W1F 7LS; Tel: 020 7297 9144.*

1.7 Modern Apprenticeships

The days of the traditional bloke in a boiler suit have gone when it comes to apprenticeships. Modern apprentices are likely to be either gender and could be working in any industry.

> 'As a country, we have many instances of world-class excellence in training and skills. But for many years we have lacked a clear system of vocational training, particularly for young people. We also have fewer people with decent skills than our major competitors. We are determined to tackle the skills gap and raise the quality and standards of vocational training across the workforce. Modern apprenticeships are central to our strategy of increasing skills across the economy. Given our lack of skills, it is particularly important for employers to consider providing modern apprenticeships in the deal that they offer to both new entrants and to existing staff.'
>
> —Tony Blair

For centuries, apprenticeships provided young people with training and experience in a number of crafts and professions. Apprentices were almost always males, engaged in manual work. On completion of the apprenticeship, having acquired their skills over a period of five, six or even seven years, they almost invariably moved into full-time employment in the same occupation and stayed there for life. Many museums and other collections hold impressive examples of 'masterpieces', the pieces of work that the apprentices produced to demonstrate that they merited the title of craftsman. However, today's employment market is much more volatile; people need to acquire high levels of skills quickly and to be able to adapt those skills to the demands of constant, often rapid, change; jobs are rarely for life.

The demise of the traditional apprenticeship in the 1980s and 1990s offered a perfect opportunity for the development and introduction of a brand new approach that would better meet the needs of modern businesses, and would continue to develop and meet those needs in the future.

Designed by employers, for employers, the Modern Apprenticeship was designed to draw on all that was best in traditional learning – hands-on training, learning in the workplace, work experience, etc. However, it combined that training with learning off-the-job, where apprentices studied both the theoretical aspects of the chosen occupation and a range of other skills that would be valuable in a variety of jobs.

At the same time, the Modern Apprenticeship did away with time-serving, gender stereotyping and the notion that apprenticeships belonged only to manual occupations in industries like construction and engineering, the classic apprentice image of a young male in a boiler suit. Today's Modern Apprentice follows a custom-designed training package that takes account of individual ability, prior learning and previous work experience. Modern Apprenticeships have been introduced into many varied sectors that had no tradition of apprenticeship training, such as Banking, Hospitality and Sports and Recreation. Today's apprentice is just as likely to be an accountant or a health and beauty specialist as they are an electrician or a motor mechanic.

The review of modern apprenticeships

In 2001, Sir John Cassels led a Government-commissioned review of Modern Apprenticeships, to take a close look at how they were performing and, where appropriate, to recommend improvements. The report of the study undertaken by the Modern Apprenticeships Advisory Committee was published in September 2001 and, at a formal launch held in November 2001 at No 11 Downing

Street, the Government and the Learning and Skills Council (LSC) broadly welcomed its recommendations and launched a new generation of Modern Apprenticeships (MAs).

The launch also heralded the start of a major, three year campaign by the DfES and the LSC '*to build the Modern Apprenticeship brand, add value to the currency of Modern Apprenticeships and increase take-up by young people and employers*'. ('Modern Apprenticeships – The Way to Work', September 2001). The implementation plan setting out how the main recommendations are being taken forward is published on the LSC's website at www.lsc.gov.uk. Progress on each of the key strands is on target.

The basic structure

MAs have two levels: Foundation at NVQ level 2, and Advanced at NVQ level 3. There are more than 150 types of MA in over 80 sectors of industry and commerce including, for example, Advice and Guidance, Cultural Heritage, Environmental Conservation and Insurance, through to Photo Imaging, Security, Telecommunications and the Water Industry.

Each MA sector has a framework produced by the appropriate Sector Skills Council, which specifies key factors like content and duration and the balance of on- and off-the-job learning, and describes the roles of apprentice, employer and apprenticeship agent (for example, a local learning provider such as a college, whose role is to advise and assist both apprentice and employer).

MAs also incorporate key skills (such as IT, communication or problem solving) which are designed not only to complement the skills necessary for the job in question, but also to provide apprentices with the skills and flexibility that will enable them to respond positively to changing markets and technology, either with their existing employers, or when moving to new jobs.

The newest addition to the MA framework is the technical certificate, recommended by Sir John Cassels: '*Technical certificates offer the prospect both of significantly upgrading apprenticeships and of forming a basis for able apprentices to progress to higher education in a subject linked to their chosen occupation.*' ('Modern Apprenticeships – The Way to Work', September 2001)

Technical certificates are proof of occupational knowledge and understanding and complement the evidence of practical skills and on-the-job knowledge provided by the NVQ. In time, all aspects of knowledge and skills acquisition within the MA will be encompassed by the Apprenticeship Diploma which is currently being developed.

So what are the advantages?

Whatever their background, education or culture, young people need jobs. Those with skills and qualifications are highly sought after. Modern Apprentices work in the real world, getting valuable hands-on experience coupled with off-the-job learning. They get qualifications and skills that are recognised and valued by employers everywhere, because MAs are designed by employers, for employers. By participating in MAs, young people get new opportunities and employers get competent and committed staff.

What's more, there is no gender stereotyping, they're for young people from all ethnic groups and they're for young people with disabilities as well as the able-bodied. And young people who have completed their MA have the opportunity to progress further. They can carry on working and take higher-level vocational qualifications, or they can move into Higher Education through the development of Foundation Degrees. In many sectors they can also undergo training for professional qualifications to gain promotion and professional status.

Facts and figures

On 28 July 2002, there were 219,500 young people undertaking MAs in England, 111,600 on Foundation and 107,900 on Advanced (DfES statistical first release 24 October 2002). 98 per cent of young people on Advanced MAs have employed status and, of those who left Advanced MAs in 2000-2001, 86 per cent were in employment six months after leaving. Since 1997, the number of young people achieving NVQ3 while on Advanced MAs has increased by 27 percentage points.

To find out more

For more information about Modern Apprenticeships in your area, contact your local Learning and Skills Council.

A national helpline is also available on 08000 150 600 and there's a campaign website at www.realworkrealpay.info.

For more general information about education and training opportunities, visit these websites, which also have many useful links:

www.dfes.gov.uk

www.connexions.gov.uk.

Learning and Skills Council

The Learning and Skills Council National Office is situated at:
Cheylesmore House
Quinton Road
Coventry CV1 2WT
Tel: 0845 019 4170
Fax: 024 76 49 3600
E-mail: info@lsc.gov.uk
Website: www.lsc.gov.uk

1.8 'More Plumbers and Fewer Graduates'

> 'Bother your 'ologies and 'ometries, let me teach him something useful!'
> The caption on a cartoon relating to a sturdy British workman (tools slung over shoulder), who is speaking to a be-gowned headmaster about a rather truculent, and academically reluctant, boy. The cartoon was from Punch (1897).

The government policy of getting more people into universities is fundamentally wrong and has led to a skills shortage of crisis proportions, writes Ruth Lea, Head of Policy at the Institute of Directors.

Introduction: skills shortages

As a business organisation, some of our main concerns are the educational standards and skill levels of the labour force, which are so vital for the competitiveness of individual businesses, on the one hand, and the overall economy, on the other. In many ways, the UK is a very competitive country, but when it comes to overall educational standards and workplace skills, the country is quite simply not world class and we believe that this holds back productivity, economic growth and prosperity. This concern was one of the main reasons behind the 'blueprint' report we released last year on education and training.

One of the most serious problems business faces is that of skills shortage (especially intermediate craft skills shortages). We believe this arises firstly, because the labour market cannot satisfactorily overcome some very fundamental basic skills deficiencies in literacy and numeracy and secondly, because far too many able school leavers are siphoned off into higher education (HE) and not enough into tough and challenging vocational training. Concerning the first issue, and the need to improve basic skills levels, we support the government's policies of improving the literacy and numeracy of school children, though we do have some concerns – not least over the considerable failure rates and the missed targets. But the policies are a step in the right direction. If the teaching of these very basic skills could be 'got right', many school leavers' employability would improve and business would be a huge beneficiary. The second issue is a different matter. Here we would argue that the government's policy of 'more and more graduates' is fundamentally mistaken.

The imbalance in the education system

The overall balance of the educational system between 'academic' HE and genuine vocational training is now badly out of kilter. Moreover, it will deteriorate further as the government struggles (including, more specifically, by the creation of 'foundation' degrees that employers will probably regard as bogus) to reach its over-ambitious 50 per cent target of young people going into HE by 2010. As already implied, the country is short of skilled craftspeople - including plumbers and people with engineering technician and ICT skills. It is not short of, for example, media studies graduates. As we said in the press release for our 'blueprint' paper, 'we need more plumbers and fewer media studies graduates'. Alas, the proposed expansion of HE is unlikely to help business's problems with skills shortages. Indeed, as already implied, the problems are likely to worsen, as even more able people are diverted from vocational training into HE.

The 50 per cent target should be unequivocally abandoned and consideration should be given to reducing the numbers going into HE. All vocational training along with further education (FE) colleges, the traditional Cinderellas of the education system, should be upgraded. We have, of course, been accused of elitism and snobbery in suggesting this policy. But behind this charge there is a strange and, yes, snobby implication that somehow 'academic' education (however debased as much of it now is) is necessarily 'better' than vocational education and training. This is wrong. How can we change the culture in this country to ensure that hard and rigorous vocational training is seen to be just as good and desirable as 'academic' education, if not better, and considerably more useful? (It is so very different in many countries, including Switzerland, where they have superb crafts training and only about 15 per cent of young people go to university. The master craftsman rightly has equal status to the graduate.) The IoD strongly promotes the value of vocational education and training. More specifically, members support National Vocational Qualifications (NVQs) and Modern Apprenticeships.

IoD members' views of in-work vocational qualifications

We have surveyed IoD members' views on NVQs on two occasions (1998 and 2000) and they gave the qualifications the overall 'thumbs-up', despite some reservations about the quality and comparability with, say, German, Swiss or Dutch vocational qualifications. In 1998 most of the IoD members who were running NVQs (a minority) thought they were worthwhile. The great majority of those who had used them said they would continue to use them, and 81 per cent said they would recommend them to other employers. In 2000, even though again only a minority of IoD members had used qualifications such as Modern Apprenticeships and NVQs, the members believed that they were a good way of equipping their workforces. The 2000 survey showed that 22 per cent had used Modern Apprenticeships and most of them (80 per cent) thought that they were equipping their employees with the required skills. Of the 36 per cent who had used NVQs, 73 per cent thought they were equipping their employees with the required skills. It is worth adding that, as few small firms have the resources to have major training courses, NVQs can be particularly useful for them – and please note that fewer small firms offer training than large ones.

Schools and vocational education and training

Our report discusses schools at some length and strongly recommends that rigorous and practical vocational education and training programmes should be introduced into our secondary schools – much along Continental lines. In countries such as Switzerland, Germany, the Netherlands and Austria there are separate 'pathways' in secondary schools according to a pupil's aptitudes, interests and abilities. This is not snobbery and 'elitism', it is common sense. The German secondary education system is tripartite, for example, whilst the Dutch system is quadripartite. We suggest a bipartite system in the UK, comprising an academic pathway (which should be made more rigorous) and a properly developed vocational pathway.

We, more specifically, recommend that the vocational pathway should be developed so that some pupils could start learning vocational craft skills from the age of 14. Such vocational training could be in school, or in an FE college, or part-time in the workplace – or in combinations of all three. Far too many young people lose interest in schooling and leave with few skills – either vocational or the basic skills of literacy and numeracy. This is little short of a national disgrace and a failure of social policy; it should be addressed as a top priority. We believe that providing a coherent alternative to the current 'one size fits all' quasi-academic GCSE system could be part of the solution.

We have recently been encouraged by policy announcements relating to 14-19 secondary schools from the DfES. The current Secretary of State for Education and Skills seems to be committed to developing an 'industry stream' (ie a vocational pathway) alongside a 'university stream' (ie an academic pathway). Moreover, the new Chief Executive of the Qualifications and Curriculum Authority (QCA), Dr Ken Boston, has suggested that there should be more practical work in the 'vocational' GCSEs and more employer involvement. We wholly support these suggestions.

At the very heart of our 'blueprint' report is the need for a greater focus on vocational education and training. The spotlight should, in our view, be unequivocally shifted from HE to FE colleges and vocational training in general. The current balance between the academic (and the 'quasi academic') and vocational is not even. It fails many young people and it also fails to deliver adequately the skills business really needs. It's not a case of 'everything's wrong' with the education system – but a lot is.

Ruth Lea, Head of Policy, Institute of Directors

Institute of Directors
116 Pall Mall
London SW1Y 5ED
Main switchboard: 020 7839 1233
Fax (main): 020 7930 1949
Website: www.iod.com
E-mail: enquiries@iod.com

1.9 People Power Key in Tackling the UK's Poor Productivity Record

British managers fall short when it comes to strategic thinking, communication, leadership and motivation. This leads to UK productivity falling further behind its main trading partners.

The UK has a well-documented and prevailingly poor productivity record. After studying more than 16,000 organisations of every conceivable type and in every major economy around the world, we can say with a fairly high degree of confidence that this is partly because most firms still operate well below their true capability.

For several years, Proudfoot Consulting has conducted an annual study to benchmark the UK's corporate productivity performance versus its traditional economic rivals. In the latest study[1], we asked Professor Nicolas Crafts of the London School of Economics to calculate the cost of inefficient working practices in some of the world's leading economies, and the results make startling reading (see figure 1).

Financial Cost (£bn) of Sub-Optimal Productivity to GDP	
Britain	110
USA	560
Germany	143
France	81

Note: Figs exclude public sector. Sources include US Bureau of Labour Statistics and OECD main economic indicators (2002)

Figure 1

As well as attempting to quantify for the first time what corporate inefficiency costs each nation, we also found that the UK is falling further behind Germany, France and the USA in the productivity performance league tables. Following our report, the DTI, citing evidence from ourselves and others, announced it was hiring Professor Michael Porter, the renowned competitiveness guru, to explore where British management is going wrong.

But is the UK's productivity problem just a symptom of low management standards? There is certainly some supporting evidence. Out of 4.5 million managers in the UK, only 20 per cent have management qualifications. And last year's report to the DTI by the Council for Excellence in Management and Leadership found British managers lacking most in four areas:

- strategic thinking
- communication
- leadership
- motivation

1 Untapped potential: the barriers to optimum corporate productivity

These qualities all underpin productivity improvement. We believe managers play a central role in improving productivity and we're not alone. Last year, a joint CBI/TUC investment working group highlighted the important link between management and productivity.

Some commentators say the UK's poor productivity record is a result of a bigger issue: a lower standard of workforce education. It's certainly true that compared with other countries we don't fare well. The UK ranks position 22 out of 24 OECD countries for adults continuing their education after age 18.

Of course, effective team-working and people management cannot be taught in the classroom alone, but it is fair to conclude from these figures that formal education appears under-valued in the UK. I believe this can make managers oblivious to what can be achieved in terms of productivity, and insecure in seeking assistance to improve.

Taking these statistics, you'd be forgiven for thinking that all firms need do is hire better-qualified people to be more productive. But it's not as simple as that. It's almost always faster and cheaper to work with the resource you already have, all the more so in the current difficult trading climate. To do this though, firm support and strong leadership from the very top of the organisation are required. It also needs a heavy dose of pragmatism, a willingness to rigorously apply some management basics and a determination to focus on the handful of specific performance measures that really count towards productivity improvement. What these measures are varies from company to company.

While it's clear that British firms have some catching up to do, how to achieve this is a different story. As a specialist management consultancy, we're not qualified to tackle macro-economic policy issues. But at the micro-level – that of the individual business – it's a different story. For any organisation seeking substantial gains in productivity, here is a ten-point framework to start from.

1. Recognise that productivity is a strategic initiative

The single most important thing is to understand that achieving substantial productivity gains, ie in excess of 20 per cent, takes more than a series of piecemeal initiatives. What's required is a top-down, CEO-led strategic initiative that is well communicated and impacts all elements of the business.

2. Aim high

Improvement goals should be 'absolute' and ambitious rather than relative targets set against peer groups. British firms have often been criticised for their 'going for bronze' attitude. Companies should aim for the absolute boundaries of achievement.

3. Be prepared to question, measure and change anything

A productivity improvement plan should seek to improve every major resource available to the firm: people, processes and management systems naturally, but also plant and equipment, premises, suppliers, raw materials and so on. There are three essential elements: discipline, sustainability and measurability. The last point may seem obvious, but companies often fail to build in the right checks and measures. I tend to hold with Porter's view that strategy without numbers is mush.

4. Tackle the basic principles of management planning and supervision

Ensure anyone promoted to a management or supervisory role has at least the basic skills for that role. It's surprising how often this still doesn't happen. Poor planning and controlling of work and inadequate management are the recurring and most significant causes of lost productivity in our studies. In the most recent, the UK fares worse than average, with 110 out of 225 productive working days per company lost, compared to France (97), Germany (83) and the USA (86).

Effective planning, assigning and follow-up of work tasks, coupled with good people practices of giving direction, providing feedback and offering coaching and support are the basic skills managers and supervisors need to quickly produce results.

5. Train people outside as well as inside the classroom

Coaching on the job is critical but often given insufficient time and not tailored to the individual. Allow at least three hours of personalised on-the-job coaching for every hour spent in formal classroom sessions.

6. Change must be physically manifested

People need to see change happening around them to believe it's going to actually happen. Even small physical changes, though subtle, can be powerful and symbolic. For example, clearing up an untidy working area or chalking an area on a factory floor to indicate where plant will be moved to both send clear signals that something is underway and taking place.

7. Speed is vital

Low inertia can kill any change programme. A strategy of small scale, separate schemes implemented sequentially will not work. Momentum will be slow, results will not appear fast enough and managers will more than likely run out of steam. Instead, design your productivity improvement plan to work concurrently across all aspects of the business. This will create drama, excitement and a high volume of early results. People will be encouraged to re-double their efforts.

8. Break it down

Understand and use 'short-interval control' methods. If you only measure how much things have been improved at the end of a day or a particular shift and you're short of the required target, there's nothing to be done. If, however, you break performance down into hourly chunks, you start to see much earlier if there's going to be a problem and can take appropriate corrective action.

9. Be patient

Major productivity improvement plans take time to reach full expectations. In our experience, around 12 weeks is the usual timescale before real changes can be seen and 16 weeks before change is locked in and sustainable.

10. Think 'continuity'

Improvement and best practice are constantly advancing targets as competitors and technology evolve. Rolling productivity improvement planning, just like quarterly financial planning, should therefore be part of every senior manager's mind-set.

Pam Hackett is Head of People Solutions at Proudfoot Consulting. The firm specialises in implementing change to achieve measurable and sustainable performance improvements. Proudfoot Consulting has carried out more than 16,000 productivity assignments globally and its client list includes Anglo American, BP, Rio Tinto, NAG, AMP, Avaya, MetLife, Peugeot Citroën and Airbus. The firm was established in Chicago in 1946 by Alexander Proudfoot and is now part of the Management Consulting Group Plc, a group of consulting businesses operating globally.

For more information, visit www.proudfootconsulting.com or contact:

Proudfoot Consulting
21 New Fetter Lane
London EC4A 1AW
Tel: 020 7832 3600
E-mail: rlanham@proudfootconsulting.com

1.10 Training of Non-Executive Directors

High profile corporate failures have put the spotlight on the role of non-executive directors. In future their preparation and training will become more formal, according to KPMG's 2002–2003 survey. Tim Copnell discusses the report's findings.

In light of an increasingly dynamic business environment, complexities in financial reporting and changes in shareholders' expectations related to financial disclosures, it is imperative that non-executive directors stay abreast of current developments. They must be in a position to ask the right questions and, more importantly, understand the answers they receive. They can keep up to speed by reading relevant industry and business publications, attending conferences, and entering into a dialogue with legislators, financiers, business leaders, technical experts, and anyone else who might be the source of useful information. Nevertheless there may well be a need for more formal education or training processes.

Non-executives were asked if they have received any formal training in a number of areas. We also asked to what extent they believe that training or guidance in those areas would be of benefit to non-executive directors in fulfilling their duties. It is apparent that many non-executive directors have not received formal training in a number of areas. What is perhaps even more surprising is that in nearly all the areas looked at, more respondents actually believed training was beneficial than had actually received formal training.

The only exception was corporate governance issues where 78 per cent had received formal training while only 73 per cent thought such training was beneficial. Perhaps this reflects the growth of formal 'governance training' in the wake of successive UK corporate governance reports.

At the other extreme, 78 per cent of respondents believed training in early warning signals would be beneficial while only 32 per cent had actually received some kind of formal training. This demonstrates the lack of formal training available for non-executive directors despite recognition of the importance of these matters – especially since the high profile corporate collapses at the beginning of the year.

Many respondents were concerned by the burden and complexity of regulations and the difficulties in keeping up to speed with rapid change. One commented that 'commercial knowledge and experience will no longer be enough to equip an individual to be an non-executive director' – how do they keep their knowledge of regulation up to speed? Previously this was done on an informal basis, but it is likely that this will become more formal. The need for a qualification in 'directorship' and compulsory post-qualification experience was raised by some respondents, but rejected in favour of a responsible approach to self learning and attending high quality courses.

Attributes

Respondents were invited to comment on what they feel are the most important skills, knowledge or attributes that are needed by non-executive directors. The responses can be broadly summarised in the following categories:

Industry processes and company knowledge

Without a clear insight into current issues facing the business, it is difficult for non-executive directors to assess potential risks and contribute more generally to corporate strategy. It is perhaps surprising that a number of respondents feel non-executive directors lack knowledge in this area.

Tenacity

The ability to 'stick to your guns' is an important attribute in dealing with overly-assertive chief executives, skills in 'constructive challenge' as one non-executive director puts it. Related attributes are independence of mind and integrity. Being able to objectively assess the executive team, especially the chief executive, is described by one non-executive director as important. Other important personal skills cited are: a probing mind, being a good listener and possessing common sense.

Ability to stand back

This skill is cited by several respondents as important. One non-executive director responded 'anything can be achieved if you do not care who gets the credit'. For some former executives, this may not be an easy transition.

Big picture

The ability to distinguish the 'wood from the trees' and only become 'involved in detail when they sense a problem looming' is how one non-executive director describes the non-executive director role. Of course, this is much more than simply doing nothing until things go wrong.

Effective relationships

Getting the right chemistry and being able to work with executives and other non-executives is important. It is also important to transcend the populist view of the non-executive is a policeman – 'non-executives must also be committed to the company's growth and success'.

Corporate governance

Keeping up to date with corporate governance developments is described by one non-executive director as being important. However, another respondent warns 'there must be a limit to what can be expected of non-executive directors'. This is why many respondents believe some sort of guidance or code for non-executive directors would be helpful.

Knowledge

Non-executive directors were asked if they had sufficient knowledge in a number of specified areas.

Financial performance and indicators

An overwhelming 94 per cent of respondents considered non-executive directors to have sufficient knowledge of financial performance and indicators. Those few respondents that consider non-executive directors to have insufficient knowledge in this area perhaps recognise that, in an age of 'smoke and mirrors' where both financial transactions and accounting standards are becoming increasingly elaborate, it is no longer possible for those non-executive audit committee members to operate effectively with only a passing knowledge of finance.

They must have expertise that goes beyond familiarity with financial statements. They must understand the principles that underpin the preparation of financial statements, why critical accounting policies are chosen, how they are applied, and satisfy themselves that they are applied consistently and that the end result fairly reflects their understanding.

Non-financial performance and indicators

In contrast to financial performance and indicators, only 60 per cent of respondents considered non-executive directors to have sufficient knowledge of non-financial performance and indicators. It is difficult to understand how business performance can be fully understood without an appreciation of non-financial critical success factors and key performance indicators.

The main reasons given for this worrying deficiency are 'lack of industry knowledge' and that the 'information provided by executives is mainly financial'. Some non-executive directors appear to blame executives for not providing this sort of information. Trust has an important role to play, as non-executive directors naturally must put a great deal of trust in their executive colleagues to tell them what they need to know. Nevertheless, they should not rely solely on what is put before them. They should ask the right questions and, perhaps more importantly, understand the answers they receive.

Business process, how value is added and customer satisfaction

One third of those responding considered non-executive directors to lack sufficient knowledge of the business process, how value is added and customer satisfaction. The main reason cited is the lack of time and lack of knowledge of the underlying business, although most agree that this is an important area. Others suggested that this type of information is often not gathered, or not provided by management – perhaps this is because certain key performance indicators (KPIs) are only reported by exception.

Cash flow analysis and projections

Although a vast majority (89 per cent) indicated that they have sufficient knowledge in this clearly fundamental area, some respondents believed that non-executive directors lacked adequate training on, and awareness of, the importance of cash flow projections. Lack of appropriate reporting by management on cash flow information/projections was also reported.

System of internal financial controls and its effectiveness

One quarter of those responding felt non-executive directors lack sufficient knowledge here. This is surprising in the post-Turnbull environment and may reflect that non-executive directors are now much more conscious of risk, control and the role they are expected to play. Again, lack of time and/or insufficient information provided by management are cited as the main reasons for knowledge deficiencies.

Exposure to financial and non-financial risk

Notwithstanding the fact that 97 per cent of those responding considered reviewing business risk to be an important part of the non-executive role, over 30 per cent considered non-executive directors to lack sufficient knowledge of exposure to financial and non-financial risk. Once again lack of time, information and training are cited as the main reasons. Many reported that financial risk is better understood than non-financial risk (mirroring their knowledge of financial and non-financial performance and indicators). It appears that non-executive directors often lack the tools or skills to understand and assess this properly. Again this may reflect their greater expectations in the post-Turnbull environment.

External benchmarking/competitor analysis

Over half of the respondents believed non-executive directors lack sufficient knowledge of competitors.

Respondents generally described the main reasons for this lack of knowledge as 'information just not provided to non-executive directors' and 'information is selective and from the eyes of the executive'. Again, while there should be trust on the board, it is also incumbent on non-executive directors to not rely solely on what is put before them, but seek out the information they require. Internal audit has a role to play in providing assurance on all the information received by all board members.

Stakeholder expectations

While only 15 per cent consider communicating with stakeholders (other than shareholders) to be an important part of their role, over 30 per cent believe that generally non-executive directors do not have sufficient knowledge of the expectations of such stakeholders. Some cited 'lack of access to quality stakeholders' as a key reason, as they only have a 'restricted view'. Others suggest that 'stakeholder relations are an executive function'. Either way, it would appear that there is often insufficient oversight by non-executive directors in this key area of reputational risk and shareholder value management.

In today's challenging global marketplace, companies require a committed and technically outstanding professional services provider who truly understands their business. For more than a century, companies have relied on KPMG to provide sound and valuable business advice and help manage their business risks.

KPMG member firms are a leading provider of assurance, tax and legal, and financial advisory services. With a global approach to service delivery, KPMG responds to clients' complex business challenges with consistent methodologies and common tools across industry sectors and national boundaries.

For more information and a full version of the report, 'Non-Executive Directors Survey 2002–2003', *contact Tim Copnell at KPMG, tel: 020 7694 8082 or e-mail: tim.copnell@kpmg.com.*

1.11 Rumours of the Demise of Supervision Remain Unfounded

Without supervisors you lose accountability – hence the re-emergence of skill undervalued in recent years.

Once in a while in the United Kingdom, national opinion about some issue swings dramatically to an extreme position, and despite all attempts to rebalance or rationalise this through reasoned debate, a pretty much unshakeable national view prevails for years, often, indeed, for decades.

Such a change of public attitude affected the terms 'supervisor' and 'supervision' during the 1980s and 1990s. This change in attitudes was caused by a complex mixture of circumstances. Some of these were the much-delayed and final death throes of the 'bad old days' of British industry. Another factor was the arrival in the workforce of Generation X, who had been brought up by their 'Boomer Generation' parents not to take any nonsense from people they didn't respect. This was underpinned by rising technology use, which meant that positional authority was being undermined by knowledge authority, perhaps for the first time since Victorian times.

Finally, the great re-structuring brought about by Information Technology was well under way, making 'overseeing' as a task seem less important, and eventually leading to the final cull. What was especially irritating to those who had to stand and watch was the almost ubiquitous refrain that supervision was all about 'standing over people to make sure they do their jobs properly'. Consequently, as so often happens, the supervision baby was thrown out with the supervisor bathwater all over the UK.

Yet in a world often rocked by front-page catastrophes, the cry 'who was supposed to be in charge?' still goes up regularly. What everyone immediately and vociferously actually wants is to know is why there was not adequate supervision before the incident. In the financial sector, in transport and healthcare, even in the 'utilities', inadequate supervision is seen as the cause of failures. Many of the cries will come from people who have grown used themselves to workplaces without supervisors, and don't necessarily like their absence.

Today however, it is increasingly accepted that the downsizing and de-layering that led to the demise of the supervisor may have been more harmful than beneficial in many cases. For example, a supervisory role was often the first step in career progression. When these positions were removed, career aspirations were limited for those at the lower levels. Career limitation pervaded workforces, and with it came less commitment, less continuity, and the loss of large amounts of the organisation's knowledge base as staff moved to other employers in search of ever-reducing promotions.

In addition, so great was the rush to de-layer and re-engineer that gaps in organisational control processes were swept under corporate carpets. That first essential check, the simple reassurance from frequent and routine exchanges between employees and their supervisor, could not be replaced when the first step became the larger hurdle of going to a manager, often one without the skill-specific understanding. We lived to see and to hear the news stories, all through the late 1990s.

But the future for supervision is once again brightening. Excellent employers have always recognised that supervision exists for the good of all. It provides the security that both employer and employees require, by limiting responsibility to those with appropriate authority, whilst at the same time steering subordinates away from the risk of making errors. Supervision – the primary quality assurance mechanism supporting the delivery of many modern services and products, supporting staff and protecting the procedures that create 'right first time', and world class, performance.

In the new century, the function that is increasingly seen as a key role of supervision is to identify performance shortfalls in the workforce, and initiate learning responses. Today's supervisor (or 'first line manager' or 'team leader') is emerging as a resource controller, a mentor, a coach and a facilitator. Many companies now provide training in coaching, facilitation, and instructional techniques for their team leaders, just as in the past thousands of supervisors were routinely sent on traditional instructional techniques courses. These companies are equipping themselves with the supervisory skills we need for the future, others must follow.

Be sure that Fred Kite is not about to re-appear. The brown coat with the row of biros, never a fashion item, is unlikely to return. Workplace discipline as a form of mass entertainment is dead for good. The woodbine is not going to burn at the workbench in the 21st century. But as long as we demand effective supervision of our companies, institutions, utilities and services, someone has to do it. And it doesn't really matter what we call the person, just so long as we train them properly, and never again let ourselves think they are unnecessary.

George Edwards, Head of Strategic Development, Institute of Leadership and Management

ILM has over half a century of experience in management development and recognition of achievement through accreditation and membership.
ILM provides distinctive and innovative services to support all individuals and organisations in building their capability in leadership and management, through membership, qualifications and awards, and representation. Formed through the merger of the Institute for Supervision and Management and NEBS Management, ILM today is the UK's largest accrediting body for management qualifications.

London office
1 Giltspur Street
London EC1A 9DD
Tel: 020 7294 2470
Fax: 020 7294 2402

Lichfield office
Stowe House
Netherstowe
Lichfield, Staffordshire WS13 6TJ
Tel: 01543 251346
Fax: 01543 266811

1.12 Corporate Universities: How the Open University is Responding

The development of corporate universities has seen a move in workplace training from training to actual learning.

COROUS (Corporate Open University Services), a company set up by the Open University, is now working with a number of large organisations and multi-national companies to provide web-based interactive learning and training. The need for this has two main drivers; one is the demand for e-learning and the second, linked to this, is the development of corporate universities.

E-learning is perceived as a means of making learning and training more cost-effective by providing it at, or near to, employee's work stations – and in 'bite size' chunks that can provide learning 'just in time' rather than conventional approach of providing learning 'just in case'. A clear model of how to make effective use of e-learning has still to emerge but the initial euphoria, associated with the dot com phenomenon, has given way to the more measured approach of integrating e-learning appropriately into a range of learning and training systems – the so called 'blended learning'.

Corporate universities (CUs) have been developed within organisations as means of raising the profile of staff development, and as reaction to dissatisfaction with the knowledge and skill-set that new graduates tend to exhibit. Some CUs are simply training departments by another name; others accredit workplace based learning and combine this with academic study to provide tightly focused degree programmes. The advantages are significant; staff development receives a boost, the focus tends to shift from training to learning, and praxis, the practical application of knowledge is applied to delivering business and organisational goals. A major personal benefit for employees is the potential growth in self-esteem that stems from attaining new knowledge and skills, and of being able to experience the improvements they can make in their working roles. The reward of widely recognised academic qualification can enhance this process.

A further reward for employees can be financial, especially if the learning outcomes match with the organisation's competency framework and rewards structure. The further benefit for the organisation can be success in the 'talent war' as the visible opportunities to gain training, qualifications and rewards can attract more applicants. There can also be improvements in staff retention and morale.

So how does e-learning fit into the picture? In some cases not at all, as some CUs are training-centre based, using conventional models of teaching and learning – but things are changing. E-learning has much more in common with the philosophy of distance teaching than it has with face-to-face teaching and training. Distance learners have to become self-motivated, independent learners who can plan and organise their own learning patterns. They need to have a sound grasp of different learning styles and strategies and the knowledge to select which are appropriate to themselves and the subject matter. They are skilled learners, able to exploit the time and resources available – and these are portable skills that are highly valuable in the workplace, especially for employers who aim to build learning organisations. Research at the Open University shows that learning is much more effective when individuals take responsibility for teaching themselves.

So, e-learning, when it is set in the context of independent and collaborative learning, can be very effective – and this is beginning to be the case when the learning environment is supported by skilled e-moderators. E-moderators ease the transition from dependent to independent learning, they facilitate online interaction between participants (who might all be from different countries) and they provide feedback on learning activities, some of which will take place offline and in the workplace.

An important advantage of e-learning that fits well with the corporate university/learning organisation model is that of knowledge management. A record of the information disseminated via lectures and the subsequent discussion in seminars might exist in a variety of individual note forms and memories – but mainly it is lost. Online materials, resources and discussions can be turned into a searchable digital archive, or even into learning objects for future use.

Studying at conventional universities is increasingly costly and is therefore placing a greater financial burden on students and the families who support them. As corporate universities become more common, they might well begin to attract young people who see an advantage in being paid, gaining work experience and have the benefit of time to study for academic qualifications. It might well be that corporate universities influence changes in a form and structure of higher education which has hardly changed in 500 years. I have a dream that one day… (the sentence is yours to complete).

For further information on corporate university listings visit: www.universityshare.com/corporate.php

Further reading on this subject can be found on: http://ts.mivu.org/default.asp?show=article&id=785

Jim Flood, Director of Leaning, COROUS

COROUS is a company wholly owned by the Open University (OU), and dedicated to the development and delivery of blended learning solutions to large organisations. This work includes advice and consultancy on strategic, educational and technical issues.

The COROUS core team draws on the unparalleled resources of the OU, including academic subject specialists, instructional designers, web developers and network specialists. The team also draws on the expertise of the Institute of Educational Technology which specialises in research into learning design and the effectiveness of teaching and learning strategies. The OU has over 30 years experience of distance teaching and 13 years experience of researching, developing and delivering online courses, including providing preparation and support to online learners. Currently, the OU supports 250,000 students in some aspect of online learning.

For more information visit www.corous.com or contact COROUS on 01908 655400

1.13 E-learning

It is a mistake to attempt to replicate traditional forms of learning on-line and call it e-learning. Instead managers and designers of e-learning initiatives need to be aware of the range of e-learning technologies and techniques that might be used to create an appropriate solution for a particular problem and an identifiable group of learners.

The advent of e-learning a few years ago was hailed as a marvellous opportunity for employees to access learning in ways that were previously not possible. However, in many organisations the concept of e-learning was seized upon as primarily a cheaper way of training staff. No longer would employees need to be sent away on courses at the other end of the country and have to stay in expensive hotels; it could all be done very cheaply and easily with them sitting at their desks – and doing their job at the same time! The answer appeared to be the purchase of online courses to replace the classroom-based ones.

But has it worked? Well, employees frequently found themselves sitting at their desktops for hours on end, clicking the 'next' button as they worked their way through an online course with no respite – not even the thought of a drink at the hotel bar at the end of the day! They soon got bored and tired of studying in this way and 'dropped out', resulting in poor completion rates. Even attempts to make the courses more compelling through the use of multimedia had little effect on keeping learners glued to their course materials to the bitter end.

The reason for this state of affairs was that it was assumed that learners could study in the same way at their computers as they could in the classroom. In other words, that the traditional classroom course could be replicated online by simply converting the content into a web-based format. But what worked in the classroom, didn't work on the desktop. It was not the wrong choice of materials per se, but the whole course paradigm. In a fast moving world, employees don't have time to study vast amounts of comprehensive course materials *just in case* they might need them in the future, they need access to *just in time* information for them to carry out an activity or task in hand.

Even today, most people equate e-learning with e-training or e-courses, and most training in organisations still takes place on a very formal basis using the traditional training object – the 'course'. However, it is now well recognised that something like 75 per cent of all learning takes place *informally* in organisations. That is, not in the classroom or working through an online course, but in everyday working life as employees carry out their jobs – finding out information, reading documents, talking to other colleagues etc. It is these kinds of informal learning activities that need to be supported and encouraged online, and they need to be firmly embedded in work processes rather than seen as a separate 'learning' activity.

Many forward thinking organisations now recognise that e-learning is more than just e-training – it is also about information, communication, collaboration, performance support and knowledge sharing. In these organisations we now see a blurring of the lines between all these areas, and in particular a move towards the provision of just-in-time, short, bite-sized learning solutions.

Managers and designers of e-learning initiatives therefore need to be aware of the whole range of e-learning technologies and techniques that might be used to create an appropriate solution for a particular problem and an identifiable group of learners.

This might well be a formal online course, but could just as easily be an online presentation, demonstration or simulation, a scheduled live e-learning class, a collaborative learning experience, a learning game, or simply a job aid or other performance support tool. Learning designers also need to understand how they can best combine a mix of online solutions with traditional, face-to-face activities to create a 'blended' solution that provides a more complete learning experience.

And with the increasing availability of broadband, which provides high-speed, 'always on' access to the internet, e-learning solutions that capitalise on broadband technologies, eg streaming audio and video, now offer learners far more interactive, engaging and collaborative experiences than ever before. But in the pursuit of more media-rich content solutions, it must not be forgotten that learning is a social activity, and that you can often provide a far more powerful and enduring learning experience through the use of online communities and networks and by encouraging collaboration between learners than you can by placing lots of content online.

It is also not a matter of building a series of ad hoc e-learning events or solutions; learning is a process that involves the continuous development of the employee. A well designed e-learning strategy also needs to be firmly aligned with business objectives, eg increasing productivity or sales, or improving customer loyalty. Many organisations are still overly concerned with the number of people being trained, and whether employees have worked through every page of a course or passed all the tests. At the end of the day, it's not about how much employees have learnt; it's about how they've applied their learning, and how the performance of the organisation has improved. E-learning, just like learning itself, is a means to an end, not the end itself.

Jane Knight, e-learning Centre

The e-learning Centre has been providing independent e-learning advice and consultancy for small and large businesses as well as for universities and colleges since 1994. The e-learning Centre website also offers a free information resource for training professionals with links to thousands of selected and reviewed e-learning resources, examples of best practice, vendors of content, technology and services, as well as a calendar of e-learning events.

The Coach House
Upper Swell
Stow on the Wold
Gloucestershire GL54 1EW

Tel: 07778 063068; Web: www.e-learningcentre.co.uk

1.14 Bringing Out the Best

Almost a third of workers think their bosses underestimate their talents. As a result business leaders are losing the war for talent by not maximising the potential of their existing workforce.

Over the past decade, organisations have invested a lot of time and money into radically flattening company structures to dispel the rigid hierarchies typified by the 1980s. While this may have improved business efficiencies, employees have not always seen the benefits, as career development paths have disappeared.

Today's more people-focused companies are well aware of the importance of investing in their staff as 'talent' becomes the latest weapon in the battle for employer supremacy. Surprising then, that Chiumento's own research into employee satisfaction, 'Bringing out the Best', reveals that so many workers feel their abilities are overlooked.

Street interviews held in cities across the UK show that people crave more responsibility, with nearly a quarter wanting to play a bigger part in their organisations. A further quarter say that they have given up showing initiative and making suggestions, claiming that no-one takes any notice anyway.

These findings provide a wake-up call to business leaders who are losing the war for talent by not maximising the potential of their existing workforce. UK businesses too often fail to engage their employees, yet for a workforce to be truly motivated, it is key.

If every employer aimed to base their reputation on 'bringing out the best' in their staff, UK organisations would be far more productive, and happier places in which to work.

Defining talent

Engagement cannot be achieved through investment in training alone, it is about creating the right working environment to nurture individual talents. But what is talent and how can companies develop it?

Talent can be defined as the individual formula that makes up people's skills, knowledge, attitudes, experiences, intelligence, judgement and motivation as well as their ability to learn, adapt and grow.

Just thinking about talent in this way makes you ask the question – how well do you know the people in your organisation? Are you frustrating the organisation's ability to spot talent and frustrating your employees' opportunities to apply their talent in a way that maximises their potential?

An important part of the process is being clear about what sort of talent will make the difference in your business, given market conditions and competitive factors. By developing a clear line of sight on future capability requirements you can spot relevant talent more easily.

Managers need to take a broad view on what constitutes talent. Talent is not intrinsically linked to intelligence. An employee can be a great team player, be very empathetic or possess amazing energy and enthusiasm – all these attributes are talents in their own right and make the person possessing them a valuable asset, particularly if for example such talents are key to delivering a critical corporate project. Would such a person really benefit from training in tangible skills or would such a person respond better to personal praise and increased recognition? I would argue the latter.

Maximising talent through achieving accountability and autonomy

A key aim for organisations is to liberate talent and creativity and maximise individual potential, yet half of respondents believe that their talents are currently underused within their organisations, with the classic symptoms of talent waste being restrictive job design, job duplication and working in perceived isolation from colleagues.

Job design is key to employee engagement with an organisation because it brings with it accountability. However, there is a new kind of hierarchy embedded in the UK workplace in which rigid job roles allow individuals the chance to perform only limited functions, with little autonomy. If a person does not feel personally responsible for their job, then why should they feel a sense of engagement?

A second cause of talent waste is job duplication – when a person's job overlaps with someone else's. Job duplication is an inefficient use of an employee's capabilities and once again, neither party feels they have total ownership for the task or process so the crucial element of personal responsibility does not exist. Why have an employee duplicate a part of another employee's role when their talents could be better maximised elsewhere?

Companies are also missing out on maximising potential by allowing staff to work in isolation. With more disparate organisational structures and increasing use of technology in workplace communication, people often work alone with little support around them. This is not conducive to nurturing talent. Instead, it's vital that workers are able to collaborate so that they can share and learn from each other's skills.

Employees also need to feel engaged in the strategic vision of the organisation – what they are aiming towards and how they fit in. This can only be achieved through regular communication from senior management, which is difficult if staff work in isolation. If a boss's vision is communicated effectively, people are more likely to share it. By taking a more creative role rather than a controlling one and allowing managers below them to be more autonomous, this culture is likely to filter positively through the organisation.

Training talent

It is a common misconception that if you simply invest in your employees then you are more likely to retain them. While it is true that investing in training does increase employees' loyalty to the organisation, it does not guarantee their engagement. The problem is that many organisations 'sheep dip' employees through fragmented training rather than leading them towards a common organisational goal and strategic vision.

Employers should not underestimate the importance of peer learning as an effective coaching tool. With 43 per cent of 'Bringing out the Best' respondents claiming that they receive little or no coaching to draw out their talents, there is a real opportunity for employers to create a culture of lifelong learning and individual recognition.

Yet training does not just come from outside an organisation. Talent also needs to be nurtured from within and the key to this lies with senior management. Research findings show that 29 per cent of workers have a negative attitude towards their bosses, yet it should be the primary duty of senior management to create organisations where employees enjoy working. By giving their team members increased accountability, senior managers can move towards creating a role where, rather than directing workers, they are able to create new opportunities for them to use their talents and create the much coveted 'great place to work'.

Engage, engage, engage

Engagement is key. It is not about financial reward or investment in training, but about company culture. Do employees feel that their role within an organisation is valued and respected? Do they feel that they have the autonomy to work through challenges and opportunities? And do they feel a sense of personal accountability for the outcome? Similarly, does the organisation have a clear line of sight on what constitutes talent in their business? Does the organisation know its people well? Is there alignment between individual and organisational goals? And do you have the right people in the right place doing the right things?

If the answer is yes, then people will truly be a company's best asset.

Top tips for employers

How to bring out the best in your employees:

- Set up and implement career development and appraisals.
- Present career development as a working partnership between managers and employees.
- Help people understand what their key skills are and work to develop them.
- Set up an 'experience and talent database' highlighting key and unusual skills held within the organisation. Draw on these and encourage staff to share wisdom with others.
- Acknowledge that people can be talented in many different ways, and it is not just linked to intelligence. For example, they can be effective team workers, energetic, intuitive, empathetic, good communicators and/or inspirational.
- Consider coaching as a way to help talented staff focus in the right direction.
- Ensure that your managers are able to motivate their staff and pull them in the best direction.
- Develop individual training programmes with staff by identifying gaps in learning.
- Recognise that every employee has different career aspirations and not all may want to be fast-tracked.
- Celebrate individual and team successes and achievements.
- Consider investing in an on-line career development system and encourage both employees and managers to be responsible for using it.

Liz McGivern, Director, Talent & Performance Management, Chiumento

Chiumento is a medium-sized HR consultancy, founded in 1994 by Richard and Sarah Chiumento. Chiumento provides outplacement, interim and strategic consultancy to blue chip clients.

Contact details are as follows: Tel: 020 7224 3307; Web: www.chiumento.co.uk;
E-mail: *info@chiumento.co.uk*

1.15 Creativity

Michael Bichard, former permanent secretary at the Department for Education & Employment and now Rector of the London Institute, regrets that too few people in the public and private sectors have the chance to express their creativity.

Increasingly, creativity matters to organisations. As technology and business systems reduce the difference in performance, creativity is the way to distinguish between products. It drives new products, new policies and profitability. In the public sector it is the key to finding solutions to social problems with limited resources. In a period of unprecedented change and uncertainty it is a 'must have'. We need it to realise the power of enhanced technology. We need it to stay ahead of the pack.

And the good news is that people want to be creative. They nearly always crave the space to innovate and thus realise their potential. The bad news is that many people have been convinced by parents, friends or tutors that they are not creative – or else they work for managers who believe that creativity is a given which cannot be enhanced. They believe it is the same as intellect – which it is not. As a result many people and many organisations don't even think about how they might become more creative – or how they might use training to enhance their creativity. And the sadness is that it's not difficult to achieve. For a start, leaders can play a key part by the way they behave. Do they welcome new ideas or discount them with a curt 'we've tried that before and it didn't work'? Do they listen to staff and clients? Do they encourage a climate where people are rewarded for critiquing new ideas rather than producing them, and where the prevailing culture is one of sarcasm?

The leader's attitude to hierarchies and status is pretty important too, because the evidence suggests that hierarchical, status-conscious organisations are not creative. But too many leaders take comfort in both, seeming to believe that an idea can only be a good idea if it comes from a senior manager. They protect hierarchical structures even though these prevent the free flow of ideas which feed innovation – often because hierarchies protect them. They show by their behaviour that they do not welcome challenge, because they are not confident in their role. So they send out a message that people are valued for what they did yesterday, which secured their place in the hierarchy, rather than what they are contributing today.

Creativity thrives in a climate of trust where people feel able to be open and share their 'off the wall' thinking. It thrives on trust too because creativity inevitably increases the level of risk and people don't take risks for those they don't trust. Developing the skills to manage risk matters as well, and successful creative leaders understand and practise risk management. They help people define risk – is it financial, political or reputational? They help people assess whether it is acceptable. They help people to minimise it and to have in place contingency plans to react to deal with the unexpected. And the likelihood is that they know how to handle a risk that goes wrong in a way that increases the likelihood of future innovation. That means that their first reaction is not to search out someone to blame.

To be creative, organisations need energy – more than is necessary merely to survive. And the best creative leaders have the ability to create it. They instil belief, legitimise passion and value the people who have the courage to be different. They work hard to reduce the ways in which organisations lose energy, often because of friction between different parts, and most frequently between the centre and the field. They seek to reduce the activities which add no value, whether these are writing unnecessarily long reports or attending pointless meetings. Creative leaders have a knack of surrounding themselves with people who create energy – and I am increasingly convinced that the world is made up of people who either create or consume energy. Creative organisations do not have too many consumers of energy!

Creative organisations tend to be outward looking. They are good at importing new ideas. They search out best practice because they want to improve the quality of what they do. They have developed the skills to develop strong partnerships – skills like negotiating, influencing and coalition building. Creative organisations encourage people to join them knowing, in the words of Arie de Geus, whether they are either fast flowing streams or stagnant puddles. Too many organisations make no real effort to connect with and listen to their clients, sometimes because the message they receive will be unwelcome, and sometimes because they don't really believe that what the client tells them can transform the way they go about the business. It can – and at the same time connecting staff with clients can be the spark which fires their motivation, as well as their creativity.

Partly that's about communication, about listening as well as informing. And that is key inside the organisation too. If people can tap into a free flow of good ideas and radical thinking they will be more inclined to be creative. If they are drowning in a sea of memos, e-mails, minutes; meetings; then they will have no time left for thinking creatively about their job or their product. But even now, how many organisations are seriously addressing the negative impact which failing to manage the e-mail is having on their creativity?

And how much effort does your organisation put into the process of business development? In the public sector, if we are honest, very little. And in the private sector, how creative is the business development process? How successful are we in our teams to encourage thinking which will develop new products, policies and services? How good are we at protecting the new ideas, at a stage when they are barely formed, so that they can be developed to the point when they can be seriously appraised? I worked with a company called What If whilst at the DfEE and they called it 'greenhousing' – the place where you protect the green shoots.

None of this is rocket science. Much of it can be learned. All of it can play a part in making our work places more fun. So what's stopping us? Creativity isn't something woolly and marginal. It is increasingly what makes the difference between success and failure.

Sir Michael Bichard KCB has worked throughout his career in the public sector – twenty years in Local Government and nearly ten in Central Government. He was Chief Executive of Brent and Gloucestershire Local Authorities and in 1990 became Chief Executive of the Government's Benefits Agency. In 1995 he was appointed Permanent Secretary of the Employment Department and then the Department for Education and Employment. In May 2001 he left the Civil Service and in September 2001 was appointed Rector of The London Institute, the largest Art and Design Institute in Europe. Further information tel: 0207 514 6002

1.16 Closing the Leadership Gap

The old days of 'command and control' are gone. In order to cope with this extreme degree of ongoing change in today's business world a collective approach is essential.

Bridging the inspiration gap

We have seen a dramatic change in what is required of good leaders over recent years; those organisations whose leaders do not operate to these required new ways of working will undoubtedly face serious problems in an ever more uncertain future.

In a major survey of over 1500 managers conducted by the Chartered Management Institute and Demos, people were asked what they would most like to see in their leaders. The single most important factor by a very significant margin, which was highlighted by 55 per cent of the sample, was 'inspiration' but only 11 per cent actually saw this 'ability to inspire' in their leaders. The top two attributes actually observed were 'knowledgeability' and 'ambition'. However, 'inspirational leadership' is vital when confronted with the biggest challenge that leaders face today, namely the unbelievable rate of change going on in the world around them.

Another startling piece of research reveals that in a single day last year there were as much world trade conducted as during the whole of 1949; as much scientific research done as during the whole of 1960; as many telephone calls made as during the whole of 1983 and as many e-mails sent as during the whole of 1990. This frighteningly dynamic environment puts effective innovation at a premium and requires leaders to have to 'inspire' their people right across and through the organisation to want and to be fully involved in continually coming up with better ways of doing things to keep ahead of the competition. The old days of 'command and control' are gone. In order to cope with this extreme degree of ongoing change, a collective approach is essential if you are to be sufficiently fleet of foot. Good modern leadership is all about sharing and involving. In the words of the Japanese proverb: 'none of us is as smart as all of us'.

Traditional leadership innovation blockers

Your archetypal traditional leader is the biggest single blocker of effective innovation. One of the great drivers of innovation is ignorance. Some of the best innovations happen because people ask naive, uninformed questions. How many traditional leaders do you know who are willing to admit to ignorance?

Another key driver for innovation is diversity, with people coming at issues from very different perspectives feeling free to express their different points of view. Innovation thrives on positive dissent. How many traditional leaders do you know who are comfortable with any form of dissent, which they see as undermining their authority?

Leading effective innovation is all about revelling in the success of other people. To foster innovation, leaders have to want other people to be more successful than they are and – even more challenging – be prepared to take the blame for other people's failures! How many traditional leaders do you know, who are happy not to take personal credit for every success and pick up the blame for the failures of others?

Innovation is also, and importantly, a very social activity within the workplace, requiring high levels of trust and collaboration. How many traditional leaders do you know, who still tend to cut themselves off from their people, which is clearly not the ideal basis for mutual trust and genuine collaboration?

Pointers to inspirational leadership

So how do we move away from the traditional leadership model and really start to close this critical leadership 'inspiration' gap to achieve optimum innovation?

Several ongoing Department of Trade and Industry (DTI) 'business sharing with business' leading-edge practice programmes are being driven with a number of lead partners, including the Institute of Directors, provide a number of powerful pointers as to what makes for inspirational leadership. These programmes include *Partnerships with People*, *Living Innovation* and the *100 Best Companies to Work For*, the latter produced by Best Companies (UK) and published annually by the *Sunday Times*.

Six essential elements of 'inspirational leadership' come through time and time again, despite the mix and broad spread of the different organisations involved:

- *Inspirational leaders genuinely care about their people.* When you ask people what it is like to work in an organisation run by an inspirational leader they talk about openness, honesty, respect and trust. These are very friendly workplaces and people feel highly valued and regarded. When you walk around there is a sort of electricity in the air and you are struck by their incredible energy and buzz. As one leader put it: 'There is no other source of competitive advantage. Others can copy our investment, technology and scale – but not the quality of our people!'
- *Inspirational leaders involve everybody.* People are given considerable freedom and support to get on with the job and are highly motivated and fulfilled as a result. As another leader put it to us: 'We never use the word "empowerment". You can't empower people, you can only create the climate and structure in which they will take responsibility'.
- *Inspirational leaders listen a lot.* They recognise that it is the people doing the job who generally know the solutions to the problems and they ask for and respect what their people tell them about how to do things better. One of the respondents in the *Partnerships with People* programme said: 'It is not the sole prerogative of the senior managers to come up with the good ideas'.
- *Inspirational leaders show lots of appreciation.* Recognition is an absolutely crucial element of inspiration, but it seems that we are not very good in the UK at saying 'thank you'. Yet those two words are a tremendous motivator when used genuinely at the right time. We came across some innovative ways in which inspirational leaders say 'thank you'. The opticians Dolland and Aitchison (whom we visited in our *Living Innovation* programme) have Incredible Colleague Awards, where staff who are successfully nominated can live out their 'incredible fantasies' courtesy of the company. Whether it is parachute jumping, driving a fast car round Silverstone or learning salsa dancing, the company will make it happen for the 'great colleague' as a very special way of saying 'thank you'.
- *Inspirational leaders ensure work is fun.* Fun is both a great indicator that an organisation is innovative and a key driver for innovation. At the *100 Best Companies to Work For* you see a lot of fun at work, ranging from lots of celebration of success (something else

we are not generally very good at in the UK!) to regular social nights out, to annual themed staff dinners. At the same time, these organisations enjoy outstanding performance.

- *Inspirational leaders and their people are deeply committed.* They are passionate about creating something special for their customers and, no matter how well they are doing, they are always looking to do things better. They are the epitome of what James Dyson describes as 'the restless company'. And they are deeply committed to the attainment of the shared vision for the organisation that they are all driving towards.
- An exciting new leadership programme is currently underway through the DTI and its partners, aimed at establishing an Inspired Leaders Index, providing clear sign-posting to the best available leadership tools and mapping and helping to further develop leadership networks across the country.
- The final word on inspirational leadership goes to another respondent from the *Partnerships with People* programme, who summed up how it feels like this: 'People are proud to work here. Proud of colleagues, proud of the company and proud of themselves'.

Nigel Crouch, Department of Trade and Industry

Nigel Crouch is a senior industrialist, who spends part of his time working with the DTI Innovation Group, where he is helping to lead on the ***'Partnerships with People', 'Living Innovation' and '100 Best Companies to Work'*** *For programmes.*
Copies of ***'Partnerships with People', 'Living Innovation' and '100 Best Companies to Work'*** *For can be obtained by: Order line telephone: 0870 150 2500; Fax: 0870 150 2333*
Websites: www.dti.gov.uk/pwp, www.lidiagnostic.com, www.Sunday-times.co.uk/bestcompanies

1.17 Building High Performance Teams

Much lip service is paid to the benefits of team-work but for team-work to really pay off more attention must be paid to what it actually means and how it can be implemented to benefit business.

Background

The idea of team-work is not always an easy one to grasp or explain. To use teams and be an effective team member, one needs to understand what is and is not a team. Most organisations, after all, organise their workforce into groups of people who work together; each has his/her own jobs to do, but these individuals are still referred to as teams. Teams can be dramatically productive. That does not mean, however, that any working group will automatically become an effective team, or that teams can simply be created and left to their own devices.

Essentially, the message of team-work is about delegation, empowerment and synergy. Team-working is about passing responsibility over to working teams, so that they get on with what they have to do without continually having to refer to higher levels in the organisation. That means that the teams need to be given enough authority to make day-to-day decisions about their work and enough power to make sure that things are done properly. Team-working also encourages people to be more professional in their approach and to take their responsibilities seriously – all of which is a tremendous benefit to any organisation.

Team performance

'Real teams'

Companies with strong performance standards seem to produce more 'real teams' than companies that promote teams per se. Teams do not become teams just because we call them teams or send them on team-building programmes. In fact, many frustrations with broad-gauged movements toward team-based organisations spring from just such imbalances. Real teams form best when management sets clear performance objectives.

High performance teams are extremely rare

Despite the attention teams have been receiving, the true high performance team – ie one that outperforms all other similar teams and outperforms expectations given its composition – is very rare. This is largely because a high degree of personal commitment to one another differentiates people on high performance teams from people on other teams. This kind of commitment cannot be managed, although it can be exploited and emulated to the great advantage of other teams and the broader organisation.

Hierarchy and teams go together almost as well as teams and performance

Teams integrate and enhance formal structures and processes. Hierarchical structures and basic processes are essential to large organisations and need not be threatened by teams. Teams, in fact, are the best way to integrate across structural boundaries and to both design and energise core processes. Those who see teams as a replacement for hierarchy are missing the true potential of teams.

Teams naturally integrate performance and learning

Few people now disagree with the aspiration implied in the learning organisation. Yet many people also express concerns over how to balance short-term performance emphasis with longer-term institution building. Teams do just that by translating longer-term purposes into definable performance goals and then developing the skills needed to meet those goals, learning not only occurs in teams but also endures.

Teams are the primary unit of performance for increasing numbers of organisations

Managers cannot master the opportunities and challenges now confronting them without emphasising teams far more than ever before. The performance challenges that face large companies in every industry (eg customer service, technological change, competitive threats and environmental constraints) demand the kind of responsiveness, speed, online customisation, and quality that is beyond the reach of individual performance. Teams can bridge this gap. Much of the success of teams lies in the disciplined pursuit of performance.

What is a team?

The working group

The difference between the working group and the team is that the working group does not have any particular need to develop and amplify its performance. But working groups are not necessarily a bad thing – for some organisations they are entirely appropriate. People participate in a working group to share information, to make decisions and to coordinate practices. The difference between that and the team is that the emphasis is always on enabling each individual to undertake his/her own area of responsibility. There is no shared responsibility and no particular need to establish it.

The pseudo team

There are a number of pitfalls, however, in moving from a working group to a real team. One of them is the danger of simply becoming a pseudo team – a group of people who are called, or who call themselves, a team and might have that potential, but who don't actually try to coordinate what they are doing or establish collective responsibility at all. Many senior management teams are of this kind: although their members may call themselves a team, in reality they act on a purely individual level and are concerned only with their own departments and responsibilities. They are a team in name only – a pseudo team. Many organisations that move into team working without really thinking through what is involved end up creating organisations consisting of pseudo teams rather than real ones. This often means that pseudo teams can be actually less effective than working groups.

The potential team

The potential team is a rather more optimistic halfway stage between the working group and the real team. This is a group that can see that there is a real need to improve performance and is really trying to do something about it. They are held back, though, mainly by a lack of clarity about shared goals and purposes and also by working practices which emphasise individual responsibilities and make it difficult to establish truly coordinated operations.

Given the right type of leadership and management, a potential team can make the change into a real team relatively straightforwardly with a corresponding increase in productivity. More commonly, however, the potential team continues to muddle along without any particularly clear direction.

A real team

A real team is a small number of people who are all jointly committed to a common purpose. They have shared goals and consider each member of the team to be equally accountable for what the team achieves, as well as for the general working approach that the team adopts. That does not mean, however, that everyone in the group is regarded as being the same.

A real team will consist of people who have complementary skills and who are also ready to learn new ones if the task demands it. But because they work together, what they are able to achieve is far more than they could have achieved if they had operated on an individual, or on a working group, basis.

The high performing team

The high performing team is the realisation of the ultimate in team potential. High performance teams have members who are deeply committed, not only to the team's success, but also to one another's personal growth and development – a relationship that has developed through the close interaction and shared responsibility of the team's activities.

These teams have extremely high performance achievements and often, in organisational terms, achieve goals that appear at the outset to be impossible. Although the team itself may have a limited life – typically, once the task has been achieved the team will dissolve – the close working relationships that emerge between team members continue to act as a positive factor throughout their subsequent organisational life.

Conclusion

In most organisations the actual dynamics of the team is rarely researched, planned for and actively added to the recruitment policy to ensure the best result in terms of performance from the group as a whole as well as the individual.

Colin Wallace, Team Dynamics International Ltd

Team Dynamics International (TDI) Ltd is one of the most established and respected operators in the fields of team development, experiential training and the dynamics of working groups. It specialises in delivering bespoke solutions, which not only deliver a motivational value to the trainee but also a bottom line and tangible benefit to the company or organisation itself. Its clients range from blue chip companies (eg Sainsbury's, Hays and Siemens) to those wishing to maximise the productivity and profitability of their employees as a team.

TDI Ltd is also responsible for the recruitment, training and management of the United Nations rapid response international emergency teams worldwide. With the help of recognised leaders in their fields, such as Dr Meredith Belbin, TDI has developed many working practises and techniques that have been taken on board and are now company policy in many of the UK's major blue chip organisations.

For more information please contact Colin Wallace, Director of Programmes Tel: 01892 535432

1.18 Coaching For Development

Executive coaching is a growth business. Amid the hype, the real power and purpose of coaching can be forgotten. Mike Brent brings coaching back to the basics of learning and development.

The aim of coaching is always to have better performance and the relationship between manager and employee is key for this. The coach helps the person being coached develop their own thinking and awareness. Many managers make the mistake of trying to solve their employees' problems with the result that they end up taking responsibility – and learning – away from the person. Coaching is about *allowing* the employee to perform to their full potential.

At Ashridge we see in our workshops many examples of managers whose default style is to go immediately to giving advice to employees, depriving them of the opportunity to work out their own solutions. Coaching helps them get out of this mindset.

A further impetus to coaching is the shift from management to leadership (although organisations still need both). Leaders must be able to coach. Coaching is essentially about creating and generating options and alternatives. If your only style is to tell people what to do, you are not empowering or enabling them.

Moreover, time is limited because the rate of change is accelerating, and the degree of complexity encountered by managers is increasing rapidly. Managers are having to deal less with simple puzzles, and more with complex problems and dilemmas (see Figure 1). The difference is that with puzzles there are answers available, and they can often be solved by an individual. Complex problems are less evident and are likely to need input from different sources to solve them.

And then there are dilemmas which don't have any solutions, only options and alternatives. For example, the question, 'What should our strategy be for the next five years?' has no single correct answer waiting to be discovered. This is a dilemma, not a puzzle or a problem. All managers

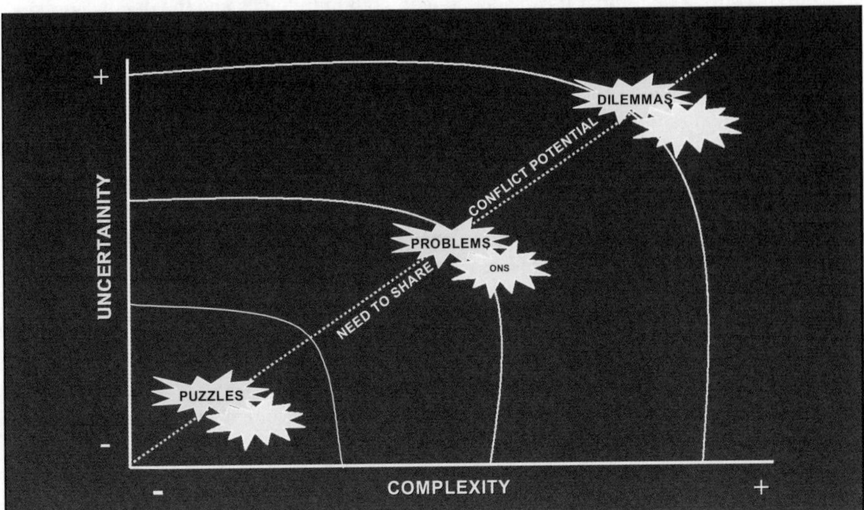

Figure 1: Coaching in a complex Environment
Source: Mike Brent, 2000. Adapted from Casey and Critchley 1985

can do is to engage in dialogue, listen, be creative and come up with different options and alternatives. If we confuse puzzles with dilemmas, then we are in danger of simplifying the issue, imposing dogma instead of looking together for alternatives.

Many managers are excellent at solving technical issues, but are not so good at dealing with human ones. One of the key roles of a manager is to develop his or her team's strengths and it's not always an easy role to play. Coaching is about helping people and enabling them to achieve something, whether it may be promotion, skills, performance, self-understanding or better balance. It has to be client-centred and not coach-, or even organisation-, centred.

The argument for coaching in terms of competitiveness is among the most straightforward. When products and services are similar, competitive advantage comes from having people with ideas, skills, responsibility and initiative. Learning makes the difference and the core idea of coaching is to help others learn. Managers cannot wait for the rest of the organisation to change before they change. We all have to take individual responsibility for learning.

There are many models which can be used in training managers to be more effective coaches. However, the real value of the coaching training lies in the actual practising of coaching, with participants bringing real issues to the workshop. In our experience, role playing is not as effective as working with real issues. After all, when you are back in the organisation, you don't have the option of saying, 'this was just a game'.

Making coaching work requires a number of things:

- Recognition that coaching is not time consuming. Simply telling people what to do is what actually consumes time. You can coach in a five minute session simply by developing the reflex of asking rather than telling. Too often managers are tempted to use the 'Why don't you' model, instead of asking people what their own thoughts and options are.
- Coaching needs a supportive organisational culture. The coaching culture has to come from a strong belief that it can add value to both individuals and the organisation.
- Workshops are not enough. Many participants in our workshops fully understand the importance of developing a coaching style, but if they go back to a boss who uses old fashioned command and control styles, and does not support coaching in practice, there is a strong possibility that they will stop using their coaching skills.
- Top management must communicate the importance of coaching. This means that they have to be visible in supporting it and, most importantly, using it themselves.
- It is important for senior members of the management team to point out the strategic importance of coaching to the participants. A coaching culture will not survive in the organisation unless it is seen to add value to the strategy of the organisation and improve the quality of organisational life.
- Resistances to the idea of managers using a coaching style must be acknowledged and brought into the open.
- Coaching must not be seen as a fad or just as remedial. The aim of coaching is to help people achieve their potential. No serious sportsman or woman would consider not using a coach – why shouldn't managers?
- When training managers to be coaches, there must be practice sessions using real issues as well as theory. The real learning comes by doing, and getting feedback.
- Coaching must take account of cross-cultural differences – especially when people are being trained to coach.

- Coaching must be linked to strategy. If we only focus on change at an individual level then the effort and initiative will be lost. On the other hand, if we work on strategy but forget implementation, then we are wasting time.
- Implementation is always carried out by individuals and a process is needed to work through the implementation of the strategy. Coaching is such a process.

Mike Brent, Ashridge

Ashridge, one of the world's leading business schools, is an independent, not for profit organisation, working with individuals and organisations in personal and corporate development (open & tailored programmes, online learning, MBA, MSc and Diploma qualifications).

Executive development is one of the activities undertaken by the Ashridge (Bonar Law Memorial) Trust based at Ashridge Estate, Berkhamsted, Hertfordshire, HP4 1NS, others being organisation consulting through Ashridge Consulting and management research. Research is carried out by the Ashridge Centre for Business and Society and the Ashridge Strategic Management Centre, the latter based in London. Ashridge is also an international conference centre, hosting meetings, seminars, workshops and conferences for a range of organisations. Ashridge is accredited by AACSB, AMBA and EQUIS.

Website: www.ashridge.org.uk

For information on Ashridge, please contact:
Toby Roe:
Tel: 01442 841289/E-mail: toby.roe@ashridge.org.uk
Jenny Reynolds:
Tel: 01442 841019/E-mail: jenny.reynolds@ashridge.org.uk

1.19 Emotional Intelligence – What Can It Do For Me and My Business?

Emotional Intelligence is possessed by people with the right attitude. People who don't have it can be taught it.

Organisations want the 'right' people. People who can learn and adapt quickly, who can solve problems without being told to, who can come up with creative ideas and not wait for others to do it for them. People with a positive attitude. In short, people with high levels of *Emotional Intelligence*.

You know when people have it and when they don't, but what exactly is Emotional Intelligence (EI)? Basically it is a set of non-cognitive abilities that influence the way we get on in life. It works with IQ to enhance performance. The term was first coined in 1985 by Dr Reuven Bar-On, an Israeli psychologist. He dedicated 17 years of his life to scientifically validating the answer to the question 'Are there factors that determine one's ability to be successful in life?'

In the mid nineteen nineties, Daniel Goleman brought the field to popular attention in his books *Emotional Intelligence* and *Working with Emotional Intelligence*. He defined the seven key emotional abilities most necessary for human beings to be successful. They are:

- the ability to motivate ourselves;
- the ability to persist against frustration;
- the ability to delay gratification;
- the ability to regulate moods;
- the ability to hope;
- the ability to empathise;
- the ability to control impulses.

The more we master these skills, the greater our level of motivation and the better developed our interpersonal skills. This in turn has an effect on what we do and how we do it. And since organisations are made of people, it is obvious that these factors are crucial to the organisation's success.

So for an organisation to be successful it needs to have the 'right' people, those with high levels of EI. How can you achieve this? You can either recruit people with high levels of EI or develop the workforce you already have. But can people really be trained in emotional intelligence? Fast? What differences will it make?

To find out, the Talent Foundation carried out a simple study comparing the attitudes of people who had been on an EI course with ones that had not. Our research showed that people who had been on the course have significant advantages in:

- 'Can do' attitude – confidence in the contribution they can make at work, attitude towards finding opportunities to use their skills at work;
- Willingness to learn – positive attitude towards learning;
- Confidence on what and how to learn;
- Win-win attitude regarding training provided by employers.

So what is an EI course and what does it take to increase your level of EI? It's all about changing the way we behave and react. Research from the fields of cognitive and behavioural science provides us with ways of doing this. Just as it is important to be able to make a connection between a particular food that we ate and a stomach ache, it is important for people to link their thoughts with their feelings and behaviours. At the Talent Foundation we have developed tools that help people remove barriers that prevent the acquisition of new skills and ways of being. One such tool is the TalentKey workshop.

Our analysis has shown that people who have attended have changed in how optimistic they feel about themselves. This kind of shift can have real and fast benefits to an organisation. Optimistic people are more positive, and more receptive to new ideas. They will respond to change more speedily and more successfully. They will assist you in the changes as opposed to resisting the change.

Lack of understanding, rivalry and not fully appreciating how the whole company works towards the common goal all prevent people working as well as they are able. All these are caused by lack of communication in the organisation. After attending TalentKey we can see that people are more willing to share their opportunities, concerns and feelings – open communication is an essential ingredient in maintaining employee motivation.

In today's changing world of work, companies need to be able to adapt and innovate. This involves a certain amount of risk taking. After attending the workshop, we found that employees are more open to taking risks. They try things that they thought were not possible in the past by exploring new avenues or changing old habits. The fast changing pace of the world of work also means that people need to keep learning and expanding what they know. £23 billion is spent on training in the UK each year, but do companies really reap the benefits? People who have attended TalentKey are 25 per cent more likely to be open to new learning than they were before the workshop.

All of this research and experience illustrates that Emotional Intelligence can be learnt. Thus, 'wrong' people, by attending EI courses and being supported, can be turned into the 'right' people.

What would life be like if we stopped looking at people in terms of them being right and wrong people, but as developed and undeveloped? Emotional Intelligence could just be the key!

The Talent Foundation
Little Russell House
22 Little Russell Street
London WC1A 2HT
Tel: 020 7430 2023
Fax: 020 7430 2024
Website: www.talentfoundation.org

1.20 Making e-business and e-commerce Strategies Pay

Investment in training and development will not produce results unless a carefully thought-out strategy to integrate technology and management is in place.

E-commerce, in simple terms, means doing business via a communication medium using modern technology, hardware and software applications. E-business, on the other hand, is the application of information technologies over public standards-based networks to improve the efficiency and effectiveness of business processes. Such a process invariably involves rethinking processes and perhaps creating entirely new business designs.

Companies introducing e-technologies sometimes have mixed results as they fail to integrate the necessary business transformations with the new e-technology initiative. In today's inter-networked world, company executives are embarking on major changes in order to grow, improve efficiency and to become more customer focused. It is important that management teams spearheading such projects have a good overview of e-business related technology to successfully blend the introduction of technology with organisation changes.

A large percentage of e-commerce software projects continue to fail to meet customer expectations, despite significant advances in the software development processes and techniques. User involvement is considered one of the most important factors contributing to the success of an IT project. It is crucial that companies initiating major e-commerce projects have the staff with the skills in e-business technology.

e-xioms

Technology is no longer an afterthought in forming business strategy, but the actual cause and driver. The new era of technology-driven business models bring about the ability to streamline the structure, influence and control of information that is dramatically more powerful and cost-effective than moving and manufacturing physical products.

The business design of the future increasingly uses reconfigurable e-business and e-commerce community models to best meet customer needs. Some of the driving forces behind the adoption of e-business include:

- rising customer expectations;
- changing manufacturing/service models;
- greater competition;
- shorter product life cycles;
- price pressures.

In order to meet these challenges, companies need to adopt a business model that incorporates flexible partnerships using electronic means. For a manufacturing company, this could mean product development and manufacturing partnerships involving many component designers and parts manufacturers. In the service sector, it could be a consortium of companies whose services complement each other and form packaged solutions to a customer need. By using electronic means to form such alliances, companies stand to gain financially.

It can also open up new business opportunities. Partnerships can reduce the cost of products/services and increase the effectiveness of communication between collaborating companies. These factors and the flexibility of such alliances can encourage companies to form such partnerships as and when needed (eg for specific products and services). Companies can provide better value for customers and reduce time to market lead time in a number of cases using a flexible outsourcing alliance. In order for such 'virtual enterprises' to succeed, it is essential that they have the IT infrastructure and inhouse to support and drive change, innovation and business goals.

e-technology

Use of innovative technology plus new business models can give companies a competitive differentiation. The Internet is one of the most widely accessible computing infrastructures and is an enabling tool in many of the e-business ventures. Some of the new forms of doing business over the Internet include:

- procurement;
- customer interaction;
- supplier management.

A number of e-business technologies and package solutions are available regarding:

- customer relationship management (CRM);
- enterprise application integration (EAI);
- supply chain management (SCM);
- sell-side solutions;
- buy-side solution.

CRM

It costs six times more to sell to a new customer than an existing one: the odds of selling to a new customer are 15 per cent while those of selling to an existing customer are 50 per cent. In addition, 70 per cent of complaining customers will do business with the company again if it quickly resolves product/service issues. However, 90 per cent of companies don't have the sales and services integration to support e-business.

CRM is a business strategy and a class of enterprise applications that seek to understand a company's customers from a multifaceted perspective. CRM's scope covers sales, marketing and customer service across multiple customer contact channels. The following are some areas in which CRM has become very effective:

- sales and marketing;
- customer service and support;
- customer email management systems;
- response and proactive email correspondence;
- interfaces to facilitate integration into other customer facing applications;
- business intelligence capabilities;
- analytics/data warehousing/data mining.

EAI

EAI are solutions that facilitate unrestricted sharing of data, application, intelligence and business processes among the many connected applications and data sources in and across enterprises. A number of inter-operable software tools are currently available, with Web Services and XML being two of the prominent technologies enabling application integration. EAI can be considered as the missing link, hiding the complexity of the underlying system from the end user.

There are a number of advantages in adopting EAI strategies:

- ability to use legacy or existing applications;
- existing databases can be integrated to new systems;
- investment in the IT infrastructure is protected;
- reduced time and cost of implementing a new system.

SCM

It is estimated that cost saving of up to seven per cent can be achieved through supply–chain integration. Changing logistics and technology introduces many challenges in the management of such extended enterprises. Despite the technical complexities in adopting SCM, companies stand to gain by reduced lead time and improved efficiency.

For companies in the service sector, a more closely related and applicable technology is Value Chain Management (VCM), where a group of organisations collaborate to deliver a complete service to the end user.

Sell-side solutions

Sell-side solutions cover a suit of software application that is focused on improving the effectiveness of sales activities. This includes product presentation, catalogue generation and automated order processing.

By using sell-side solutions, additional value can be generated through the extension of existing applications including sales related processes, warranty administration and contract administration. With the aid of electronic sell-side application, companies can benefit from:

- increased revenues and customer reach;
- convenience;
- cost reduction (including that of marketing materials);
- better customer service and enhanced customer satisfaction;
- order accuracy.

Buy-side solutions

These are software applications designed to automate the buying process and are also called e-procurement. E-procurement solutions using the Internet can make corporate purchasing activities more efficient and cost effective. The scope of e-procurement solutions includes:

- buying strategies;
- transaction processing;
- sport buying for direct and indirect materials – an emerging concept in solutions called digital marketplaces.

Digital marketplaces: bazaars of the 21st century

Digital marketplaces are totally automated environments where buyers and sellers can interact and complete a transaction. Based on the type of seller and buyer, some of the common classifications of such transactions are:

- consumer to consumer (C2C), eg eBay;
- consumer to business (C2B), eg Priceline.com;
- business to consumer (B2C), eg Amazon.com;
- business to business (B2B), eg VerticalNet;
- business to government (B2G), eg Govworks.com.

Digital marketplaces can be broadly categorised into vertical and horizontal markets. Some examples of these include:

- vertical:
  - SciQuest.com
  - E-steel
  - PlasticsNet
- horizontal;
  - Mro.com
  - Ecredit.com
  - Celarix.com

Success factors for the vertical market place include domain expertise, first mover advantage, relationships with buyers and sellers, neutrality, back-end systems integration, compelling content and partnerships. Those applicable to the success of the horizontal market place include the degree of process standardisation and generalisation, process knowledge and workflow automation expertise, the ability to customise the business process to respond to industry specific differences and back-end systems integration.

The future of e-business solutions

Widespread use of e-business solutions can result in the greater consolidation and realisation of the market place. It is possible that buy-side solutions will morph into digital market places and solution vendors will merge/acquire (be acquired by) supply chain vendors. The flexibility and cost effectiveness of setting up alliances electronically can also result in a shift towards dynamic trade where suppliers, buyers or other business partners are constantly evolving.

With the widespread use of e-business solutions in the industry, there will be a greater emphasis on integration with various enterprise procurement packages of new partners and the acquisition of skills to use such systems effectively.

The importance of training

It is important that companies venturing into using e-business technologies have a good training strategy to improve the skills of employees at all levels. Involvement of employees with domain expertise in any e-enabling project will positively contribute to its success. They can be effective decision makers in exploiting modern technology to improve business competence. Hence it is advisable that company executives take the initiative in training their employees in e-business in order to reap the benefits of doing business using the greatest network infrastructure available to all – the Internet. This could be arranged through on-the-job training, seminars or in a customised workshop.

Recommendations

E-business requires the streamlining of business processes to competitive advantage. It is essential that companies consider new processes and process integration as well as new models for doing business when adopting e-technologies. A key factor in any e-business project is the availability of inhouse expertise for developing and using business solutions based on modern technology.

Dr Muhammad Farmer, British Institute of Technology & E-commerce

The British Institute of Technology and E-commerce (BITE) aims to be one of the world's leading research and academic centres, examining the dynamics of the e-commerce industry. The Institute will use the most advanced technologies for research and education that will be a valuable resource for the world's leading businesses.

Apex House
87–89 Plashet Road
London E13 0RA
Tel: 020 8552 3071
Fax: 020 8552 3546
E-mail: info@bite.ac.uk
Website: www.bite.ac.uk

1.21 Creating a Customer Driven Culture

A customer driven culture needs to be driven from the top downwards.

One can hardly engage in any capacity with current organisations without encountering mantras about the importance of customers: 'the customer is king', 'exceeding customer expectations', 'customers are at the heart of our organisation' are but a few. Searching just one business school's website lists 874 relevant articles. It seems that customers are big news. The bad news is, few organisations live up to their mantras.

Effective organisations have always known it makes sense to invest in their customers to minimise defections and generate repeat business and referrals. Winning customers is difficult and expensive, but the lifetime value of loyal customers is significant: £5000 for a pizza eater, £200,000 for a car owner.

Customer importance is especially pertinent in today's market. It is a truism that competition and change are increasing. A fully featured quality product and a commitment to service are mandatory just to enter the sales arena. Creating a competitive advantage requires more. Today's customers, overwhelmed by choice, and ever more sophisticated, look to maximise the value added to them. Most consumer spending is no longer on functional necessities. It is about identity projects. A product's worth can only be measured by its value in the customer's world and their perception of the experience of purchasing and owning it. Success depends on their experience.

Customer driven cultures, that is using culture to promote a focus on customer experience, is a recent phenomenon. Its roots lie in the limitations of early forms of 'scientific management' as exemplified by Taylor, Foyle, Galbraith and Ford. They stressed the objective design of work, which effectively led to a separation of thought and action. Management's role was to scientifically design the best work practices and control labour, whose sole responsibility was implementation. This approach bought about enormous advances in organisational performance and the basic philosophy is still operative in many organisations, although the rhetoric may have changed.

However, it has increasingly relevant drawbacks: modern workers find mindless implementation unmotivating and the price of losing worker knowledge and discretionary effort becomes ever greater as we move to a knowledge economy. Customer knowledge, most concentrated at the customer interface, is one of the most valuable, and difficult to obtain, forms of knowledge.

If these problems are to be addressed by allowing a wider involvement in decision making, management faces a problem. If they relinquish formal control and stress customer influence, how can they maintain alignment with organisational priorities and objectives? The answer is provided by anthropology through its demonstration of the way cultures regulate behaviour.

Culture, the unconscious rules that regulate 'how things are done around here', plays a powerful role in aligning behaviour. What's more, it permeates informal systems which shape everyday behaviour. Its power is 'power with consent' leading to sincerity and authenticity instead of resigned behavioural compliance.

The best start to harnessing culture is to understand the current culture, which may be complex, multilayered or fragmentary. This is not gathering customer feedback on the organisation's offerings, but understanding how the organisation operates and relates to its customers. Many tools are available to do this: focus groups, interviews, customer forums, culture questionnaires to name a few. The important thing is to use externally validated methods which include an objective view and allow current and desired states to be compared. Without this, the results may simply be filtered to confirm existing cultural norms.

The next crucial step is to decide whether culture change is realistic given the psychological and physical resources available. Given the damage that failed culture change can do, a programme should not be undertaken lightly.

If the decision to go ahead is made, three areas need consideration: strategic processes; systems and procedures; operative culture. If they are aligned and focused on the customer, success is highly likely. If they are not, frustration, inefficiency and customer dissatisfaction are certain. As the subject of this article is customer service cultures, a critique of the strategic and procedural changes will not be given.

For culture change to succeed, change needs to be focussed on the customer interfaces, where the customer experience is shaped and customer knowledge is gained. This will only succeed if enabling conditions are created, so that the changes are supported by appropriate leadership. It is essential to remember that culture is being used to redress the shortcomings of scientific management. If scientific management is the dominant existing paradigm, the temptation will be to do culture scientifically; through bureaucracy and control. This is unlikely to succeed. What is needed is to engage, educate and enable instead of controlling. Formal systems are needed, but complementing rather than eclipsing culture.

Many employees already know, intellectually, the principles of a customer driven focus; they are consumers of innumerable products and services themselves and the concepts are straightforward. What is needed is for them to: know how their interactions impact upon customer experience; create a shared understanding of how to effect change; care about whether this change happens.

Management changes are slightly different. They also need to understand and engage in customer focus activities. Their main changes, however, are in leadership as leadership and culture are inseparably interdependent. The leader's new role is influencing culture. Their tools are: listening, coaching, role modelling, questioning, challenging, participating and caring.

Staff and managers must be vividly confronted with effects of behaviour and challenged to create and apply options for change. The focus on identifying and implementing changes must be as close to the customer interface as possible. This creates energy and engagement where it is needed.

Achieving these changes is best cascaded from the top. Commitment at the highest of levels is essential, but managerial changes will have little impact on customer experience except by creating the conditions for staff to do so.

A customer driven culture is difficult to create. It is likely to be a long, challenging and uncertain road. Paradoxically, this is its strength. For those with the courage, intelligence and determination to travel this road, the reward will be a significant source of sustainable competitive advantage. Others will find this hard to replicate.

References

1. Figures from Heskett J, Jones T, Loveman G, Sasser W, and Schlesinger L. 'Putting the Service-Profit Chain to Work', Harvard Business Review, Reprint 94204, (1994).
2. For more on these figures, see Antony P, (1994), 'Managing Culture' Open University Press, Buckingham
3. As exemplified in Deal T, and Kennedy A, (1982), 'Corporate Cultures', Addison-Wesley, MA
4. A term explored in Fairclough N, (1994), 'Language and Power'.
5. Antony, (1994).
6. Ably explained by Lupton T, 'Organisational Change: 'Top down' or 'Bottom up' Management?' In Mayn-White B, (ed), (1986), Planning and Managing Change, Paul Chapman Publishing, London

7. For example Staufer D, (1999), 'The Art of Delivering Great Customer Service', Harvard Management Update No. 9909B.
8. Schein E, (1985), 'Organisational Culture and Leadership', Jossey-Bass, San Fransisco.
9. Heskett et al (1994).

Linden Burke, Impact Development Training Group

Impact is a privately owned consultancy established in 1980 and operating from bases in the UK, Europe, US, Asia and Australasia. Its original base and current UK headquarters are in the Lake District. It employs 250 people worldwide and can mobilise multi-national, multi-lingual teams to design and deliver learning solutions locally or globally. Impact is distinguished in its market through an experimental approach to learning and development, which uses carefully constructed experiences to allow people to understand the impact of their actions. This approach involves individuals in developing their self-awareness and a sense of agency which leads to a commitment to changes in behaviour that align with improved organisational effectiveness. It is particularly renowned for its ability to target the achievement of business results through changes in cultural and social systems. Programmes typically combine research, a consultative design process, assessment tools, intensive learning events, work-based projects, support and evaluation.

Contact:
Linden Burke
Impact Development Training Group
Cragwood House
Windermere
Cumbria LA23 1LQ
Tel: 015394 88333
E-mail: linden.burke@impact-dtg.com
Website: www.impact-dtg.com

1.22 Managing Disagreement in Teams

Disagreement can be a spur to growth and innovation when handled properly.

Great teams generate a steady stream of alternative ways of getting things done. This ensures innovation and progress, but it also inevitably brings differences of opinion, which can spark off conflict. The problem is not the disagreement as such. We need disagreement as the fuel for innovation. It's when it's badly handled that it creates problems.

When people aren't communicating well, it may be because they are wrapped up in their need to win. Sometimes, the organisation and its processes are too cumbersome to make communication easy. Sometimes, personal barriers prevent a conflict being resolved. People can get anxious when someone contradicts their views. This can lead to blaming or being overly critical or others, keeping things secret and bottling it up (and later exploding).

Emotionally intelligent teams don't let conflict reach this state. They recognise the anxiety for what it is – an uncomfortable state of mind caused by leaving the comfort zone of familiar ideas. They know that no idea is so perfect that it can be allowed to get entrenched. They are able to work with the tension, so they can listen with an open mind, giving and expecting respect as they disagree.

The metaphors we use to describe conflict can affect how we deal with it. The metaphor of war implies the people involved are enemies. Changing the metaphor can help to change the attitude. For example, you can see conflict as a gateway through which we can see alternative routes created by the viewpoints of others. Conflict is a journey to somewhere new, with those disagreeing offering new paths and new possibilities. The appropriate metaphor can get us thinking of disagreement as an essential component of our discussions and plans for the future.

Creative abrasion is a concept that sees abrasion as an advantage. There are two or more views rubbing up against each other, as a match rubs against the sharp side of the matchbox. The friction results in a flame, a wild departure from match or box, but both were needed to give the flame life. When there's friction in a group, it's not necessarily helpful to reduce it, if it means diminishing the ideas that are emerging. Creative abrasion emphasises the need to bring out the opposing ideas, and to look for means of combining them in new ways.

If we accept disagreement as the norm, not as a disruptive force, we may be able to prevent ideas getting stuck as anachronisms of an old order. If we can meet disagreement, but feel respected rather than threatened, we can recognise defects in our own views, and rethink, giving more possibilities to discuss, which leads to better solutions.

When teams are too harmonious, it might be that 'groupthink' has set in. This is when teams begin to value harmony more than they value the quality of decisions, so they settle into a rut of thinking the same. When this happens, there is a barrier to changing anything. It needs strong disagreement to break free.

Disagreement can take courage, but it's important for progress that people do not omit important points for the sake of peace. Replacing 'Yes, but …' with 'Yes, and …' shows respect for the other's view, and is likely to have more influence. It's also important to accept when you have been influenced. Don't be too proud to say that you now think differently from how you thought before.

There is a need for ground rules to maintain the positive impact of disagreement. This means not allowing anything to get personal, keeping a clear view of team goals, inviting diverse viewpoints as a matter of policy, clarifying people's roles, and having a clear timetable of progress, so that disagreement does not go on for so long as to obstruct goals.

If disagreement seems to be getting hostile, it's important to acknowledge it, and take steps to get back on the right track. It's a problem like any other, and the team to get together to discuss it.

The discussion should focus firmly on ideas, not personalities. Each person should strive to understand, not necessarily agree with, the other views. This means everybody stating their views, and everybody listening to everybody else. You can then look for common ground. From there you can move towards solutions. What features must the final decision have? Get a range of options, perhaps by brainstorming. Narrow it down to a viable decision, and make an action plan. Part of this plan should be regular review meetings, so that further disagreement can be aired, and can be utilised for further progress.

The other side of the coin is managing agreement. It can be stultifying when consensus becomes so strong that the things cannot change. If outside forces change, and the team does not, it will eventually lead to disaster.

One sign of over-strong consensus, or groupthink, is a sense of moral superiority in the group, that causes them to think that outsiders are somehow different, and if they disagree it's because they don't understand. This creates a pressure to conform. They avoid any information that doesn't support the pervading view, and if things don't work, they assume someone has failed to carry out the correct action, rather than wonder if the underlying principles are right. They will find extraordinary ways to explain away flaws in their arguments. It's as though they have all donned blinkers, and can see nothing but the chosen route.

Groupthink is hard to eradicate, but steps can be taken to prevent it setting in. There need to be internal checks. There needs to be a policy of inviting, not just waiting for, different views. One way is to have sub-groups, who research and report separately, to ensure a good inflow of information and ideas.

An underlying part of this is to create a heterogeneous team. You need diversity of background, expertise and viewpoint, to ensure a continuing richness of ideas. It will bring disagreement, but if it's well handled, that disagreement will bring growth.

Contact details:
Mike Bagshaw
Trans4mation
PO Box 44
High Street
Evesham
Worcestershire WR11 4ZJ

Tel: 0870 606 4400
Direct line: 01386 422071
Fax: 01386 422076
Mobile: 07798717991

Website: www.trans4mation.com

Part 2.1

A–Z Directory

Qualifications and Curriculum Authority

With UK partners, we manage the development of standards, accredit qualifications once developed, and regulate and audit the awarding bodies to ensure that the policy standards and probity requirements of the Authority have been met.

We are responsible for the continuous development of the National Qualifications Framework.

Enquiries: 020 7509 5556 or info@qca.org.uk

Qualifications and Curriculum Authority
83 Piccadilly
London W1J 8QA

Aberdeen Business School

Robert Gordon University, Faculty of Management, Garthdee Road, Aberdeen, AB10 7QE
Tel: 01224 263825
Fax: 01224 263838
E-mail: m.brown@rgu.ac.uk

Profile: We provide high quality education training and consultancy programmes.

Services: Human resources, Leadership, Change management, Management diplomas, Psychometric testing, Games, Simulation & exercises

Aberdeen College

Gordon Centre, Ellon Road, Bridge of Don, Aberdeen, AB23 8LQ
Tel: 01224 612519
Fax: 01224 612500

Contact: Thomas Durie, H & S Education Co-ordinator

Profile: Academic and practical health and safety training and consultancy work.

Services: Health & safety

Abernethy Trust

Ardeonaig, By Killin, Perthshire, FK218SY
Tel: 01567 820523
Fax: 01567 820955

Contact: Philip Simpson MCIPD, Development Director
E-mail: at@ardeonoig.org
Website: www.ardeonaig.org

Profile: Personal development, teambuilding and leadership programmes delivered through outdoor projects.

Services: Human resources, Management development, Teamworking, Leadership, Outdoor learning, Investors in People

University of Abertay Dundee

Student Recruitment Office, Kydd Building, Bell Street, Dundee, DD1 1HG
Tel: 01382 308080
Fax: 01382 308081

Contact: Julie McEwan, Information & Recruitment Officer
E-mail: sro@abertay.ac.uk
Website: www.abertay.ac.uk

Services: Management certificates, Management diplomas, MBAs,

ABG Professional Information

40 Bernard Street, London, WClN1LD
Tel: 020 7833 3291
Fax: 020 7833 9034

Profile: The definitive accountancy information source.

Services: Courses, Books & packages, Accounting & finance

Abraham, Airey & Associates

Rochester House, 275 Baddow Road, Great Baddow, Chelmsford, Essex, CM2 7QA
Tel: 01245 262263
Fax: 01245 495705

Contact: Alison Abraham, Partner
E-mail: hq@abraham-airey.co.uk
Website: www.abraham-airey.co.uk

Profile: Friendly professional training company based in London, Chelmsford and Essex.

Services: IT, Project management, Assertiveness, Interpersonal skills, PC user skills, Presentation skills

ACA

Mill House, Mill Lane, Walessy, Newark, Nottinghamshire, NG22 9PG
Tel: 01623 835221
Fax: 01623 860803

Contact: Allen Christer, Partner
E-mail: 100642727@compuserve.com

Profile: Designing, delivering creative experiential programmes for better performance at work.

Acacia-IPS Ltd

6 Hayes Place, Bath, BA2 4QW
Tel: 01225 830040

Contact: Caroline Clarkson, Client Services Manager
E-mail: caroline@acacia-ips.com
Website: www.acacia-ips.com

Profile: IT-business courses and coaching from business analysis to information management.

Services: IT, Change management, Information systems, Innovation, Knowledge management, Project management,

ACADEMEE

Bollin House, Bollin Walk, Wilmslow, Cheshire, SK9 1DP
Tel: 01625 540540
Fax: 01625 543601

Contact: Nicola Lloyd, Marketing Executive
E-mail: marketing@academee.com
Website: www.academee.com

Profile: Provider of IM accredited management and professional e-learning certificates.

Services: Customer service, Management development, Coaching & mentoring, Emotional intelligence, Leadership, Management certificates,

The Academy of Executives & Administrators (AEA)

Academy House, Warwick Corner, 42 Warwick Road, Kenilworth, Warwickshire, CV8 1HE
Tel: 01926 855498
Fax: 01926 513100

Contact: Professor H J Manners, President and Founder

The Academy of Multi-Skills (AMS)

Academy House, Warwick Corner, 42 Warwick Road, Kenilworth, Warwickshire, CV8 1HE
Tel: 01926 855498
Fax: 01926 513100

Contact: Professor H J Manners, Chairman

Profile: Professional membership body recognising and registering multi-skilled people. Multi-skilling; courses.

act e-learning

New Oxford House, 30 Barkers Pool, Sheffield, Sl 2HB
Tel: 0114 278 0798
Fax: 0114 249 1773

Contact: John Ford, Business Development Manager
E-mail: john.ford@actlearning.com
Website: www.actlearning.com

Profile: Major learning supplier, e-learning consultancy, accreditation services and other training formats.

Services: Business Services, E-learning, Education

Action Development Group

Longsight Industrial Estate, Newton Avenue, Manchester, M12 4EY
Tel: 0161 273 1700
Fax: 0161 273 2511

Contact: Anita Wild, Director
E-mail: anita@adgroup.co.uk
Website: www.adgroup.co.uk

Profile: Action Development Group for your organisation and people development needs.

Services: Human resources, Change management, Customer service.

The Adams Consultancy Ltd

Chilterns, Bellingdon, Chesham, Buckinghamshire, HP5 2XL
Tel: 01494 791045
Fax: 01494 778045

Contact: Margaret Adams, Director
E-mail: mail@TheAdamsConsultancy.co.uk

Profile: Specialists in work-life balance consultancy and training.

Services: Management development, Interpersonal skills, Public sector

Adaptation Ltd

Mill Reach, Mill Lane, Water Newton, Cambridgeshire, PE8 6LY
Tel: 01733 361149
Fax: 01733 361459

Contact: Colin Coulson-Thomas, Chairman
E-mail: colinct@tiscali.co.uk
Website: www.ntwkfirm.com

Profile: Adaptation helps people exploit knowledge, manage change and win business.

Services: Sales & marketing, Knowledge management, Change management

Adept Consulting (Central) Ltd

76 Hazel Road, Purley on Thames, Berkshire, RG8 8HT
Tel: 0118 942 6625
Fax: 0118 942 6625

Contact: Barry Aitken, Director

Profile: Helping your business succeed through organisational change, individual career development.

Services: Human resources, Management diplomas, Interpersonal skills

AD International

Sherwood House, 7 Oxhey Road, Watford, Hertfordshire, WD19 4QF
Tel: 07000 234683
Fax: 07000 234689

Contact: J Hay, Chief Executive
E-mail: consult@adinternational.com
Website: www.adinternational.com

Profile: People skills, culture change, assessment centres, mentoring/coaching, trainer training.

Services: Management development, Coaching & mentoring, Interpersonal skills

adlib

Maidstone St Faith's Adult Education Centre, St Faith's Street, Maidstone, Kent, ME14 lLH
Tel: 01622 753290
Fax: 01622 753290

Contact: Sue Ricketts, adlib Project Manager
E-mail: adlib@Kent.gov.uk

Profile: Providing professional, flexible, high quality business language training throughout Kent.

Services: Languages, Business Services, Manufacturing & engineering

AdVal Group Plc

Triangle Business Park, Quilters Way, Aylesbury, Buckinghamshire, HP22 5BJ
Tel: 01296 616700
Fax: 01296 616710

Contact: Joe Quilter, Marketing Manager
E-mail: info@adval.co.uk
Website: www.adval.co.uk

Profile: AdVal is a highly successful learning and business services group.

Services: Human resources, IT, Change management

ADVANCE: Management Training Ltd

58 Ridgway Road, Farnham, Surrey, GU9 8NS
Tel: 01252 311366
Fax: 01252 311555

Contact: Kay Gillespie, General Manager
E-mail: info@advance-management.com

Profile: Bringing the future into your company through internationalisation, organisational transformation.

Services: E-business, Change management, Knowledge management

The Advisory Unit: Computers in Education

126 Great North Road, Hatfield, Hertfordshire, AL9 5JN
Tel: 01707 266714
Fax: 01707 856565

Contact: Mike Aston, Principal Consultant
E-mail: mike@kcited.demon.co.uk
Website: www.advisory-unit.org.uk

Profile: ICT training and consultancy for teachers, educators and managers.

Services: IT, Information systems, PC user skills

Agricola Services Ltd

Riseholme Hall, Lincoln, Lincolnshire, LN2 2LG
Tel: 01522 544756
Fax: 01522 544756

Contact: Jan De Smit, Director
E-mail: JdeSmit@dnu.ac.uk

Profile: Producers of multimedia products in software, paper, audio, video.

Airtime Communications

3 Priory Road, West Bridgford, Nottingham, NG2 5HU
Tel: 0115 981 6994
Fax: 0115 914 0332

Contact: Chris Theobald, Chief Executive
E-mail: mediatrain@airtimecomms.co.uk
Website: www.airtimecomms.co.uk

Services: Communications, advertising & PR, Presentation skills, Media skills

Akwapim Presentations Ltd

Grosvenor House, Central Park, Telford, Shropshire, TF2 9TW
Tel: 01952 290260
Fax: 01952 292270

Contact: Dennis Silverlock, Director
E-mail: enquiries@akwapim.co.uk

Profile: Presentation skills training and software. Audio visual and presentation equipment.

Services: Presentation skills

ALA International Ltd

11 Barton Close, Kingsbridge, Devon, TB7 1JU
Tel: 01548 852591
Fax: 01548 852621

Contact: George Boulden, Director
E-mail: ala@alaint.demon.co.uk
Website: www.alaint.demon.co.uk

Profile: We use action learning to help you help yourselves.

Services: Human resources, Change management, Health & safety

Alan Weaver Associates

19 Five Mile Drive, Oxford, OX2 8HT
Tel: 01865 316775
Fax: 01865 316704

Contact: Alan S Weaver, Director
E-mail: alan@aweaver.co.uk
Website: www.aweaver.co.uk

Profile: Specialist seminars on subscription marketing techniques for the publishing industry.

Services: Sales & marketing, Change management, Customer service

AL Consulting

HighTarn, Aughton, Near Lancaster, Lancashire, LA2 8LU
Tel: 01524 811890
Fax: 01524 811966

Contact: Fred Ayres, Director
E-mail: training@al-consulting.co.uk
Website: www.al-consulting.co.uk

Profile: Results oriented training designed and delivered for clients' specific needs.

Services: Human resources, Leadership

Amadeus Education Ltd

Maddox House, 1 Maddox Street, London, W1R 9WA
Tel: 020 7439 0080
Fax: 020 7439 0080

Contact: Heather Swift, Director of Training
E-mail: training@amadeus.uk.com

Profile: End user training on Microsoft, Lotus and Wordperfect products.

Services: E-business, Human resources, IT

Amethyst Learning & Development

Ty Croeso, Vauxhall Lane, Chepstow, Monmouthshire, NP16 5PZ
Tel: 01291 624725
Fax: 01291 624824

Contact: Ann Holloway, Programme Director
E-mail: ann.holloway@lineone.net
Website: www.amethyst-learning.co.uk

Profile: BESPOKE programmes group or individual, via consultancy training or mentoring.

Services: Management development, NVQs, Coaching & mentoring

Angel Productions

9 Dukes Avenue, London, N10 2PS
Tel: 020 8444 3331
Fax: 020 8444 3331

Contact: Stephen Engelhard, Partner
E-mail: info@angelproductions.co.uk
Website: www.angelproductions.co.uk

Profile: Videos and training for a fairer, more productive workplace.

Services: Blended Learning, Diversity/ Equal Opportunities, Video

Anglo-Continental

33 Wimborne Road, Bournemouth, Dorset, BH2 6NA
Tel: 01202 557414
Fax: 01202 556156

Contact: Jackie Howchin, Professional Training
E-mail: english@anglo-continental.com
Website: www.anglo-continental.com

Profile: English language training and consultancy for foreign staff and clients.

Services: Languages, Business Services, Education, Financial services, Leisure, Courses

Answers (Research) Ltd

140 Borden Lane, Sittingbourne, Kent, ME9 8HW
Tel: 01795 423778
Fax: 01795 423778

Contact: K F Lainton, Director

Profile: Marketing training for the intensively competitive 21st century provided.

Services: Communications, advertising & PR, Sales & marketing

Anthony James Management Training

Vigilant House, 120 Wilton Road, London, SWIV lJZ
Tel: 020 7233 8205
Fax: 020 7233 8206

Contact: Anthony James, Owner
E-mail: 1006602615@compuserve.com

Profile: Financial training for non-financial managers and other management development.

Services: Management development, Finance for non-finance staff

Anthony Snapes Associates, Business Psychologists

55 Clarence Gate Gardens, Glentworth Street, London, NW1 6QS
Tel: 020 7724 6731
Fax: 020 7258 1457

Contact: A W Snapes, Principal Consultant

Profile: Management development, mentoring, 360° feedback, psychometric testing, assessment, development centres.

Services: Management development, Coaching & mentoring

AP International

Heyford House, Nether Heyford, Northamptonshire, NN7 3NN
Tel: 01327 342339
Fax: 01327 349389

Contact: Dr A M Pont, Director
E-mail: a.m.pont@btinternet.com
Website: www.apinternational.co.uk

Services: Management development, Teamworking, Assertiveness

Appleton-Hill

19 Purdy Close, Old Hall, Warrington, Cheshire, WA5 9QU
Tel: 01925 413328
Fax: 01925 413328

Contact: J Hill, Partner
E-mail: appleton.hill@virgin.net

Profile: Trainer, assessor, internal verifier of NVQ advice and guidance.

Services: Competencies, Decision-making, NVQs

Architecture & Surveying Institute

St Mary House, 15 St Mary Street, Chippenham, Wiltshire, SN15 3WD
Tel: 01249 444505
Fax: 01249 443602

Contact: Mr Keith Roberts, Education & Training Executive
E-mail: mail@asi.org.uk
Website: www.asi.org.uk

Profile: ASI is the multi-disciplinary institute for professionals in construction.

Services: Teamworking, Property, Construction & facilities

Aris Education Ltd

7600 The Quorum, Oxford Business Park North, Oxford, OX4 2JZ
Tel: 0845 602 1274
Fax: 01865 334701

Contact: Ali James, Marketing Co-ordinator
E-mail: info@ariseducation.com
Website: www.ariseducation.com

Profile: Aris Education is a leading provider of blended training solutions.

Services: IT, Information systems, E-learning

Arlington Associates

5 Arlington Road, Richmond, Surrey, TW10 7BZ
Tel: 020 8948 6735

Contact: Peter Martin, Director
E-mail: consultants@arlington-associates.co.uk
Website: www.arlington-associates.co.uk

Profile: Management training group and one-to-one UK and abroad.

Services: Human resources, Presentation skills, Time management

Ashridge

Berkhamsted, Hertfordshire, HP4 lNS
Tel: 01442 841026
Fax: 01442 841036

Contact: Carol Long, Client Development Manager
E-mail: info@ashridge.org.uk
Website: www.ashridge.com

Profile: An international business school delivering executive education, consulting and research.

Services: E-learning, Management development, Leadership

ASK Europe plc

Trent House, University Way, Cranfield Technology Park, Cranfield, Bedfordshire, MK43 0AN
Tel: 01234 757575
Fax: 01234 757576

Contact: Chris Matthews, Business Development Director
E-mail: mail@askeurope.com
Website: www.askeurope.com

Profile: ASK produces development programmes that create leaders and enhance performance.

Services: Coaching & mentoring, Leadership, Management development

Association of British Professional Conference Organisers

6th Floor, Charles House, 148-149 Great Charles Street, Birmingham, B3 3HT
Tel: 0121 212 1400
Fax: 0121 212 3131

Contact: Tony Rogers, Executive Director
E-mail: information@abpco.org
Website: www.abpco.org

Profile: ABPCO runs training courses on conferences-industry related topics.

Services: Crisis & disaster management, Information & communication technologies, Conference venues

The Association of Business Executives (ABE)

William House, 14 Worple Road, Wimbledon, SW19 4DD
Tel: 020 8879 1973
Fax: 020 8946 7153

Contact: Christine Gill, Assistant CEO
E-mail: info@abeuk.com
Website: www.abeuk.com

Profile: 2003 sees ABE celebrate its 30th anniversary. Today, ABE has become a market leader in the cost-effective delivery of quality assured British management education.
The primary objective of ABE, a non-profit making organisation, is to ensure that students successfully completing its examinations will accquire the knowledge and skills needed in order to become more effective managers. ABE's awards are recognised internationally as an accepted route into the later stages of UK and overseas first degrees, professional qualifications and MBA and other Masters programmes. The provision of CD-ROM study Manuals further reduces costs for students who receive tutor support from colleges accredited by ABE.
Membership is available to both UK and overseas students and examinations are conducted twice a year worldwide.

Services: Accounting & finance, Human resources, IT

Association of Certified Book-keepers

Akhtar House, 2 Shepherds Bush Road, London, SW6 7PJ
Tel: 020 8749 7126
Fax: 020 8749 7127

Contact: Dr S Das Gupta, Secretary
E-mail: icea@enta.net

Profile: Modern professional body, producing tomorrow's financial controllers and administrators.

Services: Accounting & finance

The Association of Corporate Treasurers

Ocean House, 10-12 Little Trinity Lane, London, EC4V 2DJ
Tel: 020 7213 9728
Fax: 020 7248 2591

Contact: Makayla Rahman, Events Assistant
E-mail: enquiries@treasurers.co.uk
Website: www.treasurers.org

Profile: The world's leading provider of treasury education and training.

Services: Accounting & finance, Financial services, Risk management

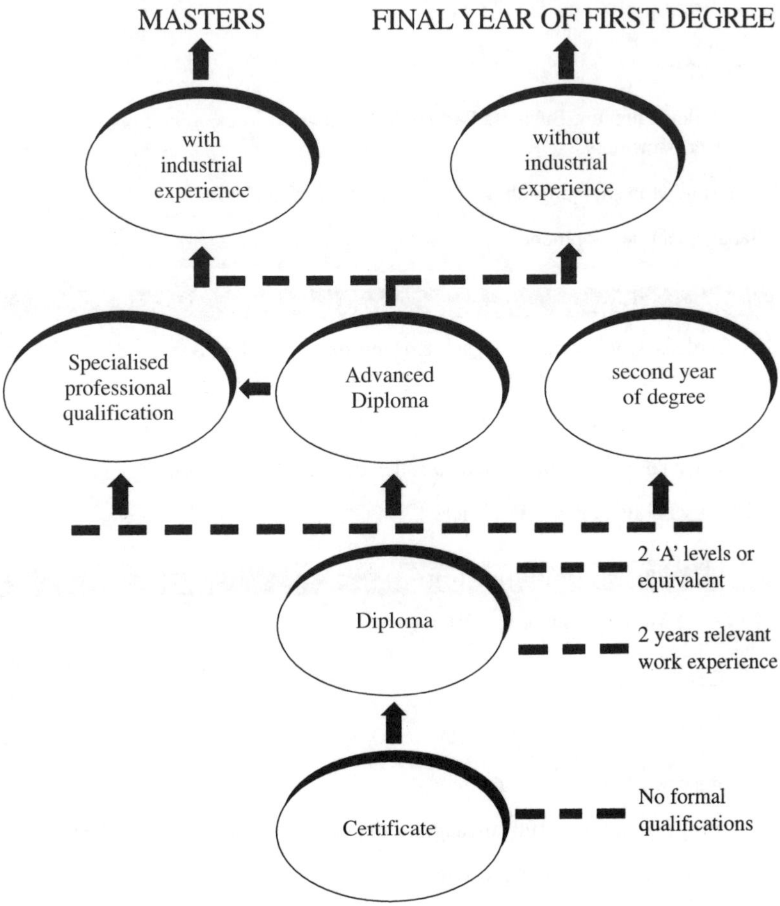

Association of Finance Controllers & Administrators

Akhtar House, 2 Shepherds Bush Road, London, SW6 7PJ
Tel: 020 8749 7126
Fax: 020 8749 7127

Contact: Dr S Das Gupta, Secretary
E-mail: icea@enta.net
Website: www.icea.enta.net

Profile: Modern professional body, producing tomorrow's financial controllers and administrators.

Services: Accounting & finance

Aston University Business Partnership Unit

Aston Triangle, Birmingham, B4 7ET
Tel: 0121 250 3646
Fax: 0121 333 5774

Contact: John Bailey, Director, Business Partnership Unit
E-mail: j.r.bailey@aston.ac.uk

Profile: Aston's one-stop shop providing services for industry and commerce.

Services: Management development

AS Training

47 Belvedere Gardens, Chineham, Basingstoke, Hampshire, RG24 8GB
Tel: 01256 358302

Contact: Susan Thorn, Training Manager

Profile: Tailor-made computer training and consultancy to suit your needs.

Services: IT, PC user skills, Financial services

Audio-Forum – The Language Source

Dept. IM, 4 Foscote Mews, London, W9 2HH
Tel: 020 7266 2202
Fax: 020 7266 2314

Contact: S C Albert, Director
E-mail: microworld@ndirect.co.uk
Website: www.microworld.ndirect.co.uk

Profile: Self-study packs for over 100 languages. Beginners, Intermediate, Advanced. Catalogue.

Services: Languages, Books & packages, Video

Aurora Business Development Ltd

9 Ferndown Close, Bristol, BS11 0UP
Tel: 0117 962 6500
Fax: 0117 962 6500

Contact: Harold James, Marketing Director
E-mail: aurora@btinternet.com
Website: www.aurora.ie

Profile: International business and manufacturing educators, trainers and consultants.

Services: Production & process control, Manufacturing & engineering, Business excellence

Austen Associates

10 Beaufort Road, St Leonards-on-Sea, East Sussex, TN37 6QA
Tel: 01424 439259

Contact: Rose Austen, Consultant
E-mail: austen@demon.co.uk

Profile: Training consultancy in team working, quality, communication, presentation, time management.

Services: Teamworking, Time management

Avon Management Services

25 Temples Court, Helpston, Peterborough, Cambridgeshire, PE6 7EV
Tel: 01733 252 510
Fax: 01733 253 599

Contact: PL Hopgood, Consultant
E-mail: plhopgood@aol.com

Profile: Management consultancy, sales and marketing consultancy and training.

Services: Sales & marketing, Education, MBAs

Axiom – MSS

PO Box 4279, Worthing, BN13 3TF
Tel: 01903 266675
Fax: 01903 694883

Contact: Justine Lewis, Course Registrar
E-mail: axiom-mss@tiscali.co.uk
Website: www.axiom-mss.co.uk

Profile: Business management and IT training. Business application computer software.

Services: IT, Business Services, PC user skills

BAB The Business Advisory Bureau Ltd

1 Britten's Court, Clifton Reynes, Olney, Buckinghamshire, MK46 5LG
Tel: 01234 241026
Fax: 01234 241593

Contact: Mrs C Francis, Director
E-mail: bab_ltd@compuserve.com
Website: www.b-a-b.co.uk

Profile: Publish successful guide to earning a living from independent consultancy.

Services: Books & packages

Babel Language & Cultural Consultants

Imperial Lodge, 33a High Street, Chislehurst, Kent, BR7 5AE
Tel: 020 8295 5877
Fax: 020 8295 5878

Contact: Sue Curry, Managing Director
E-mail: mail@babelgroup.co.uk
Website: www.babelgroup.co.uk

Profile: Babel offers award-winning language and cross-cultural training programmes.

Services: Languages

Barleythorpe Training & Conference Centre

Barleythorpe, Oakham, Rutland, LE15 7ED
Tel: 01572 723711
Fax: 01572 757657

Contact: Sue Sharpe, Training Administrator
E-mail: info@eef-eastmids.org.uk
Website: www.eef.org.uk/eastmids

Services: Assertiveness, Finance for non-finance staff, Leadership

Barlow Fraser Training and Development

3 Victoria Terrace, Musselburgh, EH21 7LW
Tel: 0131 665 6915
Fax: 0131 665 6916

Contact: Helen Barlow, Director
E-mail: info@barlow-fraser.com

Profile: Tools, theory and confidence for presenters, trainers and facilitators.

Services: Management development, Coaching & mentoring, Interpersonal skills

Barry Herd Associates

9 Ellis Close, Cottenham, Cambridge, CB4 8UN
Tel: 01954 205110

Contact: Barry Herd, Principal
E-mail: jherd@intlworld.com

Profile: Your results orientated interpersonal skills management and organisational development partner.

Services: Change management, Management development, Supervisory

BBC Learning

Corporate Sales, Room A3040, Woodlands, 80 Wood Lane, London, W12 0TT
Tel: 020 8433 1641
Fax: 020 8433 2916

Contact: Jeremy Wilcox, Channel Manager
E-mail: corporate.sales@bbc.co.uk
Website: www.bbc4biz.com

Profile: BBC produce a range of video and CD-ROM training packages.

Services: Video

BCG Consultancy

20 Eglinton Street, Irvine, Ayrshire, KA12 8AS
Tel: 01294 313177

Contact: Howard Marshall, Managing Director
E-mail: ghsm@bigfoot.com

Profile: Innovative approaches to Management Supervisory and Trainer development.

Services: Human resources, Management development, Leadership

Bernard Wynne Associates

180 Blackfen Road, Sidcup, Kent, DA15 8PT
Tel: 020 8850 6458
Fax: 020 8850 8974

Contact: Bernard Wynne, Principal
E-mail: bfwynne@aol.com

Profile: Management and people development provided in company in all sectors.

Services: Customer service, Management development, Leadership

Birkbeck, University of London

Malet Street, London, WC1E 7HX
Tel: 020 7631 6000
Fax: 020 7631 6270

Contact: Business Relations Unit
E-mail: employers@bbk.ac.uk
Website: www.birkbeck4business.com

Profile: University level part-time evening courses in central London.

Services: Accounting & finance, E-business, Human resources

Birmingham College of Food and Tourism

Summer Row, Birmingham, West Midlands, B3 1JB
Tel: 0121 693 5959
Fax: 0121 608 7100

Contact: E Pryer, Marketing
E-mail: marketing@bcftcs.ac.uk

Profile: Specialist hospitality and tourism college, offering postgraduate, degree, HND programmes.

B J O'Connor International Ltd

10 Aldenholme, Ellesmere Road, Weybridge, Surrey, KT13 0JF
Tel: 01932 851334
Fax: 01932 854298

Contact: Brian O'Connor, Director
E-mail: boconno@lineone.net
Website: www.oconnorconsultancy.com

Profile: Multilingual international consulting training company proven techniques in profits increase.

Services: Production & process control, Change management, Negotiation

Blyth Associates

1 Rigmaden Cottage, Mansergh, Carnforth, Lancashire, LA6 2ET
Tel: 015242 76484
Fax: 015242 76484

Contact: Mrs E Blyth, BA, Administrator

Profile: Training in employment, contract, pensions, law and litigation support services.

Services: Legal, Manufacturing & engineering, Business Services

BMB Management Training Consultants

285A Fore Street, Edmonton, London, N9 0PD
Tel: 020 8884 3494
Fax: 020 8884 3494

Contact: W Bolton, Proprietor

Profile: Providers of quality training programmes for all levels of management.

Services: Human resources, Management development, Leadership

Bowles Development Group

Bowles Outdoor Centre, Eridge Green, Tunbridge Wells, TN3 9LW
Tel: 01892 610600
Fax: 01892 669556

Contact: Will Grace, Development Director
E-mail: will@bowles.ac
Website: www.bowles.ac

Profile: Team building and OMD close to London. ISO 9001 approved.

Services: Change management, Management development, Teamworking

The Bracegirdle Associates

15 The Lagger, Chalfont St Giles, Buckinghamshire, HP8 4DG
Tel: 01494 872372
Fax: 01494 872372

Contact: Barbara Bracegirdle, Director

Profile: Education updating, including qualification equivalences for business personnel.

Brackenhurst College

Southwell, Nottinghamshire, NG25 0QF
Tel: 01636 817000
Fax: 01636 815404

Contact: Jamie Woolley, Marketing Manager

Profile: Specialised communicative language training for businesses, lawyers and government agencies.

Services: Languages

Bracknell and Wokingham College

Church Road, Bracknell, Berkshire, RG12 1DJ
Tel: 01344 460200
Fax: 01344 460360

Contact: Samantha While, Head of Community and Business Services
E-mail: sam.while@bracknell.ac.uk

Profile: Wide range of business training and further education for adults.

Services: IT, Health & safety, Languages, NVQs

University of Bradford Executive Development Centre

Heaton Mount, Keighley Road, Bradford, West Yorkshire, BD9 4JU
Tel: 01274 384485
Fax: 01274 384444

Contact: Patrick Allen, Management Teaching Fellow
E-mail: j.p.allen@bradford.ac.uk

Profile: Executive programmes covering all aspects of management education and development.

Services: Management development, IT, Corporate universities

Brasshouse Language Centre

50 Sheepcote Street, Birmingham, B16 8AJ
Tel: 0121 303 0114
Fax: 0121 303 4782

Contact: Nati Knight, Acting Head of Centre
E-mail: nati_knight@birmingham.gov.uk
Website: www.birmingham.gov.uk/brasshouse

Profile: Tailored language training for business and industry in 28 languages.

Services: Languages

Breakthrough Management Training Ltd

Mill House, Millness, Milnthorpe, Cumbria, LA7 7NS
Tel: 01539 567878
Fax: 01539 567007

Contact: Catherine Cousins, Office Manager
E-mail: enquiries@breakthrough-management.co.uk
Website: www.breakthrough-management.co.uk

Profile: Breakthrough Management Training. Measurably different, measurably better.

Services: Human resources, Management development, Leadership

Bridge

5-7 The Avenue, Newmarket, Suffolk, CB8 9AA
Tel: 01638 666400
Fax: 01638 666402

Contact: Lee Sears, Director
E-mail: bridge@bridge-uk.com
Website: www.bridge-uk.com

Profile: Bridge offers unique approaches in leadership development and organisational transformation.

Services: Change management, Teamworking, Coaching & mentoring

University of Brighton, Business Services

Mithras House, Lewes Road, Brighton, Sussex, BN2 4AY
Tel: 01273 643222
Fax: 01273 643227

Contact: Jennifer Wells, BSID Co-ordinator
E-mail: business.services@brighton.ac.uk
Website: www.brighton.ac.uk

Profile: Skills and training provided for organisations of all kinds.

Services: Accounting & finance, Human resources, Project management

Brinsbury College

North Heath, Pulborough, West Sussex, RH20 1DL
Tel: 01798 877400
Fax: 01798 875222

Contact: P Woodman and Irene Sylvester, Marketing Officer
E-mail: principal@brinsbury.ac.uk
Website: www.brinsbury.ac.uk

Profile: Brinsbury land-based training. The West Sussex College of the countryside.

Services: Training for trainers, IT, Courses, Change management

University of Bristol

Senate House, Tyndall Avenue, Bristol, BS8 1TH
Tel: 0117 928 9000
Fax: 0117 9251424

Contact: Registrar

Services: IT, Corporate universities

Bristol Business School

University of the West of England, Frenchay Campus, Coldharbour Lane, Bristol, BS16 1QY
Tel: 0117 344 3607
Fax: 0117 344 2925
E-mail: business@uwe.ac.uk
Website: www.uwe.ac.uk/bbs/

Profile: Provides a supportive and well-resourced learning environment, officially rated excellent by the Higher Education Funding Council for England.

Services: Accounting and finance, Human resources, Sales & marketing

British Association of Conference Destinations

6th Floor, Charles House, 148-149 Great Charles Street, Birmingham, B3 3HT
Tel: 0121 212 1400
Fax: 0121 212 3131

Contact: Tony Rogers, Executive Director
E-mail: info@bacd.org.uk
Website: www.bacd.org.uk

Profile: BACD offers free assistance in sourcing conference and training venues.

Services: Information & communication technologies, Conference venues

British Horological Institute

Upton Hall, Upton, Newark, Nottinghamshire, NG23 5TE
Tel: 01636 813795
Fax: 01636 812258

Contact: Georgina Amat, Education Officer
E-mail: clocks@bhi.co.uk
Website: www.bhi.co.uk

Profile: Multi-level training and education in watch/clock repairing/making.

The British Institute of Innkeeping

Wessex House, 80 Park Street, Camberley, Surrey, GU15 3PT
Tel: 01276 684449
Fax: 01276 23045

Contact: G Bloomfield, Qualifications Manager
E-mail: qualifications@bii.org
Website: www.bii.org

Profile: The professional institute/awarding body for the licensed retail sector.

Services: Customer service, Management development, Food & drink

British Institute of Non-DestructiveTesting

1 Spencer Parade, Northampton, Northamptonshire, NN15AA
Tel: 01604 630124
Fax: 01604 231489

Contact: M E Gallagher, Secretary
E-mail: info@bindt.org
Website: www.bindt.org

Services: Competencies

British Institute of Professional Photography

Fox Talbot House, Amwell End, Ware, Hertfordshire, SG12 9HN
Tel: 01920 464011
Fax: 01920 487056

Contact: Mark Berry, Executive Officer
E-mail: bippware@aol.com
Website: www.bipp.com

British Institute of Technology & E-commerce

Apex House, 87-89 Plashet Road, London, E13 0RA
Tel: 020 8552 3071
Fax: 020 8552 3546

Contact: Linda Unwin, Manager
E-mail: info@bite.ac.uk
Website: www.bite.ac.uk

Profile: BITE is developing e-commerce professionals for all sectors of industry.

Services: E-business, IT, Information systems, Strategy & planning, Education, Information & communication technologies, Public sector, Training for trainers, MBAs, NVQs

The British Psychological Society

48 Princess Road East, Leicester, LE1 7DR
Tel: 0116 254 9568
Fax: 0116 247 0787

Contact: Marie Elphick, Help desk
E-mail: mail@bps.org.uk
Website: www.bpsl.le.ac.uk

Profile: Chartered professional body and learned society for psychologists in UK.

British Shops & Stores Association Ltd

Middleton House, 2 Main Road, Middleton Cheney, Banbury, Oxfordshire, OX17 2TN
Tel: 01295 712277
Fax: 01295 711358

Contact: Jeanne Willis, Staff and Management Development Executive
E-mail: j.willis@bssa-dev.co.uk
Website: www.british-shops.co.uk/development

Profile: Retail selling, buying and management courses, books and distance learning.

Services: Accounting & finance, Sales & marketing, Supply chain & distribution

The British Soft Drinks Association

20-22 Stukeley Street, London, WC2B 5LR
Tel: 020 7430 0356
Fax: 020 7831 6014

Contact: Julia Broad, Training and Membership Manager
E-mail: bsda@britishsoftdrinks.com
Website: www.britishsoftdrinks.com

Services: Food & drink

Broadland District Council - Training Services

9 Hellesdon Park Road, Norwich, NR5 6DR
Tel: 01603 788950
Fax: 01603 484102

Contact: Sharon Mondy, Learning and Development Manager
E-mail: training@broadland.gov.uk
Website: www.broadlandtraining.info

Profile: Provide business and community development through training advice and guidance.

Services: Business Services, Management certificates, NVQs

Broadway Training Centre

30-31 The Broadway, Ealing, London, W5 2NP
Tel: 020 8840 2762
Fax: 020 8840 2818

Contact: Jannie Mattson, Director/Principal

Profile: RSA-approved examination centre. Specialising in word-processing, typing, shorthand, book-keeping.

Services: PC user skills

Broadway Training Ltd

56-57 Lords Drive, Wisemore, Walsall, West Midlands, WS2 8EQ
Tel: 01922 641198
Fax: 01922 720229

Contact: S Rolinson, General Manager
E-mail: srolinson@walcat.ac.uk
Website: www.broadwaytraining.co.uk

Profile: Training programmes tailor made for you. First class conference facilities.

Services: Human resources, Management development, Project management

Bromley College Business School

The Old Town Hall, Tweedy Road, Bromley, Kent, BR1 3PP
Tel: 020 8295 7000
Fax: 020 8295 7099
E-mail: info@bromley.ac.uk
Website: www.bromley.ac.uk

Profile: Management development with programmes integrating diplomas and certificates with NVQ's.

Services: Management development, Management diplomas, NVQs

Bromley College of Further & Higher Education

Rookery Lane, Bromley, Kent, BR2 8HE
Tel: 020 8295 7000
Fax: 020 8295 7099

Contact: Oliver Campayne, Marketing Manager
E-mail: info@bromley.ac.uk
Website: www.bromley.ac.uk

Bruce Nixon Associates
Consultants in Organisation Transformation and Learning

Hillway, 2 Castle Hill Avenue, Berkhamsted, Hertfordshire, HP4 1HJ
Tel: 01442 864856
Fax: 01442 864856

Contact: Bruce Nixon, Independent Management Consultant and Author
E-mail: brucenixon@hotmail.com

Profile: Helping leaders create better and more successful workplaces and contribute to a fairer and sustainable world. Bruce Nixon is also the author of 'Making a Difference' and 'Global Forces'.

Services: Change management, Management development, Strategy & planning, Teamworking, Coaching & mentoring, Leadership

Buckingham Tutors Publishing

The Old School House, School Lane, Buckingham, Buckinghamshire, MK18 1HB
Tel: 01280 813267
Fax: 01280 813267

Contact: Sidney Callis, Director
E-mail: buckinghamtutors@demon.co.uk
Website: www.buckinghamtutors.demon.co.uk

Profile: Providers of ready to use training materials for trainers.

Services: Human resources, Books & packages

Buker (UK) Ltd

Edelweiss House, Dark Lane, Kinver, Stourbridge, West Midlands, DY7 6JB
Tel: 01384 877969
Fax: 01384 877969

Contact: Burt Flannery, Senior Manufacturing Consultant

Profile: Worldwide organisation in manufacturing management education, training and consultancy.

Burnham Management Centre

1 Knight's Courtyard, Dropmore Road, Burnham, Buckinghamsbire, SLl 8NE
Tel: 01628 662858
Fax: 01628 669782

Contact: Jennifer Hetherington, Partner

Profile: Organisational and management training development consultancy. NVQs, IIP provision.

Services: Management development, NVQs

Burton College

The Business Centre, Burton College, Lichfield Street, Burton upon Trent, DE14 3RL
Tel: 01283 494768
Fax: 01283 494800

Contact: Rosemary Baker, Course Leader

Services: Health & safety, Leadership, Presentation skills

Business & Employment Skills Training Ltd

20 Eglinton Street, Irvine, Ayrshire, KA12 8AS
Tel: 01294 313144
Fax: 01294 313177

Contact: Howard Marshall, Managing Director

Profile: MCI, Institute of Management, Scotvec and NEBSM-approved management programmes.

Services: Management development

Business Centre

Bridgend College of Technology, Cowbridge Road, Bridgend, CF31 3DF

Contact: Mari Sutton, Course Co-ordinator

Profile: Contact us for engineering management, languages and computer software training.

Services: IT, Languages

Business Development Unit, Bishop Auckland College

Woodhouse Lane, Bishop Auckland, Durham, DL14 6JZ
Tel: 01388 603052/606333
Fax: 01388 609294

Contact: Clare Harley, Director

Profile: Customised training to meet needs of clients. Rapid turn round.

Business Development, University of Luton

Putteridge Bury, Hitchin Road, Luton, Bedfordshire, LU2 8LE
Tel: 01582 489026
Fax: 01582 489093

Contact: Frank Burdett, Director, Business Development
E-mail: bdinfo@luton.ac.uk
Website: www.luton.ac.uk/businessservices

Profile: Diverse range of services and practical training solutions for organisations.

Services: Innovation, Business Services, Conference venues

Business Education Publishers

The Solar Building, Admiral Way, Doxford International, Sunderland, SR3 3XW
Tel: 0191 525 2400
Fax: 0191 520 1815

Contact: Andrea Murphy, Managing Director
E-mail: sales@bepl.com

Profile: Publishers of academic learning materials in paper and electronic format.

Services: Books & packages

Business Language Bureau

The Language Institute, University of Hull, Cottingham Road, Hull, HU6 7RX
Tel: 01482 465839
Fax: 01482 466180

Contact: Dr Catherine Greensmith, Director
E-mail: cgreensmith@french.hull.ac.uk
Website: www.hull.ac.uk/langinst/blb

Profile: Translation and interpreting services. Also training courses and cultural briefing.

Services: Languages

Business Language Services

Fluency Today Programmes, Owl House, Runnington, Wellington, Somerset, TA21 0QW
Tel: 01823 662727
Fax: 01823 662727

Contact: Michael Bristow, Programmes Director
E-mail: info@fluency.force9.co.uk
Website: www.fluency-today.com/www.spanish-phrases.com

Profile: French, German and Spanish for holidays and business via Internet.

Services: Languages, Business Services, Information & communication technologies

Business Link Bolton & Bury

Bolton Business Centre, 46 Lower Bridgeman Street, Bolton, Lancashire, BL11DG
Tel: 0345 660704
Fax: 01204 372018

Contact: Tim Clarke, Business Information Manager

Profile: Business support for all businesses. Specialists in assisting growing businesses.

Business Network Ltd

93 Church Street, Bilston, West Midlands, WVl4 0BJ
Tel: 01902 404500
Fax: 01902 404545

Contact: Vivienne Harley, Training Director
E-mail: training@business-net.idiscover.co.uk

Profile: Business consultancy and training. Customer care, TQM, information technology, management.

Services: Customer service, Training for trainers, Courses

Business Skills & Services CILT

20 Bedfordbury, London, WC2N 4LB
Tel: 020 7379 5134
Fax: 020 7379 5082

Contact: Tamzin Caffrey, Communication & Publicity Officer
E-mail: blis@cilt.org.uk
Website: www.blis.org.uk

Profile: One-stop shop for all your business language needs.

Services: Languages, Business Services, NVQs

Business Skills Agency

78 The Quadrangle, Nacton Road, Ipswich, Suffolk, IP3 9QR
Tel: 01473 720575
Fax: 01473 721400

Contact: Carole Edwards, Managing Director

Profile: Business skills training: computer, management, sales, marketing, personal development.

Services: Sales & marketing, Courses, Project management

Business Skills Training & Management Solutions

100-104 Upper Ricbmond Road, Putney, London, SWl5 2SP
Tel: 020 8780 0805
Fax: 020 8780 0668

Contact: Andy Mutter, Managing Director
E-mail: enquiries@bstms.com
Website: www.bstms.com

Profile: Experienced trainers specialising in management development.

Services: Management development, Supervisory, Interpersonal skills

The Business Training Group

c/o Preston College, Trinity Building, Great Shaw Street, Preston, Lancashire
Tel: 01772 225266
Fax: 01772 225253

Contact: Malcolm Clarke, Head of The Business Training Group
E-mail: training@prestoncoll.ac.uk

Profile: A range of high-quality training to release your potential.

Services: Management development, Courses, Management certificates

Buzan Centres Ltd

54 Parkstone Road, Poole, Dorset, BH15 2PG
Tel: 01202 674676
Fax: 01202 674776

Contact: Vanda North, Managing Director
E-mail: buzan@buzancentres.com
Website: www.buzancentres.com

Profile: Buzan Brain Friendly, Intellectual Capital Development with 'stand-alone' or 'bolt-on' courses.

Services: Interpersonal skills, Communications advertising & PR

BWD Partnership

Unit 1, Forge House, 8 Summerleys Road, Princes Risborough, Buckinghamshire
Tel: 01844 275777
Fax: 01844 274102

Contact: E F Wal, Senior Partner

Profile: Providers of tailored training programmes in sales and marketing.

Services: Sales & marketing

CA Business Courses

27 Queen Street, Edinburgh, EH2 1LA
Tel: 0131 247 4861
Fax: 0131 247 4872

Contact: Anthony Winney, Sales & Marketing Manager
E-mail: cabl@icas.org.uk

Profile: CA Business Courses is the training arm of the ICAS.

Calibre Learning Ltd

The Stables, 131 Fishpool Street, St Albans, Hertfordshire, AL3 4RY
Tel: 01727 868063
Fax: 01727 846002

Contact: Alan George, Managing Director
E-mail: info@calibrelearning.co.uk
Website: www.calibrelearning.co.uk

Profile: Development programmes to support change and growth in organisations.

Services: Management development, Teamworking, Interpersonal skills, Management certificates

Cambridge International College

College House, Leoville, St. Ouen, Jersey, JE3 2DB
Tel: 01534 485485
Fax: 01534 485052

Contact: David Lawson, Director of Studies
E-mail: info@cambridgetraining.com
Website: www.cambridgecollege.co.uk

Profile: CIC conducts Diploma Programmes on a wide range of accounting, sales business, management and administration fields, as well as 'support' subjects like Business English & Letter Writing, Communications and Computers, one or more of which are often essential for Members' progress and success in their chosen careers.
All of CIC's Diploma Programmes are designed and written especially for career enhancement and development. The professional Diploma Programmes have proved outstandingly successful in achieving those objectives – as well as the goals and ambitions of the hundreds of thousands of Member who study with CIC.
As appropriate, Diploma Programmes start either from basic principles or with a revision of earlier studies, and then deal comprehensively with the important topics, with emphasis always on the practical application of what is taught.

Services: Accounting & finance, Communications, advertising & PR, Human resources, Office & secretarial, Sales & marketing, Management development, Courses, Management diplomas

Cambridge International Study Centre, St Mary's College

2 Brookside, Cambridge, CB2 1JE
Tel: 01223 305687
Fax: 01223 307352

Contact: Dolores Ditner, Director
E-mail: director@stmaryscambridge.com
Website: www.stmaryscambridge.com

Profile: Language Training for special purposes available at all levels.

Services: Languages, Presentation skills, Training for trainers

Cambridge Training & Development Ltd

Block D2, The Westbrook Centre, Milton Road, Cambridge, CB4 lYG
Tel: 01223 582582
Fax: 01223 582551

Contact: Joyce Cade, Managing Director
E-mail: postcentre@ctad.co.uk

Profile: Multi-media, electronic communications and intranet platforms developers and consultants.

Services: IT

Cameron Gill

Dykesfield House, Burgh by Sands, Carlisle, Cumbria, CA5 6AG
Tel: 01228 576631
Fax: 01228 576808

Contact: Susan Gill MA, FIPD, Principal Consultant

Profile: HRD consultancy/training. Management, supervisory, NLP including executive coaching/counselling.

Services: Human resources, Coaching & mentoring

Campaign for Learning

19 Buckingham Street, London, WC2N 6EF
Tel: 020 7930 1111
Fax: 020 7930 1551

Contact: Michelle Wake
Website: www.campaign-for-learning.org.uk

Capel Manor College

Bullsmoor Lane, Enfield, Middlesex, EN1 4RQ
Tel: 020 8366 4442
Fax: 01992 717544

Contact: Ruth Barber, Student Services Manager
E-mail: enquiries@capel.ac.uk
Website: www.capel.ac.uk

Profile: Greater London's horticulture, floristry, countryside, equine and animal studies college.

Services: Design, Management development, Coaching & mentoring

CAPITB Plc

80 Richardshaw Lane, Pudsey, Leeds, West Yorkshire, LS28 6BN
Tel: 0113 239 3355
Fax: 0113 239 3155

Contact: C Joan Cawdron, Associate Director

Profile: National organisation. Identifies, implements, and evaluates training for industry.

CAPITB Trust

80 Richardshaw Lane, Pudsey, Leeds, West Yorkshire, LS28 6BN
Tel: 0113 227 3254
Fax: 0113 227 3322

Contact: Brian Seddon, Project officer
E-mail: capitbtrust@capitbtrust.org.uk
Website: www.careers-in-clothing.co.uk

Profile: National Training Organisation for UK apparel and allied products industries.

Career Counselling Services

46 Ferry Road, London, SW13 9PW
Tel: 020 8741 0335
Fax: 020 8741 0335

Contact: Robert Nathan, Director
E-mail: careers@dialpipex.com
Website: www.career-counselling-services.co.uk

Profile: Best practice providers of training in counselling and career counselling.

Services: Human resources, Change management, Management development

Cascade Technology Ltd

5 Meadway, Ruislip, Middlesex, HA4 7QW
Tel: 01895 633449
Fax: 01896 633450

Contact: Geoff Dische, Director
E-mail: info@cascadetechnology.co.uk
Website: www.cascadetechnology.co.uk

Profile: Development of bespoke e-learning and software.

Services: IT, E-learning

Catalyst Consultants

16 Rylstone Way, Saffron Walden, Essex, CB11 3BS
Tel: 01799 516285
Fax: 01799 525626

Contact: Hilary Course, Executive Director

Profile: TNA; wide range of organisational development and personal skills training.

Services: Management development, Supervisory, Teamworking

Catalyst Training & Development Ltd

Catalyst Business Centre, Crewe Hall, Crewe, Cheshire, CWl 6UZ
Tel: 01270 250079
Fax: 01270 259321

Contact: Carole Hollins, Systems Support Manager
E-mail: admin@7reddots.com

Profile: Organisational and management development and sales and marketing training.

Services: Leadership, Sales & marketing, Change management, Outdoor learning

CBT Systems UK Ltd

5 Heathrow Boulevard, 278 Bath Road, West Drayton, Middlesex, UB7 0DQ
Tel: 020 8283 1800
Fax: 020 8283 1801

Contact: Angela Kyte, UK Marketing Manager
E-mail: cbt.heathrow@dial.pipex.com

Profile: CBT Systems is the world's largest developer of interactive IT education software professionals and business users.

Services: IT

University of Central England Business School

Perry Barr, Birmingham, B42 2SU
Tel: 0121 331 5200
Fax: 0121 331 6366

Contact: Recruitment and Admissions Unit
E-mail: business.school@uce.ac.uk
Website: www.uce.ac.uk

Profile: Generalist MBAs and specialisation in subjects of interest to professionals.

Services: Accounting & finance, E-business, MBAs

Centre for Coaching

156 Westcombe Hill, Blackheath, London, SE3 7DH
Tel: 020 8318 4448
Fax: 020 8297 5656

Contact: Professor Stephen Palmer, Director
E-mail: admin@centreforcoaching.com
Website: www.centreforcoaching.com

Profile: Stress management training consultancy with UK coverage.

Services: Stress Management, Work-Life Balance, Training for trainers

Centre for Enabling Leadership (UK) Ltd

First Base, Beacontree Plaza, Gillette Way, Reading, RG2 0BP
Tel: 0118 931 9650
Fax: 0118 931 9651

Contact: Sheila Hampshire

Profile: Focusing on all aspects of the development of the individual.

Centre for Hazard & Risk Management

Loughborough University, Loughborough, Leicestershire, LE11 3TU
Tel: 01509 222175
Fax: 01509 223991

Contact: Joyce Bostock, Administrator
E-mail: jgbostock@lboro.ac.uk

Profile: Post-graduate programme training in risk management security backcore OHES.

Services: Risk management, Health & safety, Public sector

Centre for Labour Market Studies

University of Leicester, 7-9 Salisbury Road, Leicester, LE17QR
Tel: 0116 252 5954
Fax: 0116 252 5953

Contact: Sally Gatward, Marketing co-ordinator
E-mail: sally.gatward@leicester.ac.uk

Profile: MSc and diploma distance learning courses in training and HRM.

Services: Human resources

Centre For Language Study

Leeds Metropolitan University, Jean Monnet Building, Beckett Park Campus, Leeds
Tel: 0113 283 7440
Fax: 0113 274 5966

Contact: G Webb, Head Business Language Services
Website: www.lmu.ac.uk

Profile: Tailored language courses for business including EFL for international companies.

Services: Languages

Centre for Management Creativity Ltd

High Trenhouse, Malham Moor, Settle, North Yorkshire, BD24 9PR
Tel: 01729 830322
Fax: 01729 830519

Contact: Bernadette Schutte, Managing Director
E-mail: cmc@changeandinnovation.com
Website: www.changeandinnovation.com

Profile: Whole systems approach through facilitation, creative methodologies and outdoor learning.

Services: Human resources, Strategy & planning, Coaching & mentoring

Centre for Stress Management

156 Westcombe Hill, Blackheath, London, SE3 7DH
Tel: 020 8318 5653
Fax: 020 8297 5656

Contact: Professor Stephen Palmer, Director
E-mail: admin@managingstress.com
Website: www.managingstress.com

Profile: Stress management training consultancy with UK coverage.

Services: Stress Management, Training for trainers, Work-Life Balance

Centrex National Training Centre

Harperley Hall, FirTree, Crook, Durham, DL15 8DS
Tel: 01388 762191
Fax: 01388 762191

Contact: N Tolley, Centre Support Manager
E-mail: ntcadmin@centrex.pnn.police.ik
Website: www.forensic-training.police.co.uk

Services: Crisis & disaster management, Public sector

CERT Consultancy & Training

Little Gringley, Retford, Notts, DN22 0DU
Tel: 01777 860835
Fax: 0870 1319953

Contact: Barrie Watson, Director
E-mail: cert@cert.uk.com
Website: www.cert.uk.com

Profile: Executive, management and project team development and facilitation.

Services: Human resources, Management development, Teamworking, Business writing, Presentation skills, Performance appraisal

Chamber Business Enterprises Ltd

56 Oxford Street, Churchgate House, Manchester, Greater Manchester, M60 7HJ
Tel: 0161 237 4047
Fax: 0161 236 4160

Contact: Brian White, Management Development Manager
E-mail: brian.white@cbe.co.uk
Website: www.tvc.org.uk

Profile: Management Development Programmes (NVQ L2-L5) and Best Practice Management Benchmarking Service.

Services: Management development, Business Services, Manufacturing & engineering, Public sector, Management certificates, NVQs

Change Consultancy and Training

3 The Watermill, Staithe Road, Bungay, Suffolk, NR35 1EU
Tel: 01986 896880
Fax: 01986 896880

Contact: Maria Marques, Programme Manager
E-mail: support@change-consultancy.co.uk
Website: www.change-consultancy.co.uk

Profile: CCT specialises in human resources, organisational development and management skills.

Services: Human resources, Management development, Coaching & mentoring, Business Services, Courses, Management certificates, Management diplomas, NVQs

Change Dynamics

PO Box 571, Bradwell Common, Milton Keynes, MKl3 8ZT
Tel: 01908 605033
Fax: 01908 605033

Contact: Geoff Evans
E-mail: geoff_evans@msn.com

Profile: Human resource development assessment and training.

Services: Human resources, Change management, Management development, Teamworking, Interpersonal skills, Business Services

Change Matters

29 Wolverton Road, Stony Stratford, Milton Keynes, MK11 1EA
Tel: 01908 635134
Fax: 01908 635134

Contact: Ian Welborn, Principal Consultant
E-mail: change.matters@dial.pipex.com

Profile: Leadership, organisational and personal development to public and private sector.

Services: Change management, Interpersonal skills, Leadership

The Chartered Institute of Building

Englemere, Kings Ride, Ascot, Berkshire, SL5 7TB
Tel: 01344 630765
Fax: 01344 630770
E-mail: cjoiner@ciob.org.uk
Website: www.cjob.org.uk

Contact: Cathryn Joiner AMIPR, Public Relations Manager

Profile: The Chartered Institute of Building is a modern professional body with more than 40,000 members. It has a Royal Charter to promote the science and practice of construction for public benefit, and has won recognition from Government, other professional bodies and the industry itself as being the central voice in construction. It provides expertise in all aspects of construction management, giving advice of a legal and technical nature, and sets standards in areas such as education, and health and safety.
In the past year, the Institute has made many valuable contributions to the development and improvement of the construction industry. These have included the production and implementation of a New Education Framework and a Health and Safety Action Plan, the launch of the Third Edition of Practice for Project Management, our merger with the Architectural and Surveying Institute and numerous research and innovation projects. The CIOB has also recently launched an 'Improving Site Conditions' campaign: 'Change in our Sites', in line with the aims and key issues for the industry that have been identified by the Strategic Forum for Construction.

Services: Property, construction & facilities, Change management, Crisis & disaster management, Diversity/ Equal Opportunities, Health & safety, Innovation, Management development, Project management, Risk management, Strategy & planning, Leadership, Construction, Books & packages, Conference venues, Courses, Management certificates, Management diplomas, NVQs

The Chartered Institute of Building is a modern professional body with more than 40,000 members. It has a Royal Charter to promote the science and practice of construction for public benefit, and has won recognition from Government, other professional bodies and the industry itself as being the central voice in construction, providing expertise in all aspects of construction management, giving advice of a legal and technical nature, and setting standards in areas such as education and health and safety.

In the past year, the Institute has made many valuable contributions to the development and improvement of the construction industry. These have included the production and implementation of a New Education Framework and a Health and Safety Action Plan, the launch of the Third Edition of Practice for Project Management, our merger with the Architectural and Surveying Institute and numerous research and innovation projects. The CIOB has also recently launched an 'Improving Site Conditions' campaign: 'Change in our Sites', in line with the aims and key issues for the industry that have been identified by the Strategic Forum for Construction.

Chartered Institute of Bankers in Scotland

Drumsheugh House, 38b Drumsheugh Gardens, Edinburgh, EH3 7SW
Tel: 0131 473 7777
Fax: 0131 473 7788

Contact: Derek J Langley, Director of Business Development
E-mail: info.ciobs.org.uk
Website: www.ciobs.org.uk

Profile: The professional body for the financial services sector.

Services: Accounting & finance, Books & packages

Chartered Institute of Environmental Health

Chadwick Court, 15 Hatfields, London, SE1 8DJ
Tel: 020 7827 6006
Fax: 020 7827 5866

Contact: Centre support
E-mail: cieh@cieh.org

Profile: World's largest provider of food safety qualifications, also health & safety.

Services: Health & safety

The Chartered Institute of Purchasing & Supply

Easton House, Easton on the Hill, Stamford, Lincolnshire, PE9 3NZ
Tel: 01780 756777
Fax: 01780 751610

Contact: Jill Hepburn, Training Manager
E-mail: info@cips.org
Website: www.cips.org

Profile: The leading provider of puchasing and supply chain management courses.

Services: Supply chain & distribution, Negotiation, Management diplomas

Chartered Management Institute

Management House, Cottingham Road, Corby, Northamptonshire, NN17 1TT
Tel: 01536 207373
Fax: 01536 207384

Contact: Mrs Christine Parton, Customer Services Manager
E-mail: cmd.customerservice@managers.org.uk
Website: www.managers.org.uk

Profile: Chartered Management Institute shapes and supports the managers of tomorrow.

Services: Management development, Leadership, MBAs

Chelmsford College

Moulsham Street, Chelmsford, Essex, CM2 0JQ
Tel: 01245 349009
Fax: 01245 265611

Contact: Helen Ellis, College Information Officer

Profile: We serve Essex in providing professional training for adults.

Services: Accounting & finance, Human resources, IT, Legal, Office & secretarial, Health & safety

Chester Presentations Ltd

Fern House, Eaton Lane, Cotebrook, Tarporley, Cheshire, CW6 9DP
Tel: 01829 760040
Fax: 01829 760050

Contact: Ron Pearce, Director
E-mail: 106143.556@compuserve.com

Profile: Quality personalised presentation products when making do really won't do.

Services: Presentation skills

Chris James Management Consultancy

Garden Cottage, Holcombe House, Bulls Hill, Ross-on-Wye, Herefordshire, HR9 5SD
Tel: 01989 566698
Fax: 01989 566698

Contact: Chris James, Director
E-mail: chrisjames3@compuserve.com

Profile: Investors in People, organisation development, management development, management training.

Services: Human resources, Management development, Coaching & mentoring

Chris Sangster Development

Ardochy House, Glengarry, Invergarry, PH35 4HR
Tel: 01809 511292
Fax: 01809 511293

Contact: Chris Sangster, Facilitator/ Consultant
E-mail: chris.sangster@btinternet.com
Website: www.ardochy.ukgateway.net

Profile: Chris Sangster, author of 'Brilliant Future', facilitates related development events.

Services: Emotional intelligence, Work-Life Balance, Coaching & mentoring

Chrysalis

Lulworth House, Monk Street, Abergavenny, Monmouthshire, NP7 5NP
Tel: 01873 857070
Fax: 01873 857486

Contact: Janet Dilley, Consultancy Services Manager
E-mail: jchrysa@aol.com

Profile: Management consultancy experienced in organisational development, competence based management development.

Services: Human resources, Management development, Coaching & mentoring, Manufacturing & engineering, Books & packages, NVQs

CiaTraining Ltd

Suite J, Business & Innovation Centre, Sunderland Enterprise Park, Wear Field, Sunderland, SR5 2TA
Tel: 0191 549 5002
Fax: 0191 549 9005

Contact: Kimberley Rigg, Sales & Marketing
E-mail: info@ciatraining.co.uk
Website: www.ciatraining.co.uk

Profile: Self teach ECDL training materials guides for computer software applications.

Services: PC user skills, IT, Presentation skills, Education, Books & packages, Information & communication technologies

CIMA Mastercourses

26 Chapter Street, London, SW1P 4NP
Tel: 020 8849 2244
Fax: 020 8849 2460

Contact: Evanna Morris, Courses Marketing Manager
E-mail: mastercourses@cima.org.uk
Website: www.cimaMastercourses.com

Profile: CIMA Master courses, one day management training in management accounting and business management.

Services: Accounting & finance, Finance for non-finance staff, Courses, E-learning

Circa Ltd

65 Tweedy Road, Bromley, BR1 3NH
Tel: 020 8464 5154
020 8464 5637
Fax: 020 8464 5637

Contact: Maggy Flook, Director
E-mail: maggy@circa.ltd.uk

Profile: Meeting employer and learner needs through flexible work based learning.

Services: Accounting & finance, Office & secretarial, Business Services

City & Guilds

Customer Services Enquiry Unit, City & Guilds, 1 Giltspur Street, London, EC1A 9DD
Tel: 020 7294 2800
Fax: 020 7294 2405
E-mail: enquiry@city-and-guilds.co.uk

Profile: City & Guilds is the leading provider of vocational qualifications in the United Kingdom.

City Business Seminars

10 Blyth Wood Park, Blyth Road, Bromley, BRl 3TN
Tel: 020 8460 0351
Fax: 020 8460 0351

Contact: Peter Cassidy, Director of Courses

Profile: Personalised finance training organisation.

Services: Accounting & finance, Finance for non-finance staff, Construction

City of Bath College, School of Technology Distance Education Unit

Avon Street, Bath, Bath and North East Somerset, BAl lUP
Tel: 01225 312191
Fax: 01225 444213

Contact: I Hamlen, Distance Education Unit Staff

Profile: Distance learning providers for highways, building services and marine.

City of Wolverhampton College

Wulfrun Campus, Paget Road, Wolverhampton, Staffordshire, WV6 0DU
Tel: 01902 317700
Fax: 01902 43070

Contact: Tejo Kaur, Head of School Business and Management
E-mail: kaurt@wolverhamptoncollege.ac.uk

Profile: Wolverhampton College offers a range of business and management courses.

Services: Energy, Health

CJN Management Consultancy

49 Pennard Road, London, W12 8DW
Tel: 020 8749 1210
Fax: 020 8749 1210

Contact: Chris Noonan, Principal Consultant
E-mail: consulting@cjn.co.uk

Profile: Team development covering sales management, international marketing, marketing, major accounts.

Services: Sales & marketing, Management development, Strategy & planning

Cleaning Industry National Training Organisation

3 Moulton Court, Anglia Way, Moulton Park, Northampton, NN3 6JA
Tel: 01604 645731
Fax: 01604 645988

Contact: Chris James, Chief Executive
E-mail: info@cleaningnto.org
Website: www.cleaningnto.org

Profile: Government accredited employer-led strategic training and education organisation.

Services: Health & safety, Public sector, Books & packages, NVQs

Cleveland Tertiary College

Corporation Road, Redcar, Redcar & Cleveland
Tel: 01642 473132

Contact: Glenn Preedy, Assistant Principal

Profile: Foundation to advanced level training across a broad subject range.

Clive Evans Consultancy

Orchard Barn, Tathall End, Hanslope, Buckinghamshire, MK19 7NF
Tel: 01908 511775

Contact: Clive Evans, Senior Partner
E-mail: cliveevansbsc@aol.com

Profile: Executive mentoring and organisation development.

Services: Change management, Coaching & mentoring, Strategy & planning

CMC Consultants

High Trenhouse, Malham Moor, Settle, North Yorkshire, BD24 9PR
Tel: 01729 830322
Fax: 01729 830519

E-mail: cmc@changeandinnovation.com
Website: www.changeandinnovation.com

Profile: Facilitation and coaching developing strategic team capability for change leadership.

Services: Innovation, Change management, Training for trainers

CMPS - Civil Service College Directorate

Sunningdale Park, Larch Avenue, Ascot, Berkshire, SL5 0QE
Tel: 01344 634524
Fax: 01344 634091

Contact: Jonathan Webb, Head of Marketing
E-mail: customer.services@college-cmps.gsc.gov.uk
Website: www.cmps.gov.uk

Profile: CMPS provides management development and training for the public sector.

Services: Human resources, Change management, Public sector

Coaching Solutions

PO Box 42, Watlington, Oxon, OX49 5XU
Tel: 01491 614833
Fax: 01491 614833

Contact: Mark McGuiness, Partner
E-mail: info@coachingsolutions.co.uk
Website: www.coachingsolutions.co.uk

Profile: Executive coaching, coaching skills training, online training support with coachskills.com.

Services: Human resources, Coaching & mentoring, Emotional intelligence

Co-ed Consultants

75 Crown Road, Twickenham, Middlesex, TWl 3EX
Tel: 020 88912400
Fax: 020 8744 0878

Contact: Michael J Grinter
E-mail: mj.grinter@ntlworld.com

Profile: Planning for retirement and over-50s redundancy training specialists.

Services: Human resources

Colchester Institute

Sheepen Road, Colchester, Essex, C03 3LL
Tel: 01206 518777
Fax: 01206 763041

Contact: Course Enquiry Line
E-mail: info@colch-inst.ac.uk
Website: www.colch-inst.ac.uk

Profile: College of further and higher education including services to business.

Services: Accounting & finance, Design, Office & secretarial, Construction, Education, Food & drink

Coleg Harlech WEA (North Wales)

Harlech, Gwynedd, LL46 2PU
Tel: 01766 780363
Fax: 01766 780169

Contact: David Wiltshire, Director of Studies
E-mail: ifans@harlech.ac.uk
Website: www.harlech.ac.uk

Profile: Intensive ICT training in SMEs. Residential training and conference facilities.

Services: IT, Education, Information & communication technologies

Communic-A

Silverdale House, 9 Cottage Road, Leeds, West Yorkshire, LS6 4DD
Tel: 0113 274 0219
Fax: 0113 278 4400

Contact: Janice Armstrong, Partner
E-mail: communic-a@msn.com

Profile: Executive development programmes. As unique as your top people.

Computacenter Ltd

Systems House, 90-92 Blackfriars Road, London, SE1 8HL
Tel: 01793 428142
Fax: 01793 421277

Contact: Training Administration
E-mail: training@computacenter.com
Website: www.computacenter.com/training

Profile: Computacenter offer complete IT training solutions delivering real business benefits.

Services: IT, Information systems, PC user skills, Courses, E-learning

Computer Training Centre

The ACE Centre, Burford Road, Chipping Norton, Oxfordshire, OX7 5DZ
Tel: 01608 645315
Fax: 01608 645025

Contact: Debra Barnes, Computer Centre Manager

Profile: Computer training for the community and businesses big and small.

Comtech Associates

12 Torver Close, Braintree, Essex, CM7 8XD
Tel: 01402 061951
Fax: 01376 330928

Contact: G Clarke, Senior Consultant

Profile: HRD, management, training and development, trainer training, organisational performance systems.

Services: Management development, Training for trainers

Comtest International Ltd

6th Floor, Victoria Station House, 191 Victoria Street, London, SW1E 5NE
Tel: 020 7314 3300
Fax: 020 7314 0033

Contact: Michael de Lemes, Sales and Marketing Manager
E-mail: info@comtest.uk

Profile: Specialists in datacomms and networking internetworking to improve network productivity.

Condor Training Services

PO Box 19, Princes Risborough, Buckinghamshire, HP27 9BE
Tel: 01844 275600
Fax: 0870 056 9153

Contact: Chris Wilson, Director
E-mail: info@condortraining.co.uk

Profile: Providers of classroom-based, tutor-led on-site business IT courses.

Services: IT, Presentation skills, Project management

Confederation of Tourism, Hotel & Catering Management

204 Barnett Wood Lane, Ashtead, Surrey, KT21 2DB
Tel: 013722 78572

Contact: Mrs A Keats, Secretary General
E-mail: sales@conferencesearch.co.uk
Website: www.conferencesearch.co.uk

Profile: Training in hotel, tourism, catering and travel agency management.

Services: IT, Property, construction & facilities, Conference venues

Conference Search Ltd

1st Floor, 92 Church Lane, Marple, Cheshire, SK6 7AR
Tel: 0161 427 7057
Fax: 0161 427 2415

Contact: John Waddington, Sales Manager
E-mail: sales@conferencesearch.co.uk
Website: www.conferencesearch.co.uk

Profile: Free venue finding service throughout the UK.

Services: Business Services, Public sector, Conference venues

Conflict Management Plus

Low Farm, Brook Road, Bassingbourn, Royston, Hertfordshire, SG8 5NT
Tel: 01763 852225
Fax: 01763 853313

Contact: Jenny Walsh, Marketing Officer
E-mail: info@conflictmanagementplus.com
Website: www.conflictmanagementplus.com

Profile: Conflict Management Plus Ltd are national experts in providing solutions to workplace conflicts. We have over 10 years' experience providing accredited training and running a dispute resolution service. We work with full-time trainers and specialist consultants who bring expertise and experience from a range of public and private sector backgrounds. We have clear guidelines on equal opportunities, which run throughout our training design and delivery.

We can:

- Resolve workplace disputes between colleagues and teams
- Divert harassment and bullying cases away from disciplinaries/tribunals
- Carry out independent investigations
- Coach your teams or key players to improve performance
- Sample Training Programmes
- Certificate in Mediation Skills and Practice. A six-day course leading to OCR accreditation
- Core Mediation Skills- two-day introductory course leading to OCR accreditation
- Assertiveness
- Complaints
- Conflict management skills for HR
- Constructive conflict management for managers
- Contact officers training
- Training for Colleague Support Networks
- Managing bullying and harassment
- Investigator skills training
- Managing difficult behaviour, aggression and threats of violence
- Mediation diploma – OCR qualification in mediation practice
- Mediation and counselling skills in the workplace
- Phone rage
- Win-win negotiation

Services: Human resources, Customer service, Diversity/Equal Opportunities, Teamworking, Coaching & mentoring, Conflict resolution, Emotional intelligence, Negotiation, Problem solving, Time management, Business Services, Education, Public sector

Consultancy & Training Centre

Cricklade College, Charlton Road, Andover, Hampshire, SP10 1EJ
Tel: 01264 350559
Fax: 01264 332088

Contact: Peter Richardson, Director of Workforce Development
E-mail: ctc@cricklade.ac.uk

Profile: Cost effective training providers in management, NVQs, computing, health, safety.

Services: Training for trainers, IT, Courses, Health & safety, Management certificates, Decision-making

Consultancy & Training Services

63 Wynndale Road, Woodford, London, E18 1DY
Tel: 020 8504 4639

Contact: Derrick Fellows, Sole Proprietor

Profile: Management skills courses; instructional techniques, leadership, finance, interviewing, presentation, teamwork.

Services: Leadership, Finance for non-finance staff, Presentation skills

Consultancy Skills Training Ltd

32 York Road, Cheam, Surrey, SM2 6HH
Tel: 020 8642 9568
Fax: 020 8643 0443

Contact: Diane Davies, Marketing Co-ordinator
E-mail: cst@cst-ltd.co.uk
Website: www.cst-ltd.co.uk

Profile: Developing knowledge-based business through training and consultancy.

Services: Problem solving, Interpersonal skills, Presentation skills

Corporate Capabilities Ltd

2 Hideaway Farm, Wendover Road, Stoke Mandeville, HP22 5TR
Tel: 01296 615111

Contact: Dick Byford MBA, Principal Consultant
E-mail: info@corcap.co.uk
Website: www.corcap.co.uk

Profile: Training and development for project capability improvement.

Services: Crisis & disaster management, Management development, Project management

COTU, Charter House

City College Coventry, Butts, Coventry, West Midlands, CV1 3GD
Tel: 024 7652 6709
Fax: 024 7652 6749

Contact: Clare McKenzie, Business Manager
E-mail: cotuch@staff.covcollege.ac.uk
Website: www.cotu.covcollege.ac.uk

Services: Production & process control, Management development, Finance for non-finance staff, Manufacturing & engineering, Books & packages, Management diplomas

Coulter Ford Associates

Cedarmount House, 90A Owlsmoor Road, Owlsmoor, Sandhurst, Berkshire, GU47 0SS
Tel: 01344 780240
Fax: 01344 780250

Contact: Claire Williams, Sales and Marketing Director
E-mail: coulterfordassociates@ukbusiness.co.uk

Profile: Experts in media and presentation skills open and in-house courses.

Services: Presentation skills

Coventry University

Priory Street, Coventry, West Midlands, CV1 5FB
Tel: 024 7688 7688
Fax: 024 7688 8638

Contact: Cyrrhian Macrae, Director, Corporate Affairs
E-mail: cor2@coventry.ac.uk
Website: www.coventry.ac.uk

Services: Business Services, Information & communication technologies, Manufacturing & engineering

Cranfield School of Management

Cranfield, Bedford, MK43 0AL
Tel: 01234 751122
Fax: 01234 751806

Contact: Lyn Ball, Client Services Director
E-mail: l.ball@cranfield.ac.uk
Website: www.cranfield.ac.uk/som

Profile: One of the world's major international business schools.

Services: Management development, MBAs

Cranfield University

Cranfield, Bedfordshire, MK43 0AL
Tel: 01234 754997
Fax: 01234 752259

Contact: Shirley Jones, Director of Marketing and Communication
E-mail: info@cranfield.ac.uk
Website: www.cranfield.ac.uk

Profile: Postgraduate management, manufacturing, science and engineering plus continuous professional development.

Services: Energy, Manufacturing & engineering, MBAs, Supply chain & distribution

CRG Research Consultancy & Training

209 Cathedral Road, Cardiff, CF11 9PN
Tel: 0292 0343 218
Fax: 0292 0667 328

Contact: Andrew Rix and Richard Gaunt, Director
E-mail: consult@crg.org.uk
Website: www.crgconsulting.co.uk

Profile: Research, consultancy, training solutions addressing clients' strategic and policy challenges.

Services: Management development, Human resources, Change management

Cristo HRD: Learning Resources, Training & Consultancy

The Old Mill, New Tythe Street, Long Eaton, Nottinghamshire, NG10 2DL
Tel: 0115 972 7160
Fax: 0115 9462147

Contact: Jane Oldfield, Centre Manager
E-mail: orders@cristohrd.co.uk
Website: www.cristohrd.co.uk

Profile: Learning resources centre independent free service and managemen consultancy.

Crown Agents International ManagementTraining Centre

3-10 Marine Parade, Worthing, West Sussex, BN11 3PW
Tel: 01903 234444
Fax: 01903 212622

Contact: Andy Hadfield, Centre Manager

Profile: Four lecture rooms and three seminar rooms, each specially designed using the latest tracked teaching system.

Crown College

121-129 North Road, Westcliff on Sea, Essex, SS0 7AH
Tel: 01702 340121
Fax: 01702 341167

Contact: Toni Corsini, General Manager
E-mail: tonicors@aol.com

Profile: Crown specialise in information technology, customer services, retail administrative management.

Services: Customer service, IT, Office & secretarial, Motivation, NVQs

CSA – Celebrity Speakers Ltd

90 High Street, High Street, Burnham, Buckinghamshire, SL1 7JT
Tel: 01753 747400
Fax: 01753 747401

Contact: Dagmar O'Toole, Director of Global Operations
E-mail: csa@speakers.co.uk
Website: www.speakers.co.uk

Profile: Europe's largest guest speaker bureau serving businesses and industries worldwide.

Services: Decision-making, Emotional intelligence, Interpersonal skills

Cullen Scholefield Group

Maxwelton House, 41 Boltro Road, Haywards Heath, West Sussex, RH16 lBJ
Tel: 01444 455052
Fax: 01444 459221

Contact: Philip Gott, Customer Services Manager
E-mail: enquiries@csgconsult.com
Website: www.csgconsult.com

Profile: Innovative consultancy specialising in training trainers and Human Resources people.

Services: Human resources, Coaching & mentoring, Training for trainers

Cygnet Business Development Ltd

6 Weldon Road, Loughborough, Leicestershire, LE11 5RA
Tel: 01509 241428
Fax: 01509 241429
E-mail: info@cygnet.org.uk
Website: www.cygnet.org.uk

Profile: Management and organisational development consultancy specialising in developing leader-managers.

Services: Teamworking, Management development, Leadership

Damar Training Solutions

36-38 St Petersgate, Stockport, Cheshire, SK1 1HD
Tel: 0161 480 8171
Fax: 0161 476 1429

Contact: Dale Stafford, Managing Director
E-mail: dale@damartraining.com

Profile: Effective training solutions for business. Money-back guarantee service.

Services: Communications, advertising & PR, IT, Office & secretarial, Management development, Coaching & mentoring, Interpersonal skills

David A Palmer

The Firs, Lane End, Berkhamsted, Hertfordshire, HP4 3UT
Tel: 01442 875436
Fax: 01442 875436

Contact: David A Palmer
E-mail: palmer3firs@compuserve.com
Website: www.financialmanagementdevelopement.com

Profile: Totally tailored financial management development programmes to enhance corporate profitability.

Services: Accounting & finance, Management development, Finance for non-finance staff

David Barron Associates

Tile Cottage, Stebbing Green, Dunmow, Essex, CM6 3TE
Tel: 01371 856208
Fax: 01371 856284

Contact: David Barron, Managing Partner
E-mail: david@barron211.tsnet.co.uk

Profile: Independent practitioners and trainers on employment, training and management development.

Services: Human resources, Public sector, Management development

Davies Training Services

51 Park View, New Malden, Surrey, KT3 4AX
Tel: 020 8949 3247
Fax: 020 8949 3247

Contact: Eddie Davies, Principal Consultant
E-mail: davies_training@msn.com

Profile: Focused in-company training which develops your managers' competences.

Services: Human resources, Change management, Customer service, Management development, Motivation, Project management

DBS Associates

Island House, 157 Underhill Road, Dulwich, London, SE22 0PG
Tel: 020 8693 9969
Fax: 020 8299 2111

Contact: Dennis B Sobey, Managing Director

Profile: Management sales presentation, negotiation, telephone, interviewing, coaching skills and consultancy.

Services: Coaching & mentoring

Dearne Valley College

Manvers Park, Wath-upon-Dearne, Rotherham, South Yorkshire, S63 7EW
Tel: 01709 513333
Fax: 01709 513110

Contact: Janice Driffill, Programme Area Manager
E-mail: driffill@dearne-coll.ac.uk
Website: www.dearne-coll.ac.uk

Profile: Business management and administration programmes and training including NVQs.

Services: Management diplomas, Management certificates, NVQs

Debut Computer Services Ltd

Broadway House, 7-9 Shute End, Wokingham, Berkshire, RG40 1BH
Tel: 0118 979 3030
Fax: 0118 978 9944

Contact: Jacqui Kerr, Business Development Manager
E-mail: training@debut.co.uk

Profile: Debut is an authorised training centre for Lotus and Microsoft.

Services: IT, PC user skills

Delta Computer Training Ltd

PO Box 3151, West Bergholt, Colchester, CO6 3JH
Tel: 08707 360240

Contact: Stephen Dommett, Director
Website: www.deltacom.co.uk

Profile: Training and consultancy for IT professionals and computer users.

Services: Project management, IT, Information systems

Dental Nurse Training

Glenmore, Old Bracknell Lane West, Bracknell, Berkshire, RG12 7AE
Tel: 01344 303466

Profile: Teaching dental nurses (to NEBDN examination national standard).

Derby College

Pride Parkway, Derby, DE24 8UG
Tel: 01332 757570
Fax: 01332 576301

Contact: Debbie Mace, Special Projects Manager
E-mail: enquiries@derby-college.ac.uk
Website: www.derby-college.ac.uk

Profile: Education and training provider for various qualifications at all levels.

Services: Education, Management certificates, NVQs

Developing People Associates

2 Culworth Court, Oakwood, Derby, DE21 2PR
Tel: 01332 660029
Fax: 01332 660029

Contact: Marion Parris, Principal Consultant

Profile: In company management skills development, Trainer training, IIP, Implementation consultancy.

Services: Training for trainers

Development Dimensions International (DDI) UK Ltd

Keystone Place (Building B), Sefton Park, Stoke Poges, Buckinghamshire, SL2 4JS
Tel: 01753 616000
Fax: 01753 616099

Contact: Yvonne McGowan, Marketing Executive
E-mail: info@ddi-europe.com
Website: www.ddiworld.com

Profile: DDI: global HR consultancy specialists in leadership, selection, executive development.

Services: Human resources, Management development, Leadership

Development Resources Ltd

11 Southbourne Court, Drury Lane, Dore, Sheffield, S17 3GG
Tel: 0114 262 0428
Fax: 0114 236 5396

Contact: Martin Hughes, Director
E-mail: info@developmentresources.co.uk
Website: www.developmentresources.co.uk

Profile: Management and training consultancy specialising in people skills-development.

Services: Diversity/ Equal Opportunities, Management development, Interpersonal skills

De Vere Daresbury Park Hotel

Chester Road, Daresbury, Warrington, Cheshire, WA4 4BB
Tel: 01925 267331
Fax: 01925 265615

Contact: Tracy Lavin-Barrett, Sales Development Manager
E-mail: daresburypark.salesmanager@devere-hotels.com
Website: www.devereonline.co.uk

Profile: Modern 4 star hotel, with a 'Wonderland' location, close to Daresbury Village, birthplace of author Lewis Carroll, famed for the 'Alice' books. Accessibility is second to none being situated at J11, M56, with direct access from M6, 30 minutes drive from Liverpool and Manchester City Centres and airports.
18 meeting room options for up to 300 people, 181 bedrooms and suites for up to 360 guests, Brasserie restaurant and cafe, bars, leisure club and beauty salon, free parking 400 cars, on-site AV technician and business centre.
The hotel offers you quality without compromise and is characterised by superb cuisine, superior service, and an excellent standard of accommodation and state of the art conferencing facilities. Whatever the occasion, you will be looked after by a friendly, professional team, to ensure your satisfaction is guaranteed.
Call for a range of excellent value residential and day rate packages.
Hospitality Assured Meetings Accreditation & Investor in People. Part of De Vere Group plc.

Services: Conference venues

DHP Scotland Ltd

Haymarket House, 8 Cliftom Terrace, Edinburgh, EH12 5DR
Tel: 0131 346 3700
Fax: 0131 346 3701

Contact: L McCallum, Business Development Manager
E-mail: dhp@dhped.fsnet.co.uk

Profile: Youth and adult training provider specialising in business creation/development.

DHP Southern Ltd

3rd Floor, Ambassador House, Brigstock Road, Thornton Heath, Surrey, CR7 7JG
Tel: 020 8665 5944
Fax: 020 8665 5944

Contact: Duncan Smith, Head of Communications
E-mail: enter@dhpsouthern.co.uk
Website: www.dhpsouthern.co.uk

Profile: Business skills training for the unemployed setting up in business.

Services: Business Services

DHP Training Ltd

12 Albion Road, Chesterfield, Derbyshire, S40 1LJ
Tel: 01246 297800
Fax: 01246 222998

Contact: S Spencer, Centre Co-ordinator
E-mail: dhptrain@aol.com

Profile: DHP Training Ltd provide high quality work-based NVQ training.

Services: NVQs

D J Neil Ltd

88 Great King Street, Macclesfield, Cheshire, SK11 6PW
Tel: 01625 613666
Fax: 01625 619620

Contact: D A Braddock, Company Secretary
E-mail: consult@djnl.com
Website: www.djnl.com

Profile: Design and delivery of in-house management training UK and overseas.

Services: Accounting & finance, Sales & marketing, Management development, Strategy & planning, Manufacturing & engineering

DM Management Consultants Ltd (DMMC)

19 Clarges Street, Mayfair, London, W1Y 7PG
Tel: 020 7499 8030
Fax: 020 8948 6306

Contact: Professor P M Tomkins, Chief Executive
E-mail: pmt@dmmc.co.uk
Website: www.dmmc.co.uk

Profile: Database direct marketing specialist training development consultancy.

Services: Sales & marketing, Strategy & planning, Leadership

DMC Training Associates

Kingswood, Kingswood Court, Maidenhead, Berkshire, SL6 1DE
Tel: 01628 783311
Fax: 01628 672032

Contact: Doris Chapman, Director
E-mail: chapmandoris@hotmail.com

Profile: Skills training and development including work-life balance.

Services: Coaching & mentoring, Work-Life Balance, Assertiveness

Doncaster College

Waterdale, Doncaster, South Yorkshire, DN1 3EX
Tel: 0800 358 7575
Fax: 01302 553559

Contact: J Faraday, Academic Registrar
E-mail: infocentre@don.ac.uk
Website: www.don.ac.uk

Profile: Wide range of FE, HE and customised courses available.

Dove Nest Group

The Old Corn Mill, Chrosthwaite, Kendal, Cumbria, LA8 8BS
Tel: 015395 68824
Fax: 015395 68838

Contact: John Driscoll, Managing Director
E-mail: admin@dovenest.co.uk
Website: www.dovenest.co.uk

Profile: We deliver effective behavioural change programmes for business success.

Services: Leadership, Change management, Management development

The University of Dundee

Nethergate, Dundee, Angus, DD1 4HN
Tel: 01382 344000
Fax: 01384 201604

Contact: Dr David Duncan, University secretary
E-mail: secretary@dundee.ac.uk
Website: www.dundee.ac.uk

Durham University

Mill Hill Lane, Durham City, Durham, DH1 3LB
Tel: 0191 374 2239
Fax: 0191 374 4772

Contact: Maureen McMahon, Programme Administrator
E-mail: exec.ed@durham.ac.uk

Profile: A long-established reputation for executive education programmes.

Services: IT, Corporate universities

EAP European School of Management

12 Merton Street, Oxford, OX1 4JH
Tel: 01865 263200
Fax: 01865 251960

Contact: Ian Thomas, Manager - IMDC

Profile: Specialists in cross border management development programmes.

Services: Management development

University of East London

Longbridge Road, Dagenham, Essex, RM8 2AS
Tel: 020 8223 3000
Fax: 020 8223 2900

Contact: Nicola Duffin, PR and Marketing Assistant
E-mail: publicity@uel.ac.uk
Website: www.uel.ac.uk

Profile: UEL offers courses at foundation, undergraduate and postgraduate degree level.

Services: Management diplomas, Management certificates, MBAs

University of East London Business Services

Longbridge Road, Dagenham, Essex, RM8 2AJ
Tel: 020 8849 3578
Fax: 020 8849 3576

Contact: Madeline Capel, General Manager

Profile: Consultancy research advice, education training publications: bespoke services for businesses.

Services: IT, Corporate universities

The East of England Development Agency

The Business Centre, Station Road, Histon, Cambridge, CB4 9LQ
Tel: 01223 713900
Fax: 01223 713940

E-mail: knowledge@eeda.org.uk
Website: www.eeda.org.uk

Profile: Regional Development Agency for the East of England.

Easy i Ltd

42 The Square, Kenilworth, Warwickshire, CV8 1EB
Tel: 01926 854111
Fax: 01926 854222

Contact: Andrew Breakwell, Director of Marketing & Product Development
E-mail: info@easyi.co.uk
Website: www.easyi.com

Profile: Developer of innovative and bespoke technology based training programs.

Services: Health & safety, Risk management, Energy, Financial services, E-learning, Video

eBeDo Ltd

54c High Street, Midsomer Norton, Bath, BA3 2DQ
Tel: 0845 450 0111
Fax: 0845 450 0112

Contact: Rachel Pryor
E-mail: easy@ebedo.com
Website: www.ebedo.com

ECCTIS Ltd

Oriel House, Oriel Road, Cheltenham, Gloucestershire, GL50 1XP
Tel: 01242 252627
Fax: 01242 258600

Contact: Alison West, Business Manager
E-mail: enquiries@ecctis.co.uk
Website: www.ecctis.co.uk

Profile: National database of all award bearing courses of all institutions.

Edric Audio Visual Ltd

Eagles Wood Business Park, Woodlands Lane, Bradley Stoke, Bristol, BS32 4EU
Tel: 01454 275501
Fax: 01454 616874

Contact: John Dalgarno, Sales and Marketing Director

Profile: Audiovisual equipment hire, sales, installation, conference, video and multimedia production.

Services: Video

EDTEL Consultants

34-35 Western Road, Hove, East Sussex, BM3 lAF
Tel: 01273 737183

Contact: Roland Pearne, Managing Director

Profile: Training course providers in computing, manufacturing, sales/marketing/interpersonal skills.

Services: Interpersonal skills, Sales & marketing

EEF Sheffield Association

59 Clarkehouse Road, Sheffield, S10 2LE
Tel: 0114 268 0671
Fax: 0114 266 4227

Contact: Amanda Drake, Training & Membership Co-ordinator
E-mail: adrake@eef-sheffield.org.uk
Website: www.eef.co.uk/sheffield/shtrain/shtrain

Profile: Health and safety, workforce development training, consultancy, employment, employment law advice.

EFE International Ltd

7-11 Kensington High Street, London, W8 5NP
Tel: 020 7368 3381
Fax: 020 7937 2579

Contact: Business Development Manager
Website: www.efeinternational.com/www.mbainuk.com

Profile: Business culture, country, export/import, industry briefings. Regions: Europe, Asia.

Services: E-business, Sales & marketing, Customer service

Effective Personnel Development (EPD)

Fern House, 63A Oliver's Battery Road North, Winchester, Hampshire, SO22 4JB
Tel: 01962 853232
Fax: 01962 852805

Contact: Graham Doodson, Principal Consultant
E-mail: info@epd-uk.com
Website: www.edp-uk.com

Profile: Provision of consultancy and training on quality and process improvement.

Services: Quality, Production & process control, Business Services

Electrovision UK Ltd

Hamble Point Marina, Hamble, Southampton, Hampshire, SO31 4JD
Tel: 023 8045 2221
Fax: 023 8045 5144

Contact: Brenda Thomson, Director
E-mail: sales@electrovision.com

Profile: 500+ stocked products in skills, applications, and professional IT training.

Services: IT, Management development, Leadership, Information & communication technologies, E-learning, Investors in People

Elements

Emsworth House, 13 Duke Street, Kington, Herefordshire, HR5 3BL
Tel: 01544 230059
Fax: 01544 239050

Contact: Nick Eve, Senior Partner
E-mail: elements@unisonfree.net
Website: www.elementsuk.com

Profile: Facilitation and consultancy skills training for managers and consultants.

Services: Human resources, Interpersonal skills, Management development

Elgood Effective Learning

32 West Street, Tadley, Hants, RG26 3SX
Tel: 0118 982 1115
Fax: 0118 982 1116

Contact: Christine Elgood, Director
E-mail: info@chris-elgood.co.uk
Website: www.chris-elgood.co.uk

Profile: Engaging materials, management games and business simulaitons to improve performance.

Services: Problem solving, Management development, Games, simulation & exercises

Ellerburn Consultancy

Ellerburn, Pickering, North Yorkshire, YO18 7LL
Tel: 01751 477543
Fax: 01751 477543

Contact: G G Nutt, Managing Partner

Profile: Specialists in training and recruitment for manufacturing sector.

Ellerton Training Services

Ellerton House, 125 Grange Loan, Edinburgh, EH9 2HB
Tel: 0131 667 5570
Fax: 0131 667 5570

Contact: Judith Warren, General Manager
E-mail: enquiries@ellertontraining.co.uk
Website: www.ellertontraining.co.uk

Services: Human resources, Business Services, Books & packages

Elm Training/Publications

Seaton House, Kings Ripton, Huntingdon, PE28 2NJ
Tel: 01487 773238

Contact: Sheila Ritchie
E-mail: elm@elm-training.co.uk
Website: www.elm-training.co.uk

Profile: Customised negotiation training for managers and professionals, UK and overseas.

Services: Human resources, Change management, Management development

Elmwood Business Training

Elmwood House, Carslogie Road, Cupar, Fife, KY15 4JB
Tel: 01334 658868
Fax: 01334 658880

Contact: Anne Marie Murray, Short course co-ordinator
E-mail: amurray@elmwood.ac.uk
Website: www.elmwood.ac.uk

Profile: Elmwood Business Training provider of quality training courses and consultancies.

Services: E-business, IT, Office & secretarial, Customer service, Health & safety, Project management, Supervisory, Teamworking, Corporate universities, Management certificates

Elucid

The Innovation Centre, Brunswick Street, Nelson, Lancashire, BB9 0PQ
Tel: 01282 604510
Fax: 01282 619600

Contact: Jim McGrath, Managing Director

Endeavour Training

Sheepbridge Centre, Sheepbridge Lane, Chesterfield, Derbyshire, S41 9RX
Tel: 01246 454957
Fax: 01246 261865

Contact: Richard Alexander, Manager

Profile: Leadership and teambuilding experiential outdoor programmes. Fully mobile, tailored designs.

Services: Leadership, Teamworking

Enhancement Resources Ltd

23 Kingsland Road, Hemel Hempstead, Hertfordshire, HP1 lQD
Tel: 01442 231630
Fax: 01442 213136

Contact: Marjorie Metcalfe, Director
E-mail: mm@enhancement.uk.com
Website: www.enhancement.uk.com

Profile: A company focused on realising the potential of people and organisations.

Services: Work-Life Balance, NVQs, Management development

Enlightenment Productions

1 Briars Lane, Lathorn, Ormskirk, L40 5TG
Tel: 01704 896655
Fax: 01704 895455

Contact: Adrian Tayler, Director
E-mail: mail@trainingmultimedia.co.uk
Website: www.trainingmultimedia.co.uk

Profile: Award-winning multimedia CD-ROM, DVD, e-learning and training material producer.

Services: Blended Learning, E-learning, Video

Epic Group plc

52 Old Steine, Brighton, East Sussex, BN1 1NH
Tel: 01273 728686
Fax: 01273 821567

Contact: John Helmer, Marketing Manager
E-mail: marketing@epic.co.uk
Website: www.epic.co.uk

Profile: E-learning market leader. 18 year trade record in public and private sectors.

Services: Blended Learning, E-learning, Leadership

Equal Ability

170 Benton Hill, Wakefield Road, Horbury, West Yorkshire, WF4 5HW
Tel: 01924 270335
Fax: 01924 276498

Contact: Linda Maynard
E-mail: mail@equalability.ltd.uk
Website: www.equalability.ltd.uk

Equal Opportunities Consultancy Group

Royal Holloway University of London, Egham Hill, Surrey, TW20 0EX
Tel: 01784 443815
Fax: 01784 430680

Contact: June Jackson, Manager
E-mail: j.jackson@rhul.ac.uk
Website: www.rhul.ac.uk/cems

Profile: Consultancy and applied research services on equality and diversity issues.

Services: Human resources, Diversity/ Equal Opportunities, Management certificates

Equals

12B Pownall Gardens, Hounslow, Middlesex, TW3 lYW
Tel: 020 8572 6340
Fax: 020 8814 0309

Contact: Ann Grindrod, Partner

Profile: Providers of individual solutions for personal, career and business management.

Services: Management development

Equaville Ltd – Training Services

Elmsmead, Princes Road, Bourne End, Buckinghamshire, SL8 5HZ
Tel: 01628 525210
Fax: 01628 532697

Contact: Terence Sharkey, Director
E-mail: www.equaville.com

Profile: Speaking. Media. Interviewing. Meetings. Reports. Assertiveness. Supervision. Leadership. Negotiating etc.

Services: Human resources, Management development, Leadership, Media skills, Presentation skills, Video

Ethitec

37 Millstone Lane, Leicester, LE1 5JN
Tel: 0116 247 0806
Fax: 0116 254 4172

Contact: Mike Weatherall, Technical Sales Support
E-mail: sales@ethitec.co.uk

Profile: Specialists in all IT, software engineering, training and consultancy requirements.

Services: IT

Euro View Management Services Ltd

PO Box 80, Wetherby, West Yorkshire, LS23 7EQ
Tel: 01937 541010
Fax: 01937 541083

Contact: T Burrell, MD
E-mail: euroview@compuserve.com
Website: www.euroview.co.uk

Profile: Health and safety awareness and training video supplier.

Services: Human resources, Health & safety, Video

Euro-Lang Media Courses

88 Wychwood Avenue, Knowle, Solihull, West Midlands, B93 9DQ
Tel: 01564 774452
Fax: 01564 777058

Contact: Patrick Langmead, Director

Profile: Producer/supplier of audio/video language training programmes for business.

Services: Languages

Euromoney Training

Nestor House, PlayhouseYard, London, EC4V 5EX
Tel: 020 7779 8780
Fax: 020 7779 8693

Contact: Samantha Bown, Business Development Manager
E-mail: info@euromoneytraining.com
Website: www.euromoneytraining.com/uk

Profile: Global market leader in banking and financial training.

Services: Accounting & finance, Risk management, Financial services

The Europe Japan Centre

Mutual House, 70 Conduit Street, London, W1R 9TQ
Tel: 020 7287 8605
Fax: 020 7287 8607

Contact: Richard Newton, Marketing Manager

Profile: World class workshops to help manage change and develop people.

Services: Change management

European Forum for Teamwork

2 Castle Street, Salisbury, Wiltshire, SP1 1BB
Tel: 01722 326667
Fax: 01722 410983

Contact: Judy Wilson, Administrator
E-mail: efteam@dial.pipex.com
Website: www.efteam.org

Profile: Performance improvement, change management, teamwork training for managers and teams.

Services: Change management, Quality, Teamworking, Leadership, Problem solving, Business excellence

European Language & Management Centre

15 Heath Row, Bishops Stortford, Hertfordshire, CM23 5DH
Tel: 01279 504429
Fax: 01279 506210

Contact: Chris Heath, Partner
E-mail: info@euro-consult.co.uk
Website: www.euro-consult.co.uk

Profile: Tailored management, communication and inter-cultural training to improve international effectiveness.

Services: Management diplomas, Interpersonal skills, Languages

The Evaluation Partnership

6 Cole Park Road, Twickenham, Middlesex, TW1 lHW
Tel: 020 8892 6609
Fax: 020 8891 3883

Contact: John P Watson, Principal
E-mail: jpwatson@compuserve.com
Website: www.evaluationpartnership.com

Profile: We evaluate training courses, programmes and institutions, UK and Europe.

Services: Communications, advertising & PR, Strategy & planning, Public sector

Exact

Network House, 30 Junction Road, Sheffield, S11 8XB
Tel: 0114 268 7288
Fax: 0114 268 7299

Contact: Pam Cooper, Associate Director

Profile: Healthcare resource management consultants; change management; culture change consultants.

Services: Change management

Excel Communications (HRD) Ltd

45 West Street, Marlow, Buckinghamshire, SL7 2LS
Tel: 01628 488854
Fax: 01628 488864

Contact: Neil Tappenden, Managing Director
E-mail: info@excelcom.co.uk
Website: www.excelcom.co.uk

Profile: Specialists in applying NLP to produce outstanding business results.

Services: Sales & marketing, Management development, Coaching & mentoring, Leadership, Negotiation, Presentation skills, E-learning

Excel International

Excel House, 35 Lind Road, Sutton, Surrey, SM1 4PP
Tel: 020 8770 0465
Fax: 020 8770 0468

Contact: Julie Ford, Office Manager

Profile: Consultancy/training in project and change management, leadership, interpersonal skills.

Services: Leadership, Change management

Executive Development Initiative Training (EDIT)

Littlethorpe Park, Ripon, NorthYorkshire, HE4 1UQ
Tel: 01765 604071

Contact: John Bull, Director

Profile: Without teamwork your company will fail.

Services: Teamworking

University of Exeter

CPD Unit, Northcote House, Queens Drive, Exeter, EX4 4QJ
Tel: 01392 263770
Fax: 01392 263772

Contact: Mrs M Bee, CPD Assistant
E-mail: cpd-unit@exeter.ac.uk
Website: www.ex.ac.uk/cpd

Profile: Management development programmes at Exeter short courses to masters awards.

Services: Courses, Management development, Leadership

Expert Training Systems Plc

1 Archer Mews, Windmill Road, Hampton Hill, Middlesex, TW12 1RN
Tel: 020 8941 1177
Fax: 020 8941 2332

Contact: Hazel Cranny, Business Development Manager
E-mail: hazel@experttrainingsystems.plc.uk

Profile: ETS management simulations develop managers' knowledge skills and business awareness.

Services: Knowledge management

Facilities Staff Training

7A Glebe Road, Warlingham, Surrey, CR6 9NG
Tel: 01883 623839
Fax: 01883 626365

Contact: R Bransby, Partner
E-mail: info@fastrain.co.uk
Website: www.fastrain.co.uk

Profile: Training provider: Health, safety, food, hygeine. London and south-east.

Services: Health & safety, Stress Management, Public sector

The Faraday Centre Ltd

Unit 3 Stephenson Court, Skippers Lane Industrial Estate, South Bank, Middlesbrough, TS6 6UT
Tel: 01642 467236
Fax: 01642 467236

Contact: Malcolm Bareham, Business Development Manager
E-mail: training@faradaycentre.co.uk
Website: www.faradaycentre.co.uk

Profile: Onshore, offshore and marine high voltage electrical power system training.

Services: Manufacturing & engineering

Fast Forward

Lucena House, Shaw Village Centre, Swindon, SN5 5PY
Tel: 01793 755520
Fax: 01793 755521

Contact: Emma Lacey, Business Manager
E-mail: info@fastforward.newcollege.ac.uk
Website: www.fastforward.newcollege.ac.uk

Profile: Practical training and assessment services to boost skills and profitability.

Services: Management development, Human resources, Interpersonal skills

Fielden-Cegos

The Towers, Towers Business Park, Wilmslow Road, Didsbury, Manchester, M20 2FZ
Tel: 0161 445 2426
Fax: 0161 446 2051

Contact: Krysia Makjewska, General Manager, Open Courses & Marketing
E-mail: customerservice@fielden-cegos.co.uk
Website: www.fielden-cegos.co.uk

Financial Management Development

The Firs, Lane End, Berkhamsted, Hertfordshire, HP4 3UT
Tel: 01442 875436
Fax: 01442 875436

Contact: David A Palmer
E-mail: palmer3firs@compuserve.com
Website: www.financialmanagementdevelopment.com

Profile: Totally tailored financial management development programmes to enhance corporate profitability.

Services: Finance for non-finance staff, Accounting & finance, Management development

Finchale Training College

Durham, County Durham, DH1 5RX
Tel: 0191 386 2634
Fax: 0191 386 4962

Contact: Colette Cook, Administrative Officer
E-mail: enquiries@finchalecollege.co.uk
Website: www.finchalecollege.co.uk

Profile: Residential vocational rehabilitation to assist disabled people back to work.

Services: Accounting & finance, IT, Diversity/ Equal Opportunities

FLAG Business Solutions

Phoenix House, Kingmoor Industrial Estate, Carlisle, Cumbria, CA3 9QJ
Tel: 01228 514267
Fax: 01228 512227

Contact: Gordon Clarke, Managing Partner
E-mail: info@quantec-kingfisher.com
Website: www.quantec-kingfisher.com

Profile: Multi-disciplinary business support organisation offering consultancy/training.

Services: Human resources, Production & process control, Change management

Flexible Learning Solutions

11 High Street, Hambledon, Waterlooville, Hampshire, PO7 4RS
Tel: 023 9263 2335
Fax: 023 9263 2335

Contact: Jacqui Gough
E-mail: info@flex-learning.co.uk

Profile: Specialists in flexible learning. Supply and develop multi-media training packages.

Services: Management development, Supervisory, Business writing

Flexible Learning Systems

De Montfort University, The Innovation Centre, Oxford Street, Leicester, LE1 5XY
Tel: 0116 257 7660
Fax: 0116 255 0807

Contact: Sarah Edwards, Admissions Tutor

Profile: Offer environmental training for industry and regulators by distance learning.

Force One Training Ltd

13 Basildon Business Centre, Bentalls, Basildon, Essex, SS14 3FT
Tel: 01268 284040
Fax: 01268 280565

Contact: Tracy Quick, PA to MD
E-mail: tracy@force-trg.co.uk

Profile: IT and transport related training and LearnDirect centre.

Services: Accounting & finance, IT, Management development

Forum Europe

Orion House, 5 Upper St Martin's Lane, London, WC2K 9EA
Tel: 020 7497 5555
Fax: 020 7379 9870

Contact: Mike Godliman, Marketing

Profile: Customer service.

Frank Daniels Associates Ltd

103 Hands Road, Heanor, Derbyshire, DE75 7HB
Tel: 01773 532195
Fax: 01773 532195

E-mail: info@frankdanielsassociates.co.uk
Website: www.frankdanielsassociates.co.uk

Profile: NLP specialists solve problems, develop people, and gain more choice.

Services: Management development, Interpersonal skills, Leadership

Fresh Tracks

PO Box 101, Ware, Hertfordshire, SG11 1WA
Tel: 01920 822220
Fax: 01920 822884

Contact: Dan Collins
E-mail: mail@freshtracks.co.uk
Website: www.freshtracks.co.uk

Profile: Teams that play together work together. Contact us for more.

Services: Teamworking, Coaching & mentoring, Business Services

FT Knowledge

Portland Tower, Portland Street, Manchester, M1 3LD
Tel: 0161 245 3300
Fax: 0161 245 3301

Contact: Jon Tobbell, Sales & Marketing Director
E-mail: corporatecs@ftknowledge.com
Website: www.ftknowledge.com

Profile: FT Knowledge is the world's leading provider of business education.

Services: Management development, Leadership, Sales & marketing, Management diplomas, Competencies

Fusion Training Ltd

Arena House, North End Road, Wembley, Middlesex, HA9 0AD
Tel: 020 8208 5446
Fax: 020 8795 0425

Contact: Stephen Hall, General Manager
E-mail: s.hall@fusiontraining.ltd.uk
Website: www.fusiontraining.ltd.uk

Profile: Subsidiary company of the College of North West London.

Services: Business Services, Construction, Food & drink

Gallic Exchange Ltd

1 Queenwood, Cardiff, CF3 7LE
Tel: 01222 485736
Fax: 01222 453511

Contact: Allan Dredge, Company Secretary
E-mail: plynham@msn.com

Profile: Twenty years successful experience beginners to degree level training.

Gap Ventures

Brighton Road, Shermanbury, West Sussex, RH13 8HQ
Tel: 01403 710700
Fax: 01403 710797

Contact: Eugene Roberts

Gateshead College

Durham Road, Gateshead, Tyne and Wear, NE9 5BN
Tel: 0191 490 0300
Fax: 0191 490 2313

Contact: P Prout, Curriculum Manager
E-mail: phil.prout@gateshead.ac.uk

Profile: High quality training and development. Customised to your particular needs.

Services: Human resources, Management development, Problem solving, Courses

Gateway Television Productions

Gemini House, 10 Bradgate, Cuffley, Hertfordshire, EN6 4RL
Tel: 01707 872054
Fax: 01707 888655

Contact: Graham L Smart, Director
Website: www.gatewaytelevision.co.uk

Services: Video, Human resources, Customer service

Gatleyhall & Co Ltd

Cotswold Barn, Whittington, Near Cheltenham, Gloucestershire, GL54 4HA
Tel: 01242 820009
Fax: 01242 821122

Contact: Suzanne Hall-Gibbins, Managing Director
E-mail: info@gatleyhall.co.uk
Website: www.gatleyhall.co.uk

Profile: A revolutionary approach to enhance performance for success and fulfilment.

Services: Change management, Knowledge management, Management development

GBS Training Ltd

75 Farringdon Road, London, EC1M 3JB
Tel: 020 7278 6787
Fax: 020 7833 8419

Contact: Guy Sjgren, Director, Training Services

Profile: Public and in-house training for UK and overseas based clients.

University of Glasgow

CPD Office, 12 Southpark Terrace, Glasgow, G12 8LG
Tel: 0141 330 8068
Fax: 0141 330 2961
E-mail: vshelley@admin.gla.ac.uk

Contact: Dr Viv Shelley, CPD Development Officer

Profile: Continuing Professional Development and Updating. Further information on request

Servies: Accounting & Finance, Education, MBAs

Glasgow Caledonian University

Cowcaddens Road, Glasgow, G4 0BA
Tel: 0800 027 9171
Fax: 0141 331 8685

Contact: Tom Allardyce, Schools & Colleges Liaison Assistant
E-mail: helpline@gcal.ac.uk
Website: www.caledonian.ac.uk

Profile: Please contact the institution for further information on training opportunities.

Glasgow College of Building & Printing

60 North Hanover Street, Glasgow, Strathclyde, G1 2BP
Tel: 0141 332 9969
Fax: 0141 332 5170

Contact: Eleanor Doull, Head of Marketing
E-mail: enquiries@gcbp.ac.uk
Website: www.gcbp.ac.uk

Profile: Training and education in construction, design and visual communications.

Services: Communications, advertising & PR

Glenn Ross Services

18 Greet Park, Southwell, Nottinghamshire, NG25 0EB
Tel: 01636 815449
Fax: 01636 815449

Contact: John Formoy, Senior Consultant
E-mail: johnformoy@aol.com

Profile: Customised training to your company culture and market place.

Services: Management development, Sales & marketing, Negotiation

Global Entertainment Group

HMS President (1918), Victoria Embankment, London, EC4Y 0HJ
Tel: 020 7583 0236
Fax: 020 7583 7221

Contact: Zahida Malik,
E-mail: info@globalmusicbiz.co.uk
Website: www.globalmusicbiz.co.uk

Profile: Offers training, contacts, career advice, opportunities in the music business.

Services: Sales & marketing

Goldsmiths College

University of London, New Cross, London, SE14 6NW
Tel: 020 7919 7766
Fax: 020 7717 2240

Contact: Admissions Enquiry Unit
E-mail: admissions@goldsmiths.ac.uk
Website: www.gold.ac.uk

Profile: Study and practice of creative, cultural, cognitive and social processes.

Services: Communications, advertising & PR, Information & communication technologies, Media

Gower Publishing Ltd

Gower House, Croft Road, Aldershot, Hampshire, GU11 3HR
Tel: 01252 331551
Fax: 01252 344405

Contact: Mr Luigi Fort, Promotions Manager
E-mail: gower@bookpoint.co.uk
Website: www.gowertraining.co.uk

Profile: Gower's looseleaf and hardback activity collections come with photocopying rights.

Services: Books & packages, Games, simulation & exercises, Video

Grass Routes Management Development and Consultancy Ltd

40C Apsley Road, Clifton, Bristol, BS8 2SS
Tel: 0117 973 8500
Fax: 0117 973 8500

Contact: Steven Thomas, Director
E-mail: steve@grassroutes.co.uk
Website: www.grassroutes.co.uk

Profile: Specialists in behavioural and attitudinal change through training and consultancy.

Services: Teamworking, Management development, Leadership

Groom House Holdings Ltd

Minchin Court, Forest Hill, Oxford, OX33 1EH
Tel: 01865 873007
Fax: 01865 873725

Contact: Elizabeth Harris, Director
E-mail: marketing@groomhouse.co.uk
Website: www.groomhouse.co.uk

Profile: Behavioural training to produce lost for words customer satisfaction.

Services: Change management, Customer service, Training for trainers, Coaching & mentoring, Leadership, Information & communication technologies

GSS Personnel Services Ltd

12 Ambassador Place, Stockport Road, Altringham, Cheshire, WA15 8EQ
Tel: 0161 926 9510
Fax: 0161 926 9536

Contact: Roger Crawford, Training Services Manager

Profile: Training programmes tailored to the needs of individual clients.

Services: Health & safety, Management development, Supervisory

Guildford Educational Services Ltd

3rd Floor, 1 Pickford Street, Aldershot, Hants, GU11 1TY
Tel: 01252 337500
Fax: 01252 336511

Contact: R P Twining, Director
E-mail: info@gesvt.com
Website: www.gesvt.com

Profile: Specialists in open learning, assessment and qualifications and training information.

Services: NVQs

GW Resources

Charnley House, 13 Winckley Square, Preston, Lancashire, PR1 3JJ
Tel: 01772 202722
Fax: 01772 202721

Contact: Alison Catterall, Partner

Profile: Independent advice, training products and services. Specialising in Learning Centres.

Services: Human resources, Customer service, Video

Hadlow College

Hadlow, Tonbridge, Kent, TN11 0AL
Tel: 01732 850551
Fax: 01732 853298

Contact: Lesley Terry, LSC Administration

Profile: Landbased Industry courses covering a variety of subjects.

Hall Marketing

Studio 11, Colman's Wharf, 45 Morris Road, London, E14 6PA
Tel: 020 7537 2982
Fax: 020 7537 2982

Contact: Jeremy Hall, Managing Partner
E-mail: jeremyhall@simulations.co.uk
Website: www.simulations.co.uk

Profile: Designer and provider of computer simulations for management training.

Services: Management development, Games, simulation & exercises

The Hallingbury Centre

The Hall, Great Hallingbury, Bishops Stortford, Hertfordshire, CM22 7TY
Tel: 01279 658528
Fax: 01279 652334

Contact: Jenny Baker, Chief Executive

Profile: Design and delivery of management programmes and open courses development.

Services: Management development

Halton Management Resources Ltd

Cross Keys House, 11 Bridge Street, Reading, Berkshire, RG1 2LR
Tel: 0118 950 3020
Fax: 0118 939 1404

Contact: John Tagg, Director

Profile: Customised in-house training in management, sales and IIP consultancy.

Services: Management development, Sales & marketing

Harley McKenzie

21 Lansdowne Crescent, Edinburgh, EH12 5EH
Tel: 0131 336 1454
Fax: 0131 476 4325

Contact: Bill Vivian, Owner
E-mail: harley@mactraining.fsnet.co.uk
Website: www.mactraining.fsnet.co.uk

Profile: Management and sales training - total solutions.

Services: Sales & marketing, Customer service, Management development

Harris Associates

Quadrant Court, 53 Calthorpe Road, Edgbaston, Birmingham, B15 1TH
Tel: 0121 454 5553
Fax: 0121 455 6553

Contact: Mrs Ellen Morley, Head of Organisational Development
E-mail: mail@hassoc.co.uk
Website: www.harrisassociates.co.uk

Profile: National innovative training and organisational development company based in Birmingham.

Services: Human resources, Management development, Leadership, Business Services, Training for trainers, Management certificates

Harrogate Business Enterprises (Leeds Metropolitan University)

Harrogate College, Hornbeam Park, Harrogate, North Yorkshire, HG2 8QT
Tel: 01423 878420
Fax: 01423 879829

Contact: Alison Stone, Business Development Officer
E-mail: stone_a@harrogate.ac.uk
Website: www.harrogate.ac.uk

Profile: Bespoke company training and regular open short-course programmes.

Services: Human resources, IT, Sales & marketing

HASTAM

The Old Bakehouse, Fullbridge, Maldon, Essex, CM9 4LE
Tel: 01621 854111
Fax: 01621 851756

Contact: Mike Thomas
E-mail: info@hastam.co.uk
Website: www.hastam.co.uk

Profile: Health, safety and environmental consultancy, training and evaluation software systems.

Services: Health & safety, Risk management

Health & Safety Services Ltd

6 South Bar, Banbury, Oxon, OX16 9AA
Tel: 01295 273353
Fax: 01295 253406

Contact: Bob Foster CEng, FIEE, MIOSH, MIMgt, Director
E-mail: bob@healthandsafetyservices.co.uk
Website: www.healthandsafetyservices.co.uk

Profile: Health, safety and fire training, consultancy support. Established 1985.

Services: Property, construction & facilities, Health & safety, Manufacturing & engineering

Herefordshire College of Technology

Folly Lane, Hereford, Herefordshire, HR1 1LS
Tel: 01432 365376
Fax: 01432 365357

Contact: Enquiries Officer
E-mail: enquiries@hereford-tech.ac.uk
Website: www.hereford-tech.ac.uk

Profile: HCT provides management, training and professional qualifications.

Services: Training for trainers, Management certificates, Management diplomas, NVQs

Heriot-Watt University

Riccarton, Edinburgh, EH14 4AS
Tel: 0131 451 3629
Fax: 0131 451 3886

Contact: JM Polson, Senior Staff Learning & Development Officer
E-mail: j.d.polson@hw.ac.uk

Profile: A research-led technological university with outstanding success in academic-industrial collaboration.

Services: Human resources, Customer service, Teamworking, Presentation skills, Education, Training for trainers

Highcliffe Management Development

Sunningdale House, 11 Holmhurst Avenue, Highcliffe, Christchurch, Dorset, BH23 5PG
Tel: 01425 278101

Contact: Dr Eric Hooper, Managing Partner
E-mail: ehooper@highcliffe.u-net.com

Profile: In-house training for managers and supervisors.

Services: Management development, Project management, Negotiation

Highroad Training & Consultancy

High Road, Chilwell, Nottingham, NG9 4AH
Tel: 0115 917 5225
Fax: 0115 917 5200

Contact: K Dunnill, Business Development Manager
E-mail: dunnilk@broxtowe.ac.uk

Profile: Highroad deliver high quality customised training for your organisation.

High Trenhouse Management Centre

Malham Moor, Settle, North Yorkshire, BD24 9PR
Tel: 01729 830322
Fax: 01729 830519

Contact: Bernadette Schutte, Managing Director
E-mail: bernadette@high-trenhouse.co.uk
Website: www.high-trenhouse.co.uk

Profile: Exclusive use of exceptional, beautifully located venues for management events.

Services: Conference venues, Management development, Teamworking

Hillside

Merry Hill Road, Bushey, Hertfordshire, WD23 1DR
Tel: 020 8950 7919
Fax: 020 8950 1437

Contact: Jean Gurteen, Head of Training
E-mail: training@ctcv.co.uk
Website: www.hillside-studios.co.uk

Profile: Studio-based media and presentation skills training tutored by professionals.

Services: Media skills, Presentation skills

Holme Lacy College

Holme Lacy, Hereford, HR2 6LL
Tel: 01432 870316
Fax: 01432 870566

Contact: Charlotte Gibb, Training Services Department

Profile: Delivering a comprehensive range of training and consultancy to business.

Services: IT, Health & safety, NVQs

Horwood International Ltd

PO Box 3, Hayling Island, Portsmouth, Hampshire, PO11 0DJ
Tel: 01705 466770
Fax: 01705 461949

Contact: Sylvia Teal, Office Services Manager
E-mail: horwood@compuserve.com

Profile: ISO 9001 registered. Member IMC/BQF/MCI. Specialise in Business Excellence Model.

Services: Human resources, Production & process control, Sales & marketing

Hospitality Awarding Body

3rd Floor, International House, High Street, Ealing, London, W5 5DB
Tel: 020 8579 2400
Fax: 020 8840 6217

Contact: James Wingerath, Sales Co-ordinator
E-mail: info@hab.org.uk
Website: www.hab.org.uk

Profile: HAB is the awarding body for NVQs/SVQs in hospitality.

Hospitality Training Foundation

3rd Floor, International House, High Street, Ealing, London, W5 5DB
Tel: 020 8579 2400
Fax: 020 8840 6217

Contact: Michele Peltret, Information Officer
E-mail: nto@htf.otg.uk
Website: www.htf.org.uk

Profile: The National Training Organisation (NTO) for the hospitality industry.

Host Computer Services Ltd

Haughton Hall, Haughton Lane, Shifnal, Shropshire, TF11 8HW
Tel: 01952 468300
Fax: 01952 468313

Contact: Val Watts, Director
E-mail: v.watts@hostcomputers.co.uk
Website: www.hostcomputers.co.uk

Profile: Residential training facility providing hardware training for computer service technicians.

Services: IT, Customer service, Information & communication technologies

H R Consultancy

48 Lightwoods Hill, Smethwick, Warley, West Midlands, B67 5EB
Tel: 0121 429 9041
Fax: 0870 7061 301

Contact: Helen Rushby, Senior Consultant and Trainer
E-mail: helen@helenrushby.co.uk
Website: www.helenrushby.co.uk

Profile: Consultancy training assessment to support investors in people and EFQM.

Services: Business excellence, Investors in People, Management development

The University of Huddersfield

Huddersfield, West Yorkshire, HD1 3DH
Tel: 01484 478122
Fax: 01484 478231

Contact: Mr R J McCartney, Head of Training and Quality Services
E-mail: r.j.mccartney@hud.ac.uk

Profile: Courses in management and professional development, consultancy and ISO 9000 certification.

Services: Human resources, Management development, Conflict resolution

Huddersfield University Business School (HUBS)

Queensgate, Huddersfield, Yorkshire, HD1 3DH
Tel: 01484 422288

Contact: Dr M E Waddington, Head of Department of Management
E-mail: m.e.waddington@hud.ac.uk
Website: www.hud.ac.uk

Profile: HUBS - a collaborative learning community with a clear vocational emphasis.

Services: E-business, Management development, E-learning

The University of Hull

Cottingham Road, Hull, HU6 7RX
Tel: 01482 466100
Fax: 01482 442290

Contact: Student Recruitment and Admissions Service,
E-mail: admissions@hull.ac.uk
Website: www.hull.ac.uk

Profile: Excellent teaching and learning with strong research in niche areas.

Human Potential Research Group (HPRG)

Change Agent Skills and Strategies (MSc), University of Surrey, Guildford, Surrey, GU2 7XH
Tel: 01483 689760
Fax: 01483 686191

Contact: Daniela Warr, Administrative Assistant
E-mail: cass@surrey.ac.uk
Website: www.surrey.ac.uk/Education

Services: Human resources, Change management

Human Resource Associates

FIRST BASE, Beacontree Plaza, Gillette Way, Reading, Berks, RG2 0BP
Tel: 0118 931 9650
Fax: 0118 931 9651

Contact: Lindsey Cronshaw

Humber Business School

Grimsby College, Management Centre, Grimsby, Lincolnshire, DW34 5AJ
Tel: 01472 500220
Fax: 01472 500221

Contact: Lynton Perry, Business Development Manager
E-mail: hbs@grimsby.ac.uk
Website: www.grimsby.ac.uk/business

Profile: HBS is dedicated to offering you bespoke business solutions.

Services: Accounting & finance, Design, Human resources

The Humberside Partnership

Professional Development Centre, Queen Victoria House, Alfred Gelder Street, Hull, HU1 2AY
Tel: 01482 223081
Fax: 01482 308119

Contact: Erica Rowell, External Training & Development Manager
E-mail: pdc@getting-on.co.uk
Website: www.getting-on.co.uk

Profile: We provide training and development to help realise organisations potential.

Services: NVQs, Courses

Huntingdonshire Regional College

California Road, Huntingdon, Cambridgeshire, PE29 1BL
Tel: 01480 379100
Fax: 01480 379127

Contact: Jerry Jones, Vice Principal
E-mail: college@huntingdon.ac.uk

Profile: Professionals in education and training helping individuals to achieve.

Services: Accounting & finance, Management development, Education, NVQs

HZ Management & Training Consultancy

10 Bridge Road, St Margarets, Twickenham, Middlesex, TW1 1RE
Tel: 020 8744 2845
Fax: 020 8744 2845

Contact: Harry Zutshi, Consultant
E-mail: harry@hzcm.demon.co.uk

Profile: Provision of a wide range of consultancy and training services.

The IEE

Michael Faraday House, Six Hills Way, Stevenage, Herts, SG1 1AY
Tel: 01438 767237
Fax: 01438 767291

Contact: Tricia Desborough, Courses Officer
E-mail: tdesborough@iee.org.uk
Website: www.iee.org.uk/events/courses

Profile: Your people are your most precious asset – and with the right professional guidance, you can develop their skills and abilities. The result? Enhanced individual performance – plus measurable improvements to your bottom line.
The IEE (Institution of Electrical Engineers) is one of the UK's leaders in management and business training for professionals involved with electrical engineering, IT and electronic engineering. We offer an impressive portfolio of courses for newly qualified and experienced professionals, from careers and business skills through to effective management, negotiating, presentations, marketing – plus a wide range of more technical courses.
With over 130, 000 members worldwide, the IEE is a global organisation representing the interests of IT and electrical engineering professionals - though our courses are equally applicable to other industries and commercial sectors. Most of our programmes are held in London, though we can run them at your premises, for small or large groups.
For more information about how IEE management and business training can bring out the best in your people - and your organisation - call us on 01438 767237 or log on to www.iee.org.uk

Services: Accounting & finance, Legal, Property, construction & facilities, Management diplomas, Project management, Coaching & mentoring, Interpersonal skills, Negotiation, Presentation skills, Manufacturing & engineering, Books & packages, Courses, Training for trainers

Impact Development Training Group

Cragwood House, Windermere, Cumbria, LA23 1LQ
Tel: 015394 88333
Fax: 015394 42145

Contact: David Williams, Director
E-mail: info@impact-dtg.com
Website: www.impact-dtg.com

Profile: Transforming organisations, developing talent, building high performing teams, inspiring leaders.

Services: Change management, Management development, Teamworking, Coaching & mentoring, Interpersonal skills, Leadership

Imparta Limited

14-16 Peterborough Road, London, SW6 3BN
Tel: 020 7610 8800
Fax: 020 7610 8801

Contact: Mary Dennis, General Manager
E-mail: mary@imparta.com
Website: www.imparta.com

Profile: Imparta build organisational capabilities in strategy sales and marketing.

Services: Sales & marketing, Strategy & planning, Problem solving, MBAs

Imperial College of Science, Technology and Medicine

South Kensington, London, SW7 2AZ
Tel: 020 7589 5111
Fax: 020 7594 8004

Contact: David Atkins, Senior Assistant Registrar (Admissions)
E-mail: admissions@ic.ac.uk

Profile: All aspects of communication skills, particularly presentations and media interviews.

Services: Media skills

Implementation Training Services

32 Hill Street, Totterdown, Bristol, BS3 4TW
Tel: 01275 856354
Mobile: 07941 726 890

Contact: Derek Skelcher, Proprietor

Profile: Training in communication skills particularly media interviews and news releases.

Services: Communications, advertising & PR, Business writing

In-Comm Business Services Ltd

Vigo Place, Aldridge, Walsall, West Midlands, WS9 8UG
Tel: 01922 457686
Fax: 01922 453211

Contact: G Jones, Managing Director
E-mail: geoffj@in-comm.co.uk

Profile: Training and business consultancy organisation.

Services: Management development, Supervisory, Leadership, Investors in People

Industrial Society

Robert Hyde House, 48 Bryanstone Square, London, W1H 2EA
Tel: 0870 400 1000
Fax: 0870 400 1099

Contact: Chrissie Wright, Director, London Courses
E-mail: customercentre@indosoc.co.uk

Informatics Group (UK) Ltd

Wellington House, Piccadilly, Manchester, Lancashire, M1 1TE
Tel: 0161 932 1400
Fax: 0161 932 1444

Contact: Customer Services
E-mail: info@informaticsgroup.co.uk
Website: www.informaticsgroup.co.uk

Profile: Provides Microsoft, Citrix, Comptia, Cisco, MS Office training and professional services.

Services: IT, PC user skills

Information Automation Ltd

Penbryn, Bronant, Aberystwyth, Cardigan, SY23 4TJ
Tel: 01974 251302
Fax: 01974 251302

Contact: Chris Armstrong, Director
E-mail: lisqual@cix.co.uk
Website: www.i-a-l.co.uk

Profile: Tailored training in CD-ROM, online, internet resources and searching.

Services: E-business, IT, PC user skills, Information systems, Information & communication technologies

Inner-Leadership.com Ltd

The Old Stables, Station Road, Totnes, Devon, TQ9 5HW
Tel: 01803 865154 (Totnes) 01628 639313 (Maidenhead)
Fax: 01803 840361

Contact: David England or Simon Smith, Director
E-mail: beextraordinary@inner-leadership.com
Website: www.inner-leadership.com

Profile: '*Truly life changing. Very powerful.*'
Alan Forster, General Manager, Parcelforce.

Services: Leadership, Change management, Management development

Inplant Industrial Training

4 Woodcote Green Road, Epsom, Surrey, KT18 7DH
Tel: 01372 741818
Fax: 01372 743335

Contact: Alan Briscoe, Senior Consultant

Profile: Coaching and support services for trainers of technical/production staff.

Services: Production & process control, Multi-skilling, Food & drink, Manufacturing & engineering

Insight Consulting

Holly Ridge Cottage, Ridge Lane, Diggle, Oldham, Lancashire, OL3 5LR
Tel: 01457 873884
Fax: 01457 877379

Contact: Anthony Burke, Human Resource Consultant
E-mail: insight@consulting100.freeserve.co.uk

Profile: Learning solutions designed to liberate organisational team and individual potential.

Services: Human resources, Change management, Management development

Insight Marketing and People Ltd

PO Box 997, Wexham Road, Slough, Berkshire, SL2 5JJ
Tel: 01753 877750
Fax: 01753 877342

Contact: Irene Larcombe, Training Centre Manager
E-mail: customer.service@insight-MP.com
Website: www.insight-MP.com

Profile: Providers of sales, marketing, interpersonal, finance and business development worldwide.

Services: Management development, Sales & marketing, Customer service, Business Services

Insight Training Solutions Ltd

78 Heyford Park, Upper Heyford, Oxfordshire, OX25 5HD
Tel: 01869 238023
Fax: 01869 238024

Contact: Helen Brewerton, Business Development Manager
E-mail: helen.brewerton@insighttraining.com
Website: www.insighttraining.com

Profile: Customised commercial awareness, marketing, finance, business planning and teambuilding programmes.

Services: Management development, Motivation, Project management

The Inspiration Network

PO Box 45, Truro, Cornwall, TR2 5YF
Tel: 07889 144 893
Fax: 01326 270 998

Contact: Kaye Thorne, Managing Consultant
E-mail: inspire@btinternet.com
Website: www.theinspirationnetwork.co.uk

Profile: An HR consultancy specialising in creative and inspiring learning solutions.

Services: Interpersonal skills, Communications, advertising & PR, Innovation,

Inspiration Resources

High Trenhouse, Malham Moor, Settle, North Yorkshire, BD24 9PR
Tel: 01729 830322
Fax: 01729 830519

Contact: Dan Varney, Business Manager
E-mail: cmc@changeandinnovation.com
Website: www.changeandinnovation.com

Profile: Tools and techniques for creativity and innovation.

Services: IT, Knowledge management, Problem solving

Institute for Organising in Changing Environments

Grosvenor House, 4 Kirby Park, West Kirby, Wirral, L48 2HA
Tel: 0151 625 6431
Fax: 0151 625 6431

Contact: Peter Stutt, Senior Consultant

Profile: Dealing with change: people and organisations (consulting, training and development).

Services: Management development

Institute for Supervision & Management

The Institute for Supervision & Management merged with NEBS Management in 2001 and is now called the Institute of Leadership & Management (ILM). Please see ILM entry for further details.

The Institute of Administrative Management

16 Park Crescent, London, W1B 1BA
Tel: 020 7612 7099
Fax: 020 7612 7094
E-mail: info@instam.org
Website: www.instam.org

Profile: Established in 1915, the Institute of Administrative Management is the leading Professional Body for both practising and aspiring Administrative Managers.
We can work with you to produce an internationally recognised, in-house qualification, validate your training programmes or provide our training to your employees, in house or through our provider network.

Qualifications

IAM qualifications are targeted at Supervisors, Managers, and those who aspire to these positions. Student members can progress through the Certificate, Diploma and Advanced Diploma, and on to further qualifications (such as the IAM's dedicated degree in Administrative Management) and membership of other professional institutes

Services: Human resources, Office & secretarial, Outsourcing, Production & process control, Property, construction & facilities, Induction, Information systems, Project management, Supervisory, Teamworking, Decision-making, Leadership, Business Services, Construction, Education, Energy, Financial services, Food & drink, Health, Information & communication technologies, Communications, advertising & PR, Leisure, Manufacturing & engineering, Media, Public sector, Retailing, Transport & distribution, Books & packages, Conference venues, Courses, Performance appraisal

The Institute of Cast Metal Engineers

N M C 47 Birmingham Road, West Bromwich, West Midlands, B70 6PY
Tel: 0121 601 6979
Fax: 0121 601 6981

Contact: Eur Ing A M Turner, FIBF, Secretary
E-mail: info@icme.org.uk
Website: www.icme.org.uk

Profile: Professional development for individuals in the casting industry.

Services: Sales & marketing, Manufacturing & engineering, NVQs

The Institute of Chiropodists and Podiatrists

27 Wright Street, Southport, Merseyside, PR9 0TL
Tel: 01704 546141
Fax: 01704 500477

Contact: Mrs S Kirkham, Secretary
E-mail: secretary@inst-chiropodist.org.uk
Website: www.inst-chiropodist.org.uk

Profile: Professional organisation for Chiropodists only. Further education insurance.

Services: Health & safety, Health

The Institute of Clerks of Works of Great Britain Inc

The Lawns, 33 Thorpe Road, Peterborough, PE3 6AD
Tel: 01733 564033
Fax: 01733 564632
E-mail: info@icwgb.co.uk
Website: www.icwgb.com

Profile: Qualification/membership for those engaged in site inspection for clients.

Services: Construction

Institute of Commercial Management

The Fusee, 20a Bargates, Christchurch, Dorset, BH23 1QL
Tel: 01202 490555
Fax: 01202 490666

Contact: A F S Ford, CEO
E-mail: info@icm.ac.uk
Website: www.icm.ac.uk

Profile: Provision of training services designed to raise business performance standards.

Services: Human resources, Management development, Leadership

Institute of Cost and Executive Accountants

Akhtar House, 2 Shepherd's Bush Road, London, SW6 7PJ
Tel: 020 8749 7126
Fax: 020 8749 7127

Contact: Dr S Das Gupta, Secretary General
E-mail: icea@enta.net
Website: www.icea.enta.net

Profile: Professional Examining body. Provides Training for financial decision makers.

Services: Accounting & finance, Management development, Strategy & planning

Institute of Directors

116, Pall Mall, London, SW1Y 5ED
Tel: 020 7839 1233
Fax: 020 7930 1949

Contact: David Marshall, Director of Public Affairs
E-mail: press@iod.com
Website: www.iod.com

The Institute of Financial Accountant

Burford House, 44 London Road, Sevenoaks, Kent, TN13 lAS
Tel: 01732 458080
Fax: 01732 455848

Contact: Mrs V Burrows, Membership Administrator
E-mail: mail@ifa.org.uk
Website: www.ifa.org.uk

The Institute of Food Science and Technology (UK)

5 Cambridge Court, 210 Shepherd's Bush Road, London, W6 7NJ
Tel: 020 7603 6316
Fax: 020 7602 9936
E-mail: info@ifst.org
Website: www.ifst.org

Profile: Professional qualifying body for food scientists and technologists. Educational charity.

Services: Books & packages

The Institute of Internal Auditors – UK and Ireland

13 Abbeville Mews, 88 Clapham Park Road, London, SW1 7BX
Tel: 020 7498 0101
Fax: 020 7978 2492

Contact: Ann Cantillon, Manager, Training and Conferences
Website: www.iia.org.uk

Profile: IIA – UK and Ireland. The professionals in internal audit training.

Services: Accounting & finance, Project management, Risk management

Institute of Leadership & Management

1 Giltspur Street, London, EC1A 9DD
Tel: 020 7294 3053
Fax: 020 7294 2402

Contact: Marketing team or Qualifications Divisions or Publishing Division

Stowe House, Netherstowe, Lichfield, WS13 6TJ
Tel: 01543 251346
Fax: 01543 266811

Contact: Membership team or Learning Support & Development Division

E-mail: membership@i-l-m.com
Website: www.i-l-m.com

Profile: Institute of Leadership & Management (ILM) offers membership services together with leadership and management qualifications. ILM is a professional body that supports national objectives to ensure the UK is able to develop leaders and managers of the future, with a particular focus on first line and middle levels. Offering qualifcations for managers and team leaders from Levels 2-5 of the national framework, ILM also supports individual and organisational development through endorsement, awards and learning resources. ILM is a subsidiary of the City & Guilds Group, the UK's largest provider of vocational qualifications.

We provide the following services:
Membership, Vocationally-Related Qualifications, S/NVQs, Management and team leader qualifications, Quality-Assured Awards, Open learning resources from levels 2-5 (Building Success at Level 2, ILM Super Series at Level 3 and The Universal Manager at Level 4/5), CD based assessment materials and management videos (Teams that Work and A Vision for Change).

Services: Management development, Management certificates, Management diplomas, Leadership, Supervisory, Teamworking

Institute of Linguists

Saxon House, 48 Southwark Street, London, SE1 1UN
Tel: 020 7940 3100
Fax: 020 7940 3101

Contact: Stephen Eden, Head of Publicity and Membership
E-mail: info@iol.org.uk

Profile: The Institute of Linguists is a professional membership and language examinations body.

Services: Languages

Institute of Management Services

1 Cecil Court, London Road, Enfield, Middlesex, EN2 6DD
Tel: 020 8363 7452
Fax: 020 8367 8149

Contact: Doreen Jarvis, Education Administrator

Profile: Qualified specialists for improving productivity, performance and quality.

The Institute of Management Specialists (IMS)

Head Office, Warwick Corner, 42 Warwick Road, Kenilworth, Warwickshire, CV8 1HE
Tel: 01926 855498
Fax: 01926 513100
Contact: Professor H J Manners, President and Founder

Profile: Professional membership body providing qualifications by exemption. Distance learning courses.

Services: Supervisory, Manufacturing & engineering, Management certificates, Management diplomas

The Institute of Manufacturing

Head Office, Warwick Corner, 42 Warwick Road, Kenilworth, Warwickshire, CV8 1HE
Tel: 01926 855498
Fax: 01926 513100

Contact: Professor H J Manners, President and Founder

Profile: Professional Institute. Qualifications in manufacturing, modem technology and systems.

Services: Multi-skilling, Education, Management certificates, Management diplomas

Institute of Payroll and Pensions Management

Shelly House, Farmhouse Way, Monkspath, Solihull, B90 4EH
Tel: 0121 712 1000
Fax: 0121 712 1001

Contact: M Jackson, Training Manager
E-mail: training@ippm.org
Website: www.ippm.org

Profile: Provider of payroll and pensions qualifications, consultancy and training courses.

Institute of Printing

8A Lonsdale Gardens, Tunbridge Wells, Kent, TN1 1NU
Tel: 01892 538118
Fax: 01892 518028

Contact: David Freeland, Secretary General
E-mail: iop@globalprint.com

Profile: Professional body for printing industry. Holds lectures, debates, seminars, conferences.

Institute of Professional Managers and Administrators

La Dependance, Route de Vinchelez, Jersey, JE3 2DA
Tel: 01534 485500
Fax: 01534 485072

Contact: V Carlyle, Secretary

Profile: International membership for managers offering examinations and careers training courses.

Services: Management development, Business writing, Business Services

Institute of Quality Assurance

12 Grosvenor Crescent, London, SWIX 7EE
Tel: 020 7245 6722
Fax: 020 7245 6788
E-mail: iqa@iqa.org

Profile: The IQA is the UK's leading body for the advancement of quality practice. It offers membership training courses (public and in-house), has established the Diploma in Quality and is the provider of the leading quality publication in the UK 'Quality World'.

Institute of Travel & Tourism

Mill Studio, Crane Mead, Ware, Herts, SG12 9PY
Tel: 0870 770 7960
Fax: 0870 770 7962

Contact: Steven Freudman, Chairman
E-mail: admin@itt.co.uk
Website: www.itt.co.uk

Profile: Developing the professionalism of its members within the industry.

The Institution of Occupational Safety and Health

The Grange, Highfield Drive, Wigston, Leicestershire, LE18 lNN
Tel: 0116 257 3100
Fax: 0116 2573101

Contact: C D Haynes, Commercial Training Manager

Profile: Europe's leading body for health and safety professionals.

Services: Health & safety, Risk management, Presentation skills

Intec Business Solutions (Scotland) Ltd

21-22 Lynedoch Industrial Estate, Greenock, PA15 4AX
Tel: 01475 729123
Fax: 01475 787011

Contact: Malcolm Miller, Managing Director
E-mail: malcolm.miller@surfanytime.co.uk

Profile: Experts in staff development including computing interpersonal and management skills.

Services: IT, Management development, Time management

Intech Training Group Ltd

PO Box 2, Welwyn Garden City, Hertfordshire, AL8 6NJ
Tel: 01707 320944
Fax: 01707 325930

Contact: F C Grant, Managing Director

Profile: In-company/open courses in sales, marketing, management and customer care.

Services: Customer service, Sales & marketing

Integralis Ltd

Brewery Court, 43-45 High Street, Theale, Berkshire, RG7 5AH
Tel: 01734 306060
Fax: 01734 302143

Contact: Karen Liddell, Training & Consultancy Administration
E-mail: info@integralis.co.uk

Profile: Integralis provides TCP/IP and Internet seminars consultancy and training.

Integration International

Russell House, 23 Station Road, Beamish, County Durham, DH9 0QU
Tel: 0191 370 0331
Fax: 0191 370 1492

Contact: Guy Tunnicliff, Director
E-mail: guytunnicliff@integration-int.com

Profile: Outstanding Personal leader, Team, Organisational and International Business Development.

Services: Change management, Management development, Coaching & mentoring

Intelligent Training Solutions Ltd

29 Narrow Street, London, E14 8DP
Tel: 020 7791 3000
Fax: 020 7791 3030

Contact: Steve Cousins, New Business Manager
E-mail: info@its-training.co.uk
Website: www.its-training.co.uk

Profile: Suppliers of generic and bespoke multimedia training solutions.

Services: IT, Project management, Assertiveness, Business writing, Finance for non-finance staff, PC user skills

Inter Comm

7 Barton Buildings, Bath, BA1 2JR
Tel: 01225 442839
Fax: 01225 442839

Contact: D Williams, Secretary

Profile: Studies in situational European languages for personal contact and correspondence.

Services: Languages

Interactive Training Management Ltd

Portland Chambers, 131-133 Portland Street, Manchester, Ml 4PY
Tel: 0161 228 1902
Fax: 0161 236 5974

Contact: Nicola Hardy, Contract Manager
E-mail: nicolahardy.ddi@btconnect.com

Profile: Training available in ECDL, IBT2, CLAIT, NVQs, Administration & Customer Service.

Services: Office & secretarial, IT, Customer service

The International Association of Book-keepers

Burford House, 44 London Road, Sevenoaks, Kent, TN13 1AS
Tel: 01732 458080
Fax: 01732 455848

Contact: Carmel Fitzgerald, PA to Chief Executive
E-mail: mail@iab.org.uk
Website: www.iab.org.uk

Profile: The IAB is the longest established professional body for book-keeping.

International Association of Business Computing

PO Box 2158, Swindon, SN5 3GY
Tel: 01793 772254
Fax: 01793 772254

Contact: Pippa Lewis, Administration Officer
E-mail: admin@iabc.demon.co.uk
Website: www.iabc.demon.co.uk

Profile: Examining body in computing and IT at two levels.

International Institute of Security

Suite 8, The Business Centre, 57 Torquay Road, Paignton, Devon, TQ3 3DT
Tel: 01803 663275
Fax: 01803 663251

Contact: Paula Stanbridge, Company Secretary
E-mail: iisec@btinternet.com
Website: www.iisec.co.uk

Interquad

110 Middlesex Street, London, E1 7HT
Tel: 01753 534421
Fax: 01753 577256

Contact: Julie Hunter, Marketing

Profile: Interquad provides high quality information technology training to IT professionals.

Services: IT

Invest Business Training Solutions

Hull College, Queens Gardens, Hull, HU1 3DG
Tel: 01482 598855
Fax: 01482 598780

Contact: Helen Rainey, Manager
E-mail: invest@hull-college.ac.uk
Website: http://invest.hull-college.co.uk

Profile: Invest offers training solutions to Hull and East Yorkshire Businesses.

Services: IT, Management certificates, Management diplomas

Invicta Training Ltd

240 Green Lane, New Eltham, London, SE9 3TL
Tel: 020 8851 4044
Fax: 020 8857 2443

Contact: Jacqui Roberts, Sales Manager
E-mail: info@invicta.bdx.co.uk
Website: www.invictatraining.co.uk

Profile: Specific pragmatic interactive training, consultancy, mentoring, coaching and support services.

Services: Sales & marketing, Management development, Interpersonal skills

iQ Computer Services Ltd

261 Burnt Oak, Broadway, Edgware, Middlesex, HA8 5ED
Tel: 020 8381 1188
Fax: 020 8905 7137

Contact: Janine Nyman, Director

Profile: Training for all popular business software applications and operating systems.

Services: PC user skills

IQdos Ltd

45 West Street, Marlow, SL2 2LS
Tel: 01628 488556
Fax: 01628 477491

Contact: Sue Harley, Director
E-mail: info@iqdos.com
Website: www.iqdos.com

Profile: The leading specialists in online performance measurement and development solutions.

Services: Blended Learning, Competencies, E-learning

Irenicon Ltd

Airport House, Purley Way, Croydon, CR0 0XZ
Tel: 020 8286 7770
Fax: 020 8286 9900

Contact: Annabel Kaye, Managing Director
E-mail: info@irenicon.co.uk
Website: www.irenicon.co.uk

Profile: Specialist employment law consultancy and training.

Services: Legal, Human resources, Diversity/ Equal Opportunities

IRPC Group Ltd

Stockwell House, New Buildings, Hinckley, Leicestershire, LE10 1HW
Tel: 01455 894100
Fax: 01455 894101

Contact: Anita Lange, Marketing Manager
E-mail: alange@irpc.co.uk
Website: www.irpc.co.uk

Profile: Safety and personnel training and guaranteed advice for managers/owners.

IRS Conferences & Training

Halsbury House, 35 Chancery Lane, London, WC2A 1EL
Tel: 020 7420 3500
Fax: 020 7420 3576

Contact: Sarah Hammond, Group Conference Manager
E-mail: sarah.hammond@lexisnexis.co.uk
Website: www.conferencesandtraining.com

Profile: IRS offers 30 years excellence in employment law training.

Services: Human resources, Diversity/ Equal Opportunities, Business Services

ISA 2001

9 Ferndown Close, Bristol, BS11 0UP
Tel: 0117 968 2691
Fax: 0117 962 6500

Contact: Harold James, Marketing Consultant
E-mail: Ibbc@btinternet.com
Website: www.safetyconsultantsireland.net

Profile: Providers & Trainers in Health & Safety Management Systems.

Services: Books & packages, Health & safety

The IT Partnership

Egham Training Centre, 80 High Street, Egham, Surrey, TW20 9HE
Tel: 01784 470275
Fax: 01784 470273

Contact: Adam Reid, Partner
E-mail: sales@itpart.demon.co.uk

Profile: Desktop and technical cost effective solutions throughout the UK.

Services: IT

ITE Ltd

Dominion Road, Wallisdown, Bournemouth, Dorset, BH11 8LH
Tel: 01202 570341
Fax: 01202 581116

Contact: Gill McGillivray, Marketing Assistant
E-mail: itetrain@aol.com

Profile: One of the South of England's largest independent training establishments.

i to i

One Cottage Road, Headingley, Leeds, LS6 4DD
Tel: 0870 333 2332
Fax: 0113 274 6923

Contact: Sam White, Marketing Director
E-mail: info@i-to-i.com
Website: www.i-to-i.com

Profile: Intensive TEFL training, voluntary teaching placements overseas.

Services: Education, Books & packages, E-learning

i to i Training & Development

Ashorne Hill Conference Centre, Ashorne Hill, Leamington Spa, Warwickshire, CV33 9QW
Tel: 01926 488059
Fax: 01926 488005

Contact: Carmen Caney, Business Development Co-ordinator
E-mail: carmen.caney@i2itraining.com
Website: www.i2itraining.com

Profile: Identification of needs to design and delivery of bespoke training.

Services: Change management, Project management, Teamworking

It's All About People

30 The Crossways, Wembley Park, Middlesex, HA9 9NG
Tel: 020 8904 2474
Fax: 020 8904 7773

Contact: Hoda Lacey, Senior Partner
E-mail: hodalacey@aol.com
Website: www.hodalacey.com

Profile: Management, personal and organisational development. Business Performance Coaching, Conflict Resolution.

IT Skills For All!

Grangemouth Enterprise Centre, Grangemouth, FK3 8XS
Tel: 01324 878613/21/22/23
Fax: 01324 878601

Contact: Lynne Hunter, Director
E-mail: info@itskillsforall.co.uk
Website: www.itskillsforall.co.uk

IT Training Suite, The Business and Management Centre

West Herts College, Watford Campus, Hempstead Road, Watford, Hertfordshire, WD17 3EZ
Tel: 01923 812436
Fax: 01923 812437

Contact: Nasira Alibhai, External Training Supervisor
E-mail: whbmc-it@westherts.ac.uk
Website: www.businesstraining.westherts.ac.uk

Profile: Flexible approach to IT training for professionals and individuals.

Services: IT, PC user skills

James Miles Consultants

36 Lower Hill Road, Epsom, Surrey, KT19 8LT
Tel: 01372 721582
Fax: 01372 748880

Contact: Jim Miles, Director
E-mail: jim.miles@j-m-c.demon.co.uk

Profile: Customer focused tailored training: improving processes, cycle time-flexibility-quality-cost.

Services: Production & process control, Quality, Business excellence

Jane Allan & Associates

25 High Street, Andover, Hampshire, SP10 1LJ
Tel: 01264 352755
Fax: 01264 352758

Contact: Di Swaddling, PA to Jane Allan
E-mail: ja@janeallan.com
Website: www.janeallan.com

Profile: Enjoyable training that adds pure value for salary for all.

Services: Accounting & finance, Management development, Work-Life Balance

Jaybetec Consultants Ltd

33 Kildrummy Road, Craigiebuckler, Aberdeen, AB15 8HJ
Tel: 01224 311508
Fax: 01224 311508

Contact: John B Smith, Managing Director
E-mail: info@jaybetec.com
Website: www.jaybetec.com

Profile: Consultancy and training in electrical engineering and electrical safety.

Services: Energy, PC user skills, Manufacturing & electrical engineering

Jaymedia

10A Crewe Road, Alsager, Cheshire, ST7 2ES
Tel: 01270 884453
Fax: 0870 120 9079

Contact: Nigel Jay, Director
E-mail: media@jaymedia.co.uk
Website: www.jaymedia.co.uk

Profile: Media and presenter training provided by BBL trained personnel.

Services: Media, Media skills, Presentation skills

J B Computer Management

Olumo House, 39 Luckley Road, Wokingham, Berkshire, RG41 2RS
Tel: 01734 785161
Fax: 0118 978 5161

Contact: Ann Davies, Business Development Management
E-mail: info@cdc-jbcm.com
Website: www.cdc-jbcm.com

Profile: JBCM provides HR organisation development programmes for individual and corporate.

Services: Human resources, Change management, Coaching & mentoring, Business Services, Human capital audits, Business excellence

J C Consultancy Ltd

68 Chapelfields, Charterhouse Road, Godalming, Surrey, GU7 2AA
Tel: 01483 424037
Fax: 01483 426997

Contact: Dr John Chicken, Director

Profile: Risk assessment and management training provided, tailored to clients' needs.

Services: Risk management

JD Associates

Welshpool, Gloucester Road, Alveston, Bristol, BS35 3QQ
Tel: 01454 418841

Contact: Derek Thornhill, Centre Manager
E-mail: jdassociates@bigfoot.com

Profile: NVQ Consultancy and Approved Assessment Centre.

Services: Education, Training for trainers, NVQs

Jenny Jarvis & Associates

Wood House, 31 Woodham Drive, Hatfield Peverel, Essex, CM3 2RN
Tel: 01245 381207
Fax: 01245 380904

Contact: Jane Taylor, Customer Relationship Manager
E-mail: j.jarvis@virgin.net
Website: www.jennyjarvisandassociates.co.uk

Jewel & Esk Valley Commercial Enterprises Ltd (JEVCEL)

24 Milton Road East, Milton Road Centre, Edinburgh, EH15 2PP
Tel: 0131 657 7305
Fax: 0131 657 2276

Contact: Hugh Jackson, Manager

Profile: Supplier of value for money flexible training and consultancy.

JHP Training

45 King Street, Stirling, FK8 1DN
Tel: 01786 450898

Contact: E Brown

JHP Training Ltd

Sutherland House, Matlock Road, Coventry, CV1 4JQ
Tel: 024 7666 7891
Fax: 024 7666 8075

Contact: Anne-Marie McTavish, Head of Commercial Training & Consultancy
E-mail: anne.marie.mctavish@jhp-group.com
Website: www.jhp-group.com

Profile: Customised highly interactive training developed specifically for targeted business impact.

Services: Interpersonal skills, Leadership, Training for trainers

JM Solutions Ltd

4 Heathfield Terrace, Chiswick, London, W4 4JE
Tel: 020 8994 3962
Fax: 020 8995 8170

Contact: Joan Bennett, Director
E-mail: jmsltd@surfaid.org
Website: www.jointlymanagedsolutions.com

Profile: We specialise in middle and senior management career development.

Services: Business Services, Management development, Coaching & mentoring

John Cole Management Development

186 Station Road, Sutton Coldfield, West Midlands, B73 5LH
Tel: 0121 354 7680
Fax: 0121 354 5767

Contact: John Cole, Partner
E-mail: jemcole@aol.com
Website: www.johncolemgtdev.co.uk

Profile: Publishes experiential exercises and organises management courses and team building.

Services: Management development, Teamworking, Books & packages

John Greenland

Highfield House, The Warren, Ashtead, Surrey, KT21 2SL
Tel: 01372 275094
Fax: 01372 275094

Contact: John Greenland, Director

Profile: Individual tuition and group training in business writing.

Services: Business writing, Courses

John Matchett Limited

Linden House, 55 South Bar, Banbury, Oxfordshire, OX16 9AB
Tel: 01295 256161
Fax: 01295 272108

Contact: Elaine Priestley, Marketing Manager
E-mail: sales@jmlnet.com
Website: www.jmlnet.com

Profile: Instructor lead training and skills and competence management.

Services: Accounting & finance, Project management, Leadership

John Meechan Training

5 Portland Drive, Nuneaton, Warwickshire, CV10 9HZ
Tel: 01203 744211
Fax: 01203 744211

Contact: John Meechan, Consultant

Profile: Creative managerial and interpersonal skills to meet your unique needs.

Services: Management development, Interpersonal skills

John Price Business Courses Ltd

The Old Vicarage, Poulton, Cirencester, Gloucestershire, GL7 5HU
Tel: 01285 851889
Fax: 01285 851888

Contact: A St John Price FCA
E-mail: asjohnprice@btopenworld.com

Profile: Courses & Concultancy in Value Added Tax since 1975.

Services: Accounting & finance

John Unitt Associates

9 Johnson Road, Birstall, Leicester, Leicestershire, LE4 3AT
Tel: 0116 221 7807

Contact: John Unitt, Business Owner
E-mail: johnunitt@making-a-difference.org.uk

Profile: Career management, counselling, outplacement job search, stress, supervisory, customer care.

Services: Human resources, Change management, Psychometric testing

Jon Spencer Training & Consultancy

Chestnut House Smallway, Congresbury, Bristol, BS49 5BB
Tel: 01934 833743

Contact: Jon Spencer, Principal

Profile: Management skills, managing change, training and facilitation.

Services: Change management, Management development, Coaching & mentoring

Jo Ouston & Co

Lower Ground Floor, Nelson House, Dolphin Square, London, SWlV 3NY
Tel: 020 7821 8299
Fax: 020 7798 5743

Contact: Andy Beaumont, Business Manager
E-mail: info@joouston.co.uk
Website: www.joouston.co.uk

Profile: Jo Ouston & Co take a radical new approach to personal development planning and career development.

JRTS

Maranatha, 241 Blakelow Road, Macclesfield, Cheshire, SK11 7EH
Tel: 01625 425830

Contact: J R T Spencer, Consultant

Profile: Training of trainers, youth, sales, marketing for small companies.

Services: Sales & marketing, Training for trainers

JTL

Stafford House, 120/122 High Street, Orpington, Kent, BR6 0JS
Tel: 01689 884100
Fax: 01689 891658

Contact: Helen McGrath, Marketing Manager
E-mail: helenmcgrath@jtlimited.co.uk
Website: www.jtlimited.co.uk

Profile: Training provider to the building engineering industry offering apprenticeships.

Services: Courses, Construction, NVQs

The Judge Institute of Management Studies

University of Cambridge, Trumpington Street, Cambridge, CB2 1AG
Tel: 01223 339700
Fax: 01223 339701

Services: Business writing

Julia Samways

32 Church Drive, East Keswick, Leeds, West Yorkshire, LS17 9EP
Tel: 01937 573080
Fax: 01937 573080

Contact: Julia Samways, Training Consultant
E-mail: julia@ptp.globalnet.co.uk

Profile: Tailor-made courses for managing and developing yourself and others.

Services: Courses, Coaching & mentoring, Teamworking

KB Training

White Gables, Quinton, Northampton, NN7 2DZ
Tel: 01604 862292

Contact: Kathey Bailey, Training Consultant

Profile: Training courses in time management, communication skills and self development.

Services: Business writing, Presentation skills, Time management

KD Kefford & Associates

94-96 North End, Meldreth, Royston, Hertfordshire, SG8 6NT
Tel: 01763 260513

Contact: K D Kefford, Principal

Profile: Providers of management consultancy and management and human resources training.

Services: Human resources, Management development

Keele University

Staffordshire, ST5 5BG
Tel: 01782 621111
Fax: 01782 632343

Contact: Sharne Procter, Head of Admissions and Recruitment
E-mail: aaa06@keele.ac.uk

Profile: Masters, diploma and certificate courses, full-time and part-time.

Keenan Research Limited

Victoria House, 15 Gay Street, Bath, BA1 2PH
Tel: 01225 336569
Fax: 01225 336585

Contact: Kate Keenan, Director
E-mail: kmkeenan@keenan-research.com

Profile: Managing change; motivational interviewing; handling stress; assessing risk; psychometric testing.

Services: Motivation, Books & packages, Business Services

Ken & Kate Back Ltd

Yateley Lodge, Reading Road, Yateley, Hants, GU 46 7AA
Tel: 01242 862421
Fax: 01252 890596

Contact: Chris Darwen, Training Consultant
E-mail: darwenc@kenandkateback.co.uk
Website: www.kenandkateback.co.uk

Profile: Ken & Kate Back - 'Bringing People Skills to Business.'

Services: ISO 9000, Business Services, Information & communication technologies, Public sector, Retailing

University of Kent

The Registry, University of Kent, Canterbury, Kent, CT2 7NZ
Tel: 01227 764000
Fax: 01227 452196

Contact: Hilary Saunders, Publications Manager
Website: www.kent.ac.uk

Services: Accounting & finance, Education, MBAs

Kettering Borough Training

Douglas House, 27 Station Road, Kettering, Northamptonshire, NN15 7HH
Tel: 01536 411200
Fax: 01536 412822

Contact: Angela Ellis, Manager

Profile: Industrial training broker providing vocational training within 16-24 year age group.

The Key Network

2 Low House Barn, Old Hutton, Kendal, Cumbria, LA8 0NH
Tel: 01539 730890

Contact: Simon McElroy, Training Co-ordinator
E-mail: info@thekeynetwork.com
Website: www.thekeynetwork.com

Profile: Outdoor development, team building, leadership and management development programmes UK wide.

Services: Human resources, Customer service, Management development

Keytime Management Development

72 Victoria Road, Burgess Hill, West Sussex, RH15 9LZ
Tel: 01444 235141
Fax: 01444 870004

Contact: Stephen Hannington, General Manager

Profile: Time management training, Keytime planning systems and personal development programmes.

Services: Time management

Kilmarnock College

Holehouse Road, Kilmarnock, Scotland, KA3 7AT
Tel: 01563 523501
Fax: 01563 538182

Contact: M Ruebuck, Principal

Profile: Further education college serving Ayrshire. Wide range of courses available.

Services: Courses

King Alfred's College of Higher Education

Sparkford Road, Winchester, SO22 4NR
Tel: 01962 827502
Fax: 01962 827248

Contact: Marilyn Birks, Director Business and Community Partnerships
E-mail: m.birks@wkac.ac.uk

Profile: College of Higher Education; Full time students: 3,000; Part time students: 2,000

Services: Education

King Associates

37 Elliott Square, Hampstead, London, NW3 3SU
Tel: 020 7586 3456
Fax: 020 7483 3121

Contact: Gill King, Managing Consultant
E-mail: kingassociates@aol.com
Website: www.kingassociates.org.uk

Profile: Pragmatic executive coach specialising in maximising potential, achieving positive difference.

Services: Human resources, Coaching & mentoring, Presentation skills

The King Partnership Ltd

Imber Court, High Street, Cranbrook, Kent, TN17 3DF
Tel: 01580 715635
Fax: 01580 715634

Contact: Alex King, Chairman

Profile: Support for management in education related activity, UK and overseas.

Services: Human resources, Change management, Education

Kingdom Management Training

PO Box 277, Sevenoaks, Kent, TN13 3GU
Tel: 01732 760216
Fax: 01732 763716

Contact: Jane Stevens, Business Administrator
E-mail: learn@kmtcentre.co.uk
Website: www.kmtcentre.co.uk

Profile: KMT's products and services measurably improve management of organisations.

Services: Management development, Health & safety, Risk management

Kingston Language Export Centre

Kingston University, Penrhyn Road, Kingston-upon-Thames, Surrey, KT1 2EE
Tel: 020 8547 7884
Fax: 020 8547 7388

Contact: Penny Tribe, Short Course Administrator
E-mail: p.tribe@kingston.ac.uk

Profile: Business language training, intensive and extensive, in-company or university based.

Services: Languages, Business Services, Courses, Business excellence

The Kingstree Group (UK) Ltd

68 Chandos Place, London, WC2N 4HG
Tel: 020 7836 5575
Fax: 020 72400688

Contact: Antony Finley, Consultant

Services: Business writing

KLC Advisory Services

86 Smithbrook Kilns, Cranleigh, Surrey, GU6 8JJ
Tel: 01483 267111
Fax: 01483 267322
Contact: Carolyn Chadwick, Partner
E-mail: info@klc-advisory.co.uk
Website: www.klc-advisory.co.uk

Profile: Practical training and advice in all aspects of employment law.

Services: Human resources

KMA Productions

Barford House, 40 Ditton Road, Surbiton, Surrey, KT6 6QZ
Tel: 020 8399 2009
Fax: 020 8399 8763

Contact: Mike Kirby, Producer
E-mail: kma@onetel.net
Website: www.kmaonline.com

Profile: Quality Induction and safety training packages, editing, VHS/DVD duplication services.

Services: Books & packages, Training for trainers, Video

Lakeside Management Development

YMCA National Centre, Newby Bridge, Ulverton, Cumbria, LA12 8BD
Tel: 015395 30224
Fax: 015395 30015

Contact: Chris Wells, Corporate Manager
E-mail: lmd@lmd.org.uk
Website: www.lmd.org.uk

Profile: Lakeside Corporate – one of Britain's leading experiential training providers.

Services: Change management, Management development, Project management

Lancaster and Morecambe College

Morecambe Road, Lancaster, Lancashire, LA1 2TY
Tel: 01524 66215
Fax: 01524 843078

Contact: Richard Parker, Programme Area Manager (Management Development)
E-mail: r.parker@lanmore.ac.uk
Website: www.lanmore.ac.uk

Services: Management certificates, Management diplomas, NVQs

Lancaster University

External Relations, University House, Lancaster, Lancashire, LA1 4YD
Tel: 01524 594084
Fax: 01524 594069

Contact: Tracy Bartlett, International Promotions Officer
E-mail: t.bartlett@lancaster.ac.uk

Profile: High quality training and education programmes for industry and commerce

Services: IT, Quality

Langham Management Consultants

11 Curzon Avenue, Beaconsfield, Buckinghamshire, HP9 2NN
Tel: 01494 672001
Fax: 01494 678037

Contact: Grant Stewart, Managing Director
E-mail: langham@clara.co.uk
Website: www.langham.clara.net

Profile: Sales management, sales audits, business development processes, management development training.

Services: Sales & marketing, Strategy & planning, Financial services

LD AssociatesTraining Services

18 Ruby Street, Carlinghow, Batley, West Yorkshire, WF17 8HL
Tel: 01924 475571
Fax: 01924 475571

Contact: Mr Laurie Denton, Managing Consultant
E-mail: ldassociates@btinternet.com

Profile: Provider of client specific management supervisory and trainer training programmes.

Services: Management development, Training for trainers, Supervisory

Lea, Storey & Co

Bush House, Brinsea Road, Congresbury, Bristol, BS49 5JJ
Tel: 01934 838203
Fax: 01934 838203

Contact: Robin Lea, Managing Director

Profile: Value for money, quality training services from people you trust.

Services: Human resources, Management development, Coaching & mentoring

Leadership Resources Limited

Warwick Corner, 42 Warwick Road, Kenilworth, CV8 1HE
Tel: 01926 864806
Fax: 0870 0560780

Contact: Ken Minor, Director
E-mail: info@leadreshipresources.co.uk
Website: www.leadershipresources.co.uk

Services: Knowledge management, Teamworking, Leadership

The Leadership Trust (Training) Limited

Weston-under-Penyard, Ross-on-Wye, Herefordshire, HR9 7YH
Tel: 01989 767667
Fax: 01989 768133

Contact: Margaret Pearce, New Business Co-ordinator
E-mail: enquiries@leadership.co.uk
Website: www.leadership.org.uk

Profile: Leadership development for all managers and directors.

Services: Management development, Teamworking, Leadership

Learning and Skills Council West of England

PO Box 164, St Lawrence House, 29-31 Broad Street, Bristol, BS99 7HR
Tel: 0845 019 4168
Fax: 0117 372 6433

Contact: Margaret Drury, Customer Services

Profile: Manages work-based training for young people through approved providers.

Services: NVQs

Learning Applications Ltd

Meadow House, Burrington, Umberleigh, North Devon, EX37 9LA
Tel: 01769 520609
Fax: 01769 520609

Contact: Steve Hook, Managing Director & Principal Consultant
E-mail: steve@meadowhouse.demon.co.uk
Website: www.meadowhouse.demon.co.uk

Profile: Consultancy services for specialist staff, management team and organisation development.

Services: Management diplomas, Teamworking, Coaching & mentoring

The Learning Corporation LLP

Parallel House, 32 London Road, Guildford, Surrey, GU1 2AB
Tel: 01483 454039
Fax: 01483 300145

Contact: Richard Fox, Director
E-mail: rjfox@tlc.eu.com
Website: www.tlc.eu.com

Profile: Optimising business performance through facilitation, coaching and advisory skills.

Services: Human resources, Sales & marketing, Outsourcing

Learning Curve Training Ltd

Linton House, 164-180 Union Street, London, SE1 0LH
Tel: 020 7928 5191
Fax: 020 7928 5359

Contact: Marilyn Davidson, Director

Profile: Specific recruitment industry training for managers, consultants and support staff.

Services: Human resources, Management development, Interpersonal skills, Leadership

The Learning Experience

High Trenhouse, Malham Moor, Settle, North Yorkshire, BD24 9PR
Tel: 01729 830322
Fax: 01729 830519
E-mail: cmc@changeandinnovation.com
Website: www.changeandinnovation.com

Profile: Outdoor and experiential learning for team and leadership development.

Services: Emotional intelligence, Management development, Leadership

University of Leeds

Leeds, West Yorkshire
Tel: 0113 243 1751

Services: IT, Corporate universities

Leeds College of Technology

Cookridge Street, Leeds, LS2 8BL
Tel: 0113 243 0381
Fax: 0113 2340365

Contact: Steve Marks, Director of Enterprise and Marketing

Profile: Specialises in computing, telecommunications and engineering training.

Services: IT

Leeds Training & Enterprise Counncil

Belgrave Hall, Belgrave Street, Leeds, West Yorkshire, LS2 8DD
Tel: 0113 234 7666
Fax: 0113 243 8126

Contact: Martin Ruston, Marketing Manager
E-mail: tecinfo@leedstec.co.uk

Profile: Provides support for local organisations to become investors in people.

University of Leicester

Management Centre, University of Leicester, University Road, Leicester, LEI 7RH
Tel: 0116 252 5520
Fax: 0116 252 3949
E-mail: lumc@le.ac.uk
Website: www.le.ac.uk/lumc

Profile: The University of Leicester is ranked as one of the top 20 universities in the UK. For the past 14 years The Management Centre has gained a reputation for international excellence in the development and teaching of management courses, which are intellectually stimulating and highly relevant to your career needs. Our students come from a variety of nations, cultures and professional backgrounds but have same common aim – to improve their personal and professional skills in order to advance their career opportunities.
The Management Centre offers MSc Finance; MSc Marketing and MSc Management, as well as the MBA. All courses except for MSc Management can be studied full-time on campus (12 months) or by distance learning (minimum 24 months - maximum 60 months).

Services: MBAs, Education, Courses, Management development, Management certificates, Finance, Marketing

Leisure Management International

9 Carvel Court, Terminus Road, Cowes, Isle of Wight, PO31 7TS
Tel: 01983 280641
Fax: 01983 281821

Contact: Sara Coombes, Programme Manager

Profile: Professional management training for the marine leisure industry.

Services: Management development

Les Jones & Associates

30 Beryl Avenue, Tottington, Bury, Lancashire, BL8 3NF
Tel: 01204 882950

Contact: Les Jones, Principal Consultant
E-mail: ijj4@tutor.open.ac.uk

Profile: Training and consultancy in management of change and creative management.

Services: Management development, Problem solving, Change management

Liftrain Ltd

Unit B, Spring Place Mill, Northorpe, Mirfield, West Yorkshire, WF14 0QX
Tel: 01924 490790
Fax: 01924 491107

Contact: Bob Panter, Director

Profile: Lift truck operator basic training. NVQ lift truck operations level 2.

Services: NVQs

Lindley Training

High Burton, Masham, Ripon, HG4 4XZ
Tel: 01765 689254
Fax: 01765 689604

Contact: Steve Wade, Business Development Manager
E-mail: enquiries@lindley.org
Website: www.lindley.org

Profile: Bespoke change programmes developing individuals, teams, leaders and organisational cultures.

Services: Change management, Customer service, Management development

Linguaphone Institute Ltd

Liongate Enterprise Park, 80 Morden Road, Mitcham, CR4 4PH
Tel: 020 8687 6000
Fax: 020 8687 6310

Contact: Richard Avery, Director, Sales & Marketing
E-mail: cst@linguaphone.co.uk
Website: www.linguaphone.co.uk

Profile: Self-study language courses for personal and business use.

Services: Languages

Link Training

2nd Floor, Suite 4, 38-40 High Street, Croydon, CR0 1YB
Tel: 020 8686 4644
Fax: 020 8686 4316

Contact: Graham Young, Centre Manager

Profile: Link Training are a national training organisation delivering vocational NVQ's.

Services: NVQs

Link Training

49 George Street, Walsall, West Midlands, WS1 1RT
Tel: 01922 615098
Fax: 01922 725090

Contact: M Rogers, Centre Manager

Profile: Link provide training NVQ, retail warehouse, administration and customer service.

Services: Customer service, NVQs

Liverpool Business School

98 Mount Pleasant, Liverpool, Merseyside, L3 5UZ
Tel: 0151 231 3830
Fax: 0151 231 3234

Contact: Bridget Price, Commercial Development Manager
E-mail: b.price@livjm.ac.uk
Website: www.livjm.ac.uk

Profile: Liverpool Business School for all your training needs.

Services: Information systems, Project management, Leadership

Liverpool John Moores University

JMU Tower, 24 Norton Street, Liverpool, Merseyside, L3 8PY
Tel: 0151 231 5090
Fax: 0151 231 5632

Contact: Enquiry Helpline, Enquiry Management Team
E-mail: recruitment@livjm.ac.uk
Website: www.livjmu.ac.uk

Services: Accounting & finance, Business Services, Management certificates, MBAs

Livingstone Communication

Sandhurst Place, Sandhurst Lane, Bexhill on Sea, East Sussex, TN39 4RH
Tel: 01424 844854
Fax: 01424 846970

Contact: John Livingstone-Learmonth,
E-mail: jll@livingstone.uk.com

Profile: Selling skills for brokers and portfolio managers.

Services: Sales & marketing, Financial services, Presentation skills

Livingsuccess.co.uk

7 Elm Quay Court, London, SW8 5DE
Tel: 07866 531 400
Fax: 020 7627 4053

Contact: Carole Railton Dip BPC, Director
E-mail: info@livingsuccess.co.uk
Website: www.livingsuccess.co.uk

Profile: Maximixing performance, facilitating change, increasing potential for business and individuals.

Services: Coaching & mentoring, Negotiation, Psychometric testing

LMA Training & Development

The Greyhound House, Folkingham, Sleaford, Lincolnshire, NG34 0SE
Tel: 01529 497370
Fax: 01529 497370

Contact: Philip Moon, Managing Partner

Profile: Tailored courses in personal effectiveness and communication skills.

Services: Negotiation, Stress Management, Time management

Logistics Training International Ltd

Development House, Newton Road, Heather, Coalville, Leicestershire, LE67 2RD
Tel: 01530 262666
Fax: 01530 262724
E-mail: lti.ltd@dial.pipex.com

Profile: Established: 1990. No. of consulting staff: 17 (+10 associate members)

Contact: David Jackson (General), Michael Charlesworth Mmulti-media)

London Electronics College

20 Penywern Road, London, SW5 9SU
Tel: 020 7373 8721
Fax: 020 7244 8733

Contact: Maria Mejia, Administrator
E-mail: contact@lec.org.uk
Website: www.lec.org.uk

London Languages

44 Alderney Street, London, SW1V 4EU
Tel: 020 7233 8205
Fax: 020 7233 8206

Contact: Lynn Ansell, Course Director
E-mail: mail@londonlanguages.com
Website: www.londonlanguages.com

Profile: London Languages specialises in B2B language training.

Services: Languages, Financial services

LPT Productions

Braemore House, Meigle, Blairgowrie, Perthshire, PH12 8QX
Tel: 01828 640770
Fax: 01828 640669

Contact: Lee Bushby, Partner
E-mail: lptproductions@cs.com
Website: www.lptproductions.com

Profile: Personal *Profile*s for ACL, time, behaviour, team building and empowerment.

Services: Human resources, Leadership, Time management

University of Luton

Park Square, Luton, Beds, LU1 3JU
Tel: 0800 389 6633
Fax: 01582 486 260
E-mail: www.luton.ac.uk

Profile: Quality business and management education training research and consultancy.

Services: Accounting & finance, Communications, advertising & PR, E-business, Human resources, IT, Sales & marketing

Mackenzie Training

17 Tamarind Way, Reading, Berkshire, RG6 5GR
Tel: 0118 986 8909
Fax: 0118 961 1514

Contact: Sandy Mackenzie, Partner
E-mail: sandy@mactrain.co.uk
Website: www.mactrain.com

Profile: Books, audios, videos, workshops, leadership, motivation, sales, management, customer service.

Services: Sales & marketing, Leadership, Video

MagNotes Ltd

High Trenhouse, Malharn Moor, Settle, North Yorkshire, BD24 9PR
Tel: 01729 830322
Fax: 01729 830519

Contact: Dan Varney
E-mail: cmc@changeandinnovation.com
Website: www.changeandinnovation.com

Profile: Visual thinking tools for creativity and innovation.

Services: Education, Innovation, Courses

Malpas Flexible Learning Ltd

Woodlands, 79 High Street, Greenhithe, Kent, DA9 9RD
Tel: 01322 381334
Fax: 01322 381334

Contact: Adam Ireland, Business Development Manager
E-mail: admin@malpas.co.uk
Website: www.malpas.co.uk

Profile: The leading UK provider of CIPD qualifications via flexible learning.

Services: Human resources, Management development, Leadership

Management and Technology Training

Bedford Business Centre, Suite C, Mile Road, Bedford, Bedfordshire, MK42 9TW
Tel: 01234 352163
Fax: 01234 349756

Contact: John Weekes, General Manager
E-mail: mtt@btclick.com

Profile: Specialists in HRD, customer service, QA, business skills, H & S, finance.

Services: Human resources, ISO 9000, Management certificates

The Management Centre

Moulton College, Ledge Farm, Pitsford Road, Moulton, Northampton, NN3 7RR
Tel: 01604 491131
Fax: 01604 491127

Contact: Mrs Lynn Clarke, Commercial Training Manager
E-mail: lynnc@moulton.ac.uk

Profile: Design and deliver quality training specifically tailored to industry needs.

Services: Management development, Training for trainers, IT

Management Improvements Ltd

1 Manor Wood Road, Purley, Surrey, CR8 4LG
Tel: 020 8660 9080
Fax: 020 8660 9080

Contact: Alan Speed, Managing Consultant

Profile: Process improvement and re-engineering training for banks and insurance companies.

Services: Management development, Production & process control, Courses, Business excellence, Problem solving

Management Learning Resources Ltd

PO Box 28, Carmarthen, Carmarthenshire, SA31 1DT
Tel: 01267 281661
Fax: 01267 281315

Contact: Jennifer Bott (Mrs), General Manager
E-mail: sales@mlr.co.uk
Website: www.mlruk.com

Profile: Direct marketing company distributing/producing management training and development materials.

Services: Books & packages, Games, simulation & exercises, Training for trainers

Management Magic

Pentre House, Leighton, Welshpool, Powys, SY21 8HL
Tel: 01938 553430
Fax: 01938 555355

Contact: Carol Harris, Consultant/Trainer
E-mail: management.magic@effectiveconsulting.org.uk
Website: www.border.org.uk

Profile: Development of people and organisations using NLP. Training, coaching, mentoring.

Services: Business writing, Interpersonal skills, Neuro-linguistic programming

The Management School

University of Salford, Salford, Greater Manchester, M5 4WT
Tel: 0161 295 5530
Fax: 0161 295 5022

Contact: David Lavender, Director of Marketing and Recruitment
E-mail: d.c.lavender@man-sch.salford.ac.uk

Profile: The Management School, University of Salford, MBA, MSc, Access courses.

Services: Management development

Management Training & Development

Meadow House, Dinton, Aylesbury, Buckinghamshire, HP17 8UB
Tel: 01296 747041
Fax: 01296 747441

Contact: Geoff Smith, Partner
E-mail: smith.mtd@dial.pipex.com
Website: www.geoffsmith-mtd.org.uk

Profile: We provide tailor-made courses for business organisations.

Services: Leadership, Management development, Strategy & planning

Management Training Associates

Clifton Hall, Clifton, Ashbourne, Derbyshire, DE6 25L
Tel: 01335 345642
Fax: 01335 345642

Contact: Ian Winfield, Director
E-mail: i.j.winfield@derby.ac.uk

Profile: Selection test training, Management training and development, Teambuilding, Continuous improvement.

Services: Management development

Managing and Marketing Sales Association

PO Box 11, Sandbach, Cheshire, CW11 3GE
Tel: 01270 526339
Fax: 01270 526339

Contact: Michael Whitaker, Director of Education
E-mail: info@mamsasbp.com

Profile: Professional qualifications covering management, marketing and sales, UK and overseas.

Services: Sales & marketing, Management development, Decision-making

Manchester Business School

Booth Street West, Manchester, M15 6PB
Tel: 0161 275 6333
Fax: 0161 275 5862

Contact: Janet Cusworth, Press & Information Officer
E-mail: marketing@man.mbs.ac.uk
Website: www.mbs.ac.uk

Services: Retailing, Conference venues, Management development

Manchester Open Learning

Whitworth House, Ashton Old Road, Manchester, M11 2WH
Tel: 0161 953 6000
Fax: 0161 953 6001

Contact: David Patterson, Head of Manchester Open Learning
E-mail: mol@mancat.ac.uk
Website: www.mol-openlearning.co.uk

Profile: We design, produce and deliver educational programmes covering a wide range of subjects for all levels.

Services: Education

Marketing Training Co

140 Borden Lane, Sittingbourne, Kent, ME9 8HW
Tel: 01795 423778
Fax: 01795 423778

Contact: Peter Sidlett, Manager

Profile: Marketing training covering the whole subject from introductory to MBA.

Services: Communications, advertising & PR, Sales & marketing, Strategy & planning

Marsh Business Services

36 Edwardes Square, Kensington, London, W8 6HH
Tel: 020 7603 3133
Fax: 020 7603 3133

Contact: F O Marsh, Principal
E-mail: marsh_london@compuserve.com
Website: www.marshoflondon.com

Profile: Training: intercultural relations, D-I-Y market research, development export trade.

Services: Sales & marketing, Management development, Interpersonal skills

Martin Uren

42 Carden Avenue, Patcham, Brighton, East Sussex, BN1 8NA
Tel: 01273 501113
Fax: 01273 883814

Contact: Martin Uren, Broadcast Training Consultant
E-mail: martin.uren@ntlworld.com

Profile: Provide training courses and seminars in broadcast technology and ICT.

Services: IT, Information & communication technologies, Media

Marwel & Co

Marwel House, Lee Hill Court, Lanchester, County Durham, DH7 0QE
Tel: 01207 521929
Fax: 01207 521929

Contact: Linda Marrin, Partner
E-mail: jmarrin@marwel-co.com

Profile: Specialists in realising the potential of organisations and their people.

Services: Change management, Knowledge management, Management development

Mayo Learning International Ltd

13 King Harry Lane, St Albans, Hertfordshire, AL3 4AS
Tel: 01727 843424
Fax: 01727 759185

Contact: Andrew Mayo, Director
E-mail: andrew@mliltd.com
Website: www.mliltd.com

Profile: Specialists in strategy, talent and career management and HR measurement.

Services: Human resources, Strategy & planning, Competencies, Human capital audits

McKenzie-Thorpe

42 High Street, Market Harborough, Leicestershire, LE16 7AF
Tel: 01858 410055
Fax: 01858 410443

Contact: S J Castledine, Managing Director

Profile: Innovative training solutions within selling, customer service and account management.

Services: Customer service, Accounting & finance

MDA – Management Development Associates

45 De Montfort Road, Kenilworth, Warwickshire, CV8 1DE
Tel: 01926 852547
Fax: 01926 850815

Contact: Gill Bond, Administrator
E-mail: training_mda@msn.com

Profile: Comprehensive range of in-house management supervisory and staff development programmes.

Services: Leadership, Training for trainers, Management certificates

The Meat Training Council

PO Box 141, Winterhill House, Snowdon Drive, Milton Keynes, MK6 1YY
Tel: 01908 231062
Fax: 01908 231063

Contact: S Lawton, NTO and Marketing Executive

Profile: Providers of vocational training for the meat and poultry industry.

Mechatronics International Ltd

37 Britannia Way, Lichfield, Staffordshire, WS14 9UY
Tel: 01543 255268
Fax: 01543 416717

Contact: Barry James, Director

Profile: Manufacturers/suppliers - training equipment/systems for pneumatics, hydraulics, electro-control, PLCs.

Services: Multi-skilling, Education, Manufacturing & engineering

The Media Centre@DVA Ltd

7 Campbell Court, Bramley, Basingstoke, Hampshire, RG26 5EG
Tel: 01256 882032
Fax: 01256 882024

Contact: Barrie Gibson, Managing Director
E-mail: info@dva.co.uk
Website: www.dva.co.uk

Profile: Full-service and production company. Video, Web, CD, DVD, Events.

Services: Presentation skills, Business Services, Education

Medical Indemnity Register

PO Box 12, Sutton, SM3 8ZN
Tel: 020 8644 8880
Fax: 020 8644 9499

Contact: David Guest, Registrar
E-mail: medical@btinternet.com
Website: www.medicalindemnity.com

Profile: First aid in-house training and first aid medical malpractice insurance.

Services: Health & safety, Courses, Health

Mentor Group Ltd

VER House, London Road, Markyate, Hertfordshire, AL3 8JP
Tel: 01582 842077
Fax: 01582 842122

Contact: Neil Kelly, Director
E-mail: info@mentorgroup.co.uk
Website: www.mentorgroup.co.uk

Profile: Tailored management development and training. 22 experienced consultants. Try us!

Services: Sales & marketing, Management development, Coaching & mentoring

Merlin Management Services

62 Higher Darcy Street, Darcy Lever, Bolton, Lancashire, BL2 1NQ
Tel: 01204 365332
Fax: 0797 105 6562

Contact: Janet Crummey, Senior Consultant
E-mail: merlinms@btinternet.com
Website: merlin-consultancy.co.uk

Profile: Improving business performance and profitability by developing your human assets.

Services: Customer service, Management development, Finance for non-finance staff, Presentation skills, Business Services, Manufacturing & engineering

MerlinTraining Ltd

60-62 Fulham Palace Road, London, W6 9PH
Tel: 020 8741 3221
Fax: 020 8741 0065

Contact: Neal Hutchinson, Director

Profile: Hands-on computer training covering PC hardware, windows, networking and internet.
Services: PC user skills

Metals Industry Skills & Performance Ltd (Metskill)

5 & 6 Meadowcourt, Amos Road, Sheffield, South Yorkshire, S9 1BX
Tel: 0114 244 6833
Fax: 0114 256 2855

Contact: Malcolm Leick, Development Director
E-mail: enquiries@metskill.co.uk
Website: www.metskill.co.uk

Profile: Sector skills body for the UK metals manufacturing industry.

Services: Manufacturing & engineering

Michael Adam Associates

10 Cedar Court, Edenhurst Drive, Timperley, Altrincham, Cheshire, WA15 7AH
Tel: 0161 903 9081
Fax: 0161 903 9546

Contact: Hilary Kenway, Administration Manager

Profile: Specialising in training for management directors and board members.

Services: Management development

Michael Morris Management Training & Development

Greenacres, Gypsy Lane, Marlow, Buckinghamshire, SL7 3JT
Tel: 01628 486594
Fax: 01628 890172

Contact: Michael Morris, Partner
E-mail: michael.morri@wordproc.co.uk

Profile: MMMT&D offers tailor-made executive coaching and management skills development programmes.

Services: Management development, Coaching & mentoring, Negotiation

Mid & North Wales Training Group Ltd T/A Myrick Training Services

Myrick House, Hendomen, Montgomery, Powys, SY15 6EZ
Tel: 01686 668670
Fax: 01686 668771

Contact: Janice Howells, Office Manager
E-mail: myrick@btinternet.com

Profile: Skills training, management training levels 3-5, general consultancy, short courses.

Services: Health & safety, Management development, E-learning, NVQs

Mid Career College

PO Box 20, Cambridge, Cambridgeshire, CB1 5DG
Tel: 01223 880016
Fax: 01223 881604

Contact: Mrs Ann Chapman, Registrar
E-mail: courses@mid-career-college.ac.uk
Website: www.mid-career-college.ac.uk

Profile: Established in 1986, Mid Career College is one of the most comprehensive CPD providers.

Services: Project management, Health & safety, Construction

Middlesex University

White Hart Lane, London, N17 8HR
Tel: 020 8411 5898
Fax: 020 8411 5649

Contact: Sue Scott, Publications Officer
E-mail: admissions@mdx.ac.uk
Website: www.mdx.ac.uk

Profile: London-based international university championing social inclusion and innovative courses.

Services: Accounting & finance, Human resources, Education

Milton Keynes College

Chaffron Way Campus, Woughton Campus West, Leadenhall, Milton Keynes, MK6 5LP
Tel: 01908 684444
Fax: 01908 684399

Contact: Stefan Drew, Marketing Manager
E-mail: info@mkcollege.ac.uk
Website: www.mkcollege.ac.uk

Profile: Largest provider of further education and training in North Bucks.

Services: Customer service, Management development, Business Services

Minerva Consulting

Plas Glansevin, Llangadog, Carmarthenshire, SA19 9HY
Tel: 01550 777121
Fax: 01550 777890

Contact: Harvey Peters, Head of training
E-mail: minerva@minervaconsulting.co.uk
Website: www.minervaconsulting.co.uk

Profile: Team, skills and process interventions for blue chip companies internationally.

Services: Teamworking

Mitre Group Ltd

Molyneux Business Park, Whitworh Road, Darley Dale, Matlock, Derbyshire, DE4 2HJ
Tel: 01629 734888
Fax: 01629 735666

Contact: G Todd, Director
E-mail: mail@mitregroup.com

Profile: Team development, leadership, management, coaching, single/multi-day courses.

Services: Management development, Project management, Strategy & planning

MLP Training

16 Greenmount Drive, Greenmount, Bury, Lancashire, BL8 4HA
Tel: 01635 552151
Fax: 01635 43957

Contact: Mike Le Put/Madeline White
E-mail: MLP@mlptraining.co.uk
Website: www.mlptraining.co.uk

Profile: Sales training and management development, live courses and CDs.

Services: Sales & marketing, Customer service, Problem solving

Mobile Training Ltd

Sibford Gower, Banbury, Oxfordshire, OX15 5RX
Tel: 01295 788115
Fax: 01295 780366

Contact: Beryl Pollard, Compamy Secretary
E-mail: admin@mobiletraining.co.uk
Website: www.mobiletraining.co.uk

Profile: Finance and Management Skills training both in-house and public courses.

Services: Accounting & finance, Management development, Assertiveness

MODAS (Management & Organisation Development Advisory Service)

79 Northcote Crescent, West Horsley, Leatherhead, Surrey, KT24 6LX
Tel: 01483 284765
Fax: 01483 284765

Contact: Charles Holme, Partner
E-mail: charlesholme@cs.com
Website: www.modas.org.uk

Profile: Human resources; Management development; Interpersonal skills; Training for trainers.

Services: Human resources, Management development, Interpersonal skills, Training for trainers

Momentum Business & Training Partnership

PO Box 433, Orpington, Kent, BR6 9WJ
Tel: 01689 898582
Fax: 01689 898085

Contact: David Stringer, Principal
E-mail: momentumbt@aol.com

Profile: Worldwide experience in all business sectors, large and small organisations.

Morcamation Management & Training Consultants

Management House, 156 Woodside Avenue, Chislehurst, Kent, BR7 6BS
Tel: 020 8295 5750
Fax: 020 8467 0921

Contact: Peter Forrester, Course Director
E-mail: morcamation.mc@virgin.net

Profile: Strategic business/marketing planning, quality management ISO000/TQM, managing change.

Services: Production & process control, Strategy & planning, Problem solving, ISO 9000

Mossley College (The Youth Development Association)

Old Vicarage, Mossley, Ashton-under-Lyne, Lancashire, OL5 0QY
Tel: 01457 834943
Fax: 01522 524305

Contact: C Shaw, Chair

Profile: Independent College - tutorial based. Youth & Community Services. Management Studies.

Motivation Cassettes Ltd

Dunluce, 4-8 Canfield Gardens, London, NW6 3BS
Tel: 020 7624 7785
Fax: 020 7624 4879

Contact: Nadine Levon, Marketing Executive

Profile: Audio/video cassettes created to support training courses and conferences.

Services: Video

Moulton Laidlaw

St Oswalds, Knockhundred Row, Midhurst, West Sussex, GU29 9DQ
Tel: 01730 816926
Fax: 01730 814343

Contact: Mr Moulton-Barrett, Partner
E-mail: tony@moultonlaidlaw.com
Website: www.moultonlaidlaw.com

Profile: We specialise in developing business presentation skills.

Services: Presentation skills

MRA International

TBAC Business Centre, Harvard House, Grove Technology Park, Wantage, Oxfordshire, OX12 9FE
Tel: 01235 770067
Fax: 01235 771167

Contact: Martin Gummery, MD
E-mail: headoffice@mra-int.com
Website: www.mra-int.com

Profile: The development of organisations and their people.

Services: Change management, Problem solving, Management certificates

MSB (Managing the Service Business)

Winslow House, Ashurst Park, Church Lane, Sunninghill, Berkshire, SL5 7ED
Tel: 01344 876300
Fax: 01344 873677

Contact: Andrew Shapiro, Director of Training
E-mail: andrew.shapiro@msb-ltd.co.uk
Website: www.msbconsultancy.com

Profile: Improving business performance by providing customer service excellence through training.

Services: Human resources, Sales & marketing, Customer service, Management development

Multimedia Marketing.Com

Minshull House, 47-49 Chorlton Street, Manchester, M1 3FY
Tel: 0161 2476052
Fax: 0161 2476301

Contact: Alan Pulford, Marketing Director
E-mail: Alan@multimediamarketing.com
Website: www.multimediamarketing.com

Profile: We develop and deliver marketing education and training solutions.

Services: Sales & marketing, E-learning, Management certificates

Myrick Training Services

Myrick House, Hendomen, Montgomery, Powys, SY15 6RL
Tel: 01686 668670
Fax: 01686 668771

Contact: Brian Dunlop, General Manager
E-mail: myrick@btinternet.com

Profile: Engineering management, supervisory health and safety, quality NVQs, short courses.

Services: Management development, Production & process control, Supervisory

Nacro New Careers Training

Old School, Bowman Street, Darlington, County Durham, DL3 0HE
Tel: 01325 282934
Fax: 01325 465771

Contact: Michele Armstrong, Placement Manager

Profile: Quality trainers in administration and IT up to NVQ 4.

Services: IT, NVQs

Najberg Milne

25a High Street, Kings Langley, Hertfordshire, WD4 8AB
Tel: 01923 265080
Fax: 01923 264319

Contact: Gill Baldemor, Course Manager
E-mail: gillbaldemor@najbergmilne.com
Website: www.najbergmilne.com

Profile: Our clients say we revolutionise the way they do business.

Services: Sales & marketing, Management development, Presentation skills

National Education Training Group (NETG)

1 Hogarth Business Park, Burlington Lane, Chiswick, London, W4 2TJ
Tel: 020 8994 5611

Contact: Ilke Kaufmann, PR Officer
E-mail: netg@dial.pipex.com

Profile: NETG is the world's leading provider of CBT training solutions.

The National Extension College

The Michael Young Centre, Purbeck Road, Cambridge, CB2 2HN
Tel: 01223 450300
Fax: 01223 450321

Contact: Lena Sedlan, Sales Manager
E-mail: resources@nec.ac.uk

Profile: A leading provider of flexible open learning training resources.

Services: Management development, Interpersonal skills, Customer service

National Training Organisation for Information Technology

16 Berners Street, London, W1P 3AP
Tel: 020 7580 6677
Fax: 020 7580 5577

Contact: A Russell, Chief Executive

Profile: Employer-led organisation with members drawn from IT, large corporates, training companies, HE and FE.

Services: IT

The National Training Organisation for Sport, Recreation and Allied Occupations (SPRITO)

24 Stephenson Way, London, NW1 2HD
Tel: 020 7388 7755
Fax: 020 7388 9733

Contact: Stephen Studd, Chief Executive
E-mail: the.nto@sprito.org.uk

Profile: Developing NVQs and other training programmes for sport and recreation.

Nationwide Training Ltd

The Old Pottery, Station Road, Braunton, North Devon, EX33 2AQ
Tel: 01271 815758
Fax: 01271 815251

Contact: S Hill, Consultant
E-mail: info@nationwidetraining.co.uk

Profile: Management consultants specialising in management development and salesforce training.

Services: Sales & marketing, Management development, Assertiveness, Coaching & mentoring, Negotiation, Presentation skills, Food & drink

NEBS Management

NEBS Management merged with the Institute for Supervisions & Management in 2001 and is now called the Institute of Leadership and Management (ILM). Please see ILM entry for further details.

New Directions

Royal Exchange Building, Panmure Street, Dundee, DD1 1DU
Tel: 01707 886553

Contact: Nick Heap, Managing Director
E-mail: nickheap@tesco.net
Website: http://homepages.tesco.net/nickheap

Profile: Facilitating individual, team and organisation development. Profiling, mentoring, influencing skills.

Services: Human resources, Management development, Problem solving, Training for trainers, Courses

Newham Wise Ltd

Bridge Road Depot, Abbey Road, Stratford, London, E15 3LX
Tel: 020 8557 8843
Fax: 020 8557 8844

Contact: David Crosby, Training/Personnel Manager

Profile: A charitable organisation providing youth and adult training programmes.

Nexus Learning and Development

Blencathra House, High Carleton, Penrith, Cumbria, CA11 8SW
Tel: 01768 890939
Fax: 01768 890933

Contact: David Kay, Marketing Development Manager
E-mail: enquiries@nexuslearning. co.uk
Website: www.nexuslearning.co.uk

Profile: Nexus uses diagnostics to design and deliver bespoke experential programmes.

Services: Human resources, Teamworking, Leadership

NIACE - National Institute for Adult Continuing Education

21 De Montfort Street, Leicester, LE1 7GE
Tel: 0116 204 4200
Fax: 0116 285 4514

Contact: Helen Biggs, Librarian
E-mail: enquiries@niace.org.uk
Website: www.niace.org.uk

Profile: Publications, conferences etc on Lifelong Learning.

Nigel Blagg Associates

39 Staplegrove Road, Taunton, Somerset, TA1 1DG
Tel: 01823 336204
Fax: 01823 332201
E-mail: mail@nigelblaggassociates.co.uk

Profile: Specialists in assessment, selection, psychometric testing, personal development.

Services: Management development, Coaching & mentoring, Interpersonal skills

Nigel Wyatt Financial Training

40 Tudor Gardens, Stony Stratford, Milton Keynes, Buckinghamshire, MK11 1HX
Tel: 01908 565574
Fax: 01908 567818

Contact: Nigel Wyatt, Director
E-mail: info@magentanetwork.co.uk
Website: www.magentanetwork.co.uk

Profile: Tailored in-house finance training for non-financial managers.

Services: Accounting & finance, Management development, Finance for non-finance staff

NoboVisual Aids Ltd

Alder Close, Eastbourne, East Sussex, BN23 6QB
Tel: 01323 641521
Fax: 01323 410328

Contact: Mrs T Wyatt, Customer Services Manager
E-mail: info@nobo.co.uk

Profile: Manufacture presentation products ranging from flipchart easels to overhead projectors.

North Down & ARDS Institute of Further & Higher Education

Castle Park Road, Bangor, County Down, BT20 4TF
Tel: 028 9127 6600
Fax: 028 9127 6753

Contact: Joan Caldwell, Senior Lecturer Co-ordinator
E-mail: jcaldwell@ndai.ac.uk
Website: www.ndai.ac.uk

Profile: North Down offers a wide range of management training courses.

Services: Accounting & finance, Management development, Teamworking

North Lindsey College

Kingsway, Scunthorpe, North Lincolnshire, DN17 1AJ
Tel: 01724 281111
Fax: 01724 294020

Contact: Customer Services
E-mail: info@northlindsey.ac.uk
Website: www.northlindsey.ac.uk

Profile: The largest further education college in North Lincolnshire.

Services: Education, NVQs

North West Institute of Further & Higher Education

Strand Road, Londonderry, Northern Ireland, BT48 7BX
Tel: 028 276 025/276092
Fax: 028 7137 4775

Contact: Marilyn Lento, Head of Management and Development
E-mail: marilyn.lento@nwifhe.ac.uk

Profile: Expert consultants for all Management, HR, Health & Safety areas.

Services: Communications, advertising & PR, Human resources, Sales & marketing

Northampton College

Booth Lane, Northampton, NN3 3RF
Tel: 01604 734567
Fax: 01604 734207

Contact: Central Admissions
E-mail: enquiries@northamptoncollege.ac.uk
Website: www.northamptoncollege.ac.uk

Profile: 1500 part-time and 130 full-time courses and bespoke training solutions.

Services: Accounting & finance, Design, Human resources

The Nottingham Trent University

NCL Administrative Centre, Burton Street, Nottingham, NG1 4BU
Tel: 0115 848 6409
Fax: 0115 848 6536

Contact: Sue Haslam, Head – NCL Administration Centre
E-mail: ncladmin@ntu.ac.uk

Profile: Range of one day courses including Assertiveness and Team Working.

Services: Training for trainers, Health & safety, Presentation skills, MBAs

Octave Consulting Ltd

Carr Holme, Armathwaite, Carlisle, Cumbria, CA4 0EW
Tel: 01697 472100
Fax: 01697 473883

Contact: John Taylor, Managing Director
E-mail: info@octave.edi.co.uk

Profile: Call now to discover how you can benefit today.

Odyssey Training Limited

PO Box 191, Fareham, Hampshire, PO16 8TY
Tel: 01329 230301
Fax: 01329 230304

Contact: Peter Springett, Managing Director
E-mail: peter@odysseytraining.co.uk
Website: www.odysseytraining.co.uk

Profile: IM and ISO accredited general and safety management training provider.

Services: Human resources, Supervisory, Leadership, Transport & distribution

One One Severn

9 Wedgwood Drive, Portskewett, Monmouthshire, NP6 4TL
Tel: 01291 420117

Contact: Edward Tipper, Principal

Profile: Management development training through certificate in management and NVQ assessment.

Services: Management development, NVQs

Ontrack International Ltd

Upwick House, Upwick, Albury Ware, SG11 2LA
Tel: 01279 771990
Fax: 01279 771980

Contact: Phil Bailey, Director
E-mail: info@ontracinternational.com
Website: www.ontrackinternational.com

Profile: Leading experts in developing the full potential of people.

Services: Management development, Project management, Teamworking

OPD Diagnostic Solutions

Redlands, Tapton House Road, Sheffield, Yorkshire, S10 5BY
Tel: 0114 266 4447
Fax: 0114 268 2654

Contact: Drusilla Lewis, Partner
E-mail: us@opddiagnostic.demon.co.uk
Website: www.opddiagnostic.co.uk

Profile: Flexible tailormade solutions for improving business results through development workshops.

Services: Production & process control, Manufacturing & engineering, Public sector

The Open Learning Foundation

3 Devonshire Street, London, W1N 2BA
Tel: 020 7636 4186
Fax: 020 76310132

Contact: Julia Peart, Programmes Secretary
E-mail: olf@mailbox-ulcc.ac.uk

Profile: Produces open and flexible learning materials and provides practical support and advice.

Open Mind

Delphi House, Deanfield Avenue, Henley-On-Thames, Oxfordshire, RG9 1UE
Tel: 01491 411061
Fax: 01491 411531

Contact: A Harvey, Director
E-mail: info@openmind-learning.co.uk
Website: www.openmind-learning.co.uk

Profile: 5000 learning resources on all topics in all media.

Services: Management development, Books & packages, Competencies

Open Mind Training

Delphi House, Deanfield Avenue, Henley-On-Thames, Oxfordshire, RG9 1UE
Tel: 01491 411061
Fax: 01491 411531

Contact: A Harvey, Director
E-mail: training@openmind-learning.co.uk
Website: www.openmind-learning.co.uk

Profile: Effective people through effective training and focused in-company workshops.

Services: Customer service, Management development, Finance for non-finance staff

The Open University (Human Resource Development)

Horlock Building, Milton Keynes, Buckinghamshire, MK7 6AA
Tel: 01908 654284

Contact: Janice Dolley, Senior Training Officer

Profile: Supported open learning with assessment for trainers and facilitators.

Services: Human Resources

Optimum (UK) Training Solutions Ltd

Pride Parkway, Derby, DE24 8UG
Tel: 01332 576314
Fax: 01332 576315

Contact: Karen Campbell, Optimum UK Project Manager
E-mail: info@optimum-uk.co.uk
Website: www.optimum-uk.co.uk

Profile: Providers of management and IT training at all levels.

Services: IT, Management development, Leadership

Optimum Coaching Limited

Optimum House, PO Box 61, Altrincham Road, Manchester, M22 4XL
Tel: 0800 594 2134
Fax: 01244 342135

Contact: Rebecca Bright, PA to MD
E-mail: sales@optimum-training.com
Website: www.optimum-training.com

Profile: Coaching Centre of Excellence, corporate coaching and coach training programmes.

Services: Coaching & mentoring, Education

Optimum Training Ltd

15 Castle Street, Chester, Cheshire, CH1 2DS
Tel: 01244 342133
Fax: 01244 342135

Contact: Cindy Nerney, Co-ordinator
E-mail: sales@optimum-training.com
Website: www.optimum-training.com

Profile: Health and safety training for companies plus licencing packages for trainers.

Services: Human resources, Legal, Sales & marketing

Organisation & Management Learning (OML) Associates Ltd

Willowbrook, Yarley Hill, Wells, Somerset, BA5 1PA
Tel: 01749 676103
Fax: 01749 676103

Contact: Barry Peel, Director
E-mail: oml@ukonline.co.uk
Website: www.omlassoc.co.uk

Profile: Dedicated to improving organisation performance through development of human talent.

Services: Management development, Interpersonal skills, Psychometric testing

Osmec Technology Management

Thorpeleigh House, Thorpe Waterville, Kettering, Northamtonshire, NN14 3ED
Tel: 01832 720750

Contact: Terry Robinson, Training Manager
E-mail: info@osmectraining.co.uk
Website: www.osmectraining.co.uk

Profile: Osmec provides automation, electrical engineering, electrical safety and regulations training.

Services: Production & process control, Multi-skilling, Manufacturing & engineering

Otley College

Otley, Ipswich, Suffolk, IP6 9EY
Tel: 01473 785543
Fax: 01473 785353

Contact: Delma Kirkpatrick, Student Advisor
E-mail: info@otleycollege.ac.uk
Website: www.otleycollege.ac.uk

Services: Construction, Food & drink, Information & communication technologies

The Outdoor Trust

Windy Gyle, West Street, Belford, Northumberland, NE70 7QE
Tel: 01668 213289
Fax: 01668 213289

Contact: Peter Clark, Head of Centre
E-mail: trust@outdoor.demon.co.uk
Website: www.outdoor.demon.co.uk

Profile: Successfully proven outdoor based courses tailored to meet client needs.

Services: Outdoor learning

Outdoor Wizard

Glenholme, Wigginton Bottom, Near Tring, Hertfordshire, HP23 6HW

Contact: Mark Lewis

The Outreach Organisation Tan-Y-Bwlch Centre

Llanllechid, Bangor, Gwynedd, LL57 3HY
Tel: 01248 601546
Fax: 01248 602435

Contact: Tony Griffiths, Director of Training
E-mail: outreach90@aol.com

Profile: Short programmes developing essentials for dynamic personal and organisational leadership.

Services: Human resources, Management development, Leadership

Outward Bound Scotland

Loch Eil Centre, Achdalieu, Fort William, Invernesshire, PH33 7NN
Tel: 013977 72866
Fax: 013977 72869

Contact: Simon Mann, Business Development Co-ordinator
E-mail: simonmann@outwardbound-uk.org
Website: www.outwardbound-uk.org

Profile: Management development, team building and challenge programmes using the outdoors.

Services: Teamworking, Leadership, Problem solving, Outdoor learning

University of Oxford

University Offices, Wellington Square, Oxford, OX1 2JD
Tel: 01865 270000
Fax: 01865 270708

Contact: Clare Woodcock, Information Officer
Website: www.ox.ac.uk

Oxford Brookes University

Headington Hill Campus, Headington, Oxford, OX3 0BP
Tel: 01865 484876
Fax: 01865 484884

Contact: Lindsey Major, Head of Continuing Education
E-mail: cce@brookes.ac.uk
Website: www.brookes.ac.uk/continuingeducation

Profile: High quality training competitively priced for organisations and individuals.

Services: Construction, Education, Health & safety, MBAs

Oxford Communications Group

High Cottage, The Street, Brightwell-cum-Sotwell, Wallingford, OX10 0RR
Tel: 01491 833444
Fax: 01491 833456

Contact: Eric Dore, Principal
E-mail: e.dore@btconnect.com

Profile: Business strategy, dynamic organisation improvement, investors in people. Specialists established in 1984.

Services: Change management, Management development, Investors in People

The Oxford Group, Consulting and Training

Bankside, Hanborough Business Park, Long Hanborough, Oxfordshire, OX29 8LJ
Tel: 01993 883338
Fax: 01993 883140

Contact: Sally Jackson, Principal Consultant
E-mail: enquiries@oxfordgroup.co.uk
Website: www.oxfordgroup.co.uk

Profile: Provide world-class training and consultancy – deliver solutions and measurable results.

Services: Leadership, Training for trainers, Change management

Oxford Management Consultants

29 Western Road, Henley-on-Thames, Oxfordshire, RG9 1JN
Tel: 01491 579949
Fax: 01491 579949

Contact: Bill Evans, Managing Partner
E-mail: omcbill@aol.com
Website: www.managementofchange.com

Profile: Change management, client centre consulting and influencing skills training programmes.

Services: Change management, Management development, Coaching & mentoring

The Oxford Publicity Partnership

12 Hid's Copse Road, Cumnor Hill, Oxford, OX2 9JJ
Tel: 01865 865466
Fax: 01865 862763

Contact: Sue Miller, Partner
E-mail: opp@opp.i-way.co.uk

Profile: Specialist training for those working on academic, educational and professional publications.

PACE (Performance & Communication Enterprises)

82A Hill Road, Watlington, Oxfordshire, OX49 5AF
Tel: 01491 613956
Fax: 01491 612955

Contact: Roy Johnson, Director
E-mail: pace@pacetraining.co.uk
Website: www.pacetraining.co.uk

Profile: Executive and leadership coaching for directors, senior managers, key staff.

Services: Coaching & mentoring, Human resources, Management development

Paper Education and Training Council

Papermakers House, Rivenhall Road, Swindon, Wiltshire, SN5 7BD
Tel: 01793 886086
Fax: 01793 886363

Contact: Gordon Grace, Director
E-mail: p-t@paper.org.uk

Profile: The national training organisation for the paper industry.

Parity Training Ltd

Wimbledon Bridge House, 1 Hartfield Road, Wimbledon, London, SW19 3RU
Tel: 0800 656100
Fax: 020 8545 6521

Contact: Registration and Enquiries Team
E-mail: training@parity.net
Website: www.parity.net

Profile: Parity Training delivers bespoke and public scheduled training courses in technology, management and business skills, providing training for over 40,000 delegates a year. Parity's learning consultants increasingly blend traditional training methods with e-learning initiatives to provide integrated learning solutions that ensure return on investment and effective learning outcomes.

With training centres in Antrim, Belfast, Birmingham, Bristol, Edinburgh, Fleet, Leeds, London and Manchester, Parity offers nation-wide in person (classroom based) training and support. Additionally, Parity's managed services offering provides a range of options from simple vendor management to a full outsource training and development service.
Parity's long-term partnerships with leading bodies such as the Information Systems Examination Board, DSDM Consortium, Institute of Management, Outward Bound Trust, Association for Project Management, Microsoft and Lotus Corporation keeps Parity at the forefront of the industry, able to offer an unparalleled range of certified training leading to recognised qualifications. Parity's on-going commitment to delivering effective quality training is reflected in its ISO9001 certification. In 2003 Parity Training was awarded the Instituted of IT Training's accolade of Training Company of the Year and Trainer of the Year.

Parity Training is part of Parity Group plc, the international IT consultancy and solutions group with 30 offices in the UK, mainland Europe and the USA.
For booking information or course details, call 0800 656 100, email training@parity.net or visit www.parity.net.

Services: Assertiveness, Blended learning, Books & packages, Business services, Business writing, Change management, Coaching & mentoring, Competencies, Conflict resolution, Construction, Customer service, Decision-making, Design, E-business, Education, E-learning, Emotional intelligence, Energy, Financial services, Food and drink, Games, simulation & exercises, Health, Human capital audits, Induction, Information & communication technologies, Information systems, Interpersonal skills, IT, Knowledge management, Leadership, Leisure, Management development, Manufacturing & engineering, Media, Public sector, Motivation, Multi-skilling, Needs Analysis, Negotiation, Office & secretarial, Outsourcing, PC user skills, Performance appraisal, Presentation skills, Problem solving, Project management, Psychometric testing, Retailing, Risk management, Sales & marketing, Strategy & planning, Stress management, Supervisory, Teamworking, Time management, Training for trainers, Transport & distribution, Video

Parkfields 'Exclusive Use' Venue

Pontshill, Ross-on-Wye, Herefordshire, HR9 5TH
Tel: 01989 750138
Fax: 01989 750158

Contact: Simon Ellis, Managing Director
E-mail: info@parkfields.co.uk
Website: www.parkfields.co.uk

Profile: 'Exclusive use' venue in 11 acres with 23 en-suite bedrooms.

Services: Conference venues

Paul Chapman Publishing Ltd

144 Liverpool Road, London, N1 1LA
Tel: 020 7609 5315
Fax: 020 7700 1057

Contact: Joyce Lynch, Sales Co-ordinator

Profile: Publishers in accounting, business, management and education.

Services: Management development, Accounting & finance

PDS Consulting

Innovation Way, Barnsley, South Yorkshire, S75 1JL
Tel: 01226 249590
Fax: 01226 294797

Contact: Peter Kiddell, Partner
E-mail: pds_consulting@compuserve.com

Profile: Screen and PAD (TAMPO) print vocational training. Project management, troubleshooting.

Services: Project management

Peak Training for Management

The Orchard, New Bath Hotel, New Bath Road, Matlock, Derbyshire, DE4 3PX
Tel: 01629 760297
Fax: 01629 760336
E-mail: info@peak-training.co.uk
Website: www.peak-training.co.uk

Peakdean Interactive

Snaithing Grange Annexe, Snaithing Lane, Ranmoor, Sheffield, S10 3LF
Tel: 0114 268 3700
Fax: 0114 230 5566

Contact: Jane Mort, Marketing Manager
E-mail: enquiries@peakdean.co.uk
Website: www.peakdean.co.uk

Profile: Needs analysis, training design, author training, research and development, evaluation.

Services: IT, Finance for non-finance staff, E-learning

Pearce Taylor Taxation

Sidford Road, Sidmouth, Devon, EX10 9LN
Tel: 01395 577202
Fax: 01395 515620

Contact: S Pearce, Partner

Profile: VAT consultants and lecturers. Seminars available at all levels.

Services: Accounting & finance, Financial services

Pembroke Management Development

1 High Street, St Davids, Pembrokeshire, SA62 6SA
Tel: 01437 720879
Fax: 01437 721838

Contact: Andy Middleton, CEO
E-mail: pmd@tyf.com
Website: www.thinkingatwork.com

Profile: Personal and business development that's powerful, proven and performance enhancing.

Services: Interpersonal skills, Sales & marketing, Management certificates, Multi-skilling

Penny Walker

92 Winston Road, London, N16 9LR
Tel: 020 7254 3500
Fax: 020 7275 7675

Contact: Penny Walker, Independent Practitioner
E-mail: penny.walker@btclick.com

Profile: Learning enabling corporate social responsibility, environmental management and sustainable development.

Services: Training for trainers, Strategy & planning

The Pennybank Partnership

55 Clarence Gate Gardens, Glentworth Street, London, NW1 6QS
Tel: 020 7258 1457
Fax: 020 7258 1457

Contact: Jessica Levant, Managing Partner
E-mail: 100337.704@mail.com

Profile: We develop managers and teams: tailored programmes and 360° surveys.

Services: Management development

The Pensions Management Institute

PMI House, 4-10 Artillery Lane, London, E1 7LS
Tel: 020 7247 1452
Fax: 020 7375 0603

Contact: Neil Scott, Senior Education Officer
E-mail: education@pensions-pmi.org.uk
Website: www.pensions-pmi.org.uk

Profile: Professional body for those working in pensions and employee benefits.

Services: Accounting & finance, Financial services, Books & packages

People Centred Learning

April Cottage, 7 Coverts Road, Claygate, Surrey, KT10 0JY
Tel: 01372 468695
Fax: 01372 468702

Contact: Victor Marino, Managing Director
E-mail: marino@pcl-uk.demon.co.uk

Profile: Developing excellence for individuals, groups and organisations.

People Dynamics

11 Ashley Gardens, Richmond, TW10 7BU
Tel: 020 8332 6925
Fax: 020 8948 6468

Contact: Brian Willman, Director

Profile: Leadership development of senior managers and facilitation of top teams.

Services: Management development, Leadership

People=Positive Ltd

Inverdruie House, Aviemore, Invernesshire, PH22 1QM
Tel: 01479 811900
Fax: 01479 811414

Contact: Rod Pashley, Director and Consultant
E-mail: office@peoplepositive.com
Website: www.peoplepositive.com

Profile: People=Positive is a progressive and expanding international development training company.

Services: Human resources, Change management, Teamworking, Leadership

Performance Consulting Group

Copperfields, 1 Trenchard Meadow, Lytchett Matravers, Poole, Dorset, BH16 6NA
Tel: 01761 451214
Fax: 01761 451214

Contact: Stephen M Hall, Chief Executive

Profile: The management consultants that help your return on investment grow.

Services: Negotiation, Business excellence, Human capital audits

The Performance Factor

2 Mearwood Lane, Falmouth, Cornwall, TR11 2HY
Tel: 0845 644 1641

Contact: Ginnie Sykes, Managing Director
E-mail: ready@t-p-f.demon.co.uk
Website: www.t-p-f.demon.co.uk

Profile: Effective business/personal development training, making your people powerful performers.

Services: Human resources, Change management, Teamworking

Peritas Limited

Beaumont, Burfield Road, Old Windsor, SL4 2JP
Tel: 01753 604231
Fax: 01753 604085

Contact: Jacinta Hannigan, Marketing Executive

Profile: The training services unit is a £27 million organisation employing over 200 professionals.

Personnel Management Advisory Services

Management House, 9 Park Grove, Edgware, Middlesex, HA8 7SH
Tel: 020 8958 4486

Contact: A Fiber, Senior Consultant

Profile: Professional (chartered), established 1967. Firms offered most aspects, flexibly, confidentially.

Services: Sales & marketing, Human resources, Customer service

Perth College

Crieff Road, Perth, PH1 2NX
Tel: 01738 877000
Fax: 01738 877001

Contact: Jim Ewing, Marketing Officer
E-mail: pc.enquiries@perth.uhi.ac.uk
Website: www.perth.ac.uk

Profile: One of Scotland's leading providers of further and higher education.

Services: Business Services, NVQs, Information & communication technologies

Petans

Bullock Hill, Horsham St Faith, Norwich, NR10 3HT
Tel: 01603 891255/890870
Fax: 01603 890827
Website: www.petans.co.uk

Peter Allatt Associates

Hoppy Acres, Brancepeth, Durham, County Durham, DH7 8EL
Tel: 0191 378 0454
Fax: 0191 378 0454

Contact: J P Allatt, Principal
E-mail: peter@allatt.com
Website: www.onyxnet.co.uk/clients/allatts

Profile: Helping clients to be more effective and achieve their aims.

Services: Production & process control, Business Services, Manufacturing & engineering

Peter Chapman & Associates

Hobbs Cross Business Centre, Theydon Gamon, Epping, Essex, CM16 7NY
Tel: 01995 814733
Fax: 01992 814011

Contact: Pam Evans, Research and Development Manager
E-mail: pchapmanassociates@compuserve.com
Website: www.pcatraininginternational.com

Profile: Leadership, teambuilding and management soft skills nationally and internationally.

Services: Change management, Emotional intelligence, Time management

Peter Dewrance E-Learning Ltd

Reddings Farm, Wharf Lane, Kirkby on Bain, Lincolnshire, LN10 6YW
Tel: 07775 735 058

Contact: Peter Dewrance, Managing Director/Consultant
E-mail: peterdewrance@hotmail.com

Profile: Television, video, multimedia training, e-lerning design and consultancy services international.

Services: Education, Media, E-learning

Peter Hyde Management Consulting

Woodvale House, Basingstoke Road, Spencers Wood, Reading, RG7 1AE
Tel: 0118 988 8736
Fax: 0118 988 8848

Contact: Peter Hyde
E-mail: peter@peterhyde.co.uk

Profile: Facilitation and consultancy skills, change management, TNA, strategy, design, evaluation.

Services: Human resources, Performance appraisal, Training for trainers

Peter Marsh Associates

52 Longfield Road, Tring, Hertfordshire, HP23 4DE
Tel: 01442 824309
Fax: 01442 824309

Contact: Peter Marsh, Managing Consultant
E-mail: peter_marsh@compuserve.com

Profile: Management and skills consultancy and training which makes a difference.

Services: Leadership, Sales & marketing, Business excellence

Phoenix Obsidian

Church Island House, Church Island, Staines, Middlesex, TW18 4YE
Tel: 01784 415946
Fax: 01784 415943

Contact: Thom Dennis, Sole Proprietor
E-mail: thomd@facilitation.co.uk
Website: www.facilitation.org

Profile: Executive Coaching, Culture Change, Management Development, Expert Facilitation, Leadership Skills.

Services: Change management, Management development, Coaching & mentoring

Pitman Training

Warnford Court, 29 Throgmorton Street, London, EC2N 2LT
Tel: 020 7256 6668
Fax: 020 7256 7273

Contact: Michael Cork, Senior Course Advisor
E-mail: michael.cork@pitmanlondon.co.uk
Website: www.pitmanlondon.co.uk

Profile: Helping to provide training solutions for all your office needs.

Services: IT, Office & secretarial, Information systems

Pitman Training Centre, Berkshire

23-25 High Street, Burnham, SL6 7JD
Tel: 01628 798444
Fax: 01628 782634

Contact: Ann Till, Director
E-mail: 10167.3414@compuserve.com

Profile: Flexible office skills: keyboarding, wordprocessing, shorthand, databases, presentations, spreadsheets, accounts.

Services: PC user skills

Pitman Training Centre, Colchester

First Floor, Trinity House, 1 Trinity Street, Colchester, CO1 1JN
Tel: 01206 576792
Fax: 01206 561027

Contact: Stephanie McInroy, Centre Manager

Profile: Flexible computer, bookkeeping and secretarial training.

Services: IT

Pitman Training Centre, St Albans

2 Adelaide Street, St Albans, Hertfordshire, AL3 5BH
Tel: 01727 866277
Fax: 01727 867977

Contact: Mike Busby, Manager
E-mail: 101501.3260@compuserve.com

Profile: Flexible study hours for computer, secretarial and business training.
Services: IT

PLA Training & Development

81 Chantry Avenue, Kempston, Bedfordshire, MK42 7RU
Tel: 01234 851663

Contact: Peter Akass, Consultant

Profile: Training standards advisory service including S/NVQs and training assessments.

Plain English Campaign

PO Box 3, New Mills, High Peak, SK22 4QP
Tel: 01663 744409
Fax: 01663 747038

Contact: Helen Mayo, Training Administrator
E-mail: info@plainenglish.co.uk
Website: www.plainenglish.co.uk

Profile: Plain English training - everyday, legal, medical and financial.

Services: Business writing, Books & packages, Training for trainers

Plain Language Commission

The Castle, 29 Stoneheads, Whaley Bridge, High Peak, SK23 7BB
Tel: 01663 733177
Fax: 01663 735135

Contact: Martin Cutts, Research Director
E-mail: cutts@clearest.co.uk
Website: www.clearest.co.uk

Profile: Courses on all aspects of business and legal writing skills.

Services: Business Services, Business writing, Financial services

University of Plymouth

Drake Circus, Plymouth, Devon, PL4 8AA
Tel: 01752 232141
E-mail: ncrocker@plym.ac.uk

Profile: Four campuses, one great university.

Services: IT, Corporate universities

University of Plymouth - Science Technology Short Course Unit

Drake Circus, Plymouth, Devon, PL4 8AA
Tel: 01752 233304
Fax: 01752 233310

Contact: Denise Horne, Short Course Administrator
E-mail: scuniteplymouth.ac.uk

Profile: Professional development and training for increased effectiveness and competitiveness.

Polymer Training Limited

Halesfield 7, Telford, Shropshire, TF7 4NA
Tel: 01952 587020
Fax: 01952 582065

Contact: Wendi Beamson, Project Managerr
E-mail: general@polymertraining.co.uk
Website: www.polymertraining.co.uk

Profile: Training and business development training for the polymer industry.

Services: Production & process control, Supervisory, Manufacturing & engineering

Popular Communication Courses Ltd t/a Popcomm Training

60 High Street, Bridgnorth, Shropshire, WV16 4DX
Tel: 01746 765605
Fax: 01746 767482

Contact: Colin Ringrose, Managing Director
E-mail: training@popcomm.co.uk
Website: www.popcomm.co.uk

Profile: In-house and public courses on corporate publishing, communications and PR.

Services: Communications, advertising & PR, Design, Business writing

Port Skills and Safety Ltd

Room 220 Africa House, 64-78 Kingsway, London, C2B 6AH
Tel: 020 7242 3538
Fax: 020 7430 7470

Contact: Mr Peter Bond,
E-mail: peter@portskillsandsafety.co.uk

University of Portsmouth

University House, Winston Churchill Avenue, Portsmouth, Hampshire, PO1 2UP
Tel: 023 9284 8484
Fax: 023 9284 3082

Contact: Margaret Jenkins, Assistant Academic Registrar
E-mail: admissions@port.ac.uk
Website: www.port.ac.uk

Services: Accounting & finance, Human resources, MBAs

Positive Action

17 Upper Camden Place, Bath, BAl 5HX
Tel: 01225 424027
Fax: 01225 424027

Contact: Maggie Riley, Principal Consultant
E-mail: mrileybath@aol.com

Profile: Learning and development events for trainers, developers and managers.

Services: Human resources, Teamworking, Coaching & mentoring, Conflict resolution

Positive Images

32 Hazelbourne Road, London, SW12 9NS
Tel: 020 8675 5806
Fax: 020 8673 9020

Contact: Eleri Sampson, Principal Consultant

Profile: Corporate workshops and individual coaching in image and personal impact.

Services: Games, simulation & exercises

Practice Development Consultants

Network House, 30 Junction Road, Sheffield, S11 8XB
Tel: 0114 268 7288
Fax: 0114 268 7299

Contact: Stuart Morgan, Managing Director

Profile: Management development, Organisation development, Management NVQs, Business/strategic planning.

Services: Management development, NVQs

Premiere Productions Ltd

3 Colville Place, London, W1P 1HN
Tel: 020 7255 1650

Contact: Henrietta Williams, Marketing

Profile: Multimedia training on work skills and financial subjects.

Services: Accounting & finance, Media skills

The Prestbury House Management Training Centre

The Burgage, Prestbury, Cheltenham, Gloucestershire, GL52 3DN
Tel: 01242 529533
Fax: 01242 227076

Contact: Stephen Whitbourn, Managing Director
E-mail: sandjw@freenetname.co.uk
Website: www.prestburytraining.co.uk

Profile: Operated by experienced business people with a passion for training.

Services: Management development, Teamworking, Leadership

Primary Photography

Miller House, 49 Stimpson Avenue, Northampton, NN1 4LR
Tel: 01604 31456
Fax: 01604 31456

Contact: Suzie Pay, Director
E-mail: photmart@skynet.co.uk

Profile: Photographic education in schools, a non-profit making organisation.

Priory Training Services

23 Carriage Drive, The Priory, Kettering, Northamptonshire, NN16 9EN
Tel: 01536 522792
Fax: 01536 522792

Contact: Alec McPhedran, Managing Partner
E-mail: 101377.2323@compuserve.com

Profile: Training and development services for S/NVQ's, IiP and management development.

Services: Management development, NVQs

Proaction International

PO Box 14, Grantham, Lincolnshire, NG31 7BX
Tel: 01476 577972
Fax: 01476 590862

Contact: Samantha Nicholas, Business Development Manager
E-mail: enquiries@proaction-int.com
Website: www.proaction-int.com

Profile: Provide tailor-made support to enhance the performance of organisations.

Services: Change management, Leadership, Investors in People

Pro-Active Learning

2 Cwlach Road, Llandudno, LL30 2HT
Tel: 01492 873733

Contact: Tim James, Senior Consultant
E-mail: mail@pro-active.uk.com
Website: www.pro-active.uk.com

Profile: Tailored team, management, leadership and personal development courses and events.

Services: Change management, Leadership, Outdoor learning

Proceptor Training & Consultancy

255 Edgwarebury Lane, Edgware, Middlesex, HA8 8QL
Tel: 020 8958 9709
Fax: 020 8905 4428

Contact: Paul Jackson, Partner
E-mail: paul@proceptor.net
Website: www.proceptor.net

Profile: Psychometric testing for recruitment. Negotiation skills for buyers.

Services: Sales & marketing, Customer service, Interpersonal skills

Professional Business & Technical Management (PBTM)

Head Office Warwick Corner, 42 Warwick Road, Kenilworth, Warwickshire, CV8 1HE
Tel: 01926 855498
Fax: 01926 513100

Contact: Professor H J Manners, Founder and President

Professional Computer Training

Suite 12, Eastgate Business Centre, Southernhay, Basildon, SS14 1EB
Tel: 01268 531016
Fax: 01268 527119

Contact: Joan Nettins, Partner
E-mail: info@pct.co.uk

Profile: Professional computer training service supply and technical support.

Services: IT

Professional development.co.uk

Bishop Burton College, Bishop Burton, Beverley, East Yorkshire, HU17 8QG
Tel: 01964 553034
Fax: 01964 553023

Contact: Clare Bird, Professional Development Manager
E-mail: info@professionaldevelopment.co.uk
Website: www.professionaldevelopment.co.uk

Profile: Training for businesses, management, teambuilding, short courses, NVQs and consultancy.

Services: Management development, NVQs, Teamworking

The Professional Training Centre

Sheepen House, Sheepen Road, Colchester, Essex, CO3 3LH
Tel: 01206 518181
Fax: 01206 518182

Contact: Fae Stancombe, Course Co-ordinator
E-mail: info@theptc.co.uk
Website: www.theptc.co.uk

Profile: Management, NVQs, quality, health & safety, marketing bespoke, consultancy.

Services: Coaching & mentoring, Leadership, Training for trainers

Profile (SE) Ltd

18-19 Watling Street, Canterbury, Kent, CTL 2UA
Tel: 01227 762100
Fax: 01227 769285

Contact: Simon Byers, Managing Director
Website: www.profilejobs.com

Profile: Providers of skilled staff throughout Kent, both contract and permanent.

Progress Business Consultants Ltd

2-4 High Road, Ickenham, Middlesex, UB10 8LJ
Tel: 01895 621507
Fax: 01895 624634

Contact: Serena Rayner, Marketing Manager

Profile: Supplier of windows-based products for creating unlimited tests and surveys.

Project North East

7-15 Pink Lane, Newcastle upon Tyne, NE1 5DW
Tel: 0191 261 6009
Fax: 0191 245 3785

Contact: Tracy Gee, Consultant
E-mail: tracy.gee@pne.org
Website: www.pne.org

Profile: PNE offers training and qualifications in management development subjects.

Services: Management development, Project management, Strategy & planning

Prospect CPD, University of Aberdeen

MacRobert Building, King's College, Aberdeen, AB24 5UA
Tel: 01224 272523
Fax: 01224 272079

Contact: Jacqui Allen, Development Consultant
E-mail: cpd@abdn.ac.uk
Website: www.abdn.ac.uk/cpd

Profile: Prospect CPD provides professional development from the University of Aberdeen.

Services: Project management, NVQs, Decision-making

Prospects Glasgow Ltd

Block 4 Unit 1, Cowlairs Industrial Estate, 60 Finlas Street, Glasgow, G22 5DT
Tel: 0141 557 0112
Fax: 0141 558 1773

Contact: Robert Kilpatrick, Commercial Director
E-mail: train@prospectsglasgow.co.uk
Website: www.prospectsglasgow.co.uk

Profile: Training for all in construction, horticulture and health and safety.

Services: Health & safety

PSNTO (Property Services National Training Organisation)

18 Southernhay West, Exeter, Devon, EX1 1PR
Tel: 01392 423399
Fax: 01392 423373

Contact: Richard Foxwell, Chief Executive
E-mail: rfoxwell@psnto.org
Website: www.psnto.org

Services: Property, construction & facilities, Education, E-learning

Psychology in Business

50 Milton Park, London, N6 5QA
Tel: 020 83417201

Contact: Brian Simpson MA CPsychol AFBPsS, Consultant

Profile: Consultancy and workshops for improving personal effectiveness and interpersonal skills.

Services: Interpersonal skills, Negotiation, Stress Management, Training for trainers

The Psychotherapy Centre

67 Upper Berkeley Street, London, W1H 7QX
Tel: 020 7723 6173
Website: www.the-psychotherapy-centre.org.uk

Profile: Training, therapy, publications for understanding self, others and emotional problems.

Services: Human resources, Emotional intelligence, Health

PTA Ltd

Ayston Mill, Ayston Road, Uppingham, Rutland, LE15 9RL
Tel: 01572 823899
Fax: 01572 821948

Contact: A G Hamilton, Managing Director
E-mail: fiona@pta-ltd.com

Profile: Production management and process improvement specialists working for manufacturing industries.

Services: Problem solving, Project management, Coaching & mentoring, ISO 9000

PTP Associates

32 Church Drive, East Keswick, Leeds, West Yorkshire, LS17 9EP
Tel: 01937 573080
Fax: 01937 573080

Contact: Lyn Samways, Senior Associate

Profile: Activities that help management and staff meet Business Plan requirements.

Services: Supervisory, Teamworking, Assertiveness

PTP Training & Marketing Ltd

Express House, 147 Loughborough Road, Leicester, LE4 5LR
Tel: 0116 268 0066
Fax: 0116 268 0999

Contact: Simon Cox, Director
E-mail: marc@ptp.co.uk
Website: www.ptp.co.uk

Profile: PTP provides bespoke training in management, sales and customer care.

Services: Sales & marketing, Management development, Finance for non-finance staff

The Publishing Training Centre at Book House

45 East Hill, Wandsworth, London, SW18 2QZ
Tel: 020 8874 2718
Fax: 020 8870 8985

Contact: Alex Painter, Marketing Manager
E-mail: publishing.training@bookhouse.co.uk
Website: www.train4publishing.co.uk

Profile: Open and distance learning courses for book and journal publishers.

Services: Communications, advertising & PR, Education, Negotiation

Purchasing Management Services

34 Buckingham Street, Skeldergate, York, YO1 6DW
Tel: 01904 636969
Fax: 01904 647724

Contact: David Brown, Courses Director
E-mail: training@pmsyork.co.uk
Website: www.pmsyork.co.uk

Profile: Training for buyers, stores, personnel and stock controllers.

Services: Supply chain & distribution, Manufacturing & engineering, Negotiation

PWL

PO Box 109, Henleaze, Bristol, BS9 4DH
Tel: 0117 914 6984
Fax: 0117 914 6978

Contact: Paul Keams, Director
E-mail: paulkearns@blueyonder.co.uk

Profile: Training strategy measurement, ROI and evaluation specialist.

Qorus Ltd

90 Elers Road, Ealing, London, W13 9QE
Tel: 020 8566 1683
Fax: 020 8566 1687

Contact: Jayne Finn, MD
E-mail: jayne@qorus.co.uk

Profile: Significant contributions made to client company's performance through management development.

Services: Management development, Customer service, Teamworking

QRS International Ltd

7 York Close, Kings Langley, Hertfordshire, WD4 9HX
Tel: 01923 264878
Fax: 01923 270993

Contact: Quentin Ross-Smith, Director
E-mail: qrstraining@msn.com

Profile: Specialist management, supervisory, customer care, sales trainers in service industries.

Services: Leadership, Training for trainers, Management certificates

Quadrilect

Peer House, 8-14 Verulam Street, London, WC1X 8LZ
Tel: 020 7242 4141
Fax: 020 7404 0258

Contact: Jenny Mann, Partner
E-mail: info@quadrilect.co.uk
Website: www.quadrilect.co.uk

Profile: Training courses for the British Institute of Facilities management.

Services: Property, construction & facilities, Project management, Health & safety

Qualifications for Industry Ltd

Ercall House, 8 Pearson Road, Central Park, Telford, TF2 9TX
Tel: 01952 520210
Fax: 01952 520216

Contact: Alex Nelson, Operations Manager
E-mail: qfi@qfi.co.uk
Website: www.qfi.co.uk

Profile: An awarding body accredited to award NVQs/SVQs and vocational qualifications.

Services: Human resources, Office & secretarial, Supply chain & distribution

Quality Quest Ltd

PO Box 3, Beaumont Park, Whitley Bay, Tyne and Wear, NE26 1BP
Tel: 0191 251 0789
Fax: 0191 251 7980

Contact: David Dillamore, Managing Director
E-mail: david@qualityquest.com
Website: www.qualityquest.com

Profile: Professional quality management improvement programmes tailored to support business objectives.

Services: Business excellence, ISO 9000, Quality

QUBE Ltd

Fillebrook House, 24 Fillebrook Avenue, Enfield, Middlesex, EN1 3BB
Tel: 020 8363 4011
Fax: 020 8366 0797

Contact: Karis Battram, Head of Operations

Profile: Specialists in NVQ training in hospitality and business services.

Services: Change management, Management development, Project management

The Queen's University of Belfast

University Road, Belfast, Antrim, BT7 1NN
Tel: 01232 245133
Fax: 01232 247895

Contact: A Langford, Press Officer
E-mail: info@qub.ac.uk
Website: www.qub.ac.uk

Profile: Queen's University - access to quality in teaching and research.

Services: Accounting & finance, Conference venues, MBAs

Quest Worldwide

The Manor House, Tuxley Close, Godalming, Surrey, GU7 2AS
Tel: 01483 413026
Fax: 01483 427051

Contact: Sue Matthews, Education Manager
E-mail: suem@quest-worlwide.com
Website: www.yes-you-can.co.uk

Profile: Training and consulting in strategy implementation and performance improvement.

Services: Change management, Quality, Management development

Quintilian Training Ltd

75 Harvesters Way, Weavering, Maidstone, Kent, ME14 5SH
Tel: 01622 734567
Fax: 01622 738322

Contact: Brian Kiell, Director
E-mail: qtinfo@quintiliantraining.com
Website: www.quintiliantraining.com

Profile: IT and telecommunications training.

Services: IT, Knowledge management

Quorum Training Ltd

Tavistock House, Tavistock Square, London, WC1H 9TW
Tel: 020 7388 2044
Fax: 020 7380 0377

Contact: Derek J Humphrey, Director
E-mail: courses@quorumtraining.co.uk
Website: www.quorumtraining.co.uk

Profile: Providing both public and in-house financial training courses.

Services: Accounting & finance, Financial services, Finance for non-finance staff

The Rapid Results College

27-37 St George's Road, London, SW19 4DS
Tel: 020 8944 3100
Fax: 020 8944 7099

Contact: Kate Connaire, Senior Sales Executive
E-mail: info@rrc.co.uk
Website: www.rrc.co.uk

Profile: RRC specialise in open, distance and e-learning solutions for qualifications.

Services: Quality, E-learning, Health & safety

RCMS Ltd

Windsor House, Millbrook Way, Slough, Berkshire, SL3 0HN
Tel: 01753 764436
Fax: 01753 681199

Contact: Maria Acuna, Business Development Manager
E-mail: mariaacuna@rcms.com

Profile: RCMS Ltd have been providing IT training for ten years.

Services: IT

The University of Reading

Professional Management Programmes, Building 22, London Road, Reading, RG1 5AQ
Tel: 0118 931 8180
Fax: 0118 931 6539

Contact: Caroline Guy, Programme administrator
E-mail: pmp@reading.ac.uk
Website: www.rdg.ac.uk/prof-management/

Profile: Open learning certificate and diploma of higher education in management.

Services: Management certificates, Management diplomas

Reading Adult and Community College

Wilson Road, Reading, Berkshire, RG30 2RW
Tel: 0118 901 5252
Fax: 0118 901 5250

Contact: Andrea Gewessler, Head of College
Website: www.adultlearningatreading.org.uk

Profile: General adult education and tailor-made courses in many subjects.

Services: IT, Languages, Business Services

Refractories & Building Products Training Council

c/o The University of Sheffield, 23 Shephers Street, Sheffield, S3 7BA
Tel: 0114 275 9345
Fax: 0114 275 1233

Contact: Gwyn Baker, Director
E-mail: training@rbptc.co.uk
Website: www.rbptc.co.uk

Profile: The NTO provides cost effective services to its member companies.

Services: IT, Health & safety, Management development

Rehabilitation Resource Centre City University

Northampton Square, London, EC1V 0HB
Tel: 020 7477 8377
Fax: 020 7477 8356

Contact: Dr Mike Floyd, Director
E-mail: rrc@city.ac.uk

Profile: Research and training on disability and employment.

Reid Kerr College

Renfrew Road, Paisley, PA3 4DR
Tel: 0141 581 2222
Fax: 0141 581 2204

Contact: Jim McAllister, Senior Lecturer Management
E-mail: jmcallister@reidkerr.ac.uk
Website: www.reidkerr.ac.uk

Profile: Reid Kerr College delivers effective training solutions.

Services: Management diplomas, Management certificates, NVQs

The Resource Centre

96a High Street, Ware, Hertfordshire, SG12 9AP
Tel: 01920 468000
Fax: 01920 468100

Contact: Deborah Sattler, Director
E-mail: 101644.3245@compuserve.com

Profile: Team of specialist trainers, top in their field.

The Retail Training Company

Cawley House, 96 Cliff Road, Nottingham, NG1 1CW
Tel: 0115 958 7257
Fax: 0115 950 4684

Contact: Helen Elliott,
Website: www.snta.co.uk

Profile: Expert trainers in all aspects of retail and distribution NVQs.

Services: Business Services, Health, Retailing

Retirement Education Services

16 St Mary's Street, Wallingford, Oxfordshire, OX10 0EW
Tel: 01491 833696
Fax: 01494 839913

Contact: Estelle Browne, Administrator
E-mail: res@tonywheeler.co.uk
Website: www.retirementeducationers.co.uk

Profile: Mid-life redundancy and retirement in-house or open courses and counselling.

Services: Books & packages, Presentation skills

Rhodec International

35 East Street, Brighton, East Sussex, BN1 1HL
Tel: 01273 327476
Fax: 01273 821668

Contact: Michael Dwyer, Principal
E-mail: contact@rhodec.com
Website: www.rhodec.com

Profile: Distance learning, interior design for pleasure or to professional standards.

Richard Morley

7 Fellbrook, Ham, Richmond, Surrey, TW10 7UN
Tel: 020 8948 1044
Fax: 020 8940 6764

Contact: Richard Morley, Consultant/Trainer

Profile: Management skills training/development to meet individual and organisational needs.

Services: Management development

Rigdemond Park Training & Conference Centre

Telford Avenue, Stevenage, Hertfordshire, SG2 0AU
Tel: 01438 728788
Fax: 01438 740213

Contact: Lorraine Madley, Training Manager

Profile: Commercial and industrial staff development on and off the job.

Services: Accounting & finance, IT, Office & secretarial

RKS Training Services

34A Jewry Street, Winchester, Hampshire, SO23 8RY
Tel: 01962 841851
Fax: 01962 840436

Contact: Bob Swarbrick, Owner
E-mail: rswarbrick@cwctv.net

Profile: Management, leadership, communications and inter-personal skills courses. Training consultancy.

Services: Change management, Customer service, Induction

Roadwise Safety Training

21 Delafield Drive, Calcot, Reading, Berkshire, RG31 7EB
Tel: 0118 941 5540

Contact: John Swift, Principal

Profile: Advanced driver training. One or two day courses.

Services: Transport & distribution

Rob Kelly & Associates

Hawthorn Hill, Stainton, Kendal, Cumbria, LA8 0LQ
Tel: 015395 61311
Fax: 015395 61310

Contact: Rob Kelly, Director
E-mail: robkelly@rkanda.co.uk
Website: www.rkanda.co.uk

Profile: Developing people in organisations to work effectively in teams.

Services: Human resources, Management development, Teamworking, Leadership, Manufacturing & engineering, Outdoor learning

The Robert Gordon University

Schoolhill, Aberdeen, AB10 1FR
Tel: 01224 262180
Fax: 01224 262185

Contact: Laura Brodie, Information Centre Officer
E-mail: i.centre@rgu.ac.uk
Website: www.rgu.ac.uk

Robert Rainsbury Associates

101 Lonsdale Road, Bames, London, SW13 9DA
Tel: 020 8748 0125
Fax: 020 87414980

Contact: Robert Rainsbury, Principal
E-mail: r.rainsbury@btinternet.com

Profile: Hands-on business skills in maximising management potential through change.

Services: Motivation, Assertiveness, Interpersonal skills

Robson Training Services

33 Lloyd Road, Rugby, Warwickshire, CV21 1JW
Tel: 01788 542622
Fax: 01788 542622

Contact: John Robson, Consultant

Profile: Management and supervisory training for the transport and distribution industries.

Services: Management development

Roffey Park Institute

Forest Road, Horsham, West Sussex, RH12 4TD
Tel: 01293 851644
Fax: 01293 851565

Contact: Kate Bridge, Marketing Manager
E-mail: info@roffeypark.com
Website: www.roffeypark.com

Profile: Renowned providers of management development programmes, consultancy and research.

Services: Management development, Leadership, MBAs

Role Plays for Training

38 Springbank Road, London, SE13 6SN
Tel: 020 8318 3892
Fax: 020 8318 3892

Contact: Andrew Baguley, Managing Director
E-mail: mail@roleplays.co.uk
Website: www.roleplays.co.uk

Profile: Suppliers of excellent professional role players.

Services: Games, simulation & exercises, Customer service, Video

The Royal Agricultural College

Cirencester, Gloucestershire, GL7 6JS
Tel: 01285 652531
Fax: 01285 641282

Contact: Helen Pattison, Marketing Executive
E-mail: helen.pattison@royagcol.ac.uk
Website: www.royagcol.ac.uk

Profile: Providing excellence in education/training at undergraduate and postgraduate level.

Services: Sales & marketing, MBAs, Property, construction & facilities

The Royal Society for the Prevention of Accidents

Edgbaston Park, 353 Bristol Road, Birmingham, B5 7ST
Tel: 0121 248 2000
Fax: 0121 248 2001

Contact: John Phillips, Training and Consultancy Manager
E-mail: jphillips@rospa.co.uk
Website: www.rospa.co.uk

Profile: Provision of health and safety training courses and consultancy services.

Services: Human resources, Health & safety, Stress Management

RRC Business Training

27-37 St Georges Road, London, SW19 4DS
Tel: 020 8944 3100
Fax: 020 8944 7099

Contact: Kate Connaire, Senior Sales Executive
E-mail: info@rrc.co.uk
Website: www.rrc.co.uk

Profile: Providing businesses and individuals with top quality, innovative, professional training.

Services: Health & safety, Risk management, Blended Learning

Rycotewood College

Priest End, Thame, Oxfordshire, OX9 2AF
Tel: 01844 212501
Fax: 01844 218809

Contact: Liz Myles, Deputy Principal
E-mail: enquiries@rycote.ac.uk

Profile: We offer flexible professional and training services to employers.

Services: Supervisory, Construction, Information & communication technologies

S A Associates Management Training Company

Ullet Nest, Elterwater, Ambleside, Cumbria, LA22 9HY
Tel: 01539 437436
Fax: 01539 437196

Contact: S Allum, Managing Director
E-mail: online@training-uk.com

Profile: Management skills, environmental health and safety. Training. Over 32 trainers.

Safety & Hygiene Consultants

7 South Avenue, Stoke Park, Coventry, West Midlands, CV2 4DQ
Tel: 024 7645 6929
Fax: 024 7645 3811

Contact: Jeremy Stranks, Partner
E-mail: jeremystranks@btinternet.com

Profile: In-house training on health and safety law and practical issues.

Services: Health & safety, Risk management

University of Salford

Salford, Greater Manchester, M5 4WT
Tel: 0161 295 5000
Fax: 0161 295 5999

Contact: Gary Wright, Head of Marketing Services

Profile: Education, training, research, continuing professional development, for industry and commerce.

Services: IT, Corporate universities

Salon 2000 Training Centre

2 Henry Street, Keighley, West Yorkshire, BD21 3DR
Tel: 01535 661776
Fax: 01535 661353

Contact: Joanne Angus, Proprieter
E-mail: bibop@salon2k.f9.co.uk
Website: www.salon2k.co.uk

Profile: Dog grooming training - for beginners to experienced groomers.

Sandra Burrows Associates

Ash House, 8 Second Cross Road, Twickenham, TW2 5RF
Tel: 07966 199 350
Fax: 0208 893 4092

Contact: Sandra Burrows, Principal Consultant/Proprietor
E-mail: sba.consult@virgin.net

Profile: Management development, employment law training, developing your personal effectiveness workshops.

Services: Management development, Assertiveness, Interpersonal skills

Sandstone Ltd

PO Box 400, Tarporley, Cheshire, CW6 0FW
Tel: 01829 733669
Fax: 01829 733617

Contact: Alan Hunt, Director
E-mail: email@sandstone.co.uk
Website: www.sandstone.co.uk

Profile: Professional training and development resources. Exceptional training and consultancy services.

Services: Management development, Teamworking, Management diplomas

Sankofa Exchange Limited (SEL)

Head Office, Africa House, 21 Shorwell Road, Nottingham, NG3 7HG
Tel: 0115 911 0111
Fax: 0115 911 0110

Contact: B I Horsford, Chief Executive
E-mail: marketing@sankofa.demon.co.uk

Profile: High quality trainers/consultants in human resources and equal opportunities.

Services: Human resources

The Saville Group Limited

Unit 5, Millfield Lane, Nether Poppleton, York, YO2 6PQ
Tel: 01904 782782
Fax: 01904 782700

Contact: E J Everard, Group Sales & Marketing Director
E-mail: head.office@saville.co.uk
Website: www.saville-av.com

Profile: Audio visual specialists, presentation materials and conference hire equipment.

Services: Video

SBP Consultants Ltd

PO Box 2455, London, W2 5XJ
Tel: 020 7229 3958
Fax: 020 72214539

Contact: R Lutz, Director

Profile: Providing international business-to-business marketing research/marketing strategy consultancy.

Services: Sales & marketing

School for Policy Studies, University of Bristol

Rodney Lodge, Grange Road, Bristol, BS8 4EA
Tel: 0117 974 1117
Fax: 0117 973 7308

Contact: Carroll Pierce, Public Relations/Publicity Officer
E-mail: carroll.pierce@bris.ac.uk

Profile: Research, consultancy and teaching in public and social policy.

The School of Management

University of Bath, Bath, BA2 7AY
Tel: 01225 826902
Fax: 01225 323902

Contact: David Grove, Manager, Executive Development
E-mail: mnsdkg@management.bath.ac.uk

Profile: A full service business school offering world class products.

Services: Human resources, Supply chain & distribution, Management development

The School of Management

The University of Surrey, Guildford, Surrey, GU2 7XH
Tel: 01483 686300
Fax: 01483 686301

Contact: Alison Pike, Marketing Officer
E-mail: management@surrey.ac.uk
Website: www.som.surrey.ac.uk

Profile: Professional development at University of Surrey. Email wbl@surrey.ac.uk for details.

Services: Management development, Retailing, Management diplomas

School of Postgraduate Medical & Dental Education

University of Wales, College of Medicine, Heath Park, Cardiff, CF14 4XN
Tel: 029 2074 5076
Fax: 029 2075 4966

Contact: Pia Towell, Course Co-ordinator for Health Service Management

Profile: Experts in health- providing academic programmes to develop services.

Services: Management development, Health, Courses

Science, Engineering and Manufacturing Technologies Alliance

14 Upton Rd, Watford, Hertfordshire, WD18 0JT
Tel: 01923 238441
Fax: 01923 256086

Contact: David C. Nicoll, Head of Marketing Communications
E-mail: dnicoll@semta.org.uk
Website: www.semta.org.uk

Profile: The sector skills council for stem industries.

Services: Needs Analysis, Business excellence, NVQs

Scitech Educational Ltd

Kent Innovation Centre, Millenium Way, Thanet Reach Business Park, Broadstairs, Kent, CT10 2QQ
Tel: 01843 609300
Fax: 01843 609301

Contact: Maria Thompson, Product Sales and Marketing Manager
E-mail: info@scitech-ed.com
Website: www.scitech-ed.com

Profile: Blended learning, learning support, management and customer service resources.

Services: Blended Learning, Books & packages, E-learning

SCOTS

1 Princes Street, Stirling, FK8 1HQ
Tel: 01786 479731
Fax: 01786 451320

Contact: Kevin Short, Manager
E-mail: admin@scotservices.com

Profile: We provide occupational safety consultancy and training services throughout Scotland.

Services: Health & safety, Risk management, Business Services, Manufacturing & engineering, Management certificates, Construction

Scottish Association of Master Bakers

Atholl House, 4 Torphichen Street, Edinburgh, EH3 8JQ
Tel: 0131 229 1401
Fax: 0131 229 8239

Contact: Kirk Hunter, Chief Executive
E-mail: master.bakers@samb.co.uk

Profile: Awarding body and training provider for craft baking vocational qualifications.

Services: Production & process control, Supervisory, Food & drink, NVQs

Scottish Bakery Training Council

Atholl House, 4 Torphichen Street, Edinburgh, EH3 8JQ
Tel: 0131 229 1401
Fax: 0131 229 8239

Contact: Arthur Rayer, Head of Skills Training
E-mail: master.bakers@samb.co.uk
Website: www.bakerytraining.co.uk

Profile: National training organisation for the Scottish baking industry.

Services: Production & process control, Supervisory, Food & drink

Scottish Centres

Loaningdale House, Carwood Road, Biggar, ML12 6LX
Tel: 01899 221115
Fax: 01899 220644

Contact: Audrey Brown, Bookings
E-mail: enquiries@scottish-centres.org.uk
Website: www.scottish-centres.org.uk

Profile: Four outdoor centres in Scotland suitable for outdoor management development.

Services: Teamworking, Leadership, Problem solving

Secker Training & Development

16 Bridgehill Close, Guildford, Surrey, GU2 8BA
Tel: 01483 567308
Fax: 01483 567308

Contact: Muriel Secker, Director
E-mail: muriel@secker-td.com
Website: www.secker-td.com

Profile: Coaching and distance learning on equality issues for senior professionals.

Services: Human resources, Management development, Diversity/ Equal Opportunities, Coaching & mentoring, Presentation skills

Selby College Business Services

Abbot's Road, Selby, North Yorkshire, YO8 8AT
Tel: 01757 211091
Fax: 01757 213137

Contact: Emma Stones, Administrative Officer
E-mail: scbs@selby.ac.uk
Website: www.selbycollege.co.uk

Profile: Flexible training delivered within your organisation by highly qualified staff.

Services: Neuro-linguistic programming, Training for trainers, Business Services

Sheffield TEC

St Mary's Court, 55 St Mary's Road, Sheffield, South Yorkshire, S10 5FX
Tel: 0114 270 1911
Fax: 0114 275 2634

Profile: Practical support for personnel development within all types of businesses.

Skern Lodge Development Training

Skern Lodge, Appledore, Bideford, North Devon, EX39 1NG
Tel: 01237 475992
Fax: 01237 421203

Contact: John Watson, Partner
E-mail: john@skernlodge.co.uk

Profile: Practical programmes using the outdoors; exceptional staff, residential training centre.

Services: Courses, Teamworking, Leadership

SkilladvanceTraining

707 High Road, Finchley, London, N12 0BT
Tel: 020 8446 6481
Fax: 020 8446 9143

Contact: Azmina Mukadam, Marketing Manager
E-mail: training@skilladvance.co.uk
Website: www.skilladvance.com

Profile: Unix, Oracle, Programming, Informix, Internet, security, scheduled and closed courses.

Services: Information & communication technologies, Manufacturing & engineering, Public sector

SkillSoft E M E A

5 Heathrow Boulevard, 278 Bath Road, West Drayton, Middlesex, UB7 0DQ
Tel: 020 8283 1800

Contact: Kay Baldwin-Evans, Director of Marketing
E-mail: internationalinfo@skillsoft.com
Website: www.skillsoft.com

Profile: Skillsoft offers e-learning in business and IT skills.

Services: Leadership, Information & communication technologies, Needs Analysis

Sleaford Foyer

81 Eastgate, Sleaford, Lincolnshire, NG34 7EA
Tel: 01529 415394
Fax: 01529 415394

Contact: R Manhire, Training Manager

Profile: Part of Grantham College, training centre offering variety of courses.

Small Business Council

6th Floor, Kingsgate House, 66-74 Victoria Street, London, SW1E 6SW
Tel: 020 7215 8494
Fax: 020 7215 8111
E-mail: sbcsecretariat@sbs.gsi.gov.uk
Website: www.sbs.gov.uk/organisation/sbc.asp

Smallpeice Enterprises Ltd

27 Newbold Terrace East, Leamington Spa, Warwickshire, CV32 4ES
Tel: 01926 336423
Fax: 01926 450679

Contact: Lorraine Shearsby, Marketing Assistant
E-mail: train@smallpeice.co.uk
Website: www.smallpeice.co.uk

Profile: Public/Private courses in Management Development, Project Management and business skills.

Services: Quality, Management development, Manufacturing & engineering

SML Training & Consultancy Ltd

Grove House, Devenish Lane, Sunningdale, Ascot, SL5 9QU
Tel: 01344 620508

Contact: Sue Lovegrove, Managing Psychologist
E-mail: smlcons@aol.com

Profile: 'People skills' training offered by psychologists for all sectors.

Services: Assertiveness, Coaching & mentoring, Interpersonal skills

Society of Business Practitioners

PO Box 10, Hazel Grove, Stockport, Cheshire, SK7 4AD
Tel: 01270 526339
Fax: 01270 526339

Contact: D M Whitaker, President
E-mail: info@mamsasbp.com

Profile: British professional institute offering recognised awards in business administration.

Services: Management certificates, Management diplomas

Solutions by Interact Ltd

1-3 Threshers Yard, Kingham, Oxfordshire, OX7 6YF
Tel: 01608 659 500
Fax: 01608 659 555

Contact: Sue Jowsey, Training Support Manager
E-mail: info@interactwin.com

Profile: Interact has expertise in sales training consultancy and software.

Services: Management development, Business writing

Somerset Training & Enterprise Council

East Reach House, East Reach, Taunton, Somerset, TA1 3EN
Tel: 01823 321188
Fax: 01823 256174

Contact: Sally House, Director of Planning and Communications

Profile: Improving the long-term economic growth and development of Somerset.

South Kent College

Business Development, The Shakespeare Centre, 145-147 Sandgate Road, Folkestone, Kent, CT20 2DA
Tel: 01303 226238
Fax: 01303 226238

Contact: Linda Hooton, Business Development Administrator
E-mail: businessdev@southkent.ac.uk
Website: www.southkent.ac.uk

Profile: SKC has an enviable record for NVQs and accredited training.

Services: Management certificates, Management diplomas, NVQs

South Kent College

Stanhope Road, Ashford, Kent, TN23 5RN
Tel: 01233 655610
Fax: 01233 655611

Contact: Adrian Goodson, Head of Division

Profile: Providing a range of FE, commercial, TEC and ES programmes.

South Nottingham College

Greythorn Drive, West Bridgford, Nottingham, NG2 7GA
Tel: 0115 914 6400
Fax: 0115 914 6444

Contact: Terry Breheny, Course team leader professional and management studies
E-mail: brehenyt@south-nottingham.ac.uk
Website: www.south-nottingham.ac.uk

Profile: Specialists in multi-media, printing, business, computing, management, TUC education, NVQs.

Services: Supply chain & distribution, Public sector, E-learning

Southampton City College

St. Mary Street, Southampton, Hampshire, SO14 1AR
Tel: 023 8057 7426
Fax: 023 8057 7473

Contact: Julie Broomfeld, Enterprise Manager
E-mail: enterprise@southampton-city.ac.uk
Website: www.southampton-city.ac.uk

Profile: Provider of high quality, successful training/consultancy services to business.

Services: Management diplomas, Management certificates, NVQs

Speakers International Corporate Development Ltd

Blythe Road, London, W14 0HN
Tel: 020 7602 9498
Fax: 020 7602 9101

Contact: Mr Dominic Sharpe, Event Manager

Profile: World class peak performance coaching for quality organisations.

Services: E-business, Sales & marketing, Supply chain & distribution

Spearhead Training Group Ltd

Thorpe Close, Thorpe WayTrading Estate, Banbury, Oxfordshire, OX16 4SW
Tel: 01295 250010
Fax: 01295 268382

Contact: David Stone, Managing Director
E-mail: info@spearhead-training.co.uk
Website: www.spearhead-training.co.uk

Profile: The UK's leading provider of sales management and marketing courses.

Services: Sales & marketing, Management development, Leadership

Specialist Horticulture Services

8 Merlin Court, Netherton, Huddersfield, West Yorkshire, HD4 7SP
Tel: 01484 319781
Fax: 01484 319781

Contact: Graham Porter MIHORT, CERTEd, FIVA, Sole Trader
E-mail: graham.porter@ntlworld.com

Profile: Training and internal verification for NVQ's in horticulture.

Services: NVQs

Spring Skills

Seymour House, 30-34 Muspole Street, Norwich, Norfolk, NR3 1DJ
Tel: 01603 614321
Fax: 01603 616449

Contact: Kate Woods, Programmes Manager
E-mail: kate_woods@spring.com

Profile: Professional development and training services for managers and training personnel.

Services: Human resources, Management certificates, NVQs

The Springboard Consultancy

Holwell, East Down, Barnstaple, Devon, EX31 4NZ
Tel: 01271 850828
Fax: 01271 850130

Contact: Jenny Daisley, Chief Executive
E-mail: springboard@compuserve.com

Profile: Specialists in women's/men's development training, consultancy and training trainers.

Services: Management development, Supervisory, Assertiveness

University of St Andrews

79 North Street, Admissions Office, St Andrews, Fife, KY16 9AJ
Tel: 01334 462150
Fax: 01334 463388

Contact: Mr S R Magee, Director of Admissions
E-mail: admissions@st-andrews.ac.uk

Services: IT

STACS Training Ltd

Second Floor, The Kingsway Post Office, 35 The Kingsway, Swansea, SA1 5LF
Tel: 01792 463453
Fax: 01792 644131

Contact: Colin Palacio, Managing Director
E-mail: business@stacs.co.uk
Website: www.stacs.co.uk

Services: Human resources, Quality, Management development

Staff Education & Development Centre

Royal Free Hampstead NHS Trust, 50 Lawn Road, Hampstead, London, NW3 2XD
Tel: 020 7830 2532
Fax: 020 7830 2537

Contact: Mr Joseph L Serra, Senior Lecturer
E-mail: rfheducat@compuserve.com

Profile: Staff education and development centre for the Royal Free Trust.

Services: Public sector, Management certificates, Management diplomas

Stairway Consultancy Ltd

PO Box 720, Bourne End, Buckinghamshire, SL8 5YT

Contact: Sarah Cook, Director

Profile: Customer service and leadership consultancy and tailor-made training courses.

Services: Management development, Financial services, Competencies

Statistics for Industry Ltd

4 Victoria Avenue, Knaresborough, North Yorkshire, HG5 9EU
Tel: 01423 865955
Fax: 01423 865711

Contact: A Mann, Courses Manager
E-mail: s4i@aol.com
Website: www.s4i.co.uk

Profile: Practical statistical courses/consultancy aimed at scientists/technologists in industry.

Services: Production & process control, Project management, Manufacturing & engineering

Stehle Associates

212 Piccadilly, London, W1J 9HG
Tel: 020 7917 9943
Fax: 020 7917 9944

Contact: David Beaumont, Partner
E-mail: info@stehle.co.uk
Website: www.stehle.co.uk

Profile: Award winning training from Stehle Associates. We offer a complete training service, including public and in-house courses, project facilitation and consultancy for all levels of staff from senior management to new hires. Our expertise covers Information Systems Development, Project Management, Management and Leadership skills, Interpersonal skills, and Customer Service. For in-house programmes we work closely with our clients to agree the required outcomes and preferred delivery methods. Then we tailor materials from our extensive course portfolio to provide innovative training solutions which match the requirements exactly. To ensure that learning is successful we provide follow-up facilitation and consultancy to reinforce in the workplace these newly acquired skills. All our training is focused on equipping staff with the essential skills required in their job role, and on providing cost-effective results. Whatever the content or duration of our programmes we aim to achieve capabilities which can be applied immediately the training is completed and which can be transferred to new roles as staff develop. We are accredited by the Institute of IT Training as a Gold Standard training provider and abide by their code of practice.

Services: Information Systems Development, Project Management, IT, Management and Leadership skills, Interpersonal Skills, Customer Service

Stephen M Hall & Associates Ltd

Copperfields, 1 Trenchard Meadow, Lytchett Matravers, Poole, BH16 6NA
Tel: 01761 451214
Fax: 01761 451214

Contact: Stephen Hall, Director

Profile: The management consultants that help your managers and business grow.

Services: Human resources, Leadership, IT, Courses, Change management, Business excellence, Human capital audits

Stevenson Business Training Ltd

Bankhead Avenue, Edinburgh, Lothian, EH11 4DE
Tel: 0131 535 4800
Fax: 0131 535 4655

Contact: Melanie Duncan, Sales Executive
E-mail: mduncan@stevenson.ac.uk
Website: www.stevensonbusiness.com

Profile: We are a commercial training and consultancy company.

Services: Health & safety, Management development, Coaching & mentoring

Stirling Associates

Marlborough House, 679 Warwick Road, Solihull, West Midlands, B91 3DA
Tel: 0121 704 4141
Fax: 0121 704 0744

Contact: Jill Stirling, Director
Website: www.stirling-assocates.co.uk

Profile: Small professional company delivering PC courses in Solihull or on-site.

Stirling Management Centre

University of Stirling, Stirling, FK9 4LA
Tel: 01786 451712
Fax: 01786 449940

Contact: Gail Miller, Business Manager
E-mail: smc.sales@stir.ac.uk

Profile: 19 Purpose built training rooms, 75 deluxe bedrooms and suite; bar and restaurant.

Services: Conference venues

Stirling Training Consultants

The Courtyard, Park Royal Road, London, W3 6XA
Tel: 020 8993 6663
Fax: 020 8993 6664

Contact: Deirdre Skies, Course Administration
E-mail: stc@stirlingtraining.co.uk
Website: www.stirlingtraining.co.uk

Profile: STC is an established consultancy offering results focused, practical training.

Services: Interpersonal skills, Presentation skills, Training for trainers

St James's College

4 Wetherby Gardens, London, SW5 0JN
Tel: 020 7373 3852
Fax: 020 7370 3303

Contact: Tess Housden, Principal
E-mail: information@stjamesscollege.co.uk
Website: www.stjamesscollege.co.uk

Profile: Keyboarding, computing, shorthand, public relations, marketing, advertising, personal development training.

Services: Assertiveness, Presentation skills, Time management

Stockport College of F&HE

The Business School, Wellington Road South, Stockport, Cheshire, SK1
Tel: 0161 958 3606

Contact: Gill Humphrey, Area Manager, Business and Management

Profile: The Business School offers a wide range of management training.

Services: Human resources, Interpersonal skills, Training for trainers

Stockport College of Further & Higher Education

Wellington Road South, Stockport, SK1 3QU
Tel: 0161 958 3605/06
Fax: 0161 958 3384

Contact: Alison Denholm, Head of vocational training services
E-mail: stockcoll@cs.stockport.ac.uk

Profile: The Business School at Stockport College provides courses in accounting, law, personnel and training, business and administration and management.

Stoke-on-Trent College Commercial Unit

Cauldon Campus, Stoke Road, Shelton, Stoke-on-Trent, ST4 2DG
Tel: 01782 208208
Fax: 01782 603565

Contact: Mark Dethick, Commercial Development Manager

Profile: The commercial unit provides training and consultancy.

Stonebow

Third Floor, International House, High Street, Ealing, London, W5 5DB
Tel: 020 8567 5591
Fax: 020 8579 4805

Contact: Jo Frank, Business Development Executive
E-mail: info@stonebow.co.uk
Website: www.stonebow.co.uk

Profile: Training, consultancy and management development for the hospitality industry.

Services: Human resources, Production & process control, Coaching & mentoring

Stotts Correspondence College

Dept. IM, 4 Foscote Mews, London, W9 2HH
Tel: 020 7266 2202
Fax: 020 7266 2314

Contact: S C Albert, Director
E-mail: microworld@ndirect.co.uk
Website: www.microworld.ndirect.co.uk

Profile: Distance learning: locksmithing/calligraphy/fitness and nutrition/dressmaking correspondence courses.

Services: Human resources, Leisure, Books & packages

Stradling Training & Consultancy

Swan House, 54 Station Lane, Hornchurch, Essex, RM12 6NB
Tel: 0845 126 0662
Fax: 01708 478064

Contact: Ron Stradling, Proprietor
E-mail: ron@stradlingtandc.fsbusiness.co.uk
Website: www.traineurope.co.uk

Profile: The best value holistic approach to management guidance and training.

Services: Leadership, Change management, Management development

Straightforward Training Ltd

54 Grand Avenue, Surbiton, Surrey, KT5 9HU
Tel: 020 8399 4332
Fax: 020 8399 4332

Contact: Bill Peters, Director
E-mail: info@stltd.co.uk
Website: www.stltd.co.uk

Profile: Management, supervisory, customer care and teambuilding, training and development.

Services: Customer service, Management development, Teamworking

Strategic Management Partners

'Meadows', Roedean Way, Brighton, Sussex, BN2 5RJ
Tel: 01273 675924
Fax: 01273 673960

Contact: Clive Bonny, Chief Executive
E-mail: clivebonny@aol.com
Website: www.consult-smp.com

Services: Human resources, Sales & marketing, Risk management

Strategy Workshop Facilitators Limited

Trafalgar House, 11/12 Waterloo Place, London, SW1Y 4AU
Tel: 020 7863 8805
Fax: 020 7863 8805

Contact: Roger Handley, Managing Director
E-mail: mail@strategy-workshops.co.uk
Website: www.strategy-workshops.co.uk

Profile: Professional facilitators of Strategic Thinking, Innovation and Decision Making processes.

Services: Innovation, Strategy & planning, Decision-making

University of Strathclyde

16 Richmond Street, Glasgow, G1 1XQ
Tel: 0141 552 4400
Fax: 0141 552 0775

Profile: The University aims to be a place of useful learning.

Services: IT, Corporate universities

Stresswise

Department of Biological Sciences, The Manchester Metropolitan University, Manchester, M1 5GD
Tel: 0161 247 1234
Fax: 0161 247 6325

Contact: Terry Looker, Head of Department
E-mail: t.looker@mmu.ac.uk
Website: www.sci-eng.mmu.ac.uk/biology

Profile: Stress awareness and management. Handling pressures and demands effectively.

Structured Training Ltd

Prospero Barn, The Green, Snitterfield, Stratford-upon-Avon, Warwickshire, CV37 0TR
Tel: 01789 734300
Fax: 01789 730791

Contact: Andrew Brown, Chairman
E-mail: info@structured-training.com
Website: www.structured-training.com

Profile: Open and bespoke sales, management and customer service training courses.

Services: Problem solving, Manufacturing & engineering, E-learning

Suffolk College

Suffolk College, Ipswich, Suffolk, IP4 1LT
Tel: 01473 255885
Fax: 01473 230054

Contact: Tracey Bailey, Promotions & Information Centre Manager
E-mail: info@suffolk.ac.uk
Website: www.suffolk.ac.uk

Profile: The largest provider of education and training in Suffolk.

Services: IT, Corporate universities

University of Sunderland

Langham Tower, Ryhope Road, Sunderland, SR2 7EE
Tel: 0191 515 3000
Fax: 0191 515 3805
E-mail: student-helpline@sunderland.ac.uk
Website: www.sunderland.ac.uk

Services: Customer service, Information systems, E-learning

Sunderland City Training & Enterprise Ltd

Business & Innovation Centre, Sunderland Enterprise Park, Sunderland, Tyne and Wear, SR1 2TA
Tel: 0191 516 0222
Fax: 0191 516 8159

Contact: P M Eldon, Financial Controller

Profile: Administration of government funded training and enterprise programmes.

Sunley Management Centre

University College Northampton, Boughton Green Road, Northampton, NN2 7AL
Tel: 01604 719531
Fax: 01604 77201

Contact: Lesley Roach, Business Development
E-mail: lesley.roach@northampton.ac.uk
Website: www.sunley-northampton.co.uk

Profile: Sunley Management Centre is a management training and conference centre.

Services: Management development, Leadership, Management certificates

Superboss Ltd

PO Box 813, Windsor, Berkshire, SL4 2XU
Tel: 01753 833226
Fax: 01753 863412

Contact: Dr David Freemantle, Chairman
E-mail: team@superboss.co.uk

Profile: Motivational customer service and leadership seminars for managers.

Services: Human resources, Management development, Emotional intelligence

University of Surrey

Guildford, GU2 7XH
Tel: 01483 300800
Fax: 01483 300803

Contact: P Elliott, Corporate Marketing Manager
E-mail: information@surrey.ac.uk
Website: www.surrey.ac.uk

Profile: University of Surrey provides scholarship attuned to today's technological society.

Services: Business Services, Conference venues, MBAs

Survey Force Ltd

140 Borden Lane, Sittingbourne, Kent, ME9 8HW
Tel: 01795 423778
Fax: 01795 423778
Contact: Peter Sidlett, Manager

Profile: Survey Force is a well established experience provider of marketing training.

Services: Design, Supply chain & distribution, Supervisory

Sussex Publications

Dept IM, Sussex Publications, 4 Foscote Mews, London, W9 2HH
Tel: 020 7266 2202
Fax: 020 7266 2314

Contact: S C Albert, Director
E-mail: microworld@ndirect.co.uk
Website: www.microworld.ndirect.co.uk

Profile: Video/audio learning resources: English, History, Music, Languages. Catalogue.

Services: Education, Leisure, Books & packages

System Concepts Ltd

2 Savoy Court, Strand, London, WC2R 0EZ
Tel: 020 7240 3388
Fax: 020 7240 5212

Contact: Andrea Caws, Director
E-mail: andy@system-concepts.com
Website: www.system-concepts.com

Profile: Specialists in office and industrial ergonomics and health and safety.

Services: Health & safety, Risk management, Property, construction & facilities

Target Resources

The Stables, Southfield Cloisters, Aston Flamville, Leicestershire, LE10 3AQ
Tel: 01455 239090
Fax: 01455 239090

Contact: Ted Garratt, Partner
E-mail: target_resources@lineone.net
Website: www.targetresources.co.uk

Services: Coaching & mentoring, Interpersonal skills, Leadership

Tatum's Word

9 Melbourne Court, Meadway, Twickenham, Middlesex, TW2 6PH
Tel: 020 8898 3837

Contact: Sylvie Tatum, Director

Profile: Computer software training, leading software applications.

Services: IT

Taylor-Stewart Associates Ltd

201 Hatton Square, 16 Baldwins Gardens, London, EC1N 7RJ
Tel: 020 7922 8846
Fax: 020 7922 8878

Contact: Dr Marie Stewart, Director

Profile: Equal opportunities consultancy and training: recruitment, management and service delivery.

Services: Management development

TBL Organisational Development Ltd

Hallburn House, Pitkeathly Mains, Bridge of Earn, Perthshire, PH2 9HL
Tel: 01738 813644
Fax: 01738 813644

Contact: Oliver Crance, Director
E-mail: enquiries@tbl.uk.com
Website: www.tbl.uk.com

Profile: Team building, leadership, facilitation and graduate development throughout the UK.

Services: Teamworking, Emotional intelligence, Leadership

TDS

95 Great Victoria Street, Belfast, Antrim, BT2 7AG
Tel: 01232 233433
Fax: 01232 777669

Contact: Paul McCallion, Director

Profile: Management development programmes.

Services: Management development

Team Training International

Team Training House, Bellingdon, Chesham, Buckinghamshire, HP5 2XU
Tel: 01494 758995
Fax: 01494 758808

Contact: Margaret Lewis, Marketing Director
E-mail: teamtrng@aol.com
Website: www.teamtrainingint.com

Profile: Services offered: team problem solving, planning, leadership management, communication skills.

Services: Change management, Management development, Teamworking

Teleconomy Peoples Development

The Mews, 62A Main Street, Kirkby Lonsdale, Cumbria, LA6 2AJ
Tel: 015242 71866
Fax: 015242 72599

Contact: Ailsa Hulme, Director

Profile: Telephone communications skills development and training.

Services: Communications, advertising & PR

Telematica Ltd

Newburn Centre, Newburn Crescent, Swindon, SN1 5ES
Tel: 01793 530844
Fax: 01793 530521

Contact: Ken Street, CEO
E-mail: info@telematica.co.uk
Website: www.telematica.co.uk

Profile: E-learning infrastructure products and services including learning & content management systems.

Services: Competencies, Corporate universities, Performance appraisal

Thames Valley CCi Training Ltd

Training Centre, 467 Malton Avenue, Slough, Berkshire, SL1 4QU
Tel: 01753 824541
Fax: 01753 538844

Contact: Karyn Buck, Training Courses Manager
E-mail: trainingsales@thamesvalleychambers.co.uk
Website: www.thamesvalleychamber.co.uk

Profile: Short courses and tailored training in all areas business.

Services: Management development, Assertiveness, Business Services

Thanet Community Learning Centre

Unit 5, The St John Business Centre, St Peter's Road, Margate, CT9 1TE
Tel: 01843 232111

Contact: Miriam Ibbotson, Manager

Profile: Provision of text and computer-based self study courses.

Services: IT

The Thinking Consultancy Ltd

Greystones, Medlake Road, Egham, Surrey, TW20 8HU
Tel: 01784 440404
Fax: 01784 740750

Contact: Paul Hobbs, Managing Director
E-mail: paul@thethinkingconsultancy.com
Website: www.quantum-reading.com

Profile: Development of personal thinking skills and related behaviours.

Services: Management development

Tidalfire

91 Hanover Street, Edinburgh, EH2 1DJ
Tel: 0131 718 4245
Fax: 0131 718 4750

Contact: Ros Lavery, Customer Services Manager
E-mail: info@tidalfire.com
Website: www.tidalfire.com

Profile: Training and consulting for web and internet, design and print.

Services: Communications, advertising & PR

Tim Russell and Company

112 Defoe House, Barbican, London, EC2Y 8ND
Tel: 020 7638 5357
Fax: 020 7638 5357

Contact: Tim Russell, Managing Partner
E-mail: timrussell1@compuserve.com

Profile: Transforming organisations with the amazing microskills system of interpersonal skills.

Services: Interpersonal skills, Leadership, Supervisory

Time for People Ltd

Newsons Farm, Thorpe Morieux, Bury St Edmunds, Suffolk, IP30 0PB
Tel: 01284 828284
Fax: 01284 828285

Contact: Roland Bee, Director
E-mail: bee@anglianet.co.uk

Profile: Training and consultancy in TNA, training evaluation and time management.

TMS Development International Ltd

128 Holgate Rd, York, North Yorkshire, YO24 4FL
Tel: 01904 641640
Fax: 01904 640076

Contact: Corrine Lightowler, Sales Executive
E-mail: enquiry@tmsdi.com
Website: www.tmsdi.com

Tony Wheeler Associates

16 St Mary's Street, Wallingford, Oxfordshire, OX10 0EW
Tel: 01491 839913
Fax: 01491 839913

Contact: Estelle Browne, Administrator

Profile: Providers of a wide range of in-house courses and seminars.

Services: Customer service, Presentation skills, Books & packages

Top Performance Communication Consultants

Manor House, Gribthorpe, Howden, East Yorkshire, DN14 7ST
Tel: 01757 288243
Fax: 01757 288243

Contact: Alan Ram, Partner
E-mail: topcoaching@easynet.co.uk

Profile: Consultancy and coaching in written communication and advanced presentation techniques.

Services: Human resources, Sales & marketing, E-learning

Trainers at Work

19 Glebe Road, London, N8 7DA
Tel: 020 83413461
Fax: 020 8292 0832

Contact: Valerie Thackeray, Senior Associate

Training & Consultancy Unit

Kensington & Chelsea College, Wornington Road, London, W10 5QQ
Tel: 020 7573 5322
Fax: 020 8968 4797

Contact: Clare Dawson, Manager Training and Consultancy Unit
E-mail: tacu@kcc.ac.uk
Website: www.kcc.ac.uk

Profile: Training customised to clients needs, delivered conveniently on your premises.

Services: Management diplomas, Management development, Management certificates

Training Business

63 Cheyneys Avenue, Edgware, Middlesex, HA8 6SD
Tel: 020 89513732

Contact: Daniel Yadin, Director
E-mail: daniel@creativemarcoms.co.uk
Website: www.creativemarcoms.co.uk

Profile: Courses and seminars in creative, marketing, management and media communications.

Services: Communications, advertising & PR, Sales & marketing, Business writing

The Training Company

Dean Haven House, Viney Woodside, Lydney, Gloucestershire, GL15 4LX
Tel: 01594 510613
Fax: 01594 826495
E-mail: info@trainingco.co.uk

Profile: High quality training in people development skills.

Services: Assertiveness, Coaching & mentoring, Conflict resolution

Training Direct

Edinburgh Gate, Marlow, Essex, CM20 2JE
Tel: 01279 623927
Fax: 01279 623795

Contact: Sean Hart, Direct Marketing Executive

Profile: Recognised as the leading provider of world-class training resources.

Training Exchange Services

59 Broomfield Avenue, Glasgow, G77 5JR
Tel: 0141 585 3711
Fax: 0141 639 0362

Contact: Mike Gillen, Chief Executive Officer
E-mail: info@trainexe.com
Website: www.trainexe.com

Profile: Producer of training software in management and practical topics.

Services: E-business, Management development, Business Services

Training for Excellence

5 Magna Close, Harpenden, Hertfordshire, AL5 1RH
Tel: 01582 761555
Fax: 01582 620225

Contact: Tony Fowler, Senior Partner
E-mail: training4excellence@ntlworld.com
Website: www.abovethesalt.co.uk

Profile: Since 1987 TFE has helped people to achieve their potential.

Services: Sales & marketing, Interpersonal skills, Presentation skills

Training Leads

61/63b Westgate, Grantham, Lincolnshire, NG31 6JZ
Tel: 01476 570525

Contact: David Allenby, Managing Director

Profile: Providers of quality bespoke management and supervisory training and development.

Services: Management development

Training Opportunities

Hanover House, 61-64 Dudley Road, Wolverhampton, WV2 2BY
Tel: 01902 877920
Fax: 01902 877921

Contact: Dawn Bennett, Trustee
E-mail: busnet@wavender.co.uk
Website: www.topps.ukpc.net

Profile: Quality training for busy people. Learn online or on site.

Services: IT, Management development, Assertiveness

Training Plus

54 Pheasants Way, Rickmansworth, Hertfordshire, WD3 7HA
Tel: 01923 774283
Fax: 01923 897587

Contact: Michael Owen, Director
E-mail: michael.d.owen@btopenworld.com

Profile: Bespoke training and coaching with helpline, distance learning available.

Services: Interpersonal skills, Presentation skills, Business writing

The Training Store Ltd

23-25 High Street, Burnham, SL1 7JD
Tel: 01628 776070
Fax: 01628 782634

Contact: Graham Till, Managing Director
E-mail: 10167.3414@compuserve.com

Profile: Single/mixed media materials for businesses, publishers, universities, professional bodies.

Services: Media skills

Training Video Associates (TVA)

1A Kent Avenue, Harrogate, North Yorkshire, HG1 2ES
Tel: 01423 531727
Fax: 01423 567727

Contact: Alan Davies, Partner
E-mail: mail@dtva.co.uk
Website: www.tva.co.uk

Profile: Training media production including video DVD print.

Services: Health & safety, Induction, Video

Transglobal Languages Limited

Merchants Court, Borough Road, Altrincham, Greater Manchester, WA15 9RA
Tel: 0161 233 0888
Fax: 0161 233 0666

Contact: Ela Linton, Training Manager
E-mail: training@transgloballanguages.co.uk
Website: www.transgloballanguages.co.uk

Profile: Language training and testing, country and culture briefings, translation, interpreting.

Services: Change management, Teamworking, Languages

Transitional Space

99 High Street, Marshfield, Wiltshire, SN14 8LT
Tel: 01225 891478

Contact: Michael Green, Partner
E-mail: enquiries@transitionalspace.co.uk
Website: www.transitionalspace.co.uk

Profile: Enabling change through individual, team and organisational development.

Services: Leadership, Change management, Coaching & mentoring

Tregalic (UK) Ltd

The Old Magazine, 8 & 9 Northern Galleries, Fort Fareham Business Park, Newgate Lane, Fareham, Hampshire, PO14 1AH
Tel: 01329 284562
Fax: 01329 284565

Contact: Jeff Murphy, Trainer Consultant
E-mail: jeff@tregalic.co.uk
Website: www.tregalic.co.uk

Profile: NVQ consultancy D32/33 D34/36 training support applications for approved centre.

Services: Human resources, Supervisory, Coaching & mentoring, Courses, Training for trainers, NVQs

Trent Transport Training Ltd

Arlic Way, Kimberley, Nottingham, NG16 2HP
Tel: 0115 938 4982
Fax: 0115 945 9806

Contact: G R Newton, Managing Director

Triangle Group (UK) Ltd

Hanover House, The Roe, St Asaph, LL17 0LT
Tel: 01745 585857

Contact: Laurence Waxman, Managing Director

Profile: Organisation/management development, training courses, programmes and resources.

Services: Management development

Trident Training Services

Suite 5, 155 Fawe Park Road, London, SW15 2EG
Tel: 020 8874 3610
Fax: 020 8874 3610

Contact: Jane Hammond, Director
E-mail: trident@btconnect.com
Website: www.tridenttraining.co.uk

Profile: Specialises in tailor-made public relations training for individuals or groups.

Services: Media skills, Public sector, NVQs

The Triforium

16 Warwick Street, Rugby, Warwickshire, CV21 3DH
Tel: 01788 575090
Fax: 01788 575411

Contact: Paul Talbot, Operations Manager, Consultancy
Website: www.intechq.demon.co.uk

Profile: Competence based management development programmes approved by Institute of Management

Services: Supervisory, Business Services, Financial services

Trubody Training Associates

55 Willow Road, Bourneville, Birmingham, West Midlands, B30 2AT
Tel: 0121 472 1421
Fax: 0121 472 1421

Contact: Roger Trubody, Managing Director
E-mail: roger.trubody@tiscali.co.uk

Profile: In-company courses in manufacturing systems, quality techniques and lean manufacturing.

Services: Production & process control, Management development, Manufacturing & engineering

TSL Training

The Chantry, Rooks Bridge, Axbridge, Somerset, BS26 2TR
Tel: 01934 750224
Fax: 01934 750224

Contact: Terry Yeadon, Director
E-mail: terry.yeadon@btinternet.com

Profile: Specialists in tailor-made in-house management development and people skills training.

Services: Interpersonal skills, Presentation skills, Time management

TTC Training Ltd

The Cornerstone, The Broadway, Woking, Surrey, GU21 5AR
Tel: 01483 727321
Fax: 01483 756698

Contact: Camilla Nichols-Wilson, Sales Support
E-mail: alliance@ttctraining.co.uk
Website: www.ttctraining.co.uk

Profile: NVQ and other training from entry level to management.

Services: Financial services, Transport & distribution, Books & packages

Tullos Training Ltd

Craigshaw Drive, West Tullos, Aberdeen, AB12 3AL
Tel: 01224 872316
Fax: 01224 894677

Contact: I R Garrett, Chief Executive
E-mail: info@tullostraining.co.uk
Website: www.tullostraining.co.uk

Profile: Providers of engineering skills training, modern apprenticeships and vocational qualifications.

Services: Health & safety, Manufacturing & engineering, NVQs

TV Choice

22 Charing Cross Road, London, WC2H 0HR
Tel: 020 7379 0873
Fax: 020 7379 0263

Contact: Norman Thomas, Director
E-mail: tvchoiceuk@aol.com
Website: www.tvchoice.uk.com

Profile: We provide realistic videos which highlight human and organisational issues.

Services: Business writing, Change management, Coaching & mentoring

Values Education for Life (Training) Ltd

51 - 54 Hockley Hill, Birmingham, West Midlands, B18 5AQ
Tel: 0121 753 3715
Fax: 0121 753 3715

Contact: H L Owen, Co-ordinator

Profile: Consult the experts for quality advice on all your needs.

Venture Wales

23 Park Place, Cardiff, CF10 3BA
Tel: 0290 203 75940
Fax: 0290 2037 5949

Contact: Mark Goodwin, Training and Development Manager
E-mail: mgoodwin@venturewales.com
Website: www.venturewales.com

Services: Management development, Finance for non-finance staff, Business Services

Verax International Ltd

Taplins Court, Hartley Wintney, Hampshire, RG27 8XU
Tel: 01252 849300
Fax: 01252 849333

Contact: K Bedingham, Director
E-mail: info@verax.co.uk
Website: www.verax.co.uk

Profile: Providers of best practice diagnostics for managing change and development.

Services: Human resources, Customer service, Teamworking

Vertex

Downlands, 73 Oathall Road, Haywards Heath, West Sussex, RH16 3EL
Tel: 01444 456473

Contact: Vic Hartley, Partner

Profile: Consultants in organisation and management development.

Vetlink Information Services

Cats Drove House, 19 Station Road, Ashcott, Near Bridgwater, TA7 9QP
Tel: 01458 210818
Fax: 01458 210040

Contact: John R Corsan, Principal
E-mail: john.corsan@vetlink.co.uk
Website: www.vetlink.co.uk

Services: Customer service, Coaching & mentoring, Courses

Vets in Business Ltd

c/o 2 The Spinney, Bath Road, Ashcott, Bridgwater, TA7 9QS
Tel: 01458 210468

Contact: Mark Moran, Director
E-mail: info@vetsinbusiness.co.uk
Website: www.vetsinbusiness.co.uk

Profile: Training for veterinary partners and practice staff.

Services: Customer service, Strategy & planning, Teamworking

Video Arts

Dumbarton House, 68 Oxford Street, London, WlN 0LH
Tel: 020 7637 7288
Fax: 020 7580 8103

Contact: Martin Addison, Director - Learning Solutions
E-mail: enquiries@videoarts.co.uk
Website: www.videoarts.co.uk

Profile: Inspirational learning solutions.

Services: Motivation, Project management, Teamworking

Videotel

84 Newman Street, London, W1T 3EU
Tel: 020 7299 1800
Fax: 020 7299 1818

Contact: Barbara Steinberg, Marketing Manager
E-mail: mail@videotelmail.com
Website: www.videotel.co.uk

Profile: Training videos and CD-Roms producers specialising in safety subjects.

Services: Crisis & disaster management, Health & safety, Video

Visuals

55 Selwood Road, Chessington, Surrey, KT9 1PT
Tel: 020 8397 1567
Fax: 020 8287 8618

Contact: Alan Moss, Consultant
E-mail: visuals@bigfoot.com
Website: www.visuals.freeserve.co.uk

Profile: Consultants specialising in audio - video and multi-media technology.

Services: Media skills, Business Services, Video

Voss Training International Ltd T/A VossTraining Services

The Coach Services, 61/62 Hamilton Square, Birkenhead, Wirral, CH41 5AT
Tel: 0151 650 6600
Fax: 0151 650 6606

Contact: Morris Dickie, Managing Director
E-mail: enquiries@vosstrainingservices.co.uk
Website: www.vosstrainingservices.co.uk

Profile: National lift truck training provider- RTITB accredited- 24 hour service.

Services: Health & safety, Food & drink, Manufacturing & engineering

The Wadenhoe Consultancy

Wadenhoe House, Wadenhoe, Peterborough, Cambridgeshire, PE8 5SR
Tel: 01832 720123
Fax: 01832 720125

Contact: John Fawson, Consultant
E-mail: john@wadenhoe.com
Website: www.wadenhoe.com

Profile: Strategic management developers. IOM accredited coaching middle/senior level managers.

Services: Change management, Management development, Motivation

Wakefield Skillcentre

Units 41-43, Monckton Industrial Estate, Denby Dale Road, Wakefield, WFZ 7AL
Tel: 01924 375823
Fax: 01924 362811
E-mail: info@skill-centre.co.uk
Website: www.skill-centre.co.uk

Profile: A leading provider of training services to industry and individuals.

Services: Production & process control, Health & safety, Management development

University of Wales College, Newport

University Information Centre, Caerleon Campus, PO Box 101, Newport, NP18 3YH
Tel: 01633 432432
Fax: 01633 432850

Contact: Ms Karen Fishlock, Head of Admissions
E-mail: uic@newport.ac.uk
Website: www.newport.ac.uk

Profile: The university where we bring learning to life.

Services: Accounting & finance, Design, Human resources

Walford & North Shropshire College

Baschurch, Shrewsbury, Shropshire, SY4 2HL
Tel: 01939 262100
Fax: 01939 261112

Contact: Michelle Hay, Marketing Manager

Profile: Providing high quality education courses for the land-based industries.

Warwick Business School

University of Warwick, Coventry, CV4 7AL
Tel: 024 7652 4306
Fax: 024 7652 3719

Contact: Diana Holton, Press Information Officer
E-mail: enquiries@wbs.ac.uk
Website: www.wbs.ac.uk

Profile: Internationally accredited, WBS is highly ranked for teaching and research.

Services: Strategy & planning, Management diplomas, MBAs

Webb Associates

41 Warwick Avenue, Coventry, West Midlands, CV5 6DJ
Tel: 024 7671 7671
Fax: 024 7671 7671

Contact: Neville Webb, Managing Partner
E-mail: info@webb-associates.co.uk

Profile: Effectiveness through people.

Services: Change management, Management development, Leadership

Wentworth Consultants (UK) Ltd

Clifton Lodge, Clifton Lane, Meltham, Huddersfield, HD9 4AH
Tel: 01484 850770
Fax: 01484 852437

Contact: Mary Harrison, Company Administrator
E-mail: mad@wentworthconsultants.co.uk

Services: Change management, Management development, Teamworking

West Herts College

Hempstead Road, Watford, Hertfordshire, WD17 3EZ
Tel: 01923 812000
Fax: 01923 812000

Contact: Helen Free, Head of Marketing
E-mail: admissions@westherts.ac.uk
Website: www.westherts.ac.uk

Services: Business Services, Leisure, Media

Williams Learning Network (UK) Ltd

Henwood Pavilion, Hythe Road, Ashford, Kent, TN24 8DH
Tel: 01233 633605
Fax: 01233 633609

Contact: Ed Acock, Operations Manager
E-mail: 106261.2632@compuserve.com

Profile: Providers of integrated solutions to the process and manufacturing industries.

The Winning Post

Calvorde House, Kings Drive, Newmarket, Suffolk, CB8 8DG
Tel: 01638 668581
Fax: 01638 668581

Contact: C Poole, Manager
E-mail: winningpost@cpoole100.freeserve.co.uk

Profile: Provide training in bookkeeping, accounting and personal and business development.

Services: Management development, Problem solving, Training for trainers

WLT Safety Advisory Service

Talfryn, Ystrad Aeron Lampeter, Ceredigion, SA48 7PG
Tel: 01570 470102
Fax: 01570 470102

Contact: W Lynford Thomas, Proprietor
E-mail: wlt.safety@virgin.net

Profile: Health and safety training for all sectors of business.

Services: Health & safety, Construction, Food & drink

WMC ManagementTraining Consultants

Engineers' House, The Promenade, Clifton Down, Bristol, BS8 3NB
Tel: 0117 973 1471
Fax: 0117 974 4288

Contact: Pat Strickland, Administration Officer
E-mail: enquiries@eef-west.org.uk
Website: www.eeftraining.org.uk

Profile: Management development, health and safety, environmental and employment law training.

Services: Management development, Project management, Teamworking

Woodcote Technical Services

4-6 Woodcote Green Road, Epsom, Surrey, KT18 7DH
Tel: 01372 741818
Fax: 01372 743335

Contact: Roger W Elliott, Technical Director

Profile: Bespoke technical training for manufacturing companies including providing illustrated materials.

Services: Production & process control, Multi-skilling, Presentation skills, Food & drink

Woodlyn Training & Consultancy Services

Northern College, Northern College, Gardyne Road, Dundee, DD5 1NY
Tel: 01382 454921
Fax: 01382 454921

Contact: Jim Waddell, Principal Consultant

Profile: Supervisor training (NEBSM), training needs analysis, investing in people consultancy.

Woolhampton Management Services

Cherrington, Ryefield Road, Ross-on-Wye, Herefordshire, HR9 5LS
Tel: 01989 562463
Fax: 01989 768349

Contact: R J Pope, Director
E-mail: r.j.pope@btinternet.com

Profile: Consultancy in performance improvement and development of teams and individuals.

Services: Management development, Change management, Teamworking

Worcester College of Technology

Deansway, Worcester, Hereford and Worcester, WRl 2JF
Tel: 01905 725555
Fax: 01905 28906

Contact: T A Dillingham, Assistant Principal
E-mail: tad@wortech.ac.uk
Website: www.wortech.ac.uk

Profile: Major provider of NVQ and professional qualifications; all levels.

Worcestershire College of Agriculture Hindlip

Worcester, WR3 8SS
Tel: 01905 754760
Contact: Lesley Archer, Marketing

Profile: Agriculture, equine studies, animal care. Motor vehicle mechanics, conservation forestry.

Work-Based Learning Unit (SES)

University of Surrey, Guildford, Surrey, GU2 7XH
Tel: 01483 686157
Fax: 01483 689522

Contact: Kirsten Cartland-Glover, Administrator
E-mail: wbl@surrey.ac.uk

Profile: In-house/campus-based courses for enhancing performance at work.

World Microfilms

Dept. IM, Microworld House, 4 Foscote Mews, London, W9 2HH
Tel: 020 7266 2202
Fax: 020 7266 2314

Contact: S C Albert, Director
E-mail: microworld@ndirect.co.uk
Website: www.microworld.ndirect.co.uk

Profile: Audiovisual learning resources for architecture and design students. Catalogue.

Services: Design, Construction, Education, Leisure

Writtle College

Writtle, Chelmsford, Essex, CM1 3RR
Tel: 01245 424200
Fax: 01245 420456

Contact: Mike Hall, Director of Industrial Development
E-mail: mjh@writtle.ac.uk
Website: www.writtle.ac.uk

Profile: The leading land-based college, linked to the University of Essex.

Services: Management certificates, Management diplomas, MBAs

WSC Ltd

3rd Floor, Broadway House, The Broadway, London, SW19 1RL
Tel: 020 8540 2282
Fax: 020 8540 5024

Contact: D Jeffwate, Director

Profile: Trainers and training room for hire for computer training.

Services: IT

WTI Training Group

Tadley Court, Tadley, Hampshire, RG26 3TB
Tel: 0118 981 3011
Fax: 0118 981 7000

Contact: Customer Services
E-mail: customer.services@wti.co.uk
Website: www.wti.co.uk

Profile: Open courses, customised and on site training.

Services: Property, construction & facilities, Health & safety, Construction

The Wye Group Ltd

Lawness Barns, Mountnessing Road, Billericay, Essex, CM12 0TS
Tel: 01277 634638
Fax: 01277 634639

Contact: Amanda Stephens, Director
E-mail: enquiries@wye.net
Website: www.wye.net

Profile: Tailored management development and communication skills plus experiential learning programmes.

Services: Change management, Teamworking, Coaching & mentoring

Xansa

4 West Links, Tollgate Business Park, Chandlers Ford, Eastleigh, Hampshire, SO50 3TG
Tel: 023 8064 6700
Fax: 023 8064 6740

Contact: Sue Lindsay, Account Manager
E-mail: training@xansa.com
Website: www.xansa.com/training

Profile: PRINCE2, programme management, project management service, management ISEB qualifications.

Services: Change management, Project management, Risk management

Xebec Multi Media Solutions Ltd

Wellington House, Bath Road, Woodchester, Gloucestershire, GL5 5EY
Tel: 01453 832241

Contact: Chris Horseman, Managing Director
E-mail: postbox@xebec.co.uk

Profile: Leading publishers of multimedia training courses on CD-ROM.

YH Training Services

37-39 Falsgrave Road, Scarborough, North Yorkshire, YO12 5EA
Tel: 01723 371481
Fax: 01723 374286

Contact: Christine Fisher, Marketing Co-ordinator
E-mail: enquiries@yh-group.co.uk
Website: www.yh-group.co.uk

Profile: High calibre training and employment opportunities for individuals and businesses.

Services: Customer service, Accounting & finance, Conference venues

YMCA Training

54 Holly Bush Lane, Sevenoaks, Kent, TN13 3TL
Tel: 01732 458024
Fax: 01732 742367

Contact: Lynn Coutts, Manager

Profile: YMCA training provides vocational and personal development programmes nationally.

Services: Management development, Motivation, Supervisory

Ystrad Mynach College

Twyn Road, Ystrad Mynach, Caerphilly, CF82 7XR
Tel: 01443 816888
Fax: 01443 816973

Contact: Lee-Anne Leyshon, Marketing Officer

Profile: Tailor-made and off the shelf programmes to suit all employers.

Services: Training for trainers, IT, Health & safety, NVQs

Part 2.2

Functional Skills

Accounting & finance

ABG Professional Information
The definitive accountancy information source.
76

The Association of Business Executives (ABE)
2003 sees ABE celebrate its 30th anniversary. Today, ABE has become a market leader in the cost-effictive delivery of quality assured British management education.
The primary objective of ABE, a non-profit making organisation, is to ensure that students successfully completing its examinations will accquire the knowledge and skills needed in order to become more effective managers. ABE's awards are recognised internationally as an accepted route into the later stages of UK and overseas first degrees, professional qualifications and MBA and other Masters programmes. The provision of CD-ROM study Manuals further reduces costs for students who receive tutor support from colleges accredited by ABE.
Membership is available to both UK and overseas students and examinations are conducted twice a year worldwide.
86

Association of Certified Book-keepers
Modern professional body, producing tomorrow's financial controllers and administrators.
86

The Association of Corporate Treasurers
The world's leading provider of treasury education and training.
86

Association of Finance Controllers & Administrators
Modern professional body, producing tomorrow's financial controllers and administrators.
88

Birkbeck, University of London
University level part-time evening courses in central London.
92

University of Brighton, Business Services
Skills and training provided for organisations of all kinds.
95

Bristol Business School
Provides a supportive and well-resourced learning environment, officially rated excellent by the Higher Education Funding Council for England.
96

British Shops & Stores Association Ltd
Retail selling, buying and management courses, books and distance learning.
98

Cambridge International College
CIC conducts Diploma Programmes on a wide range of accounting, sales business, management and administration fields, as well as 'support' subjects like Business English & Letter Writing, Communications and Computers, one or more of which are often essential for Members' progress and success in their chosen careers.
All of CIC's Diploma Programmes are designed and written especially for career enhancement and development. The professional Diploma Programmes have proved outstandingly successful in achieving those objectives – as well as the goals and ambitions of the hundreds of thousands of Member who study with CIC.
As appropriate, Diploma Programmes start either from basic principles or with a revision of earlier studies, and then deal comprehensively with the important topics, with emphasis always on the practical application of what is taught.
105

University of Central England Business School
Generalist MBAs and specialisation in subjects of interest to professionals.
108

Chartered Institute of Bankers in Scotland
The professional body for the financial services sector.
114

Chelmsford College
We serve Essex in providing professional training for adults.
116

CIMA Mastercourses
CIMA Master courses, one day management training in management accounting and business management.
117

Circa Ltd
Meeting employer and learner needs through flexible work based learning.
118

City Business Seminars
Personalised finance training organisation.
118

Colchester Institute
College of further and higher education including services to business.
121

David A Palmer
Totally tailored financial management development programmes to enhance corporate profitability.
129

D J Neil Ltd
Design and delivery of in-house management training UK and overseas.
133

Euromoney Training
Global market leader in banking and financial training.
143

Financial Management Development
Totally tailored financial management development programmes to enhance corporate profitability.
147

Finchale Training College
Residential vocational rehabilitation to assist disabled people back to work.
147

Force One Training Ltd
IT and transport related training and LearnDirect centre.
148

Humber Business School
HBS is dedicated to offering you bespoke business solutions.
161

Huntingdonshire Regional College
Professionals in education and training helping individuals to achieve.
161

The IEE
Your people are your most precious asset – and with the right professional guidance, you can develop their skills and abilities. The result? Enhanced individual performance – plus measurable improvements to your bottom line. The IEE (Institution of Electrical Engineers) is one of the UK's leaders in management and business training for professionals involved with electrical engineering, IT and electronic engineering. We offer an impressive portfolio of courses for newly qualified and experienced professionals, from careers and business skills through to effective management, negotiating, presentations, marketing – plus a wide range of more technical courses. With over 130,000 members worldwide, the IEE is a global organisation representing the interests of IT and electrical engineering professionals - though our courses are equally applicable to other industries and commercial sectors. Most of our programmes are held in London, though we can run them at your premises, for small or large groups. For more information about how IEE management and business training can bring out the best in your people - and your organisation - call us on 01438 767237 or log on to www.iee.org.uk
162

Institute of Cost and Executive Accountants
Professional Examining body. Provides Training for financial decision makers.
169

The Institute of Internal Auditors – UK and Ireland
IIA – UK and Ireland. The professionals in internal audit training.
170

Jane Allan & Associates
Enjoyable training that adds pure value for salary for all.
181

Communications, advertising & PR

Airtime Communications

80

Buzan Centres Ltd

Buzan Brain Friendly, Intellectual Capital Development with 'stand-alone' or 'bolt-on' courses.

104

Cambridge International College

CIC conducts Diploma Programmes on a wide range of accounting, sales business, management and administration fields, as well as 'support' subjects like Business English & Letter Writing, Communications and Computers, one or more of which are often essential for Members' progress and success in their chosen careers.

All of CIC's Diploma Programmes are designed and written especially for career enhancement and development. The professional Diploma Programmes have proved outstandingly successful in achieving those objectives – as well as the goals and ambitions of the hundreds of thousands of Member who study with CIC.

As appropriate, Diploma Programmes start either from basic principles or with a revision of earlier studies, and then deal comprehensively with the important topics, with emphasis always on the practical application of what is taught.

105

Damar Training Solutions

Effective training solutions for business. Money-back guarantee service.

129

The Evaluation Partnership

We evaluate training courses, programmes and institutions, UK and Europe.

144

Glasgow College of Building & Printing

Training and education in construction, design and visual communications.

152

Goldsmiths College

Study and practice of creative, cultural, cognitive and social processes.

152

Implementation Training Services

Training in communication skills particularly media interviews and news releases.

164

The Inspiration Network

An HR consultancy specialising in creative and inspiring learning solutions.

166

The Institute of Administrative Management

Established in 1915, the Institute of Administrative Management is the leading Professional Body for both practising and aspiring Administrative Managers.

We can work with you to produce an internationally recognised, in-house qualification, validate your training programmes or provide our training to your employees, in house or through our provider network.

Qualifications

IAM qualifications are targeted at Supervisors, Managers, and those who aspire to these positions. Student members can progress through the Certificate, Diploma and Advanced Diploma, and on to further qualifications (such as the IAM's dedicated degree in Administrative Management) and membership of other professional institutes

168

University of Luton

Quality business and management education training research and consultancy.

199

Marketing Training Co

Marketing training covering the whole subject from introductory to MBA.

203

North West Institute of Further & Higher Education

Expert consultants for all Management, HR, Health & Safety areas.

216

Popular Communication Courses Ltd t/a Popcomm Training

In-house and public courses on corporate publishing, communications and PR.

233

The Publishing Training Centre at Book House
Open and distance learning courses for book and journal publishers.
240

Teleconomy Peoples Development
Telephone communications skills development and training.
271

Tidalfire
Training and consulting for web and internet, design and print.
272

Training Business
Courses and seminars in creative, marketing, management and media communications.
274

Design

Capel Manor College
Greater London's horticulture, floristry, countryside, equine and animal studies college.
106

Colchester Institute
College of further and higher education including services to business.
121

Humber Business School
HBS is dedicated to offering you bespoke business solutions.
161

Northampton College
1500 part-time and 130 full-time courses and bespoke training solutions.
216

Parity Training Ltd
Parity Training delivers bespoke and public scheduled training courses in technology, management and business skills, providing training for over 40,000 delegates a year. Parity's learning consultants increasingly blend traditional training methods with e-learning initiatives to provide integrated learning solutions that ensure return on investment and effective learning outcomes.
With training centres in Antrim, Belfast, Birmingham, Bristol, Edinburgh, Fleet, Leeds, London and Manchester, Parity offers nation-wide in person (classroom based) training and support. Additionally, Parity's managed services offering provides a range of options from simple vendor management to a full outsource training and development service.
Parity's long-term partnerships with leading bodies such as the Information Systems Examination Board, DSDM Consortium, Institute of Management, Outward Bound Trust, Association for Project Management, Microsoft and Lotus Corporation keeps Parity at the forefront of the industry, able to offer an unparalleled range of certified training leading to recognised qualifications. Parity's on-going commitment to delivering effective quality training is reflected in its ISO9001 certification. In 2003 Parity Training was awarded the Institued of IT Training's accolade of Training Company of the Year and Trainer of the Year.
Parity Training is part of Parity Group plc, the international IT consultancy and solutions group with 30 offices in the UK, mainland Europe and the USA.
For booking information or course details, call 0800 656 100, email training@parity.net or visit www.parity.net.
224

Popular Communication Courses Ltd t/a Popcomm Training
In-house and public courses on corporate publishing, communications and PR.
233

Survey Force Ltd
Survey Force is a well established experience provider of marketing training.
269

University of Wales College, Newport
The university where we bring learning to life.
283

World Microfilms
Audiovisual learning resources for architecture and design students. Catalogue.
287

E-business

ADVANCE: Management Training Ltd
Bringing the future into your company through internationalisation, organisational transformation.
79

Amadeus Education Ltd
End user training on Microsoft, Lotus and Wordperfect products.
81

Birkbeck, University of London
University level part-time evening courses in central London.
92

British Institute of Technology & E-commerce
BITE is developing e-commerce professionals for all sectors of industry.
97

University of Central England Business School
Generalist MBAs and specialisation in subjects of interest to professionals.
108

EFE International Ltd
Business culture, country, export/import, industry briefings. Regions: Europe, Asia.
138

Elmwood Business Training
Elmwood Business Training provider of quality training courses and consultancies.
140

Huddersfield University Business School (HUBS)
HUBS - a collaborative learning community with a clear vocational emphasis.
160

Information Automation Ltd
Tailored training in CD-ROM, online, internet resources and searching.
165

University of Luton
Quality business and management education training research and consultancy.
199

Parity Training Ltd
Parity Training delivers bespoke and public scheduled training courses in technology, management and business skills, providing training for over 40,000 delegates a year. Parity's learning consultants increasingly blend traditional training methods with e-learning initiatives to provide integrated learning solutions that ensure return on investment and effective learning outcomes.
With training centres in Antrim, Belfast, Birmingham, Bristol, Edinburgh, Fleet, Leeds, London and Manchester, Parity offers nation-wide in person (classroom based) training and support. Additionally, Parity's managed services offering provides a range of options from simple vendor management to a full outsource training and development service.
Parity's long-term partnerships with leading bodies such as the Information Systems Examination Board, DSDM Consortium, Institute of Management, Outward Bound Trust, Association for Project Management, Microsoft and Lotus Corporation keeps Parity at the forefront of the industry, able to offer an unparalleled range of certified training leading to recognised qualifications. Parity's on-going commitment to delivering effective quality training is reflected in its ISO9001 certification. In 2003 Parity Training was awarded the Instituted of IT Training's accolade of Training Company of the Year and Trainer of the Year.
Parity Training is part of Parity Group plc, the international IT consultancy and solutions group with 30 offices in the UK, mainland Europe and the USA. For booking information or course details, call 0800 656 100, email training@parity.net or visit www.parity.net.
224

Speakers International Corporate Development Ltd
World class peak performance coaching for quality organisations.
259

Training Exchange Services
Producer of training software in management and practical topics.
275

Human resources

Aberdeen Business School
We provide high quality education training and consultancy programmes.
75

Abernethy Trust
Personal development, teambuilding and leadership programmes delivered through outdoor projects.
75

Action Development Group
Action Development Group for your organisation and people development needs.
78

Adept Consulting (Central) Ltd
Helping your business succeed through organisational change, individual career development.
78

AdVal Group Plc
AdVal is a highly successful learning and business services group.
79

ALA International Ltd
We use action learning to help you help yourselves.
81

AL Consulting
Results oriented training designed and delivered for clients' specific needs.
81

Amadeus Education Ltd
End user training on Microsoft, Lotus and Wordperfect products.
81

Arlington Associates
Management training group and one-to-one UK and abroad.
84

The Association of Business Executives (ABE)
2003 sees ABE celebrate its 30th anniversary. Today, ABE has become a market leader in the cost-effective delivery of quality assured British management education.
The primary objective of ABE, a non-profit making organisation, is to ensure that students successfully completing its examinations will accquire the knowledge and skills needed in order to become more effective managers. ABE's awards are recognised internationally as an accepted route into the later stages of UK and overseas first degrees, professional qualifications and MBA and other Masters programmes. The provision of CD-ROM study Manuals further reduces costs for students who receive tutor support from colleges accredited by ABE.
Membership is available to both UK and overseas students and examinations are conducted twice a year worldwide.
86

BCG Consultancy
Innovative approaches to Management Supervisory and Trainer development.
91

Birkbeck, University of London
University level part-time evening courses in central London.
92

BMB Management Training Consultants
Providers of quality training programmes for all levels of management.
93

Breakthrough Management Training Ltd
Breakthrough Management Training. Measurably different, measurably better.
94

IT

RCMS Ltd
RCMS Ltd have been providing IT training for ten years.
244

Reading Adult and Community College
General adult education and tailor-made courses in many subjects.
244

Refractories & Building Products Training Council
The NTO provides cost effective services to its member companies.
245

Rigdemond Park Training & Conference Centre
Commercial and industrial staff development on and off the job.
247

University of Salford
Education, training, research, continuing professional development, for industry and commerce.
250

University of St Andrews
260

Stehle Associates
Award winning training from Stehle Associates. We offer a complete training service, including public and in-house courses, project facilitation and consultancy for all levels of staff from senior management to new hires. Our expertise covers Information Systems Development, Project Management, Management and Leadership skills, Interpersonal skills, and Customer Service. For in-house programmes we work closely with our clients to agree the required outcomes and preferred delivery methods. Then we tailor materials from our extensive course portfolio to provide innovative training solutions which match the requirements exactly. To ensure that learning is successful we provide follow-up facilitation and consultancy to reinforce in the workplace these newly acquired skills. All our training is focused on equipping staff with the essential skills required in their job role, and on providing cost-effective results. Whatever the content or duration of our programmes we aim to achieve capabilities which can be applied immediately the training is completed and which can be transferred to new roles as staff develop. We are accredited by the Institute of IT Training as a Gold Standard training provider and abide by their code of practice.
262

Stephen M Hall & Associates Ltd
The management consultants that help your managers and business grow.
262

University of Strathclyde
The University aims to be a place of useful learning.
266

Suffolk College
The largest provider of education and training in Suffolk.
267

Tatum's Word
Computer software training, leading software applications.
270

Thanet Community Learning Centre
Provision of text and computer-based self study courses.
272

Training Opportunities
Quality training for busy people. Learn online or on site.
276

WSC Ltd
Trainers and training room for hire for computer training.
288

Ystrad Mynach College
Tailor-made and off the shelf programmes to suit all employers.
289

Legal

Blyth Associates
Training in employment, contract, pensions, law and litigation support services.

92

Chelmsford College
We serve Essex in providing professional training for adults.

116

The IEE
Your people are your most precious asset – and with the right professional guidance, you can develop their skills and abilities. The result? Enhanced individual performance – plus measurable improvements to your bottom line.
The IEE (Institution of Electrical Engineers) is one of the UK's leaders in management and business training for professionals involved with electrical engineering, IT and electronic engineering. We offer an impressive portfolio of courses for newly qualified and experienced professionals, from careers and business skills through to effective management, negotiating, presentations, marketing – plus a wide range of more technical courses.
With over 130,000 members worldwide, the IEE is a global organisation representing the interests of IT and electrical engineering professionals - though our courses are equally applicable to other industries and commercial sectors. Most of our programmes are held in London, though we can run them at your premises, for small or large groups.
For more information about how IEE management and business training can bring out the best in your people - and your organisation - call us on 01438 767237 or log on to www.iee.org.uk

162

Irenicon Ltd
Specialist employment law consultancy and training.

178

Optimum Training Ltd
Health and safety training for companies plus licencing packages for trainers.

220

Office & secretarial

Cambridge International College
CIC conducts Diploma Programmes on a wide range of accounting, sales business, management and administration fields, as well as 'support' subjects like Business English & Letter Writing, Communications and Computers, one or more of which are often essential for Members' progress and success in their chosen careers.
All of CIC's Diploma Programmes are designed and written especially for career enhancement and development. The professional Diploma Programmes have proved outstandingly successful in achieving those objectives – as well as the goals and ambitions of the hundreds of thousands of Member who study with CIC.
As appropriate, Diploma Programmes start either from basic principles or with a revision of earlier studies, and then deal comprehensively with the important topics, with emphasis always on the practical application of what is taught.

105

Chelmsford College
We serve Essex in providing professional training for adults.

116

Circa Ltd
Meeting employer and learner needs through flexible work based learning.

118

Colchester Institute
College of further and higher education including services to business.

121

Crown College
Crown specialise in information technology, customer services, retail administrative management.

128

Damar Training Solutions
Effective training solutions for business. Money-back guarantee service.

129

Elmwood Business Training
Elmwood Business Training provider of quality training courses and consultancies.

140

The Institute of Administrative Management
Established in 1915, the Institute of Administrative Management is the leading Professional Body for both practising and aspiring Administrative Managers.
We can work with you to produce an internationally recognised, in-house qualification, validate your training programmes or provide our training to your employees, in house or through our provider network.

Qualifications
IAM qualifications are targeted at Supervisors, Managers, and those who aspire to these positions. Student members can progress through the Certificate, Diploma and Advanced Diploma, and on to further qualifications (such as the IAM's dedicated degree in Administrative Management) and membership of other professional institutes

168

Interactive Training Management Ltd
Training available in ECDL, IBT2, Clait, NVQs, Administration & Customer Service.

175

Parity Training Ltd
Parity Training delivers bespoke and public scheduled training courses in technology, management and business skills, providing training for over 40,000 delegates a year. Parity's learning consultants increasingly blend traditional training methods with e-learning initiatives to provide integrated learning solutions that ensure return on investment and effective learning outcomes.
With training centres in Antrim, Belfast, Birmingham, Bristol, Edinburgh, Fleet, Leeds, London and Manchester, Parity offers nation-wide in person (classroom based) training and support. Additionally, Parity's managed services offering provides a range of options from simple vendor management to a full outsource training and development service.
Parity's long-term partnerships with leading bodies such as the Information Systems Examination Board, DSDM Consortium, Institute of Management, Outward Bound Trust, Association for Project Management, Microsoft and Lotus Corporation keeps Parity at the forefront of the industry, able to offer an unparalleled range of certified training leading to recognised qualifications. Parity's on-going commitment to delivering effective quality training is reflected in its ISO9001 certification. In 2003 Parity Training was awarded the Instituted of IT Training's accolade of Training Company of the Year and Trainer of the Year.
Parity Training is part of Parity Group plc, the international IT consultancy and solutions group with 30 offices in the UK, mainland Europe and the USA.
For booking information or course details, call 0800 656 100, email training@parity.net or visit www.parity.net.

224

Pitman Training
Helping to provide training solutions for all your office needs.

231

Qualifications for Industry Ltd
An awarding body accredited to award NVQs/ SVQs and vocational qualifications.

242

Rigdemond Park Training & Conference Centre
Commercial and industrial staff development on and off the job.

247

Outsourcing

The Institute of Administrative Management
Established in 1915, the Institute of Administrative Management is the leading Professional Body for both practising and aspiring Administrative Managers.
We can work with you to produce an internationally recognised, in-house qualification, validate your training programmes or provide our training to your employees, in house or through our provider network.

Qualifications
IAM qualifications are targeted at Supervisors, Managers, and those who aspire to these positions. Student members can progress through the Certificate, Diploma and Advanced Diploma, and on to further qualifications (such as the IAM's dedicated degree in Administrative Management) and membership of other professional institutes

168

The Learning Corporation LLP
Optimising business performance through facilitation, coaching and advisory skills.

193

Parity Training Ltd
Parity Training delivers bespoke and public scheduled training courses in technology, management and business skills, providing training for over 40,000 delegates a year. Parity's learning consultants increasingly blend traditional training methods with e-learning initiatives to provide integrated learning solutions that ensure return on investment and effective learning outcomes.
With training centres in Antrim, Belfast, Birmingham, Bristol, Edinburgh, Fleet, Leeds, London and Manchester, Parity offers nation-wide in person (classroom based) training and support.
Additionally, Parity's managed services offering provides a range of options from simple vendor management to a full outsource training and development service.
Parity's long-term partnerships with leading bodies such as the Information Systems Examination Board, DSDM Consortium, Institute of Management, Outward Bound Trust, Association for Project Management, Microsoft and Lotus Corporation keeps Parity at the forefront of the industry, able to offer an unparalleled range of certified training leading to recognised qualifications. Parity's on-going commitment to delivering effective quality training is reflected in its ISO9001 certification. In 2003 Parity Training was awarded the Institued of IT Training's accolade of Training Company of the Year and Trainer of the Year.
Parity Training is part of Parity Group plc, the international IT consultancy and solutions group with 30 offices in the UK, mainland Europe and the USA.
For booking information or course details, call 0800 656 100, email training@parity.net or visit www.parity.net.

224

Production & process control

Aurora Business Development Ltd
International business and manufacturing educators, trainers and consultants.

89

B J O'Connor International Ltd
Multilingual international consulting training company proven techniques in profits increase.

92

COTU, Charter House

125

Effective Personnel Development (EPD)
Provision of consultancy and training on quality and process improvement.

138

FLAG Business Solutions
Multi-disciplinary business support organisation offering consultancy/training.
147

Horwood International Ltd
ISO 9001 registered. Member IMC/BQF/MCI. Specialise in Business Excellence Model.
158

Inplant Industrial Training
Coaching and support services for trainers of technical/production staff.
165

The Institute of Administrative Management
Established in 1915, the Institute of Administrative Management is the leading Professional Body for both practising and aspiring Administrative Managers.
We can work with you to produce an internationally recognised, in-house qualification, validate your training programmes or provide our training to your employees, in house or through our provider network.
Qualifications
IAM qualifications are targeted at Supervisors, Managers, and those who aspire to these positions. Student members can progress through the Certificate, Diploma and Advanced Diploma, and on to further qualifications (such as the IAM's dedicated degree in Administrative Management) and membership of other professional institutes
168

James Miles Consultants
Customer focused tailored training: improving processes, cycle time-flexibility-quality-cost.
180

Management Improvements Ltd
Process improvement and re-engineering training for banks and insurance companies.
201

Morcamation Management & Training Consultants
Strategic business/marketing planning, quality management ISO000/TQM, managing change.
210

Myrick Training Services
Engineering management, supervisory health and safety, quality NVQs, short courses.
212

OPD Diagnostic Solutions
Flexible tailormade solutions for improving business results through development workshops.
218

Osmec Technology Management
Osmec provides automation, electrical engineering, electrical safety and regulations training.
220

Peter Allatt Associates
Helping clients to be more effective and achieve their aims.
229

Polymer Training Limited
Training and business development training for the polymer industry.
233

Scottish Association of Master Bakers
Awarding body and training provider for craft baking vocational qualifications.
254

Scottish Bakery Training Council
National training organisation for the Scottish baking industry.
254

Statistics for Industry Ltd
Practical statistical courses/consultancy aimed at scientists/technologists in industry.
261

Stonebow
Training, consultancy and management development for the hospitality industry.
265

Trubody Training Associates
In-company courses in manufacturing systems, quality techniques and lean manufacturing.
279

Wakefield Skillcentre
A leading provider of training services to industry and individuals.
283

Woodcote Technical Services
Bespoke technical training for manufacturing companies including providing illustrated materials.
286

Property, construction & facilities

Architecture & Surveying Institute
ASI is the multi-disciplinary institute for professionals in construction.

84

The Chartered Institute of Building
The Chartered Institute of Building is a modern professional body with more than 40,000 members. It has a Royal Charter to promote the science and practice of construction for public benefit, and has won recognition from Government, other professional bodies and the industry itself as being the central voice in construction. It provides expertise in all aspects of construction management, giving advice of a legal and technical nature, and sets standards in areas such as education, and health and safety.
In the past year, the Institute has made many valuable contributions to the development and improvement of the construction industry. These have included the production and implementation of a New Education Framework and a Health and Safety Action Plan, the launch of the Third Edition of Practice for Project Management, our merger with the Architectural and Surveying Institute and numerous research and innovation projects. The CIOB has also recently launched an 'Improving Site Conditions' campaign: 'Change in our Sites', in line with the aims and key issues for the industry that have been identified by the Strategic Forum for Construction.

112

Confederation of Tourism, Hotel & Catering Management
Training in hotel, tourism, catering and travel agency management.

123

Health & Safety Services Ltd
Health, safety and fire training, consultancy support. Established 1985.

156

The IEE
Your people are your most precious asset – and with the right professional guidance, you can develop their skills and abilities. The result? Enhanced individual performance – plus measurable improvements to your bottom line.
The IEE (Institution of Electrical Engineers) is one of the UK's leaders in management and business training for professionals involved with electrical engineering, IT and electronic engineering. We offer an impressive portfolio of courses for newly qualified and experienced professionals, from careers and business skills through to effective management, negotiating, presentations, marketing – plus a wide range of more technical courses.
With over 130, 000 members worldwide, the IEE is a global organisation representing the interests of IT and electrical engineering professionals - though our courses are equally applicable to other industries and commercial sectors. Most of our programmes are held in London, though we can run them at your premises, for small or large groups.
For more information about how IEE management and business training can bring out the best in your people - and your organisation - call us on 01438 767237 or log on to www.iee.org.uk

162

The Institute of Administrative Management
Established in 1915, the Institute of Administrative Management is the leading Professional Body for both practising and aspiring Administrative Managers.

We can work with you to produce an internationally recognised, in-house qualification, validate your training programmes or provide our training to your employees, in house or through our provider network.

Qualifications
IAM qualifications are targeted at Supervisors, Managers, and those who aspire to these positions. Student members can progress through the Certificate, Diploma and Advanced Diploma, and on to further qualifications (such as the IAM's dedicated degree in Administrative Management) and membership of other professional institutes

168

PSNTO (Property Services National Training Organisation)

239

Quadrilect
Training courses for the British Institute of Facilities management.
242

The Royal Agricultural College
Providing excellence in education/training at undergraduate and postgraduate level.
249

System Concepts Ltd
Specialists in office and industrial ergonomics and health and safety.
269

WTI Training Group
Open courses, customised and on site training.
288

Sales & marketing

Adaptation Ltd
Adaptation helps people exploit knowledge, manage change and win business.
78

Alan Weaver Associates
Specialist seminars on subscription marketing techniques for the publishing industry.
81

Answers (Research) Ltd
Marketing training for the intensively competitive 21st century provided.
82

Avon Management Services
Management consultancy, sales and marketing consultancy and training.
89

Bristol Business School
Provides a supportive and well-resourced learning environment, officially rated excellent by the Higher Education Funding Council for England.
96

British Shops & Stores Association Ltd
Retail selling, buying and management courses, books and distance learning.
98

Business Skills Agency
Business skills training: computer, management, sales, marketing, personal development.
103

BWD Partnership
Providers of tailored training programmes in sales and marketing.
104

Cambridge International College
CIC conducts Diploma Programmes on a wide range of accounting, sales business, management and administration fields, as well as 'support' subjects like Business English & Letter Writing, Communications and Computers, one or more of which are often essential for Members' progress and success in their chosen careers.
All of CIC's Diploma Programmes are designed and written especially for career enhancement and development. The professional Diploma Programmes have proved outstandingly successful in achieving those objectives – as well as the goals and ambitions of the hundreds of thousands of Member who study with CIC.
As appropriate, Diploma Programmes start either from basic principles or with a revision of earlier studies, and then deal comprehensively with the important topics, with emphasis always on the practical application of what is taught.
105

Catalyst Training & Development Ltd
Organisational and management development and sales and marketing training.
108

CJN Management Consultancy
Team development covering sales management, international marketing, marketing, major accounts.
119

Supply chain & distribution

Qualifications for Industry Ltd
An awarding body accredited to award NVQs/SVQs and vocational qualifications.
242

The School of Management
A full service business school offering world class products.
252

South Nottingham College
Specialists in multi-media, printing, business, computing, management, TUC education, NVQs.
258

Speakers International Corporate Development Ltd
World class peak performance coaching for quality organisations.
259

Survey Force Ltd
Survey Force is a well established experience provider of marketing training.
269

Part 2.3

Organisational Skills

Change management

Aberdeen Business School
We provide high quality education training and consultancy programmes.
75

Acacia-IPS Ltd
IT-business courses and coaching from business analysis to information management.
76

Action Development Group
Action Development Group for your organisation and people development needs.
78

Adaptation Ltd
Adaptation helps people exploit knowledge, manage change and win business.
78

AdVal Group Plc
AdVal is a highly successful learning and business services group.
79

ADVANCE: Management Training Ltd
Bringing the future into your company through internationalisation, organisational transformation.
79

ALA International Ltd
We use action learning to help you help yourselves.
81

Alan Weaver Associates
Specialist seminars on subscription marketing techniques for the publishing industry.
81

Barry Herd Associates
Your results orientated interpersonal skills management and organisational development partner.
91

B J O'Connor International Ltd
Multilingual international consulting training company proven techniques in profits increase.
92

Bowles Development Group
Team building and OMD close to London. ISO 9001 approved.
93

Bridge
Bridge offers unique approaches in leadership development and organisational transformation.
95

Brinsbury College
Brinsbury land-based training. The West Sussex College of the countryside.
95

Bruce Nixon AssociatesConsultants in Organisation Transformation and Learning
Helping leaders create better and more successful workplaces and contribute to a fairer and sustainable world. Bruce Nixon is also the author of 'Making a Difference' and 'Global Forces'.
99

Career Counselling Services
Best practice providers of training in counselling and career counselling.
107

Catalyst Training & Development Ltd
Organisational and management development and sales and marketing training.
108

Change Dynamics
Human resource development assessment and training.
111

Change Matters
Leadership, organisational and personal development to public and private sector.
112

Integration International
Outstanding Personal leader, Team, Organisational and International Business Development.
175

i to i Training & Development
Identification of needs to design and delivery of bespoke training.
179

J B Computer Management
JBCM provides HR organisation development programmes for individual and corporate.
182

John Unitt Associates
Career management, counselling, outplacement job search, stress, supervisory, customer care.
185

Jon Spencer Training & Consultancy
Management skills, managing change, training and facilitation.
185

The King Partnership Ltd
Support for management in education related activity, UK and overseas.
189

Lakeside Management Development
Lakeside Corporate – one of Britain's leading experiential training providers.
191

Les Jones & Associates
Training and consultancy in management of change and creative management.
195

Lindley Training
Bespoke change programmes developing individuals, teams, leaders and organisational cultures.
196

Marwel & Co
Specialists in realising the potential of organisations and their people.
204

MRA International
The development of organisations and their people.
211

Oxford Communications Group
Business strategy, dynamic organisation improvement, investors in people. Specialists established in 1984.
222

The Oxford Group, Consulting and Training
Provide world-class training and consultancy – deliver solutions and measurable results.
222

Oxford Management Consultants
Change management, client centre consulting and influencing skills training programmes.
223

Parity Training Ltd
Parity Training delivers bespoke and public scheduled training courses in technology, management and business skills, providing training for over 40,000 delegates a year. Parity's learning consultants increasingly blend traditional training methods with e-learning initiatives to provide integrated learning solutions that ensure return on investment and effective learning outcomes.
With training centres in Antrim, Belfast, Birmingham, Bristol, Edinburgh, Fleet, Leeds, London and Manchester, Parity offers nation-wide in person (classroom based) training and support. Additionally, Parity's managed services offering provides a range of options from simple vendor management to a full outsource training and development service.
Parity's long-term partnerships with leading bodies such as the Information Systems Examination Board, DSDM Consortium, Institute of Management, Outward Bound Trust, Association for Project Management, Microsoft and Lotus Corporation keeps Parity at the forefront of the industry, able to offer an unparalleled range of certified training leading to recognised qualifications. Parity's on-going commitment to delivering effective quality training is reflected in its ISO9001 certification. In 2003 Parity Training was awarded the Institued of IT Training's accolade of Training Company of the Year and Trainer of the Year.
Parity Training is part of Parity Group plc, the international IT consultancy and solutions group with 30 offices in the UK, mainland Europe and the USA. For booking information or course details, call 0800 656 100, email training@parity.net or visit www.parity.net.
224

Crisis & disaster management

Association of British Professional Conference Organisers
ABPCO runs training courses on conferences-industry related topics.
85

Centrex National Training Centre
110

The Chartered Institute of Building
The Chartered Institute of Building is a modern professional body with more than 40,000 members. It has a Royal Charter to promote the science and practice of construction for public benefit, and has won recognition from Government, other professional bodies and the industry itself as being the central voice in construction. It provides expertise in all aspects of construction management, giving advice of a legal and technical nature, and sets standards in areas such as education, and health and safety. In the past year, the Institute has made many valuable contributions to the development and improvement of the construction industry. These have included the production and implementation of a New Education Framework and a Health and Safety Action Plan, the launch of the Third Edition of Practice for Project Management, our merger with the Architectural and Surveying Institute and numerous research and innovation projects. The CIOB has also recently launched an 'Improving Site Conditions' campaign: 'Change in our Sites', in line with the aims and key issues for the industry that have been identified by the Strategic Forum for Construction.
112

Corporate Capabilities Ltd
Training and development for project capability improvement.
125

Videotel
Training videos and CD-Roms producers specialising in safety subjects.
282

Customer service

ACADEMEE
Provider of IM accredited management and professional e-learning certificates.
77

Action Development Group
Action Development Group for your organisation and people development needs.
78

Alan Weaver Associates
Specialist seminars on subscription marketing techniques for the publishing industry.
81

Bernard Wynne Associates
Management and people development provided in company in all sectors.
91

The British Institute of Innkeeping
The professional institute/awarding body for the licensed retail sector.
96

Business Network Ltd
Business consultancy and training.
Customer care, TQM, information technology, management.
102

Conflict Management Plus
Conflict Management Plus Ltd are national experts in providing solutions to workplace conflicts. We have over 10 years' experience providing accredited training and running a dispute resolution service. We work with full-time trainers and specialist consultants who bring expertise and experience from a range of public and private sector backgrounds. We have clear guidelines on equal opportunities, which run throughout our training design and delivery.

We can:

- Resolve workplace disputes between colleagues and teams
- Divert harassment and bullying cases away from disciplinaries/tribunals
- Carry out independent investigations
- Coach your teams or key players to improve performance
- Sample Training Programmes
- Certificate in Mediation Skills and Practice. A six-day course leading to OCR accreditation
- Core Mediation Skills- two-day introductory course leading to OCR accreditation
- Assertiveness
- Complaints
- Conflict management skills for HR
- Constructive conflict management for managers
- Contact officers training
- Training for Colleague Support Networks
- Managing bullying and harassment
- Investigator skills training
- Managing difficult behaviour, aggression and threats of violence
- Mediation diploma – OCR qualification in mediation practice
- Mediation and counselling skills in the workplace
- Phone rage
- Win-win negotiation

124

Crown College
Crown specialise in information technology, customer services, retail administrative management.

128

Davies Training Services
Focused in-company training which develops your managers' competences.

130

EFE International Ltd
Business culture, country, export/import, industry briefings. Regions: Europe, Asia.

138

Elmwood Business Training
Elmwood Business Training provider of quality training courses and consultancies.

140

Gateway Television Productions

150

Groom House Holdings Ltd
Behavioural training to produce lost for words customer satisfaction.

153

GW Resources
Independent advice, training products and services. Specialising in Learning Centres.

154

Harley McKenzie
Management and sales training - total solutions.

155

Heriot-Watt University
A research-led technological university with outstanding success in academic-industrial collaboration.

157

Host Computer Services Ltd
Residential training facility providing hardware training for computer service technicians.

159

Insight Marketing and People Ltd
Providers of sales, marketing, interpersonal, finance and business development worldwide.

166

Intech Training Group Ltd
In-company/open courses in sales, marketing, management and customer care.

174

Interactive Training Management Ltd
Training available in ECDL, IBT2, Clait, NVQs, Administration & Customer Service.

175

The Key Network
Outdoor development, team building, leadership and management development programmes UK wide.
188

Lindley Training
Bespoke change programmes developing individuals, teams, leaders and organisational cultures.
196

Link Training
Link provide training NVQ, retail warehouse, administration and customer service.
197

McKenzie-Thorpe
Innovative training solutions within selling, customer service and account management.
204

Merlin Management Services
Improving business performance and profitability by developing your human assets.
206

Milton Keynes College
Largest provider of further education and training in North Bucks.
208

MLP Training
Sales training and management development, live courses and cds.
209

MSB (Managing the Service Business)
Improving business performance by providing customer service excellence through training.
211

The National Extension College
A leading provider of flexible open learning training resources.
213

Open Mind Training
Effective people through effective training and focused in-company workshops.
219

Parity Training Ltd
Parity Training delivers bespoke and public scheduled training courses in technology, management and business skills, providing training for over 40,000 delegates a year. Parity's learning consultants increasingly blend traditional training methods with e-learning initiatives to provide integrated learning solutions that ensure return on investment and effective learning outcomes.
With training centres in Antrim, Belfast, Birmingham, Bristol, Edinburgh, Fleet, Leeds, London and Manchester, Parity offers nation-wide in person (classroom based) training and support. Additionally, Parity's managed services offering provides a range of options from simple vendor management to a full outsource training and development service.
Parity's long-term partnerships with leading bodies such as the Information Systems Examination Board, DSDM Consortium, Institute of Management, Outward Bound Trust, Association for Project Management, Microsoft and Lotus Corporation keeps Parity at the forefront of the industry, able to offer an unparalleled range of certified training leading to recognised qualifications. Parity's on-going commitment to delivering effective quality training is reflected in its ISO9001 certification. In 2003 Parity Training was awarded the Instituted of IT Training's accolade of Training Company of the Year and Trainer of the Year.
Parity Training is part of Parity Group plc, the international IT consultancy and solutions group with 30 offices in the UK, mainland Europe and the USA.
For booking information or course details, call 0800 656 100, email training@parity.net or visit www.parity.net.
224

Personnel Management Advisory Services
Professional (chartered), established 1967. Firms offered most aspects, flexibly, confidentially.
229

Proceptor Training & Consultancy
Psychometric testing for recruitment. Negotiation skills for buyers.
236

Diversity/ Equal Opportunities

and a Health and Safety Action Plan, the launch of the Third Edition of Practice for Project Management, our merger with the Architectural and Surveying Institute and numerous research and innovation projects. The CIOB has also recently launched an 'Improving Site Conditions' campaign: 'Change in our Sites', in line with the aims and key issues for the industry that have been identified by the Strategic Forum for Construction.

112

Conflict Management Plus

Conflict Management Plus Ltd are national experts in providing solutions to workplace conflicts. We have over 10 years' experience providing accredited training and running a dispute resolution service. We work with full-time trainers and specialist consultants who bring expertise and experience from a range of public and private sector backgrounds. We have clear guidelines on equal opportunities, which run throughout our training design and delivery.

We can:

- Resolve workplace disputes between colleagues and teams
- Divert harassment and bullying cases away from disciplinaries/tribunals
- Carry out independent investigations
- Coach your teams or key players to improve performance
- Sample Training Programmes
- Certificate in Mediation Skills and Practice. A six-day course leading to OCR accreditation
- Core Mediation Skills- two-day introductory course leading to OCR accreditation
- Assertiveness
- Complaints
- Conflict management skills for HR
- Constructive conflict management for managers
- Contact officers training
- Training for Colleague Support Networks
- Managing bullying and harassment
- Investigator skills training
- Managing difficult behaviour, aggression and threats of violence
- Mediation diploma – OCR qualification in mediation practice
- Mediation and counselling skills in the workplace
- Phone rage
- Win-win negotiation

124

Development Resources Ltd

Management and training consultancy specialising in people skills-development.

132

Equal Opportunities Consultancy Group

Consultancy and applied research services on equality and diversity issues.

141

Finchale Training College

Residential vocational rehabilitation to assist disabled people back to work.

147

Irenicon Ltd

Specialist employment law consultancy and training.

178

IRS Conferences & Training

IRS offers 30 years excellence in employment law training.

178

Secker Training & Development

Coaching and distance learning on equality issues for senior professionals.

255

Health & safety

Aberdeen College

Academic and practical health and safety training and consultancy work.

75

ALA International Ltd

We use action learning to help you help yourselves.

81

Induction

Information systems

Acacia-IPS Ltd
IT-business courses and coaching from business analysis to information management.
76

The Advisory Unit: Computers in Education
ICT training and consultancy for teachers, educators and managers.
80

Aris Education Ltd
Aris Education is a leading provider of blended training solutions.
84

British Institute of Technology & E-commerce
BITE is developing e-commerce professionals for all sectors of industry.
97

Computacenter Ltd
Computacenter offer complete IT training solutions delivering real business benefits.
122

Delta Computer Training Ltd
Training and consultancy for IT professionals and computer users.
131

Information Automation Ltd
Tailored training in CD-ROM, online, internet resources and searching.
165

The Institute of Administrative Management
Established in 1915, the Institute of Administrative Management is the leading Professional Body for both practising and aspiring Administrative Managers.
We can work with you to produce an internationally recognised, in-house qualification, validate your training programmes or provide our training to your employees, in house or through our provider network.

Qualifications
IAM qualifications are targeted at Supervisors, Managers, and those who aspire to these positions. Student members can progress through the Certificate, Diploma and Advanced Diploma, and on to further qualifications (such as the IAM's dedicated degree in Administrative Management) and membership of other professional institutes
168

Liverpool Business School
Liverpool Business School for all your training needs.
197

Parity Training Ltd
Parity Training delivers bespoke and public scheduled training courses in technology, management and business skills, providing training for over 40,000 delegates a year. Parity's learning consultants increasingly blend traditional training methods with e-learning initiatives to provide integrated learning solutions that ensure return on investment and effective learning outcomes.
With training centres in Antrim, Belfast, Birmingham, Bristol, Edinburgh, Fleet, Leeds, London and Manchester, Parity offers nation-wide in person (classroom based) training and support. Additionally, Parity's managed services offering provides a range of options from simple vendor management to a full outsource training and development service.
Parity's long-term partnerships with leading bodies such as the Information Systems Examination Board, DSDM Consortium, Institute of Management, Outward Bound Trust, Association for Project Management, Microsoft and Lotus Corporation keeps Parity at the forefront of the industry, able to offer an unparalleled range of certified training leading to recognised qualifications. Parity's on-going commitment to delivering effective quality training is reflected in its ISO9001 certification. In 2003 Parity Training was awarded the Instituted of IT Training's accolade of Training Company of the Year and Trainer of the Year.
Parity Training is part of Parity Group plc, the international IT consultancy and solutions group with 30 offices in the UK, mainland Europe and the USA. For booking information or course details, call 0800 656 100, email training@parity.net or visit www.parity.net.
224

Pitman Training
Helping to provide training solutions for all your office needs.

231

Stehle Associates
Award winning training from Stehle Associates. We offer a complete training service, including public and in-house courses, project facilitation and consultancy for all levels of staff from senior management to new hires. Our expertise covers Information Systems Development, Project Management, Management and Leadership skills, Interpersonal skills, and Customer Service. For in-house programmes we work closely with our clients to agree the required outcomes and preferred delivery methods. Then we tailor materials from our extensive course portfolio to provide innovative training solutions which match the requirements exactly. To ensure that learning is successful we provide follow-up facilitation and consultancy to reinforce in the workplace these newly acquired skills. All our training is focused on equipping staff with the essential skills required in their job role, and on providing cost-effective results. Whatever the content or duration of our programmes we aim to achieve capabilities which can be applied immediately the training is completed and which can be transferred to new roles as staff develop. We are accredited by the Institute of IT Training as a Gold Standard training provider and abide by their code of practice.

262

University of Sunderland

267

Innovation

Acacia-IPS Ltd
IT-business courses and coaching from business analysis to information management.

76

Business Development, University of Luton
Diverse range of services and practical training solutions for organisations.

101

The Chartered Institute of Building
The Chartered Institute of Building is a modern professional body with more than 40,000 members. It has a Royal Charter to promote the science and practice of construction for public benefit, and has won recognition from Government, other professional bodies and the industry itself as being the central voice in construction. It provides expertise in all aspects of construction management, giving advice of a legal and technical nature, and sets standards in areas such as education, and health and safety.
In the past year, the Institute has made many valuable contributions to the development and improvement of the construction industry. These have included the production and implementation of a New Education Framework and a Health and Safety Action Plan, the launch of the Third Edition of Practice for Project Management, our merger with the Architectural and Surveying Institute and numerous research and innovation projects. The CIOB has also recently launched an 'Improving Site Conditions' campaign: 'Change in our Sites', in line with the aims and key issues for the industry that have been identified by the Strategic Forum for Construction.

112

CMC Consultants
Facilitation and coaching developing strategic team capability for change leadership.

120

The Inspiration Network
An HR consultancy specialising in creative and inspiring learning solutions.

166

MagNotes Ltd
Visual thinking tools for creativity and innovation.

200

Strategy Workshop Facilitators Limited
Professional facilitators of Strategic Thinking, Innovation and Decision Making processes.

266

Knowledge management

Acacia-IPS Ltd
IT-business courses and coaching from business analysis to information management.
76

Adaptation Ltd
Adaptation helps people exploit knowledge, manage change and win business.
78

ADVANCE: Management Training Ltd
Bringing the future into your company through internationalisation, organisational transformation.
79

Expert Training Systems Plc
ETS management simulations develop managers' knowledge skills and business awareness.
146

Gatleyhall & Co Ltd
A revolutionary approach to enhance performance for success and fulfilment.
151

Inspiration Resources
Tools and techniques for creativity and innovation.
167

Leadership Resources Limited
192

Marwel & Co
Specialists in realising the potential of organisations and their people.
204

Parity Training Ltd
Parity Training delivers bespoke and public scheduled training courses in technology, management and business skills, providing training for over 40,000 delegates a year. Parity's learning consultants increasingly blend traditional training methods with e-learning initiatives to provide integrated learning solutions that ensure return on investment and effective learning outcomes.
With training centres in Antrim, Belfast, Birmingham, Bristol, Edinburgh, Fleet, Leeds, London and Manchester, Parity offers nation-wide in person (classroom based) training and support. Additionally, Parity's managed services offering provides a range of options from simple vendor management to a full outsource training and development service.
Parity's long-term partnerships with leading bodies such as the Information Systems Examination Board, DSDM Consortium, Institute of Management, Outward Bound Trust, Association for Project Management, Microsoft and Lotus Corporation keeps Parity at the forefront of the industry, able to offer an unparalleled range of certified training leading to recognised qualifications. Parity's on-going commitment to delivering effective quality training is reflected in its ISO9001 certification. In 2003 Parity Training was awarded the Institued of IT Training's accolade of Training Company of the Year and Trainer of the Year.
Parity Training is part of Parity Group plc, the international IT consultancy and solutions group with 30 offices in the UK, mainland Europe and the USA.
For booking information or course details, call 0800 656 100, email training@parity.net or visit www.parity.net.
224

Quintilian Training Ltd
IT and telecommunications training.
243

Management development

The Chartered Institute of Building
The Chartered Institute of Building is a modern professional body with more than 40,000 members. It has a Royal Charter to promote the science and practice of construction for public benefit, and has won recognition from Government, other professional bodies and the industry itself as being the central voice in construction. It provides expertise in all aspects of construction management, giving advice of a legal and technical nature, and sets standards in areas such as education, and health and safety.
In the past year, the Institute has made many valuable contributions to the development and improvement of the construction industry. These have included the production and implementation of a New Education Framework and a Health and Safety Action Plan, the launch of the Third Edition of Practice for Project Management, our merger with the Architectural and Surveying Institute and numerous research and innovation projects. The CIOB has also recently launched an 'Improving Site Conditions' campaign: 'Change in our Sites', in line with the aims and key issues for the industry that have been identified by the Strategic Forum for Construction.
112

Chartered Management Institute
Chartered Management Institute shapes and supports the managers of tomorrow.
114

Chris James Management Consultancy
Investors in People, organisation development, management development, management training.
116

Chrysalis
Management consultancy experienced in organisational development, competence based management development.
117

CJN Management Consultancy
Team development covering sales management, international marketing, marketing, major accounts.
119

Comtech Associates
HRD, management, training and development, trainer training, organisational performance systems.
122

Corporate Capabilities Ltd
Training and development for project capability improvement.
125

COTU, Charter House
125

Cranfield School of Management
One of the world's major international business schools.
126

CRG Research Consultancy & Training
Research, consultancy, training solutions addressing clients' strategic and policy challenges.
127

Cygnet Business Development Ltd
Management and organisational development consultancy specialising in developing leader-managers.
128

Damar Training Solutions
Effective training solutions for business. Money-back guarantee service.
129

David A Palmer
Totally tailored financial management development programmes to enhance corporate profitability.
129

David Barron Associates
Independent practitioners and trainers on employment, training and management development.
129

Davies Training Services
Focused in-company training which develops your managers' competences.
130

Development Dimensions International (DDI) UK
DDI: global HR consultancy specialists in leadership, selection, executive development.
132

Development Resources Ltd
Management and training consultancy specialising in people skills-development.
132

D J Neil Ltd
Design and delivery of in-house management training UK and overseas.
133

Dove Nest Group
We deliver effective behavioural change programmes for business success.
134

EAP European School of Management
Specialists in cross border management development programmes.
135

Electrovision UK Ltd
500+ stocked products in skills, applications, and professional IT training.
138

Elements
Facilitation and consultancy skills training for managers and consultants.
138

Elgood Effective Learning
Engaging materials, management games and business simulaitons to improve performance.
139

Elm Training/Publications
Customised negotiation training for managers and professionals, UK and overseas.
139

Enhancement Resources Ltd
A company focused on realising the potential of people and organisations.
140

Equals
Providers of individual solutions for personal, career and business management.
142

Equaville Ltd – Training Services
Speaking. Media. Interviewing. Meetings. Reports. Assertiveness. Supervision. Leadership. Negotiating etc.
142

Excel Communications (HRD) Ltd
Specialists in applying NLP to produce outstanding business results.
145

University of Exeter
Management development programmes at Exeter short courses to masters awards.
145

Fast Forward
Practical training and assessment services to boost skills and profitability.
146

Financial Management Development
Totally tailored financial management development programmes to enhance corporate profitability.
147

Flexible Learning Solutions
Specialists in flexible learning. Supply and develop multi-media training packages.
148

Force One Training Ltd
IT and transport related training and LearnDirect centre.
148

Frank Daniels Associates Ltd
NLP specialists solve problems, develop people, and gain more choice.
149

FT Knowledge
FT Knowledge is the world's leading provider of business education.
149

Gateshead College
High quality training and development. Customised to your particular needs.
150

Gatleyhall & Co Ltd
A revolutionary approach to enhance performance for success and fulfilment.
151

Glenn Ross Services
Customised training to your company culture and market place.
152

Grass Routes Management Development and Consultancy Ltd
Specialists in behavioural and attitudinal change through training and consultancy.
153

Institute of Leadership & Management
Institute of Leadership & Management (ILM) offers membership services together with leadership and management qualifications. ILM is a professional body that supports national objectives to ensure the UK is able to develop leaders and managers of the future, with a particular focus on first line and middle levels. Offering qualifcations for managers and team leaders from Levels 2-5 of the national framework, ILM also supports individual and organisational development through endorsement, awards and learning resources. ILM is a subsidiary of the City & Guilds Group, the UK's largest provider of vocational qualifications.
We provide the following services:
Membership, Vocationally-Related Qualifications, S/NVQs, Management and team leader qualifications, Quality-Assured Awards, Open learning resources from levels 2-5 (Building Success at Level 2, ILM Super Series at Level 3 and The Universal Manager at Level 4/5), CD based assessment materials and management videos (Teams that Work and A Vision for Change).
171

Institute of Professional Managers and Administrators
International membership for managers offering examinations and careers training courses.
173

Intec Business Solutions (Scotland) Ltd
Experts in staff development including computing interpersonal and management skills.
174

Integration International
Outstanding Personal leader, Team, Organisational and International Business Development.
175

Invicta Training Ltd
Specific pragmatic interactive training, consultancy, mentoring, coaching and support services.
177

Jane Allan & Associates
Enjoyable training that adds pure value for salary for all.
181

JM Solutions Ltd
We specialise in middle and senior management career development.
183

John Cole Management Development
Publishes experiential exercises and organises management courses and team building.
184

John Meechan Training
Creative managerial and interpersonal skills to meet your unique needs.
184

Jon Spencer Training & Consultancy
Management skills, managing change, training and facilitation.
185

KD Kefford & Associates
Providers of management consultancy and management and human resources training.
187

The Key Network
Outdoor development, team building, leadership and management development programmes UK wide.
188

Kingdom Management Training
KMT's products and services measurably improve management of organisations.
190

Lakeside Management Development
Lakeside Corporate – one of Britain's leading experiential training providers.
191

LD AssociatesTraining Services
Provider of client specific management supervisory and trainer training programmes.
192

Lea, Storey & Co
Value for money, quality training services from people you trust.
192

The Leadership Trust (Training) Limited
Leadership development for all managers and directors.
193

Motivation

Crown College
Crown specialise in information technology, customer services, retail administrative management.
128

Davies Training Services
Focused in-company training which develops your managers' competences.
130

Insight Training Solutions Ltd
Customised commercial awareness, marketing, finance, business planning and teambuilding programmes.
166

Keenan Research Limited
Managing change; motivational interviewing; handling stress; assessing risk; psychometric testing.
187

Parity Training Ltd
Parity Training delivers bespoke and public scheduled training courses in technology, management and business skills, providing training for over 40,000 delegates a year. Parity's learning consultants increasingly blend traditional training methods with e-learning initiatives to provide integrated learning solutions that ensure return on investment and effective learning outcomes.
With training centres in Antrim, Belfast, Birmingham, Bristol, Edinburgh, Fleet, Leeds, London and Manchester, Parity offers nation-wide in person (classroom based) training and support. Additionally, Parity's managed services offering provides a range of options from simple vendor management to a full outsource training and development service.
Parity's long-term partnerships with leading bodies such as the Information Systems Examination Board, DSDM Consortium, Institute of Management, Outward Bound Trust, Association for Project Management, Microsoft and Lotus Corporation keeps Parity at the forefront of the industry, able to offer an unparalleled range of certified training leading to recognised qualifications. Parity's on-going commitment to delivering effective quality training is reflected in its ISO9001 certification. In 2003 Parity Training was awarded the Institued of IT Training's accolade of Training Company of the Year and Trainer of the Year.
Parity Training is part of Parity Group plc, the international IT consultancy and solutions group with 30 offices in the UK, mainland Europe and the USA.
For booking information or course details, call 0800 656 100, email training@parity.net or visit www.parity.net.
224

Robert Rainsbury Associates
Hands-on business skills in maximising management potential through change.
248

Video Arts
Inspirational learning solutions.
281

The Wadenhoe Consultancy
Strategic management developers. IOM accredited coaching middle/senior level managers.
283

YMCA Training
YMCA training provides vocational and personal development programmes nationally.
289

Multi-skilling

Inplant Industrial Training
Coaching and support services for trainers of technical/production staff.
165

The Institute of Manufacturing
Professional Institute. Qualifications in manufacturing, modem technology and systems.
172

Mechatronics International Ltd
Manufacturers/suppliers - training equipment/systems for pneumatics, hydraulics, electro-control, PLCs.
205

Osmec Technology Management
Osmec provides automation, electrical engineering, electrical safety and regulations training.
220

Parity Training Ltd
Parity Training delivers bespoke and public scheduled training courses in technology, management and business skills, providing training for over 40,000 delegates a year. Parity's learning consultants increasingly blend traditional training methods with e-learning initiatives to provide integrated learning solutions that ensure return on investment and effective learning outcomes.
With training centres in Antrim, Belfast, Birmingham, Bristol, Edinburgh, Fleet, Leeds, London and Manchester, Parity offers nation-wide in person (classroom based) training and support. Additionally, Parity's managed services offering provides a range of options from simple vendor management to a full outsource training and development service.
Parity's long-term partnerships with leading bodies such as the Information Systems Examination Board, DSDM Consortium, Institute of Management, Outward Bound Trust, Association for Project Management, Microsoft and Lotus Corporation keeps Parity at the forefront of the industry, able to offer an unparalleled range of certified training leading to recognised qualifications. Parity's on-going commitment to delivering effective quality training is reflected in its ISO9001 certification. In 2003 Parity Training was awarded the Institued of IT Training's accolade of Training Company of the Year and Trainer of the Year.
Parity Training is part of Parity Group plc, the international IT consultancy and solutions group with 30 offices in the UK, mainland Europe and the USA.
For booking information or course details, call 0800 656 100, email training@parity.net or visit www.parity.net.
224

Pembroke Management Development
Personal and business development that's powerful, proven and performance enhancing.
226

Woodcote Technical Services
Bespoke technical training for manufacturing companies including providing illustrated materials.
286

Project management

Abraham, Airey & Associates
Friendly professional training company based in London, Chelmsford and Essex.
76

Acacia-IPS Ltd
IT-business courses and coaching from business analysis to information management.
76

University of Brighton, Business Services
Skills and training provided for organisations of all kinds.
95

Broadway Training Ltd
Training programmes tailor made for you. First class conference facilities.
99

Business Skills Agency
Business skills training: computer, management, sales, marketing, personal development.
103

The Chartered Institute of Building
The Chartered Institute of Building is a modern professional body with more than 40,000 members. It has a Royal Charter to promote the science and practice of construction for public benefit, and has won recognition from Government, other professional bodies and the industry itself as being the central voice in construction. It provides expertise in all aspects of construction management, giving advice of a legal and technical nature, and sets standards in areas such as education, and health and safety.

In the past year, the Institute has made many valuable contributions to the development and improvement of the construction industry. These have included the production and implementation of a New Education Framework and a Health and Safety Action Plan, the launch of the Third Edition of Practice for Project Management, our merger with the Architectural and Surveying Institute and numerous research and innovation projects. The CIOB has also recently launched an 'Improving Site Conditions' campaign: 'Change in our Sites', in line with the aims and key issues for the industry that have been identified by the Strategic Forum for Construction.

112

Condor Training Services
Providers of classroom-based, tutor-led on-site business IT courses.

123

Corporate Capabilities Ltd
Training and development for project capability improvement.

125

Davies Training Services
Focused in-company training which develops your managers' competences.

130

Delta Computer Training Ltd
Training and consultancy for IT professionals and computer users.

131

Elmwood Business Training
Elmwood Business Training provider of quality training courses and consultancies.

140

Highcliffe Management Development
In-house training for managers and supervisors.

157

The IEE
Your people are your most precious asset – and with the right professional guidance, you can develop their skills and abilities. The result? Enhanced individual performance – plus measurable improvements to your bottom line.

The IEE (Institution of Electrical Engineers) is one of the UK's leaders in management and business training for professionals involved with electrical engineering, IT and electronic engineering. We offer an impressive portfolio of courses for newly qualified and experienced professionals, from careers and business skills through to effective management, negotiating, presentations, marketing – plus a wide range of more technical courses.
With over 130, 000 members worldwide, the IEE is a global organisation representing the interests of IT and electrical engineering professionals - though our courses are equally applicable to other industries and commercial sectors. Most of our programmes are held in London, though we can run them at your premises, for small or large groups.
For more information about how IEE management and business training can bring out the best in your people - and your organisation - call us on 01438 767237 or log on to www.iee.org.uk

162

Insight Training Solutions Ltd
Customised commercial awareness, marketing, finance, business planning and teambuilding programmes.

166

The Institute of Administrative Management
Established in 1915, the Institute of Administrative Management is the leading Professional Body for both practising and aspiring Administrative Managers.
We can work with you to produce an internationally recognised, in-house qualification, validate your training programmes or provide our training to your employees, in house or through our provider network.

Qualifications
IAM qualifications are targeted at Supervisors, Managers, and those who aspire to these positions. Student members can progress through the Certificate, Diploma and Advanced Diploma, and on to further qualifications (such as the IAM's dedicated degree in Administrative Management) and membership of other professional institutes

168

The Institute of Internal Auditors – UK and Ireland
IIA – UK and Ireland. The professionals in internal audit training.
170

Intelligent Training Solutions Ltd
Suppliers of generic and bespoke multimedia training solutions.
175

i to i Training & Development
Identification of needs to design and delivery of bespoke training.
179

John Matchett Limited
Instructor lead training and skills and competence management.
184

Lakeside Management Development
Lakeside Corporate – one of Britain's leading experiential training providers.
191

Liverpool Business School
Liverpool Business School for all your training needs.
197

Mid Career College
Established in 1986, Mid Career College is one of the most comprehensive CPD providers.
207

Mitre Group Ltd
Team development, leadership, management, coaching, single/multi-day courses.
208

Ontrack International Ltd
Leading experts in developing the full potential of people.
218

Parity Training Ltd
Parity Training delivers bespoke and public scheduled training courses in technology, management and business skills, providing training for over 40,000 delegates a year. Parity's learning consultants increasingly blend traditional training methods with e-learning initiatives to provide integrated learning solutions that ensure return on investment and effective learning outcomes.
With training centres in Antrim, Belfast, Birmingham, Bristol, Edinburgh, Fleet, Leeds, London and Manchester, Parity offers nation-wide in person (classroom based) training and support. Additionally, Parity's managed services offering provides a range of options from simple vendor management to a full outsource training and development service.
Parity's long-term partnerships with leading bodies such as the Information Systems Examination Board, DSDM Consortium, Institute of Management, Outward Bound Trust, Association for Project Management, Microsoft and Lotus Corporation keeps Parity at the forefront of the industry, able to offer an unparalleled range of certified training leading to recognised qualifications. Parity's on-going commitment to delivering effective quality training is reflected in its ISO9001 certification. In 2003 Parity Training was awarded the Instited of IT Training's accolade of Training Company of the Year and Trainer of the Year.
Parity Training is part of Parity Group plc, the international IT consultancy and solutions group with 30 offices in the UK, mainland Europe and the USA. For booking information or course details, call 0800 656 100, email training@parity.net or visit www.parity.net.
224

PDS Consulting
Screen and PAD (TAMPO) print vocational training. Project management, troubleshooting.
225

Project North East
PNE offers training and qualifications in management development subjects.
238

Prospect CPD, University of Aberdeen
Prospect CPD provides professional development from the University of Aberdeen.
238

PTA Ltd
Production management and process improvement specialists working for manufacturing industries.
240

Quadrilect
Training courses for the British Institute of Facilities management.
242

QUBE Ltd
Specialists in NVQ training in hospitality and business services.
242

Statistics for Industry Ltd
Practical statistical courses/consultancy aimed at scientists/technologists in industry.
261

Stehle Associates
Award winning training from Stehle Associates. We offer a complete training service, including public and in-house courses, project facilitation and consultancy for all levels of staff from senior management to new hires. Our expertise covers Information Systems Development, Project Management, Management and Leadership skills, Interpersonal skills, and Customer Service. For in-house programmes we work closely with our clients to agree the required outcomes and preferred delivery methods. Then we tailor materials from our extensive course portfolio to provide innovative training solutions which match the requirements exactly. To ensure that learning is successful we provide follow-up facilitation and consultancy to reinforce in the workplace these newly acquired skills. All our training is focused on equipping staff with the essential skills required in their job role, and on providing cost-effective results. Whatever the content or duration of our programmes we aim to achieve capabilities which can be applied immediately the training is completed and which can be transferred to new roles as staff develop. We are accredited by the Institute of IT Training as a Gold Standard training provider and abide by their code of practice.
262

Video Arts
Inspirational learning solutions.
281

WMC ManagementTraining Consultants
Management development, health and safety, environmental and employment law training.
285

Xansa
PRINCE2, programme management, project management service, management ISEB qualifications.
288

Quality

Effective Personnel Development (EPD)
Provision of consultancy and training on quality and process improvement.
138

European Forum for Teamwork
Performance improvement, change management, teamwork training for managers and teams.
143

James Miles Consultants
Customer focused tailored training: improving processes, cycle time-flexibility-quality-cost.
180

Lancaster University
High quality training and education programmes for industry and commerce
191

Quality Quest Ltd
Professional quality management improvement programmes tailored to support business objectives.
242

Quest Worldwide
Training and consulting in strategy implementation and performance improvement.
243

The Rapid Results College
RRC specialise in open, distance and e-learning solutions for qualifications.
244

Smallpeice Enterprises Ltd
Public/Private courses in Management Development, Project Management and business skills.
257

STACS Training Ltd
260

Risk management

The Association of Corporate Treasurers
The world's leading provider of treasury education and training.
86

Centre for Hazard & Risk Management
Post-graduate programme training in risk management security backcore OHES.
109

The Chartered Institute of Building
The Chartered Institute of Building is a modern professional body with more than 40,000 members. It has a Royal Charter to promote the science and practice of construction for public benefit, and has won recognition from Government, other professional bodies and the industry itself as being the central voice in construction. It provides expertise in all aspects of construction management, giving advice of a legal and technical nature, and sets standards in areas such as education, and health and safety.
In the past year, the Institute has made many valuable contributions to the development and improvement of the construction industry. These have included the production and implementation of a New Education Framework and a Health and Safety Action Plan, the launch of the Third Edition of Practice for Project Management, our merger with the Architectural and Surveying Institute and numerous research and innovation projects. The CIOB has also recently launched an 'Improving Site Conditions' campaign: 'Change in our Sites', in line with the aims and key issues for the industry that have been identified by the Strategic Forum for Construction.
112

Easy i Ltd
Developer of innovative and bespoke technology based training programs.
136

Euromoney Training
Global market leader in banking and financial training.
143

HASTAM
Health, safety and environmental consultancy, training and evaluation software systems.
156

The Institute of Internal Auditors – UK and Ireland
IIA – UK and Ireland. The professionals in internal audit training.
170

The Institution of Occupational Safety and Health
Europe's leading body for health and safety professionals.
174

J C Consultancy Ltd
Risk assessment and management training provided, tailored to clients' needs.
182

Kingdom Management Training
KMT's products and services measurably improve management of organisations.
190

Parity Training Ltd
Parity Training delivers bespoke and public scheduled training courses in technology, management and business skills, providing training for over 40,000 delegates a year. Parity's learning consultants increasingly blend traditional training methods with e-learning initiatives to provide integrated learning solutions that ensure return on investment and effective learning outcomes.
With training centres in Antrim, Belfast, Birmingham, Bristol, Edinburgh, Fleet, Leeds, London and Manchester, Parity offers nation-wide in person (classroom based) training and support. Additionally, Parity's managed services offering provides a range of options from simple vendor management to a full outsource training and development service.
Parity's long-term partnerships with leading bodies such as the Information Systems Examination Board, DSDM Consortium, Institute of Management, Outward Bound Trust, Association for Project Management, Microsoft and Lotus Corporation

keeps Parity at the forefront of the industry, able to offer an unparalleled range of certified training leading to recognised qualifications. Parity's on-going commitment to delivering effective quality training is reflected in its ISO9001 certification. In 2003 Parity Training was awarded the Institued of IT Training's accolade of Training Company of the Year and Trainer of the Year.
Parity Training is part of Parity Group plc, the international IT consultancy and solutions group with 30 offices in the UK, mainland Europe and the USA. For booking information or course details, call 0800 656 100, email training@parity.net or visit www.parity.net.

224

RRC Business Training
Providing businesses and individuals with top quality, innovative, professional training.

249

Safety & Hygiene Consultants
In-house training on health and safety law and practical issues.

250

SCOTS
We provide occupational safety consultancy and training services throughout Scotland.

254

Strategic Management Partners

266

System Concepts Ltd
Specialists in office and industrial ergonomics and health and safety.

269

Xansa
PRINCE2, programme management, project management service, management ISEB qualifications.

288

Strategy & planning

Answers (Research) Ltd
Marketing training for the intensively competitive 21st century provided.

82

British Institute of Technology & E-commerce
BITE is developing e-commerce professionals for all sectors of industry.

97

Bruce Nixon AssociatesConsultants in Organisation Transformation and Learning
Helping leaders create better and more successful workplaces and contribute to a fairer and sustainable world. Bruce Nixon is also the author of 'Making a Difference' and 'Global Forces'.

99

Centre for Management Creativity Ltd
Whole systems approach through facilitation, creative methodologies and outdoor learning.

110

The Chartered Institute of Building
The Chartered Institute of Building is a modern professional body with more than 40,000 members. It has a Royal Charter to promote the science and practice of construction for public benefit, and has won recognition from Government, other professional bodies and the industry itself as being the central voice in construction. It provides expertise in all aspects of construction management, giving advice of a legal and technical nature, and sets standards in areas such as education, and health and safety.
In the past year, the Institute has made many valuable contributions to the development and improvement of the construction industry. These have included the production and implementation of a New Education Framework and a Health and Safety Action Plan, the launch of the Third Edition of Practice for Project Management, our merger with the Architectural and Surveying Institute and numerous research and innovation projects. The CIOB has also recently launched an 'Improving Site Conditions' campaign: 'Change in our Sites', in line with the aims and key issues for the industry that have been identified by the Strategic Forum for Construction.

112

CJN Management Consultancy
Team development covering sales management, international marketing, marketing, major accounts.
119

Clive Evans Consultancy
Executive mentoring and organisation development.
120

D J Neil Ltd
Design and delivery of in-house management training UK and overseas.
133

DM Management Consultants Ltd (DMMC)
Database direct marketing specialist training development consultancy.
134

The Evaluation Partnership
We evaluate training courses, programmes and institutions, UK and Europe.
144

Imparta Limited
Imparta build organisational capabilities in strategy sales and marketing.
163

Institute of Cost and Executive Accountants
Professional Examining body. Provides Training for financial decision makers.
169

Langham Management Consultants
Sales management, sales audits, business development processes, management development training.
192

Management Training & Development
We provide tailor-made courses for business organisations.
202

Marketing Training Co
Marketing training covering the whole subject from introductory to MBA.
203

Mayo Learning International Ltd
Specialists in strategy, talent and career management and HR measurement.
204

Mitre Group Ltd
Team development, leadership, management, coaching, single/multi-day courses.
208

Morcamation Management & Training Consultants
Strategic business/marketing planning, quality management ISO000/TQM, managing change.
210

Parity Training Ltd
Parity Training delivers bespoke and public scheduled training courses in technology, management and business skills, providing training for over 40,000 delegates a year. Parity's learning consultants increasingly blend traditional training methods with e-learning initiatives to provide integrated learning solutions that ensure return on investment and effective learning outcomes.
With training centres in Antrim, Belfast, Birmingham, Bristol, Edinburgh, Fleet, Leeds, London and Manchester, Parity offers nation-wide in person (classroom based) training and support. Additionally, Parity's managed services offering provides a range of options from simple vendor management to a full outsource training and development service.
Parity's long-term partnerships with leading bodies such as the Information Systems Examination Board, DSDM Consortium, Institute of Management, Outward Bound Trust, Association for Project Management, Microsoft and Lotus Corporation keeps Parity at the forefront of the industry, able to offer an unparalleled range of certified training leading to recognised qualifications. Parity's on-going commitment to delivering effective quality training is reflected in its ISO9001 certification. In 2003 Parity Training was awarded the Instituted of IT Training's accolade of Training Company of the Year and Trainer of the Year.
Parity Training is part of Parity Group plc, the international IT consultancy and solutions group

with 30 offices in the UK, mainland Europe and the USA.
For booking information or course details, call 0800 656 100, email training@parity.net or visit www.parity.net.

224

Penny Walker
Learning enabling corporate social responsibility, environmental management and sustainable development.

226

Project North East
PNE offers training and qualifications in management development subjects.

238

Strategy Workshop Facilitators Limited
Professional facilitators of Strategic Thinking, Innovation and Decision Making processes.

266

Vets in Business Ltd
Training for veterinary partners and practice staff.

281

Warwick Business School
Internationally accredited, WBS is highly ranked for teaching and research.

284

Supervisory

Barry Herd Associates
Your results orientated interpersonal skills management and organisational development partner.

91

Business Skills Training & Management Solutions
Experienced trainers specialising in management development.

103

Catalyst Consultants
TNA; wide range of organisational development and personal skills training.

107

Elmwood Business Training
Elmwood Business Training provider of quality training courses and consultancies.

140

Flexible Learning Solutions
Specialists in flexible learning. Supply and develop multi-media training packages.

148

GSS Personnel Services Ltd
Training programmes tailored to the needs of individual clients.

153

In-Comm Business Services Ltd
Training and business consultancy organisation.

164

The Institute of Administrative Management
Established in 1915, the Institute of Administrative Management is the leading Professional Body for both practising and aspiring Administrative Managers.
We can work with you to produce an internationally recognised, in-house qualification, validate your training programmes or provide our training to your employees, in house or through our provider network.

Qualifications
IAM qualifications are targeted at Supervisors, Managers, and those who aspire to these positions. Student members can progress through the Certificate, Diploma and Advanced Diploma, and on to further qualifications (such as the IAM's dedicated degree in Administrative Management) and membership of other professional institutes

168

Institute of Leadership & Management
Institute of Leadership & Management (ILM) offers membership services together with leadership and management qualifications. ILM is a professional body that supports national objectives to ensure the UK is able to develop leaders and managers of the future, with a particular focus on first line and middle levels. Offering qualifcations for managers and team leaders from Levels 2-5 of the national framework, ILM also supports individual and organisational development through endorsement, awards and learning resources. ILM is a subsidiary of the City & Guilds Group, the UK's largest provider of vocational qualifications.
We provide the following services:
Membership, Vocationally-Related Qualifications, S/NVQs, Management and team leader qualifications, Quality-Assured Awards, Open learning resources from levels 2-5 (Building Success at Level 2, ILM Super Series at Level 3 and The Universal Manager at Level 4/5), CD based assessment materials and management videos (Teams that Work and A Vision for Change).

171

The Institute of Management Specialists (IMS)
Professional membership body providing qualifications by exemption. Distance learning courses.

172

LD AssociatesTraining Services
Provider of client specific management supervisory and trainer training programmes.358

192

Myrick Training Services
Engineering management, supervisory health and safety, quality NVQs, short courses.

212

Odyssey Training Limited
IM and ISO accredited general and safety management training provider.

217

Parity Training Ltd
Parity Training delivers bespoke and public scheduled training courses in technology, management and business skills, providing training for over 40,000 delegates a year. Parity's learning consultants increasingly blend traditional training methods with e-learning initiatives to provide integrated learning solutions that ensure return on investment and effective learning outcomes.
With training centres in Antrim, Belfast, Birmingham, Bristol, Edinburgh, Fleet, Leeds, London and Manchester, Parity offers nation-wide in person (classroom based) training and support. Additionally, Parity's managed services offering provides a range of options from simple vendor management to a full outsource training and development service.
Parity's long-term partnerships with leading bodies such as the Information Systems Examination Board, DSDM Consortium, Institute of Management, Outward Bound Trust, Association for Project Management, Microsoft and Lotus Corporation keeps Parity at the forefront of the industry, able to offer an unparalleled range of certified training leading to recognised qualifications. Parity's on-going commitment to delivering effective quality training is reflected in its ISO9001 certification. In 2003 Parity Training was awarded the Instituted of IT Training's accolade of Training Company of the Year and Trainer of the Year.
Parity Training is part of Parity Group plc, the international IT consultancy and solutions group with 30 offices in the UK, mainland Europe and the USA.
For booking information or course details, call 0800 656 100, email training@parity.net or visit www.parity.net.

224

Polymer Training Limited
Training and business development training for the polymer industry.

233

PTP Associates
Activities that help management and staff meet Business Plan requirements.

240

Rycotewood College
We offer flexible professional and training services to employers.

250

Teamworking

Conflict Management Plus
Conflict Management Plus Ltd are national experts in providing solutions to workplace conflicts. We have over 10 years' experience providing accredited training and running a dispute resolution service. We work with full-time trainers and specialist consultants who bring expertise and experience from a range of public and private sector backgrounds. We have clear guidelines on equal opportunities, which run throughout our training design and delivery.

We can:

- Resolve workplace disputes between colleagues and teams
- Divert harassment and bullying cases away from disciplinaries/tribunals
- Carry out independent investigations
- Coach your teams or key players to improve performance
- Sample Training Programmes
- Certificate in Mediation Skills and Practice. A six-day course leading to OCR accreditation
- Core Mediation Skills- two-day introductory course leading to OCR accreditation
- Assertiveness
- Complaints
- Conflict management skills for HR
- Constructive conflict management for managers
- Contact officers training
- Training for Colleague Support Networks
- Managing bullying and harassment
- Investigator skills training
- Managing difficult behaviour, aggression and threats of violence
- Mediation diploma – OCR qualification in mediation practice
- Mediation and counselling skills in the workplace
- Phone rage
- Win-win negotiation

124

Cygnet Business Development Ltd
Management and organisational development consultancy specialising in developing leader-managers.

128

Elmwood Business Training
Elmwood Business Training provider of quality training courses and consultancies.

140

Endeavour Training
Leadership and teambuilding experiential outdoor programmes. Fully mobile, tailored designs.

140

European Forum for Teamwork
Performance improvement, change management, teamwork training for managers and teams.

143

Executive Development Initiative Training (EDIT)
Without teamwork your company will fail.

145

Fresh Tracks
Teams that play together work together. Contact us for more.

149

Grass Routes Management Development and Consultancy Ltd
Specialists in behavioural and attitudinal change through training and consultancy.

153

Heriot-Watt University
A research-led technological university with outstanding success in academic-industrial collaboration.

157

High Trenhouse Management Centre
Exclusive use of exceptional, beautifully located venues for management events.

157

Impact Development Training Group
Transforming organisations, developing talent, building high performing teams, inspiring leaders.

162

The Institute of Administrative Management
Established in 1915, the Institute of Administrative Management is the leading Professional Body for both practising and aspiring Administrative Managers.
We can work with you to produce an internationally recognised, in-house qualification, validate your training programmes or provide our training to your employees, in house or through our provider network.

Qualifications
IAM qualifications are targeted at Supervisors, Managers, and those who aspire to these positions. Student members can progress through the Certificate, Diploma and Advanced Diploma, and on to further qualifications (such as the IAM's dedicated degree in Administrative Management) and membership of other professional institutes

168

Institute of Leadership & Management
Institute of Leadership & Management (ILM) offers membership services together with leadership and management qualifications. ILM is a professional body that supports national objectives to ensure the UK is able to develop leaders and managers of the future, with a particular focus on first line and middle levels. Offering qualifcations for managers and team leaders from Levels 2-5 of the national framework, ILM also supports individual and organisational development through endorsement, awards and learning resources. ILM is a subsidiary of the City & Guilds Group, the UK's largest provider of vocational qualifications.
We provide the following services:
Membership, Vocationally-Related Qualifications, S/NVQs, Management and team leader qualifications, Quality-Assured Awards, Open learning resources from levels 2-5 (Building Success at Level 2, ILM Super Series at Level 3 and The Universal Manager at Level 4/5), CD based assessment materials and management videos (Teams that Work and A Vision for Change).

171

i to i Training & Development
Identification of needs to design and delivery of bespoke training.

179

John Cole Management Development
Publishes experiential exercises and organises management courses and team building.

184

Julia Samways
Tailor-made courses for managing and developing yourself and others.

186

Leadership Resources Limited

192

The Leadership Trust (Training) Limited
Leadership development for all managers and directors.

193

Learning Applications Ltd
Consultancy services for specialist staff, management team and organisation development.

193

Minerva Consulting
Team, skills and process interventions for blue chip companies internationally.

208

Nexus Learning and Development
Nexus uses diagnostics to design and deliver bespoke experential programmes.

214

North Down & ARDS Institute of Further & Higher Education
North Down offers a wide range of management training courses.

216

Ontrack International Ltd
Leading experts in developing the full potential of people.

218

Outward Bound Scotland
Management development, team building and challenge programmes using the outdoors.

221

Parity Training Ltd
Parity Training delivers bespoke and public scheduled training courses in technology, management and business skills, providing training for over 40,000 delegates a year. Parity's learning consultants increasingly blend traditional training methods with e-learning initiatives to provide integrated learning solutions that ensure return on investment and effective learning outcomes.
With training centres in Antrim, Belfast, Birmingham, Bristol, Edinburgh, Fleet, Leeds, London and Manchester, Parity offers nation-wide in person (classroom based) training and support. Additionally, Parity's managed services offering provides a range of options from simple vendor

management to a full outsource training and development service.

Parity's long-term partnerships with leading bodies such as the Information Systems Examination Board, DSDM Consortium, Institute of Management, Outward Bound Trust, Association for Project Management, Microsoft and Lotus Corporation keeps Parity at the forefront of the industry, able to offer an unparalleled range of certified training leading to recognised qualifications. Parity's on-going commitment to delivering effective quality training is reflected in its ISO9001 certification. In 2003 Parity Training was awarded the Institued of IT Training's accolade of Training Company of the Year and Trainer of the Year.

Parity Training is part of Parity Group plc, the international IT consultancy and solutions group with 30 offices in the UK, mainland Europe and the USA.

For booking information or course details, call 0800 656 100, email training@parity.net or visit www.parity.net.

224

People=Positive Ltd

People=Positive is a progressive and expanding international development training company.

228

The Performance Factor

Effective business/personal development training, making your people powerful performers.

228

Positive Action

Learning and development events for trainers, developers and managers.

234

The Prestbury House Management Training Centre

Operated by experienced business people with a passion for training.

235

Professional development.co.uk

Training for businesses, management, teambuilding, short courses, NVQs and consultancy.

237

PTP Associates

Activities that help management and staff meet Business Plan requirements.

240

Qorus Ltd

Significant contributions made to client company's performance through management development.

241

Rob Kelly & Associates

Developing people in organisations to work effectively in teams.

247

Sandstone Ltd

Professional training and development resources. Exceptional training and consultancy services.

251

Scottish Centres

Four outdoor centres in Scotland suitable for outdoor management development.

254

Skern Lodge Development Training

Practical programmes using the outdoors; exceptional staff, residential training centre.

255

Straightforward Training Ltd

Management, supervisory, customer care and teambuilding, training and development.

266

TBL Organisational Development Ltd

Team building, leadership, facilitation and graduate development throughout the UK.

270

Team Training International

Services offered: team problem solving, planning, leadership management, communication skills.

271

Transglobal Languages Limited

Language training and testing, country and culture briefings, translation, interpreting.

277

Part 2.4

Personal Skills

Assertiveness

Abraham, Airey & Associates
Friendly professional training company based in London, Chelmsford and Essex.
76

AP International
83

Barleythorpe Training & Conference Centre
90

DMC Training Associates
Skills training and development including work-life balance.
134

Intelligent Training Solutions Ltd
Suppliers of generic and bespoke multimedia training solutions.
175

Mobile Training Ltd
Finance and Management Skills training both in-house and public courses.
209

Nationwide Training Ltd
Management consultants specialising in management development and salesforce training.
213

Parity Training Ltd
Parity Training delivers bespoke and public scheduled training courses in technology, management and business skills, providing training for over 40,000 delegates a year. Parity's learning consultants increasingly blend traditional training methods with e-learning initiatives to provide integrated learning solutions that ensure return on investment and effective learning outcomes.
With training centres in Antrim, Belfast, Birmingham, Bristol, Edinburgh, Fleet, Leeds, London and Manchester, Parity offers nation-wide in person (classroom based) training and support. Additionally, Parity's managed services offering provides a range of options from simple vendor management to a full outsource training and development service.
Parity's long-term partnerships with leading bodies such as the Information Systems Examination Board, DSDM Consortium, Institute of Management, Outward Bound Trust, Association for Project Management, Microsoft and Lotus Corporation keeps Parity at the forefront of the industry, able to offer an unparalleled range of certified training leading to recognised qualifications. Parity's on-going commitment to delivering effective quality training is reflected in its ISO9001 certification. In 2003 Parity Training was awarded the Institued of IT Training's accolade of Training Company of the Year and Trainer of the Year.
Parity Training is part of Parity Group plc, the international IT consultancy and solutions group with 30 offices in the UK, mainland Europe and the USA.
For booking information or course details, call 0800 656 100, email training@parity.net or visit www.parity.net.
224

PTP Associates
Activities that help management and staff meet Business Plan requirements.
240

Robert Rainsbury Associates
Hands-on business skills in maximising management potential through change.
248

Sandra Burrows Associates
Management development, employment law training, developing your personal effectiveness workshops.
251

SML Training & Consultancy Ltd
'People skills' training offered by psychologists for all sectors.
257

The Springboard Consultancy
Specialists in women's/men's development training, consultancy and training trainers.
260

Business writing

Parity Training Ltd
Parity Training delivers bespoke and public scheduled training courses in technology, management and business skills, providing training for over 40,000 delegates a year. Parity's learning consultants increasingly blend traditional training methods with e-learning initiatives to provide integrated learning solutions that ensure return on investment and effective learning outcomes.
With training centres in Antrim, Belfast, Birmingham, Bristol, Edinburgh, Fleet, Leeds, London and Manchester, Parity offers nation-wide in person (classroom based) training and support. Additionally, Parity's managed services offering provides a range of options from simple vendor management to a full outsource training and development service.
Parity's long-term partnerships with leading bodies such as the Information Systems Examination Board, DSDM Consortium, Institute of Management, Outward Bound Trust, Association for Project Management, Microsoft and Lotus Corporation keeps Parity at the forefront of the industry, able to offer an unparalleled range of certified training leading to recognised qualifications. Parity's on-going commitment to delivering effective quality training is reflected in its ISO9001 certification. In 2003 Parity Training

was awarded the Instituted of IT Training's accolade of Training Company of the Year and Trainer of the Year.
Parity Training is part of Parity Group plc, the international IT consultancy and solutions group with 30 offices in the UK, mainland Europe and the USA. For booking information or course details, call 0800 656 100, email training@parity.net or visit www.parity.net.

224

Plain English Campaign
Plain English training - everyday, legal, medical and financial.

232

Plain Language Commission
Courses on all aspects of business and legal writing skills.

232

Popular Communication Courses Ltd t/a Popcomm Training
In-house and public courses on corporate publishing, communications and PR.

233

Solutions by Interact Ltd
Interact has expertise in sales training consultancy and software.

257

Training Business
Courses and seminars in creative, marketing, management and media communications.

274

Training Plus
Bespoke training and coaching with helpline, distance learning available.

276

TV Choice
We provide realistic videos which highlight human and organisational issues.

280

Coaching & mentoring

ACADEMEE
Provider of IM accredited management and professional e-learning certificates.

77

AD International
People skills, culture change, assessment centres, mentoring/coaching, trainer training.

79

Amethyst Learning & Development
BESPOKE programmes group or individual, via consultancy training or mentoring.

82

Anthony Snapes Associates, Business Psychologists
Management development, mentoring, 360° feedback, psychometric testing, assessment, development centres.

83

ASK Europe plc
ASK produces development programmes that create leaders and enhance performance.

85

Barlow Fraser Training and Development
Tools, theory and confidence for presenters, trainers and facilitators.

90

Bridge
Bridge offers unique approaches in leadership development and organisational transformation.

95

Bruce Nixon AssociatesConsultants in Organisation Transformation and Learning
Helping leaders create better and more successful workplaces and contribute to a fairer and sustainable world. Bruce Nixon is also the author of 'Making a Difference' and 'Global Forces'.

99

Cameron Gill
HRD consultancy/training. Management, supervisory, NLP including executive coaching/ counselling.
106

Capel Manor College
Greater London's horticulture, floristry, countryside, equine and animal studies college.
106

Centre for Management Creativity Ltd
Whole systems approach through facilitation, creative methodologies and outdoor learning.
110

Change Consultancy and Training
CCT specialises in human resources, organisational development and management skills.
111

Chris James Management Consultancy
Investors in People, organisation development, management development, management training.
116

Chris Sangster Development
Chris Sangster, author of 'Brilliant Future', facilitates related development events.
116

Chrysalis
Management consultancy experienced in organisational development, competence based management development.
117

Clive Evans Consultancy
Executive mentoring and organisation development.
120

Coaching Solutions
Executive coaching, coaching skills training, online training support with coachskills.com.
120

Conflict Management Plus
Conflict Management Plus Ltd are national experts in providing solutions to workplace conflicts. We have over 10 years' experience providing accredited training and running a dispute resolution service. We work with full-time trainers and specialist consultants who bring expertise and experience from a range of public and private sector backgrounds. We have clear guidelines on equal opportunities, which run throughout our training design and delivery.

We can:

- Resolve workplace disputes between colleagues and teams
- Divert harassment and bullying cases away from disciplinaries/tribunals
- Carry out independent investigations
- Coach your teams or key players to improve performance
- Sample Training Programmes
- Certificate in Mediation Skills and Practice. A six-day course leading to OCR accreditation
- Core Mediation Skills- two-day introductory course leading to OCR accreditation
- Assertiveness
- Complaints
- Conflict management skills for HR
- Constructive conflict management for managers
- Contact officers training
- Training for Colleague Support Networks
- Managing bullying and harassment
- Investigator skills training
- Managing difficult behaviour, aggression and threats of violence
- Mediation diploma – OCR qualification in mediation practice
- Mediation and counselling skills in the workplace
- Phone rage
- Win-win negotiation

124

Cullen Scholefield Group
Innovative consultancy specialising in training trainers and Human Resources people.
128

Damar Training Solutions
Effective training solutions for business. Money-back guarantee service.
129

DBS Associates
Management sales presentation, negotiation, telephone, interviewing, coaching skills and consultancy.
130

DMC Training Associates
Skills training and development including work-life balance.
134

Excel Communications (HRD) Ltd
Specialists in applying NLP to produce outstanding business results.
145

Fresh Tracks
Teams that play together work together. Contact us for more.
149

Groom House Holdings Ltd
Behavioural training to produce lost for words customer satisfaction.
153

The IEE
Your people are your most precious asset – and with the right professional guidance, you can develop their skills and abilities. The result? Enhanced individual performance – plus measurable improvements to your bottom line. The IEE (Institution of Electrical Engineers) is one of the UK's leaders in management and business training for professionals involved with electrical engineering, IT and electronic engineering. We offer an impressive portfolio of courses for newly qualified and experienced professionals, from careers and business skills through to effective management, negotiating, presentations, marketing – plus a wide range of more technical courses. With over 130, 000 members worldwide, the IEE is a global organisation representing the interests of IT and electrical engineering professionals - though our courses are equally applicable to other industries and commercial sectors. Most of our programmes are held in London, though we can run them at your premises, for small or large groups. For more information about how IEE management and business training can bring out the best in your people - and your organisation - call us on 01438 767237 or log on to www.iee.org.uk
162

Impact Development Training Group
Transforming organisations, developing talent, building high performing teams, inspiring leaders.
162

Integration International
Outstanding Personal leader, Team, Organisational and International Business Development.
175

J B Computer Management
JBCM provides HR organisation development programmes for individual and corporate.
182

JM Solutions Ltd
We specialise in middle and senior management career development.
183

Jon Spencer Training & Consultancy
Management skills, managing change, training and facilitation.
185

Julia Samways
Tailor-made courses for managing and developing yourself and others.
186

King Associates
Pragmatic executive coach specialising in maximising potential, achieving positive difference.
189

Lea, Storey & Co
Value for money, quality training services from people you trust.
192

Learning Applications Ltd
Consultancy services for specialist staff, management team and organisation development.
193

Livingsuccess.co.uk
Maximixing performance, facilitating change, increasing potential for business and individuals.
198

Mentor Group Ltd
Tailored management development and training. 22 experienced consultants. Try us!
206

Michael Morris Management Training & Development
MMMT&D offers tailor-made executive coaching and management skills development programmes.
207

Nationwide Training Ltd
Management consultants specialising in management development and salesforce training.
213

Nigel Blagg Associates
Specialists in assessment, selection, psychometric testing, personal development.
215

Optimum Coaching Limited
Coaching Centre of Excellence, corporate coaching and coach training programmes.
219

Oxford Management Consultants
Change management, client centre consulting and influencing skills training programmes.
223

PACE (Performance & Communication Enterprises)
Executive and leadership coaching for directors, senior managers, key staff.
223

Parity Training Ltd
Parity Training delivers bespoke and public scheduled training courses in technology, management and business skills, providing training for over 40,000 delegates a year. Parity's learning consultants increasingly blend traditional training methods with e-learning initiatives to provide integrated learning solutions that ensure return on investment and effective learning outcomes.
With training centres in Antrim, Belfast, Birmingham, Bristol, Edinburgh, Fleet, Leeds, London and Manchester, Parity offers nation-wide in person (classroom based) training and support. Additionally, Parity's managed services offering provides a range of options from simple vendor management to a full outsource training and development service.
Parity's long-term partnerships with leading bodies such as the Information Systems Examination Board, DSDM Consortium, Institute of Management, Outward Bound Trust, Association for Project Management, Microsoft and Lotus Corporation keeps Parity at the forefront of the industry, able to offer an unparalleled range of certified training leading to recognised qualifications. Parity's on-going commitment to delivering effective quality training is reflected in its ISO9001 certification. In 2003 Parity Training was awarded the Instituted of IT Training's accolade of Training Company of the Year and Trainer of the Year.
Parity Training is part of Parity Group plc, the international IT consultancy and solutions group with 30 offices in the UK, mainland Europe and the USA.
For booking information or course details, call 0800 656 100, email training@parity.net or visit www.parity.net.
224

Phoenix Obsidian
Executive Coaching, Culture Change, Management Development, Expert Facilitation, Leadership Skills.
231

Positive Action
Learning and development events for trainers, developers and managers.
234

The Professional Training Centre
Management, NVQs, quality, health & safety, marketing bespoke, consultancy.
237

PTA Ltd
Production management and process improvement specialists working for manufacturing industries.
240

Secker Training & Development
Coaching and distance learning on equality issues for senior professionals.
255

SML Training & Consultancy Ltd
'People skills' training offered by psychologists for all sectors.
257

Stevenson Business Training Ltd
We are a commercial training and consultancy company.
263

Stonebow
Training, consultancy and management development for the hospitality industry.
265

Target Resources
269

The Training Company
High quality training in people development skills.
274

Transitional Space
Enabling change through individual, team and organisational development.
277

Tregalic (UK) Ltd
NVQ consultancy D32/33 D34/36 training support applications for approved centre.
277

TV Choice
We provide realistic videos which highlight human and organisational issues.
280

Vetlink Information Services
281

The Wye Group Ltd
Tailored management development and communication skills plus experiential learning programmes.
288

Conflict resolution

Conflict Management Plus
Conflict Management Plus Ltd are national experts in providing solutions to workplace conflicts. We have over 10 years' experience providing accredited training and running a dispute resolution service. We work with full-time trainers and specialist consultants who bring expertise and experience from a range of public and private sector backgrounds. We have clear guidelines on equal opportunities, which run throughout our training design and delivery.

We can:

- Resolve workplace disputes between colleagues and teams
- Divert harassment and bullying cases away from disciplinaries/tribunals
- Carry out independent investigations
- Coach your teams or key players to improve performance
- Sample Training Programmes
- Certificate in Mediation Skills and Practice. A six-day course leading to OCR accreditation
- Core Mediation Skills- two-day introductory course leading to OCR accreditation
- Assertiveness
- Complaints
- Conflict management skills for HR
- Constructive conflict management for managers
- Contact officers training
- Training for Colleague Support Networks
- Managing bullying and harassment
- Investigator skills training
- Managing difficult behaviour, aggression and threats of violence
- Mediation diploma – OCR qualification in mediation practice
- Mediation and counselling skills in the workplace
- Phone rage
- Win-win negotiation

124

The University of Huddersfield
Courses in management and professional development, consultancy and ISO 9000 certification.
159

Parity Training Ltd
Parity Training delivers bespoke and public scheduled training courses in technology, management and business skills, providing training for over 40,000 delegates a year. Parity's learning consultants increasingly blend traditional training methods with e-learning initiatives to provide integrated learning solutions that ensure return on investment and effective learning outcomes.
With training centres in Antrim, Belfast, Birmingham, Bristol, Edinburgh, Fleet, Leeds, London and Manchester, Parity offers nation-wide in person (classroom based) training and support.
Additionally, Parity's managed services offering provides a range of options from simple vendor management to a full outsource training and development service.
Parity's long-term partnerships with leading bodies such as the Information Systems Examination Board, DSDM Consortium, Institute of Management, Outward Bound Trust, Association for Project Management, Microsoft and Lotus Corporation keeps Parity at the forefront of the industry, able to offer an unparalleled range of certified training leading to recognised qualifications. Parity's on-going commitment to delivering effective quality training is reflected in its ISO9001 certification. In 2003 Parity Training was awarded the Instituted of IT Training's accolade of Training Company of the Year and Trainer of the Year.
Parity Training is part of Parity Group plc, the international IT consultancy and solutions group with 30 offices in the UK, mainland Europe and the USA.
For booking information or course details, call 0800 656 100, email training@parity.net or visit www.parity.net.
224

Positive Action
Learning and development events for trainers, developers and managers.
234

The Training Company
High quality training in people development skills.
274

Decision-making

Appleton-Hill
Trainer, assessor, internal verifier of NVQ advice and guidance.
84

Consultancy & Training Centre
Cost effective training providers in management, NVQs, computing, health, safety.
124

CSA – Celebrity Speakers Ltd
Europe's largest guest speaker bureau serving businesses and industries worldwide.
128

The Institute of Administrative Management
Established in 1915, the Institute of Administrative Management is the leading Professional Body for both practising and aspiring Administrative Managers.
We can work with you to produce an internationally recognised, in-house qualification, validate your training programmes or provide our training to your employees, in house or through our provider network.

Qualifications
IAM qualifications are targeted at Supervisors, Managers, and those who aspire to these positions. Student members can progress through the Certificate, Diploma and Advanced Diploma, and on to further qualifications (such as the IAM's dedicated degree in Administrative Management) and membership of other professional institutes
168

Managing and Marketing Sales Association
Professional qualifications covering management, marketing and sales, UK and overseas.
202

Parity Training Ltd
Parity Training delivers bespoke and public scheduled training courses in technology, management and business skills, providing training for over 40,000 delegates a year. Parity's learning consultants increasingly blend traditional training methods with e-learning initiatives to provide integrated learning solutions that ensure return on investment and effective learning outcomes.

With training centres in Antrim, Belfast, Birmingham, Bristol, Edinburgh, Fleet, Leeds, London and Manchester, Parity offers nation-wide in person (classroom based) training and support. Additionally, Parity's managed services offering provides a range of options from simple vendor management to a full outsource training and development service.
Parity's long-term partnerships with leading bodies such as the Information Systems Examination Board, DSDM Consortium, Institute of Management, Outward Bound Trust, Association for Project Management, Microsoft and Lotus Corporation keeps Parity at the forefront of the industry, able to offer an unparalleled range of certified training leading to recognised qualifications. Parity's on-going commitment to delivering effective quality training is reflected in its ISO9001 certification. In 2003 Parity Training was awarded the Instituted of IT Training's accolade of Training Company of the Year and Trainer of the Year.
Parity Training is part of Parity Group plc, the international IT consultancy and solutions group with 30 offices in the UK, mainland Europe and the USA.
For booking information or course details, call 0800 656 100, email training@parity.net or visit www.parity.net.

224

Prospect CPD, University of Aberdeen
Prospect CPD provides professional development from the University of Aberdeen.

238

Strategy Workshop Facilitators Limited
Professional facilitators of Strategic Thinking, Innovation and Decision Making processes.

266

Emotional intelligence

ACADEMEE
Provider of IM accredited management and professional e-learning certificates.

77

Chris Sangster Development
Chris Sangster, author of 'Brilliant Future', facilitates related development events.

116

Coaching Solutions
Executive coaching, coaching skills training, online training support with coachskills.com.

120

Conflict Management Plus
Conflict Management Plus Ltd are national experts in providing solutions to workplace conflicts. We have over 10 years' experience providing accredited training and running a dispute resolution service. We work with full-time trainers and specialist consultants who bring expertise and experience from a range of public and private sector backgrounds. We have clear guidelines on equal opportunities, which run throughout our training design and delivery.

We can:

- Resolve workplace disputes between colleagues and teams
- Divert harassment and bullying cases away from disciplinaries/tribunals
- Carry out independent investigations
- Coach your teams or key players to improve performance
- Sample Training Programmes
- Certificate in Mediation Skills and Practice. A six-day course leading to OCR accreditation
- Core Mediation Skills- two-day introductory course leading to OCR accreditation
- Assertiveness
- Complaints
- Conflict management skills for HR
- Constructive conflict management for managers
- Contact officers training
- Training for Colleague Support Networks
- Managing bullying and harassment
- Investigator skills training
- Managing difficult behaviour, aggression and threats of violence
- Mediation diploma – OCR qualification in mediation practice
- Mediation and counselling skills in the workplace
- Phone rage
- Win-win negotiation

124

CSA – Celebrity Speakers Ltd
Europe's largest guest speaker bureau serving businesses and industries worldwide.
128

The Learning Experience
Outdoor and experiential learning for team and leadership development.
194

Parity Training Ltd
Parity Training delivers bespoke and public scheduled training courses in technology, management and business skills, providing training for over 40,000 delegates a year. Parity's learning consultants increasingly blend traditional training methods with e-learning initiatives to provide integrated learning solutions that ensure return on investment and effective learning outcomes.
With training centres in Antrim, Belfast, Birmingham, Bristol, Edinburgh, Fleet, Leeds, London and Manchester, Parity offers nation-wide in person (classroom based) training and support. Additionally, Parity's managed services offering provides a range of options from simple vendor management to a full outsource training and development service.
Parityà:'s long-term partnerships with leading bodies such as the Information Systems Examination Board, DSDM Consortium, Institute of Management, Outward Bound Trust, Association for Project Management, Microsoft and Lotus Corporation keeps Parity at the forefront of the industry, able to offer an unparalleled range of certified training leading to recognised qualifications. Parity's on-going commitment to delivering effective quality training is reflected in its ISO9001 certification. In 2003 Parity Training was awarded the Institued of IT Training's accolade of Training Company of the Year and Trainer of the Year.
Parity Training is part of Parity Group plc, the international IT consultancy and solutions group with 30 offices in the UK, mainland Europe and the USA.
For booking information or course details, call 0800 656 100, email training@parity.net or visit www.parity.net.
224

Peter Chapman & Associates
Leadership, teambuilding and management soft skills nationally and internationally.
230

The Psychotherapy Centre
Training, therapy, publications for understanding self, others and emotional problems.
239

Superboss Ltd
Motivational customer service and leadership seminars for managers.
268

TBL Organisational Development Ltd
Team building, leadership, facilitation and graduate development throughout the UK.
270

Finance for non-finance staff

Anthony James Management Training
Financial training for non-financial managers and other management development.
83

Barleythorpe Training & Conference Centre
90

CIMA Mastercourses
CIMA Master courses, one day management training in management accounting and business management.
117

City Business Seminars
Personalised finance training organisation.
118

Consultancy & Training Services
Management skills courses; instructional techniques, leadership, finance, interviewing, presentation, teamwork.
125

COTU, Charter House
125

Interpersonal skills

Management Magic
Development of people and organisations using NLP. Training, coaching, mentoring.
201

Marsh Business Services
Training: intercultural relations, D-I-Y market research, development export trade.
203

MODAS (Management & Organisation Development Advisory Service)
Human resources; Management development; Interpersonal skills; Training for trainers.
209

The National Extension College
A leading provider of flexible open learning training resources.q:
213

Nigel Blagg Associates
Specialists in assessment, selection, psychometric testing, personal development.
215

Organisation & Management Learning (OML) Associates Ltd
Dedicated to improving organisation performance through development of human talent.
220

Parity Training Ltd
Parity Training delivers bespoke and public scheduled training courses in technology, management and business skills, providing training for over 40,000 delegates a year. Parity's learning consultants increasingly blend traditional training methods with e-learning initiatives to provide integrated learning solutions that ensure return on investment and effective learning outcomes.
With training centres in Antrim, Belfast, Birmingham, Bristol, Edinburgh, Fleet, Leeds, London and Manchester, Parity offers nation-wide in person (classroom based) training and support. Additionally, Parity's managed services offering provides a range of options from simple vendor management to a full outsource training and development service.
Parity's long-term partnerships with leading bodies such as the Information Systems Examination Board, DSDM Consortium, Institute of Management, Outward Bound Trust, Association for Project Management, Microsoft and Lotus Corporation keeps Parity at the forefront of the industry, able to offer an unparalleled range of certified training leading to recognised qualifications. Parity's on-going commitment to delivering effective quality training is reflected in its ISO9001 certification. In 2003 Parity Training was awarded the Instituted of IT Training's accolade of Training Company of the Year and Trainer of the Year.
Parity Training is part of Parity Group plc, the international IT consultancy and solutions group with 30 offices in the UK, mainland Europe and the USA.
For booking information or course details, call 0800 656 100, email training@parity.net or visit www.parity.net.
224

Pembroke Management Development
Personal and business development that's powerful, proven and performance enhancing.
226

Proceptor Training & Consultancy
Psychometric testing for recruitment. Negotiation skills for buyers.
236

Psychology in Business
Consultancy and workshops for improving personal effectiveness and interpersonal skills.
239

Robert Rainsbury Associates
Hands-on business skills in maximising management potential through change.
248

Sandra Burrows Associates
Management development, employment law training, developing your personal effectiveness workshops.
251

SML Training & Consultancy Ltd
'People skills' training offered by psychologists for all sectors.
257

Stehle Associates
Award winning training from Stehle Associates. We offer a complete training service, including public and in-house courses, project facilitation and consultancy for all levels of staff from senior management to new hires. Our expertise covers Information Systems Development, Project Management, Management and Leadership skills, Interpersonal skills, and Customer Service. For in-house programmes we work closely with our clients to agree the required outcomes and preferred delivery methods. Then we tailor materials from our extensive course portfolio to provide innovative training solutions which match the requirements exactly. To ensure that learning is successful we provide follow-up facilitation and consultancy to reinforce in the workplace these newly acquired skills. All our training is focused on equipping staff with the essential skills required in their job role, and on providing cost-effective results. Whatever the content or duration of our programmes we aim to achieve capabilities which can be applied immediately the training is completed and which can be transferred to new roles as staff develop. We are accredited by the Institute of IT Training as a Gold Standard training provider and abide by their code of practice.
262

Stirling Training Consultants
STC is an established consultancy offering results focused, practical training.
263

Stockport College of F&HE
The Business School offers a wide range of management training.
264

Target Resources
269

Tim Russell and Company
Transforming organisations with the amazing microskills system of interpersonal skills.
272

Training for Excellence
Since 1987 TFE has helped people to achieve their potential.
275

Training Plus
Bespoke training and coaching with helpline, distance learning available.
276

TSL Training
Specialists in tailor-made in-house management development and people skills training.
279

Languages

adlib
Providing professional, flexible, high quality business language training throughout Kent.
79

Anglo-Continental
English language training and consultancy for foreign staff and clients.
82

Audio-Forum – The Language Source
Self-study packs for over 100 languages. Beginners, Intermediate, Advanced. Catalogue.
88

Babel Language & Cultural Consultants
Babel offers award-winning language and cross-cultural training programmes.
90

Brackenhurst College
Specialised communicative language training for businesses, lawyers and government agencies.
93

Bracknell and Wokingham College
Wide range of business training and further education for adults.
94

Brasshouse Language Centre
Tailored language training for business and industry in 28 languages.
94

Business Centre
Contact us for engineering management, languages and computer software training.
101

Business Language Bureau
Translation and interpreting services. Also training courses and cultural briefing.
102

Business Language Services
French, German and Spanish for holidays and business via Internet.
102

Business Skills & Services CILT
One-stop shop for all your business language needs.
103

Cambridge International Study Centre, St Mary's College
Language Training for special purposes available at all levels.
105

Centre For Language Study
Tailored language courses for business including EFL for international companies.
109

Euro-Lang Media Courses
Producer/supplier of audio/video language training programmes for business.
143

European Language & Management Centre
Tailored management, communication and inter-cultural training to improve international effectiveness.
144

Institute of Linguists
The Institute of Linguists is a professional membership and language examinations body.
171

Inter Comm
Studies in situational European languages for personal contact and correspondence.
175

Kingston Language Export Centre
Business language training, intensive and extensive, in-company or university based.
190

Linguaphone Institute Ltd
Self-study language courses for personal and business use.
196

London Languages
London Languages specialises in B2B language training.
199

Reading Adult and Community College
General adult education and tailor-made courses in many subjects.
244

Transglobal Languages Limited
Language training and testing, country and culture briefings, translation, interpreting.
277

Leadership

Aberdeen Business School
We provide high quality education training and consultancy programmes.
75

Abernethy Trust
Personal development, teambuilding and leadership programmes delivered through outdoor projects.
75

ACADEMEE
Provider of IM accredited management and professional e-learning certificates.
77

AL Consulting
Results oriented training designed and delivered for clients' specific needs.
81

DM Management Consultants Ltd (DMMC)
Database direct marketing specialist training development consultancy.
134

Dove Nest Group
We deliver effective behavioural change programmes for business success.
134

Electrovision UK Ltd
500+ stocked products in skills, applications, and professional IT training.
138

Endeavour Training
Leadership and teambuilding experiential outdoor programmes. Fully mobile, tailored designs.
140

Epic Group plc
E-learning market leader. 18 year trade record in public and private sectors.
141

Equaville Ltd – Training Services
Speaking. Media. Interviewing. Meetings. Reports. Assertiveness. Supervision. Leadership. Negotiating etc.
142

European Forum for Teamwork
Performance improvement, change management, teamwork training for managers and teams.
143

Excel Communications (HRD) Ltd
Specialists in applying NLP to produce outstanding business results.
145

Excel International
Consultancy/training in project and change management, leadership, interpersonal skills.
145

University of Exeter
Management development programmes at Exeter short courses to masters awards.
145

Frank Daniels Associates Ltd
NLP specialists solve problems, develop people, and gain more choice.
149

FT Knowledge
FT Knowledge is the world's leading provider of business education.
149

Grass Routes Management Development and Consultancy Ltd
Specialists in behavioural and attitudinal change through training and consultancy.
153

Groom House Holdings Ltd
Behavioural training to produce lost for words customer satisfaction.
153

Harris Associates
National innovative training and organisational development company based in Birmingham.
155

Impact Development Training Group
Transforming organisations, developing talent, building high performing teams, inspiring leaders.
162

In-Comm Business Services Ltd
Training and business consultancy organisation.
164

Inner-Leadership.com Ltd
'Truly life changing. Very powerful.'
165

The Institute of Administrative Management
Established in 1915, the Institute of Administrative Management is the leading Professional Body for both practising and aspiring Administrative Managers.
We can work with you to produce an internationally recognised, in-house qualification, validate your training programmes or provide our training to your employees, in house or through our provider network.

Qualifications
IAM qualifications are targeted at Supervisors, Managers, and those who aspire to these positions. Student members can progress through the Certificate, Diploma and Advanced Diploma, and on to further qualifications (such as the IAM's dedicated degree in Administrative Management) and membership of other professional institutes
168

The Outreach Organisation Tan-Y-Bwlch Centre
Short programmes developing essentials for dynamic personal and organisational leadership.
221

Outward Bound Scotland
Management development, team building and challenge programmes using the outdoors.
221

The Oxford Group, Consulting and Training
Provide world-class training and consultancy – deliver solutions and measurable results.
222

Parity Training Ltd
Parity Training delivers bespoke and public scheduled training courses in technology, management and business skills, providing training for over 40,000 delegates a year. Parity's learning consultants increasingly blend traditional training methods with e-learning initiatives to provide integrated learning solutions that ensure return on investment and effective learning outcomes.
With training centres in Antrim, Belfast, Birmingham, Bristol, Edinburgh, Fleet, Leeds, London and Manchester, Parity offers nation-wide in person (classroom based) training and support. Additionally, Parity's managed services offering provides a range of options from simple vendor management to a full outsource training and development service.
Parity's long-term partnerships with leading bodies such as the Information Systems Examination Board, DSDM Consortium, Institute of Management, Outward Bound Trust, Association for Project Management, Microsoft and Lotus Corporation keeps Parity at the forefront of the industry, able to offer an unparalleled range of certified training leading to recognised qualifications. Parity's on-going commitment to delivering effective quality training is reflected in its ISO9001 certification. In 2003 Parity Training was awarded the Instituted of IT Training's accolade of Training Company of the Year and Trainer of the Year.
Parity Training is part of Parity Group plc, the international IT consultancy and solutions group with 30 offices in the UK, mainland Europe and the USA.
For booking information or course details, call 0800 656 100, email training@parity.net or visit www.parity.net.
224

People Dynamics
Leadership development of senior managers and facilitation of top teams.
227

People=Positive Ltd
People=Positive is a progressive and expanding international development training company.
228

Peter Marsh Associates
Management and skills consultancy and training which makes a difference.
230

The Prestbury House Management Training Centre
Operated by experienced business people with a passion for training.
235

Proaction International
Provide tailor-made support to enhance the performance of organisations.
236

Pro-Active Learning
Tailored team, management, leadership and personal development courses and events.
236

The Professional Training Centre
Management, NVQs, quality, health & safety, marketing bespoke, consultancy.
237

QRS International Ltd
Specialist management, supervisory, customer care, sales trainers in service industries.
241

Rob Kelly & Associates
Developing people in organisations to work effectively in teams.
247

Roffey Park Institute
Renowned providers of management development programmes, consultancy and research.
248

Manufacturing & electrical engineering

Media skills

Airtime Communications 80

Equaville Ltd – Training Services
Speaking. Media. Interviewing. Meetings. Reports. Assertiveness. Supervision. Leadership. Negotiating etc.
142

Hillside
Studio-based media and presentation skills training tutored by professionals.
158

Imperial College of Science, Technology and Medicine
All aspects of communication skills, particularly presentations and media interviews.
163

Jaymedia
Media and presenter training provided by BBL trained personnel.
181

Premiere Productions Ltd
Multimedia training on work skills and financial subjects.
235

The Training Store Ltd
Single/mixed media materials for businesses, publishers, universities, professional bodies.
276

Trident Training Services
Specialises in tailor-made public relations training for individuals or groups.
278

Visuals
Consultants specialising in audio - video and multi-media technology.
282

Negotiation

B J O'Connor International Ltd
Multilingual international consulting training company proven techniques in profits increase.
92

The Chartered Institute of Purchasing & Supply
The leading provider of puchasing and supply chain management courses.
114

Conflict Management Plus
Conflict Management Plus Ltd are national experts in providing solutions to workplace conflicts. We have over 10 years' experience providing accredited training and running a dispute resolution service. We work with full-time trainers and specialist consultants who bring expertise and experience from a range of public and private sector backgrounds. We have clear guidelines on equal opportunities, which run throughout our training design and delivery.
We can:

- Resolve workplace disputes between colleagues and teams
- Divert harassment and bullying cases away from disciplinaries/tribunals
- Carry out independent investigations
- Coach your teams or key players to improve performance
- Sample Training Programmes
- Certificate in Mediation Skills and Practice. A six-day course leading to OCR accreditation
- Core Mediation Skills- two-day introductory course leading to OCR accreditation
- Assertiveness
- Complaints
- Conflict management skills for HR
- Constructive conflict management for managers
- Contact officers training
- Training for Colleague Support Networks
- Managing bullying and harassment
- Investigator skills training
- Managing difficult behaviour, aggression and threats of violence
- Mediation diploma – OCR qualification in mediation practice
- Mediation and counselling skills in the workplace
- Phone rage
- Win-win negotiation

124

Excel Communications (HRD) Ltd
Specialists in applying NLP to produce outstanding business results.
145

Glenn Ross Services
Customised training to your company culture and market place.
152

Highcliffe Management Development
In-house training for managers and supervisors.
157

The IEE
Your people are your most precious asset – and with the right professional guidance, you can develop their skills and abilities. The result? Enhanced individual performance – plus measurable improvements to your bottom line.
The IEE (Institution of Electrical Engineers) is one of the UK's leaders in management and business training for professionals involved with electrical engineering, IT and electronic engineering. We offer an impressive portfolio of courses for newly qualified and experienced professionals, from careers and business skills through to effective management, negotiating, presentations, marketing – plus a wide range of more technical courses.
With over 130, 000 members worldwide, the IEE is a global organisation representing the interests of IT and electrical engineering professionals - though our courses are equally applicable to other industries and commercial sectors. Most of our programmes are held in London, though we can run them at your premises, for small or large groups.
For more information about how IEE management and business training can bring out the best in your people - and your organisation - call us on 01438 767237 or log on to www.iee.org.uk
162

Livingsuccess.co.uk
Maximixing performance, facilitating change, increasing potential for business and individuals.
198

LMA Training & Development
Tailored courses in personal effectiveness and communication skills.
198

Michael Morris Management Training & Development
MMMT&D offers tailor-made executive coaching and management skills development programmes.
207

Nationwide Training Ltd
Management consultants specialising in management development and salesforce training.
213

Parity Training Ltd
Parity Training delivers bespoke and public scheduled training courses in technology, management and business skills, providing training for over 40,000 delegates a year. Parity's learning consultants increasingly blend traditional training methods with e-learning initiatives to provide integrated learning solutions that ensure return on investment and effective learning outcomes.
With training centres in Antrim, Belfast, Birmingham, Bristol, Edinburgh, Fleet, Leeds, London and Manchester, Parity offers nation-wide in person (classroom based) training and support. Additionally, Parity's managed services offering provides a range of options from simple vendor management to a full outsource training and development service.
Parity's long-term partnerships with leading bodies such as the Information Systems Examination Board, DSDM Consortium, Institute of Management, Outward Bound Trust, Association for Project Management, Microsoft and Lotus Corporation keeps Parity at the forefront of the industry, able to offer an unparalleled range of certified training leading to recognised qualifications. Parity's on-going commitment to delivering effective quality training is reflected in its ISO9001 certification. In 2003 Parity Training was awarded the Institued of IT Training's accolade of Training Company of the Year and Trainer of the Year.
Parity Training is part of Parity Group plc, the international IT consultancy and solutions group with 30 offices in the UK, mainland Europe and the USA.
For booking information or course details, call 0800 656 100, email training@parity.net or visit www.parity.net.
224

Performance Consulting Group
The management consultants that help your return on investment grow.
228

Psychology in Business
Consultancy and workshops for improving personal effectiveness and interpersonal skills.
239

The Publishing Training Centre at Book House
Open and distance learning courses for book and journal publishers.
240

Purchasing Management Services
Training for buyers, stores, personnel and stock controllers.
241

Neuro-linguistic programming

Management Magic
Development of people and organisations using NLP. Training, coaching, mentoring.
201

Selby College Business Services
Flexible training delivered within your organisation by highly qualified staff.
255

PC user skills

Abraham, Airey & Associates
Friendly professional training company based in London, Chelmsford and Essex.
76

The Advisory Unit: Computers in Education
ICT training and consultancy for teachers, educators and managers.
80

AS Training
Tailor-made computer training and consultancy to suit your needs.
88

Axiom – MSS
Business management and IT training. Business application computer software.
89

Broadway Training Centre
RSA-approved examination centre. Specialising in word-processing, typing, shorthand, book-keeping.
98

CiaTraining Ltd
Self teach ECDL training materials guides for computer software applications.
117

Computacenter Ltd
Computacenter offer complete IT training solutions delivering real business benefits.
122

Debut Computer Services Ltd
Debut is an authorised training centre for Lotus and Microsoft.
130

Informatics Group (UK) Ltd
Provides Microsoft, Citrix, Comptia, Cisco, MS Office training and professional services.
164

Information Automation Ltd
Tailored training in CD-ROM, online, internet resources and searching.
165

Intelligent Training Solutions Ltd
Suppliers of generic and bespoke multimedia training solutions.
175

IQ Computer Services Ltd
Training for all popular business software applications and operating systems.
177

IT Training Suite, The Business and Management Centre
Flexible approach to IT training for professionals and individuals.
180

Jaybetec Consultants Ltd
Consultancy and training in electrical engineering and electrical safety.
181

MerlinTraining Ltd
Hands-on computer training covering PC hardware, windows, networking and internet.
206

Parity Training Ltd
Parity Training delivers bespoke and public scheduled training courses in technology, management and business skills, providing training for over 40,000 delegates a year. Parity's learning consultants increasingly blend traditional training methods with e-learning initiatives to provide integrated learning solutions that ensure return on investment and effective learning outcomes.
With training centres in Antrim, Belfast, Birmingham, Bristol, Edinburgh, Fleet, Leeds, London and Manchester, Parity offers nation-wide in person (classroom based) training and support. Additionally, Parity's managed services offering provides a range of options from simple vendor management to a full outsource training and development service.
Parity's long-term partnerships with leading bodies such as the Information Systems Examination Board, DSDM Consortium, Institute of Management, Outward Bound Trust, Association for Project Management, Microsoft and Lotus Corporation keeps Parity at the forefront of the industry, able to offer an unparalleled range of certified training leading to recognised qualifications. Parity's on-going commitment to delivering effective quality training is reflected in its ISO9001 certification. In 2003 Parity Training was awarded the Institued of IT Training's accolade of Training Company of the Year and Trainer of the Year.
Parity Training is part of Parity Group plc, the international IT consultancy and solutions group with 30 offices in the UK, mainland Europe and the USA. For booking information or course details, call 0800 656 100, email training@parity.net or visit www.parity.net.
224

Pitman Training Centre, Berkshire
Flexible office skills: keyboarding, wordprocessing, shorthand, databases, presentations, spreadsheets, accounts.
231

Presentation skills

Abraham, Airey & Associates
Friendly professional training company based in London, Chelmsford and Essex.
76

Airtime Communications
80

Akwapim Presentations Ltd
Presentation skills training and software. Audio visual and presentation equipment.
80

Arlington Associates
Management training group and one-to-one UK and abroad.
84

Burton College
100

Cambridge International Study Centre, St Mary's College
Language Training for special purposes available at all levels.
105

CERT Consultancy & Training
Executive, management and project team development and facilitation.
110

Chester Presentations Ltd
Quality personalised presentation products when making do really won't do.
116

CiaTraining Ltd
Self teach ECDL training materials guides for computer software applications.
117

Condor Training Services
Providers of classroom-based, tutor-led on-site business IT courses.
123

Consultancy & Training Services
Management skills courses; instructional techniques, leadership, finance, interviewing, presentation, teamwork.
125

Consultancy Skills Training Ltd
Developing knowledge-based business through training and consultancy.
125

Coulter Ford Associates
Experts in media and presentation skills open and in-house courses.
126

Equaville Ltd – Training Services
Speaking. Media. Interviewing. Meetings. Reports. Assertiveness. Supervision. Leadership. Negotiating etc.
142

Excel Communications (HRD) Ltd
Specialists in applying NLP to produce outstanding business results.
145

Heriot-Watt University
A research-led technological university with outstanding success in academic-industrial collaboration.
157

Hillside
Studio-based media and presentation skills training tutored by professionals.
158

The IEE
Your people are your most precious asset – and with the right professional guidance, you can develop their skills and abilities. The result? Enhanced individual performance – plus measurable improvements to your bottom line.
The IEE (Institution of Electrical Engineers) is one of the UK's leaders in management and business training for professionals involved with electrical engineering, IT and electronic engineering. We offer an impressive portfolio of courses for newly qualified and experienced professionals, from careers and business skills through to effective management, negotiating, presentations, marketing – plus a wide range of more technical courses.
With over 130, 000 members worldwide, the IEE is a global organisation representing the interests of IT and electrical engineering professionals - though our courses are equally applicable to other industries and commercial sectors. Most of our programmes are held in London, though we can run them at your premises, for small or large groups.
For more information about how IEE management and business training can bring out the best in your people - and your organisation - call us on 01438 767237 or log on to www.iee.org.uk
162

The Institution of Occupational Safety and Health
Europe's leading body for health and safety professionals.
174

Jaymedia
Media and presenter training provided by BBL trained personnel.
181

KB Training
Training courses in time management, communication skills and self development.
186

King Associates
Pragmatic executive coach specialising in maximising potential, achieving positive difference.
189

Livingstone Communication
Selling skills for brokers and portfolio managers.
197

Training Plus
Bespoke training and coaching with helpline, distance learning available.
276

TSL Training
Specialists in tailor-made in-house management development and people skills training.
279

Woodcote Technical Services
Bespoke technical training for manufacturing companies including providing illustrated materials.
286

Problem solving

Conflict Management Plus
Conflict Management Plus Ltd are national experts in providing solutions to workplace conflicts. We have over 10 years' experience providing accredited training and running a dispute resolution service. We work with full-time trainers and specialist consultants who bring expertise and experience from a range of public and private sector backgrounds. We have clear guidelines on equal opportunities, which run throughout our training design and delivery.

We can:

- Resolve workplace disputes between colleagues and teams
- Divert harassment and bullying cases away from disciplinaries/tribunals
- Carry out independent investigations
- Coach your teams or key players to improve performance
- Sample Training Programmes
- Certificate in Mediation Skills and Practice. A six-day course leading to OCR accreditation
- Core Mediation Skills- two-day introductory course leading to OCR accreditation
- Assertiveness
- Complaints
- Conflict management skills for HR
- Constructive conflict management for managers
- Contact officers training
- Training for Colleague Support Networks
- Managing bullying and harassment
- Investigator skills training
- Managing difficult behaviour, aggression and threats of violence
- Mediation diploma – OCR qualification in mediation practice
- Mediation and counselling skills in the workplace
- Phone rage
- Win-win negotiation

124

Consultancy Skills Training Ltd
Developing knowledge-based business through training and consultancy.
125

Elgood Effective Learning
Engaging materials, management games and business simulaitons to improve performance.
139

European Forum for Teamwork
Performance improvement, change management, teamwork training for managers and teams.
143

Gateshead College
High quality training and development. Customised to your particular needs.
150

Imparta Limited
Imparta build organisational capabilities in strategy sales and marketing.
163

Inspiration Resources
Tools and techniques for creativity and innovation.
167

Les Jones & Associates
Training and consultancy in management of change and creative management.
195

Management Improvements Ltd
Process improvement and re-engineering training for banks and insurance companies.
201

MLP Training
Sales training and management development, live courses and cds.
209

Morcamation Management & Training Consultants
Strategic business/marketing planning, quality management ISO000/TQM, managing change.
210

MRA International
The development of organisations and their people.
211

New Directions
Facilitating individual, team and organisation development. Profiling, mentoring, influencing skills.
214

Outward Bound Scotland
Management development, team building and challenge programmes using the outdoors.
221

Parity Training Ltd
Parity Training delivers bespoke and public scheduled training courses in technology, management and business skills, providing training for over 40,000 delegates a year. Parity's learning consultants increasingly blend traditional training methods with e-learning initiatives to provide integrated learning solutions that ensure return on investment and effective learning outcomes.
With training centres in Antrim, Belfast, Birmingham, Bristol, Edinburgh, Fleet, Leeds, London and Manchester, Parity offers nation-wide in person (classroom based) training and support. Additionally, Parity's managed services offering provides a range of options from simple vendor management to a full outsource training and development service.
Parity's long-term partnerships with leading bodies such as the Information Systems Examination Board, DSDM Consortium, Institute of Management, Outward Bound Trust, Association for Project Management, Microsoft and Lotus Corporation keeps Parity at the forefront of the industry, able to offer an unparalleled range of certified training leading to recognised qualifications. Parity's on-going commitment to delivering effective quality training is reflected in its ISO9001 certification. In 2003 Parity Training was awarded the Institued of IT Training's accolade of Training Company of the Year and Trainer of the Year.
Parity Training is part of Parity Group plc, the international IT consultancy and solutions group with 30 offices in the UK, mainland Europe and the USA.
For booking information or course details, call 0800 656 100, email training@parity.net or visit www.parity.net.
224

PTA Ltd
Production management and process improvement specialists working for manufacturing industries.
240

Scottish Centres
Four outdoor centres in Scotland suitable for outdoor management development.
254

Structured Training Ltd
Open and bespoke sales, management and customer service training courses.
267

The Winning Post
Provide training in bookkeeping, accounting and personal and business development.
285

Stress Management

Centre for Coaching
Stress management training consultancy with UK coverage.
108

Centre for Stress Management
Stress management training consultancy with UK coverage.
110

Facilities Staff Training
Training provider: Health, safety, food, hygeine. London and south-east.
146

John Unitt Associates
Career management, counselling, outplacement job search, stress, supervisory, customer care.
185

LMA Training & Development
Tailored courses in personal effectiveness and communication skills.
198

Parity Training Ltd
Parity Training delivers bespoke and public scheduled training courses in technology, management and business skills, providing training for over 40,000 delegates a year. Parity's learning consultants increasingly blend traditional training methods with e-learning initiatives to provide integrated learning solutions that ensure return on investment and effective learning outcomes.
With training centres in Antrim, Belfast, Birmingham, Bristol, Edinburgh, Fleet, Leeds, London and Manchester, Parity offers nation-wide in person (classroom based) training and support. Additionally, Parity's managed services offering provides a range of options from simple vendor management to a full outsource training and development service.
Parity's long-term partnerships with leading bodies such as the Information Systems Examination Board, DSDM Consortium, Institute of Management, Outward Bound Trust, Association for Project Management, Microsoft and Lotus Corporation keeps Parity at the forefront of the industry, able to offer an unparalleled range of certified training leading to recognised qualifications. Parity's on-going commitment to delivering effective quality training is reflected in its ISO9001 certification. In 2003 Parity Training was awarded the Instituted of IT Training's accolade of Training Company of the Year and Trainer of the Year.
Parity Training is part of Parity Group plc, the international IT consultancy and solutions group with 30 offices in the UK, mainland Europe and the USA.
For booking information or course details, call 0800 656 100, email training@parity.net or visit www.parity.net.
224

Psychology in Business
Consultancy and workshops for improving personal effectiveness and interpersonal skills.
239

The Royal Society for the Prevention of Accidents
Provision of health and safety training courses and consultancy services.
249

Time management

Arlington Associates
Management training group and one-to-one UK and abroad.
84

Austen Associates
Training consultancy in team working, quality, communication, presentation, time management.
89

Conflict Management Plus

Conflict Management Plus Ltd are national experts in providing solutions to workplace conflicts. We have over 10 years' experience providing accredited training and running a dispute resolution service. We work with full-time trainers and specialist consultants who bring expertise and experience from a range of public and private sector backgrounds. We have clear guidelines on equal opportunities, which run throughout our training design and delivery.

We can:

- Resolve workplace disputes between colleagues and teams
- Divert harassment and bullying cases away from disciplinaries/tribunals
- Carry out independent investigations
- Coach your teams or key players to improve performance
- Sample Training Programmes
- Certificate in Mediation Skills and Practice. A six-day course leading to OCR accreditation
- Core Mediation Skills- two-day introductory course leading to OCR accreditation
- Assertiveness
- Complaints
- Conflict management skills for HR
- Constructive conflict management for managers
- Contact officers training
- Training for Colleague Support Networks
- Managing bullying and harassment
- Investigator skills training
- Managing difficult behaviour, aggression and threats of violence
- Mediation diploma – OCR qualification in mediation practice
- Mediation and counselling skills in the workplace
- Phone rage
- Win-win negotiation

124

Intec Business Solutions (Scotland) Ltd

Experts in staff development including computing interpersonal and management skills.

174

KB Training

Training courses in time management, communication skills and self development.

186

Keytime Management Development

Time management training, Keytime planning systems and personal development programmes.

188

LMA Training & Development

Tailored courses in personal effectiveness and communication skills.

198

LPT Productions

Personal Profiles for ACL, time, behaviour, team building and empowerment.

199

Parity Training Ltd

Parity Training delivers bespoke and public scheduled training courses in technology, management and business skills, providing training for over 40,000 delegates a year. Parity's learning consultants increasingly blend traditional training methods with e-learning initiatives to provide integrated learning solutions that ensure return on investment and effective learning outcomes.

With training centres in Antrim, Belfast, Birmingham, Bristol, Edinburgh, Fleet, Leeds, London and Manchester, Parity offers nation-wide in person (classroom based) training and support. Additionally, Parity's managed services offering provides a range of options from simple vendor management to a full outsource training and development service.

Parity's long-term partnerships with leading bodies such as the Information Systems Examination Board, DSDM Consortium, Institute of Management, Outward Bound Trust, Association for Project Management, Microsoft and Lotus Corporation keeps Parity at the forefront of the industry, able to offer an unparalleled range of certified training leading to recognised qualifications. Parity's on-going commitment to delivering effective quality training is reflected in its ISO9001 certification. In 2003 Parity Training was awarded the Institued of IT Training's accolade of Training Company of the Year and Trainer of the Year.

Parity Training is part of Parity Group plc, the international IT consultancy and solutions group with 30 offices in the UK, mainland Europe and the USA.

For booking information or course details, call 0800 656 100, email training@parity.net or visit www.parity.net.

224

Peter Chapman & Associates
Leadership, teambuilding and management soft skills nationally and internationally.
230

St James's College
Keyboarding, computing, shorthand, public relations, marketing, advertising, personal development training.
264

TSL Training
Specialists in tailor-made in-house management development and people skills training.
279

Work-Life Balance

Centre for Coaching
Stress management training consultancy with UK coverage.
108

Centre for Stress Management
Stress management training consultancy with UK coverage.
110

Chris Sangster Development
Chris Sangster, author of 'Brilliant Future', facilitates related development events.
116

DMC Training Associates
Skills training and development including work-life balance.
134

Enhancement Resources Ltd
A company focused on realising the potential of people and organisations.
140

Jane Allan & Associates
Enjoyable training that adds pure value for salary for all.
181

Part 2.5

Sectors

Business Services

- Constructive conflict management for managers
- Contact officers training
- Training for Colleague Support Networks
- Managing bullying and harassment
- Investigator skills training
- Managing difficult behaviour, aggression and threats of violence
- Mediation diploma – OCR qualification in mediation practice
- Mediation and counselling skills in the workplace
- Phone rage
- Win-win negotiation

124

Coventry University

126

DHP Southern Ltd
Business skills training for the unemployed setting up in business.

133

Effective Personnel Development (EPD)
Provision of consultancy and training on quality and process improvement.

138

Ellerton Training Services

139

Fresh Tracks
Teams that play together work together. Contact us for more.

149

Fusion Training Ltd
Subsidiary company of the College of North West London.

149

Harris Associates
National innovative training and organisational development company based in Birmingham.

155

Insight Marketing and People Ltd
Providers of sales, marketing, interpersonal, finance and business development worldwide.

166

The Institute of Administrative Management
Established in 1915, the Institute of Administrative Management is the leading Professional Body for both practising and aspiring Administrative Managers.
We can work with you to produce an internationally recognised, in-house qualification, validate your training programmes or provide our training to your employees, in house or through our provider network.

Qualifications
IAM qualifications are targeted at Supervisors, Managers, and those who aspire to these positions. Student members can progress through the Certificate, Diploma and Advanced Diploma, and on to further qualifications (such as the IAM's dedicated degree in Administrative Management) and membership of other professional institutes

168

Institute of Professional Managers and Administrators
International membership for managers offering examinations and careers training courses.

173

IRS Conferences & Training
IRS offers 30 years excellence in employment law training.

178

J B Computer Management
JBCM provides HR organisation development programmes for individual and corporate.

182

JM Solutions Ltd
We specialise in middle and senior management career development.

183

Keenan Research Limited
Managing change; motivational interviewing; handling stress; assessing risk; psychometric testing.

187

Training Exchange Services
Producer of training software in management and practical topics.>2:

275

The Triforium
Competence based management development programmes approved by Institute of Management

278

Venture Wales

280

Visuals
Consultants specialising in audio - video and multi-media technology.

282

West Herts College

284

Construction

The Chartered Institute of Building
The Chartered Institute of Building is a modern professional body with more than 40,000 members. It has a Royal Charter to promote the science and practice of construction for public benefit, and has won recognition from Government, other professional bodies and the industry itself as being the central voice in construction. It provides expertise in all aspects of construction management, giving advice of a legal and technical nature, and sets standards in areas such as education, and health and safety.
In the past year, the Institute has made many valuable contributions to the development and improvement of the construction industry.
These have included the production and implementation of a New Education Framework and a Health and Safety Action Plan, the launch of the Third Edition of Practice for Project Management, our merger with the Architectural and Surveying Institute and numerous research and innovation projects.
The CIOB has also recently launched an 'Improving Site Conditions' campaign: 'Change in our Sites', in line with the aims and key issues for the industry that have been identified by the Strategic Forum for Construction.

112

City Business Seminars
Personalised finance training organisation.

118

Colchester Institute
College of further and higher education including services to business.

121

Fusion Training Ltd
Subsidiary company of the College of North West London.

149

The Institute of Administrative Management
Established in 1915, the Institute of Administrative Management is the leading Professional Body for both practising and aspiring Administrative Managers.
We can work with you to produce an internationally recognised, in-house qualification, validate your training programmes or provide our training to your employees, in house or through our provider network.

Qualifications
IAM qualifications are targeted at Supervisors, Managers, and those who aspire to these positions. Student members can progress through the Certificate, Diploma and Advanced Diploma, and on to further qualifications (such as the IAM's dedicated degree in Administrative Management) and membership of other professional institutes

168

The Institute of Clerks of Works of Great Britain
Qualification/membership for those engaged in site inspection for clients.

169

JTL
Training provider to the building engineering industry offering apprenticeships.

186

Mid Career College
Established in 1986, Mid Career College is one of the most comprehensive CPD providers.
207

Otley College
220

Oxford Brookes University
High quality training competitively priced for organisations and individuals.
222

Parity Training Ltd
Parity Training delivers bespoke and public scheduled training courses in technology, management and business skills, providing training for over 40,000 delegates a year. Parity's learning consultants increasingly blend traditional training methods with e-learning initiatives to provide integrated learning solutions that ensure return on investment and effective learning outcomes.
With training centres in Antrim, Belfast, Birmingham, Bristol, Edinburgh, Fleet, Leeds, London and Manchester, Parity offers nation-wide in person (classroom based) training and support. Additionally, Parity's managed services offering provides a range of options from simple vendor management to a full outsource training and development service.
Parity's long-term partnerships with leading bodies such as the Information Systems Examination Board, DSDM Consortium, Institute of Management, Outward Bound Trust, Association for Project Management, Microsoft and Lotus Corporation keeps Parity at the forefront of the industry, able to offer an unparalleled range of certified training leading to recognised qualifications. Parity's on-going commitment to delivering effective quality training is reflected in its ISO9001 certification. In 2003 Parity Training was awarded the Instituted of IT Training's accolade of Training Company of the Year and Trainer of the Year.
Parity Training is part of Parity Group plc, the international IT consultancy and solutions group with 30 offices in the UK, mainland Europe and the USA.
For booking information or course details, call 0800 656 100, email training@parity.net or visit www.parity.net.
224

Rycotewood College
We offer flexible professional and training services to employers.
250

SCOTS
We provide occupational safety consultancy and training services throughout Scotland.
254

WLT Safety Advisory Service
Health and safety training for all sectors of business.
285

World Microfilms
Audiovisual learning resources for architecture and design students. Catalogue.
287

WTI Training Group
Open courses, customised and on site training.
288

Education

act e-learning
Major learning supplier, e-learning consultancy, accreditation services and other training formats.
77

Anglo-Continental
English language training and consultancy for foreign staff and clients.
82

Avon Management Services
Management consultancy, sales and marketing consultancy and training.
89

British Institute of Technology & E-commerce
BITE is developing e-commerce professionals for all sectors of industry.
97

CiaTraining Ltd
Self teach ECDL training materials guides for computer software applications.

117

Colchester Institute
College of further and higher education including services to business.

121

Coleg Harlech WEA (North Wales)
Intensive ICT training in SMEs. Residential training and conference facilities.

121

Conflict Management Plus
Conflict Management Plus Ltd are national experts in providing solutions to workplace conflicts. We have over 10 years' experience providing accredited training and running a dispute resolution service. We work with full-time trainers and specialist consultants who bring expertise and experience from a range of public and private sector backgrounds. We have clear guidelines on equal opportunities, which run throughout our training design and delivery.
We can:

- Resolve workplace disputes between colleagues and teams
- Divert harassment and bullying cases away from disciplinaries/tribunals
- Carry out independent investigations
- Coach your teams or key players to improve performance
- Sample Training Programmes
- Certificate in Mediation Skills and Practice. A six-day course leading to OCR accreditation
- Core Mediation Skills- two-day introductory course leading to OCR accreditation
- Assertiveness
- Complaints
- Conflict management skills for HR
- Constructive conflict management for managers
- Contact officers training
- Training for Colleague Support Networks
- Managing bullying and harassment
- Investigator skills training
- Managing difficult behaviour, aggression and threats of violence
- Mediation diploma – OCR qualification in mediation practice
- Mediation and counselling skills in the workplace
- Phone rage
- Win-win negotiation

124

Derby College
Education and training provider for various qualifications at all levels.

131

Heriot-Watt University
A research-led technological university with outstanding success in academic-industrial collaboration.

157

Huntingdonshire Regional College
Professionals in education and training helping individuals to achieve.

161

The Institute of Administrative Management
Established in 1915, the Institute of Administrative Management is the leading Professional Body for both practising and aspiring Administrative Managers.
We can work with you to produce an internationally recognised, in-house qualification, validate your training programmes or provide our training to your employees, in house or through our provider network.

Qualifications
IAM qualifications are targeted at Supervisors, Managers, and those who aspire to these positions. Student members can progress through the Certificate, Diploma and Advanced Diploma, and on to further qualifications (such as the IAM's dedicated degree in Administrative Management) and membership of other professional institutes

168

The Institute of Manufacturing
Professional Institute. Qualifications in manufacturing, modem technology and systems.

172

i to i
Intensive TEFL training, voluntary teaching placements overseas.

179

JD Associates
NVQ Consultancy and Approved Assessment Centre.
182

University of Kent
188

King Alfred's College of Higher Education
College of Higher Education; Full time students: 3,000; Part time students: 2,000
189

The King Partnership Ltd
Support for management in education related activity, UK and overseas.
189

MagNotes Ltd
Visual thinking tools for creativity and innovation.
200

Manchester Open Learning
We design, produce and deliver educational programmes covering a wide range of subjects for all levels.
203

Mechatronics International Ltd
Manufacturers/suppliers - training equipment/systems for pneumatics, hydraulics, electro-control, PLCs.
205

The Media Centre@DVA Ltd
Full-service and production company. Video, Web, CD, DVD, Events.
205

Middlesex University
London-based international university championing social inclusion and innovative courses.
208

North Lindsey College
The largest further education college in North Lincolnshire.
216

Optimum Coaching Limited
Coaching Centre of Excellence, corporate coaching and coach training programmes.
219

Oxford Brookes University
High quality training competitively priced for organisations and individuals.
222

Parity Training Ltd
Parity Training delivers bespoke and public scheduled training courses in technology, management and business skills, providing training for over 40,000 delegates a year. Parity's learning consultants increasingly blend traditional training methods with e-learning initiatives to provide integrated learning solutions that ensure return on investment and effective learning outcomes.
With training centres in Antrim, Belfast, Birmingham, Bristol, Edinburgh, Fleet, Leeds, London and Manchester, Parity offers nation-wide in person (classroom based) training and support. Additionally, Parity's managed services offering provides a range of options from simple vendor management to a full outsource training and development service.
Parity's long-term partnerships with leading bodies such as the Information Systems Examination Board, DSDM Consortium, Institute of Management, Outward Bound Trust, Association for Project Management, Microsoft and Lotus Corporation keeps Parity at the forefront of the industry, able to offer an unparalleled range of certified training leading to recognised qualifications. Parity's on-going commitment to delivering effective quality training is reflected in its ISO9001 certification. In 2003 Parity Training was awarded the Instituted of IT Training's accolade of Training Company of the Year and Trainer of the Year.
Parity Training is part of Parity Group plc, the international IT consultancy and solutions group with 30 offices in the UK, mainland Europe and the USA. For booking information or course details, call 0800 656 100, email training@parity.net or visit www.parity.net.
224

Peter Dewrance E-Learning Ltd
Television, video, multimedia training, e-lerning design and consultancy services international.
230

PSNTO (Property Services National Training Organisation)
239

The Publishing Training Centre at Book House
Open and distance learning courses for book and journal publishers.
240

Sussex Publications
Video/audio learning resources: English, History, Music, Languages. Catalogue.

269

World Microfilms
Audiovisual learning resources for architecture and design students. Catalogue.

287

Energy

City of Wolverhampton College
Wolverhampton College offers a range of business and management courses.

119

Cranfield University
Postgraduate management, manufacturing, science and engineering plus continuous professional development.

127

Easy i Ltd
Developer of innovative and bespoke technology based training programs.

136

The Institute of Administrative Management
Established in 1915, the Institute of Administrative Management is the leading Professional Body for both practising and aspiring Administrative Managers.
We can work with you to produce an internationally recognised, in-house qualification, validate your training programmes or provide our training to your employees, in house or through our provider network.

Qualifications
IAM qualifications are targeted at Supervisors, Managers, and those who aspire to these positions. Student members can progress through the Certificate, Diploma and Advanced Diploma, and on to further qualifications (such as the IAM's dedicated degree in Administrative Management) and membership of other professional institutes

168

Jaybetec Consultants Ltd
Consultancy and training in electrical engineering and electrical safety.

181

Parity Training Ltd
Parity Training delivers bespoke and public scheduled training courses in technology, management and business skills, providing training for over 40,000 delegates a year. Parity's learning consultants increasingly blend traditional training methods with e-learning initiatives to provide integrated learning solutions that ensure return on investment and effective learning outcomes.
With training centres in Antrim, Belfast, Birmingham, Bristol, Edinburgh, Fleet, Leeds, London and Manchester, Parity offers nation-wide in person (classroom based) training and support. Additionally, Parity's managed services offering provides a range of options from simple vendor management to a full outsource training and development service.
Parity's long-term partnerships with leading bodies such as the Information Systems Examination Board, DSDM Consortium, Institute of Management, Outward Bound Trust, Association for Project Management, Microsoft and Lotus Corporation keeps Parity at the forefront of the industry, able to offer an unparalleled range of certified training leading to recognised qualifications. Parity's on-going commitment to delivering effective quality training is reflected in its ISO9001 certification. In 2003 Parity Training was awarded the Institued of IT Training's accolade of Training Company of the Year and Trainer of the Year.
Parity Training is part of Parity Group plc, the international IT consultancy and solutions group with 30 offices in the UK, mainland Europe and the USA.
For booking information or course details, call 0800 656 100, email training@parity.net or visit www.parity.net.

224

Financial services

Anglo-Continental
English language training and consultancy for foreign staff and clients.
82

The Association of Corporate Treasurers
The world's leading provider of treasury education and training.
86

AS Training
Tailor-made computer training and consultancy to suit your needs.
88

Easy i Ltd
Developer of innovative and bespoke technology based training programs.
136

Euromoney Training
Global market leader in banking and financial training.
143

The Institute of Administrative Management
Established in 1915, the Institute of Administrative Management is the leading Professional Body for both practising and aspiring Administrative Managers.
We can work with you to produce an internationally recognised, in-house qualification, validate your training programmes or provide our training to your employees, in house or through our provider network.

Qualifications
IAM qualifications are targeted at Supervisors, Managers, and those who aspire to these positions. Student members can progress through the Certificate, Diploma and Advanced Diploma, and on to further qualifications (such as the IAM's dedicated degree in Administrative Management) and membership of other professional institutes
168

Langham Management Consultants
Sales management, sales audits, business development processes, management development training.
192

Livingstone Communication
Selling skills for brokers and portfolio managers.
197

London Languages
London Languages specialises in B2B language training.
199

Parity Training Ltd
Parity Training delivers bespoke and public scheduled training courses in technology, management and business skills, providing training for over 40,000 delegates a year. Parity's learning consultants increasingly blend traditional training methods with e-learning initiatives to provide integrated learning solutions that ensure return on investment and effective learning outcomes.
With training centres in Antrim, Belfast, Birmingham, Bristol, Edinburgh, Fleet, Leeds, London and Manchester, Parity offers nation-wide in person (classroom based) training and support. Additionally, Parity's managed services offering provides a range of options from simple vendor management to a full outsource training and development service.
Parity's long-term partnerships with leading bodies such as the Information Systems Examination Board, DSDM Consortium, Institute of Management, Outward Bound Trust, Association for Project Management, Microsoft and Lotus Corporation keeps Parity at the forefront of the industry, able to offer an unparalleled range of certified training leading to recognised qualifications. Parity's on-going commitment to delivering effective quality training is reflected in its ISO9001 certification. In 2003 Parity Training was awarded the Instituted of IT Training's accolade of Training Company of the Year and Trainer of the Year.
Parity Training is part of Parity Group plc, the international IT consultancy and solutions group with 30 offices in the UK, mainland Europe and the USA.
For booking information or course details, call 0800 656 100, email training@parity.net or visit www.parity.net.
224

Food & drink

training methods with e-learning initiatives to provide integrated learning solutions that ensure return on investment and effective learning outcomes.

With training centres in Antrim, Belfast, Birmingham, Bristol, Edinburgh, Fleet, Leeds, London and Manchester, Parity offers nation-wide in person (classroom based) training and support. Additionally, Parity's managed services offering provides a range of options from simple vendor management to a full outsource training and development service.

Parity's long-term partnerships with leading bodies such as the Information Systems Examination Board, DSDM Consortium, Institute of Management, Outward Bound Trust, Association for Project Management, Microsoft and Lotus Corporation keeps Parity at the forefront of the industry, able to offer an unparalleled range of certified training leading to recognised qualifications. Parity's on-going commitment to delivering effective quality training is reflected in its ISO9001 certification. In 2003 Parity Training was awarded the Instiued of IT Training's accolade of Training Company of the Year and Trainer of the Year.

Parity Training is part of Parity Group plc, the international IT consultancy and solutions group with 30 offices in the UK, mainland Europe and the USA.

For booking information or course details, call 0800 656 100, email training@parity.net or visit www.parity.net.

224

Scottish Association of Master Bakers
Awarding body and training provider for craft baking vocational qualifications.

254

Scottish Bakery Training Council
National training organisation for the Scottish baking industry.

254

Voss Training International Ltd T/A VossTraining Services
National lift truck training provider- RTITB accredited- 24 hour service.

282

WLT Safety Advisory Service
Health and safety training for all sectors of business.

285

Woodcote Technical Services
Bespoke technical training for manufacturing companies including providing illustrated materials.

286

Health

City of Wolverhampton College
Wolverhampton College offers a range of business and management courses.

119

The Institute of Administrative Management
Established in 1915, the Institute of Administrative Management is the leading Professional Body for both practising and aspiring Administrative Managers.

We can work with you to produce an internationally recognised, in-house qualification, validate your training programmes or provide our training to your employees, in house or through our provider network.

Qualifications

IAM qualifications are targeted at Supervisors, Managers, and those who aspire to these positions. Student members can progress through the Certificate, Diploma and Advanced Diploma, and on to further qualifications (such as the IAM's dedicated degree in Administrative Management) and membership of other professional institutes

168

The Institute of Chiropodists and Podiatrists
Professional organisation for Chiropodists only. Further education insurance.

169

Medical Indemnity Register
First aid in-house training and first aid medical malpractice insurance.

205

Parity Training Ltd
Parity Training delivers bespoke and public scheduled training courses in technology, management and business skills, providing training for over 40,000 delegates a year. Parity's learning consultants increasingly blend traditional training methods with e-learning initiatives to provide integrated learning solutions that ensure return on investment and effective learning outcomes.
With training centres in Antrim, Belfast, Birmingham, Bristol, Edinburgh, Fleet, Leeds, London and Manchester, Parity offers nation-wide in person (classroom based) training and support. Additionally, Parity's managed services offering provides a range of options from simple vendor management to a full outsource training and development service.
Parity's long-term partnerships with leading bodies such as the Information Systems Examination Board, DSDM Consortium, Institute of Management, Outward Bound Trust, Association for Project Management, Microsoft and Lotus Corporation keeps Parity at the forefront of the industry, able to offer an unparalleled range of certified training leading to recognised qualifications. Parity's on-going commitment to delivering effective quality training is reflected in its ISO9001 certification. In 2003 Parity Training was awarded the Instituted of IT Training's accolade of Training Company of the Year and Trainer of the Year.
Parity Training is part of Parity Group plc, the international IT consultancy and solutions group with 30 offices in the UK, mainland Europe and the USA.
For booking information or course details, call 0800 656 100, email training@parity.net or visit www.parity.net.

224

The Psychotherapy Centre
Training, therapy, publications for understanding self, others and emotional problems.

239

The Retail Training Company
Expert trainers in all aspects of retail and distribution NVQs.

246

School of Postgraduate Medical & Dental Education
Experts in health- providing academic programmes to develop services.

253

Information & communication technologies

Association of British Professional Conference Organisers
ABPCO runs training courses on conferences-industry related topics.

85

British Association of Conference Destinations
BACD offers free assistance in sourcing conference and training venues.

96

British Institute of Technology & E-commerce
BITE is developing e-commerce professionals for all sectors of industry.

97

Business Language Services
French, German and Spanish for holidays and business via Internet.

102

CiaTraining Ltd
Self teach ECDL training materials guides for computer software applications.

117

Coleg Harlech WEA (North Wales)
Intensive ICT training in SMEs. Residential training and conference facilities.

121

Coventry University

126

Electrovision UK Ltd
500+ stocked products in skills, applications, and professional IT training.
138

Goldsmiths College
Study and practice of creative, cultural, cognitive and social processes.
152

Groom House Holdings Ltd
Behavioural training to produce lost for words customer satisfaction.
153

Host Computer Services Ltd
Residential training facility providing hardware training for computer service technicians.
159

Information Automation Ltd
Tailored training in CD-ROM, online, internet resources and searching.
165

The Institute of Administrative Management
Established in 1915, the Institute of Administrative Management is the leading Professional Body for both practising and aspiring Administrative Managers.
We can work with you to produce an internationally recognised, in-house qualification, validate your training programmes or provide our training to your employees, in house or through our provider network.

Qualifications
IAM qualifications are targeted at Supervisors, Managers, and those who aspire to these positions. Student members can progress through the Certificate, Diploma and Advanced Diploma, and on to further qualifications (such as the IAM's dedicated degree in Administrative Management) and membership of other professional institutes
168

Ken & Kate Back Ltd
Ken & Kate Back - 'Bringing People Skills to Business.'
187

Martin Uren
Provide training courses and seminars in broadcast technology and ICT.
203

Otley College
220

Parity Training Ltd
Parity Training delivers bespoke and public scheduled training courses in technology, management and business skills, providing training for over 40,000 delegates a year. Parity's learning consultants increasingly blend traditional training methods with e-learning initiatives to provide integrated learning solutions that ensure return on investment and effective learning outcomes.
With training centres in Antrim, Belfast, Birmingham, Bristol, Edinburgh, Fleet, Leeds, London and Manchester, Parity offers nation-wide in person (classroom based) training and support. Additionally, Parity's managed services offering provides a range of options from simple vendor management to a full outsource training and development service.
Parity's long-term partnerships with leading bodies such as the Information Systems Examination Board, DSDM Consortium, Institute of Management, Outward Bound Trust, Association for Project Management, Microsoft and Lotus Corporation keeps Parity at the forefront of the industry, able to offer an unparalleled range of certified training leading to recognised qualifications. Parity's on-going commitment to delivering effective quality training is reflected in its ISO9001 certification. In 2003 Parity Training was awarded the Institued of IT Training's accolade of Training Company of the Year and Trainer of the Year.
Parity Training is part of Parity Group plc, the international IT consultancy and solutions group with 30 offices in the UK, mainland Europe and the USA.
For booking information or course details, call 0800 656 100, email training@parity.net or visit www.parity.net.
224

Perth College
One of Scotland's leading providers of further and higher education.
229

Rycotewood College
We offer flexible professional and training services to employers.
250

SkilladvanceTraining
Unix, Oracle, Programming, Informix, Internet, security, scheduled and closed courses.
256

SkillSoft E M E A
Skillsoft offers e-learning in business and IT skills.
256

Leisure

Anglo-Continental
English language training and consultancy for foreign staff and clients.
82

The Institute of Administrative Management
Established in 1915, the Institute of Administrative Management is the leading Professional Body for both practising and aspiring Administrative Managers.
We can work with you to produce an internationally recognised, in-house qualification, validate your training programmes or provide our training to your employees, in house or through our provider network.

Qualifications
IAM qualifications are targeted at Supervisors, Managers, and those who aspire to these positions. Student members can progress through the Certificate, Diploma and Advanced Diploma, and on to further qualifications (such as the IAM's dedicated degree in Administrative Management) and membership of other professional institutes
168

Parity Training Ltd
Parity Training delivers bespoke and public scheduled training courses in technology, management and business skills, providing training for over 40,000 delegates a year. Parity's learning consultants increasingly blend traditional training methods with e-learning initiatives to provide integrated learning solutions that ensure return on investment and effective learning outcomes.
With training centres in Antrim, Belfast, Birmingham, Bristol, Edinburgh, Fleet, Leeds, London and Manchester, Parity offers nation-wide in person (classroom based) training and support. Additionally, Parity's managed services offering provides a range of options from simple vendor management to a full outsource training and development service.
Parity's long-term partnerships with leading bodies such as the Information Systems Examination Board, DSDM Consortium, Institute of Management, Outward Bound Trust, Association for Project Management, Microsoft and Lotus Corporation keeps Parity at the forefront of the industry, able to offer an unparalleled range of certified training leading to recognised qualifications. Parity's on-going commitment to delivering effective quality training is reflected in its ISO9001 certification. In 2003 Parity Training was awarded the Institued of IT Training's accolade of Training Company of the Year and Trainer of the Year.
Parity Training is part of Parity Group plc, the international IT consultancy and solutions group with 30 offices in the UK, mainland Europe and the USA.
For booking information or course details, call 0800 656 100, email training@parity.net or visit www.parity.net.
224

Stotts Correspondence College
Distance learning: locksmithing/calligraphy/fitness and nutrition/dressmaking correspondence courses.
265

Sussex Publications
Video/audio learning resources: English, History, Music, Languages. Catalogue.
269

West Herts College
284

World Microfilms
Audiovisual learning resources for architecture and design students. Catalogue.
287

Manufacturing & engineering

adlib
Providing professional, flexible, high quality business language training throughout Kent.
79

Aurora Business Development Ltd
International business and manufacturing educators, trainers and consultants.
89

Blyth Associates
Training in employment, contract, pensions, law and litigation support services.
92

Chamber Business Enterprises Ltd
Management Development Programmes (NVQ L2-L5) and Best Practice Management Benchmarking Service.
111

Chrysalis
Management consultancy experienced in organisational development, competence based management development.
117

COTU, Charter House 125

Coventry University 126

Cranfield University
Postgraduate management, manufacturing, science and engineering plus continuous professional development.
127

D J Neil Ltd
Design and delivery of in-house management training UK and overseas.
133

The Faraday Centre Ltd
Onshore, offshore and marine high voltage electrical power system training.
146

Health & Safety Services Ltd
Health, safety and fire training, consultancy support. Established 1985.
156

The IEE
Your people are your most precious asset – and with the right professional guidance, you can develop their skills and abilities. The result? Enhanced individual performance – plus measurable improvements to your bottom line.
The IEE (Institution of Electrical Engineers) is one of the UK's leaders in management and business training for professionals involved with electrical engineering, IT and electronic engineering. We offer an impressive portfolio of courses for newly qualified and experienced professionals, from careers and business skills through to effective management, negotiating, presentations, marketing – plus a wide range of more technical courses.
With over 130, 000 members worldwide, the IEE is a global organisation representing the interests of IT and electrical engineering professionals - though our courses are equally applicable to other industries and commercial sectors. Most of our programmes are held in London, though we can run them at your premises, for small or large groups.
For more information about how IEE management and business training can bring out the best in your people - and your organisation - call us on 01438 767237 or log on to www.iee.org.uk
162

Inplant Industrial Training
Coaching and support services for trainers of technical/production staff.
165

The Institute of Administrative Management
Established in 1915, the Institute of Administrative Management is the leading Professional Body for both practising and aspiring Administrative Managers.
We can work with you to produce an internationally recognised, in-house qualification, validate your training programmes or provide our training to your employees, in house or through our provider network.

Qualifications
IAM qualifications are targeted at Supervisors, Managers, and those who aspire to these positions. Student members can progress through the Certificate, Diploma and Advanced Diploma, and on to further qualifications (such as the IAM's dedicated degree in Administrative Management) and membership of other professional institutes
168

Statistics for Industry Ltd
Practical statistical courses/consultancy aimed at scientists/technologists in industry.

261

Structured Training Ltd
Open and bespoke sales, management and customer service training courses.

267

Trubody Training Associates
In-company courses in manufacturing systems, quality techniques and lean manufacturing.

279

Tullos Training Ltd
Providers of engineering skills training, modern apprenticeships and vocational qualifications.

279

Voss Training International Ltd T/A VossTraining Services
National lift truck training provider- RTITB accredited- 24 hour service.

282

Media

Goldsmiths College
Study and practice of creative, cultural, cognitive and social processes.

152

The Institute of Administrative Management
Established in 1915, the Institute of Administrative Management is the leading Professional Body for both practising and aspiring Administrative Managers. We can work with you to produce an internationally recognised, in-house qualification, validate your training programmes or provide our training to your employees, in house or through our providernetwork.

Qualifications
IAM qualifications are targeted at Supervisors, Managers, and those who aspire to these positions. Student members can progress through the Certificate, Diploma and Advanced Diploma, and on to further qualifications (such as the IAM's dedicated degree in Administrative Management) and membership of other professional institutes

168

Jaymedia
Media and presenter training provided by BBL trained personnel.

181

Martin Uren
Provide training courses and seminars in broadcast technology and ICT.

203

Parity Training Ltd
Parity Training delivers bespoke and public scheduled training courses in technology, management and business skills, providing training for over 40,000 delegates a year. Parity's learning consultants increasingly blend traditional training methods with e-learning initiatives to provide integrated learning solutions that ensure return on investment and effective learning outcomes.
With training centres in Antrim, Belfast, Birmingham, Bristol, Edinburgh, Fleet, Leeds, London and Manchester, Parity offers nation-wide in person (classroom based) training and support. Additionally, Parity's managed services offering provides a range of options from simple vendor management to a full outsource training and development service.
Parity's long-term partnerships with leading bodies such as the Information Systems Examination Board, DSDM Consortium, Institute of Management, Outward Bound Trust, Association for Project Management, Microsoft and Lotus Corporation keeps Parity at the forefront of the industry, able to offer an unparalleled range of certified training leading to recognised qualifications. Parity's on-going commitment to delivering effective quality training is reflected in its ISO9001 certification. In 2003 Parity Training was awarded the Instituted of IT Training's accolade of Training Company of the Year and Trainer of the Year.
Parity Training is part of Parity Group plc, the international IT consultancy and solutions group with 30 offices in the UK, mainland Europe and the USA. For booking information or course details, call 0800 656 100, email training@parity.net or visit www.parity.net.

224

Peter Dewrance E-Learning Ltd
Television, video, multimedia training, e-lerning design and consultancy services international.
230

West Herts College
284

Public sector

The Adams Consultancy Ltd
Specialists in work-life balance consultancy and training.
78

British Institute of Technology & E-commerce
BITE is developing e-commerce professionals for all sectors of industry.
97

Centre for Hazard & Risk Management
Post-graduate programme training in risk management security backcore OHES.
109

Centrex National Training Centre
110

Chamber Business Enterprises Ltd
Management Development Programmes (NVQ L2-L5) and Best Practice Management Benchmarking Service.
111

Cleaning Industry National Training Organisation
Government accredited employer-led strategic training and education organisation.
119

CMPS - Civil Service College Directorate
CMPS provides management development and training for the public sector.
120

Conference Search Ltd
Free venue finding service throughout the UK.
123

Conflict Management Plus
Conflict Management Plus Ltd are national experts in providing solutions to workplace conflicts. We have over 10 years' experience providing accredited training and running a dispute resolution service. We work with full-time trainers and specialist consultants who bring expertise and experience from a range of public and private sector backgrounds. We have clear guidelines on equal opportunities, which run throughout our training design and delivery.
We can:

- Resolve workplace disputes between colleagues and teams
- Divert harassment and bullying cases away from disciplinaries/tribunals
- Carry out independent investigations
- Coach your teams or key players to improve performance
- Sample Training Programmes
- Certificate in Mediation Skills and Practice. A six-day course leading to OCR accreditation
- Core Mediation Skills- two-day introductory course leading to OCR accreditation
- Assertiveness
- Complaints
- Conflict management skills for HR
- Constructive conflict management for managers
- Contact officers training
- Training for Colleague Support Networks
- Managing bullying and harassment
- Investigator skills training
- Managing difficult behaviour, aggression and threats of violence
- Mediation diploma – OCR qualification in mediation practice
- Mediation and counselling skills in the workplace
- Phone rage
- Win-win negotiation

124

David Barron Associates
Independent practitioners and trainers on employment, training and management development.
129

The Evaluation Partnership
We evaluate training courses, programmes and institutions, UK and Europe.
144

Facilities Staff Training
Training provider: Health, safety, food, hygeine. London and south-east.
146

The Institute of Administrative Management
Established in 1915, the Institute of Administrative Management is the leading Professional Body for both practising and aspiring Administrative Managers.
We can work with you to produce an internationally recognised, in-house qualification, validate your training programmes or provide our training to your employees, in house or through our provider network.

Qualifications
IAM qualifications are targeted at Supervisors, Managers, and those who aspire to these positions. Student members can progress through the Certificate, Diploma and Advanced Diploma, and on to further qualifications (such as the IAM's dedicated degree in Administrative Management) and membership of other professional institutes
168

Ken & Kate Back Ltd
Ken & Kate Back - 'Bringing People Skills to Business.'
187

OPD Diagnostic Solutions
Flexible tailormade solutions for improving business results through development workshops.
218

Parity Training Ltd
Parity Training delivers bespoke and public scheduled training courses in technology, management and business skills, providing training for over 40,000 delegates a year. Parity's learning consultants increasingly blend traditional training methods with e-learning initiatives to provide integrated learning solutions that ensure return on investment and effective learning outcomes.
With training centres in Antrim, Belfast, Birmingham, Bristol, Edinburgh, Fleet, Leeds, London and Manchester, Parity offers nation-wide in person (classroom based) training and support. Additionally, Parity's managed services offering provides a range of options from simple vendor management to a full outsource training and development service.
Parity's long-term partnerships with leading bodies such as the Information Systems Examination Board, DSDM Consortium, Institute of Management, Outward Bound Trust, Association for Project Management, Microsoft and Lotus Corporation keeps Parity at the forefront of the industry, able to offer an unparalleled range of certified training leading to recognised qualifications. Parity's on-going commitment to delivering effective quality training is reflected in its ISO9001 certification. In 2003 Parity Training was awarded the Instiued of IT Training's accolade of Training Company of the Year and Trainer of the Year.
Parity Training is part of Parity Group plc, the international IT consultancy and solutions group with 30 offices in the UK, mainland Europe and the USA.
For booking information or course details, call 0800 656 100, email training@parity.net or visit www.parity.net.
224

SkilladvanceTraining
Unix, Oracle, Programming, Informix, Internet, security, scheduled and closed courses.
256

South Nottingham College
Specialists in multi-media, printing, business, computing, management, TUC education, NVQs.
258

Staff Education & Development Centre
Staff education and development centre for the Royal Free Trust.
261

Trident Training Services
Specialises in tailor-made public relations training for individuals or groups.No:
278

Retailing

The Institute of Administrative Management
Established in 1915, the Institute of Administrative Management is the leading Professional Body for both practising and aspiring Administrative Managers.
We can work with you to produce an internationally recognised, in-house qualification, validate your training programmes or provide our training to your employees, in house or through our provider network.

Qualifications
IAM qualifications are targeted at Supervisors, Managers, and those who aspire to these positions. Student members can progress through the Certificate, Diploma and Advanced Diploma, and on to further qualifications (such as the IAM's dedicated degree in Administrative Management) and membership of other professional institutes

168

Ken & Kate Back Ltd
Ken & Kate Back - 'Bringing People Skills to Business.'

187

Manchester Business School

202

Parity Training Ltd
Parity Training delivers bespoke and public scheduled training courses in technology, management and business skills, providing training for over 40,000 delegates a year. Parity's learning consultants increasingly blend traditional training methods with e-learning initiatives to provide integrated learning solutions that ensure return on investment and effective learning outcomes.
With training centres in Antrim, Belfast, Birmingham, Bristol, Edinburgh, Fleet, Leeds, London and Manchester, Parity offers nation-wide in person (classroom based) training and support. Additionally, Parity's managed services offering provides a range of options from simple vendor management to a full outsource training and development service.
Parity's long-term partnerships with leading bodies such as the Information Systems Examination Board, DSDM Consortium, Institute of Management, Outward Bound Trust, Association for Project Management, Microsoft and Lotus Corporation keeps Parity at the forefront of the industry, able to offer an unparalleled range of certified training leading to recognised qualifications. Parity's on-going commitment to delivering effective quality training is reflected in its ISO9001 certification. In 2003 Parity Training was awarded the Instituted of IT Training's accolade of Training Company of the Year and Trainer of the Year.
Parity Training is part of Parity Group plc, the international IT consultancy and solutions group with 30 offices in the UK, mainland Europe and the USA.
For booking information or course details, call 0800 656 100, email training@parity.net or visit www.parity.net.

224

The Retail Training Company
Expert trainers in all aspects of retail and distribution NVQs.

246

The School of Management
Professional development at University of Surrey. Email wbl@surrey.ac.uk for details.

253

Transport & distribution

The Institute of Administrative Management
Established in 1915, the Institute of Administrative Management is the leading Professional Body for both practising and aspiring Administrative Managers.

We can work with you to produce an internationally recognised, in-house qualification, validate your training programmes or provide our training to your employees, in house or through our provider network.

Qualifications

IAM qualifications are targeted at Supervisors, Managers, and those who aspire to these positions. Student members can progress through the Certificate, Diploma and Advanced Diploma, and on to further qualifications (such as the IAM's dedicated degree in Administrative Management) and membership of other professional institutes

168

Odyssey Training Limited

IM and ISO accredited general and safety management training provider.

217

Parity Training Ltd

Parity Training delivers bespoke and public scheduled training courses in technology, management and business skills, providing training for over 40,000 delegates a year. Parity's learning consultants increasingly blend traditional training methods with e-learning initiatives to provide integrated learning solutions that ensure return on investment and effective learning outcomes.

With training centres in Antrim, Belfast, Birmingham, Bristol, Edinburgh, Fleet, Leeds, London and Manchester, Parity offers nation-wide in person (classroom based) training and support. Additionally, Parity's managed services offering provides a range of options from simple vendor management to a full outsource training and development service.

Parity's long-term partnerships with leading bodies such as the Information Systems Examination Board, DSDM Consortium, Institute of Management, Outward Bound Trust, Association for Project Management, Microsoft and Lotus Corporation keeps Parity at the forefront of the industry, able to offer an unparalleled range of certified training leading to recognised qualifications. Parity's on-going commitment to delivering effective quality training is reflected in its ISO9001 certification. In 2003 Parity Training was awarded the Institued of IT Training's accolade of Training Company of the Year and Trainer of the Year.

Parity Training is part of Parity Group plc, the international IT consultancy and solutions group with 30 offices in the UK, mainland Europe and the USA.

For booking information or course details, call 0800 656 100, email training@parity.net or visit www.parity.net.

224

Roadwise Safety Training

Advanced driver training. One or two day courses.

247

TTC Training Ltd

NVQ and other training from entry level to management.

279

Part 2.6

Trainer Support Services

Blended Learning

Angel Productions
Videos and training for a fairer, more productive workplace.
82

Enlightenment Productions
Award-winning multimedia CD-ROM, DVD, e-learning and training material producer.
141

Epic Group plc
E-learning market leader. 18 year trade record in public and private sectors.
141

IQdos Ltd
The leading specialists in online performance measurement and development solutions.
177

Parity Training Ltd
Parity Training delivers bespoke and public scheduled training courses in technology, management and business skills, providing training for over 40,000 delegates a year. Parity's learning consultants increasingly blend traditional training methods with e-learning initiatives to provide integrated learning solutions that ensure return on investment and effective learning outcomes.
With training centres in Antrim, Belfast, Birmingham, Bristol, Edinburgh, Fleet, Leeds, London and Manchester, Parity offers nation-wide in person (classroom based) training and support. Additionally, Parity's managed services offering provides a range of options from simple vendor management to a full outsource training and development service.
Parity's long-term partnerships with leading bodies such as the Information Systems Examination Board, DSDM Consortium, Institute of Management, Outward Bound Trust, Association for Project Management, Microsoft and Lotus Corporation keeps Parity at the forefront of the industry, able to offer an unparalleled range of certified training leading to recognised qualifications. Parity's on-going commitment to delivering effective quality training is reflected in its ISO9001 certification. In 2003 Parity Training was awarded the Instituted of IT Training's accolade of Training Company of the Year and Trainer of the Year.
Parity Training is part of Parity Group plc, the international IT consultancy and solutions group with 30 offices in the UK, mainland Europe and the USA.
For booking information or course details, call 0800 656 100, email training@parity.net or visit www.parity.net.
224

RRC Business Training
Providing businesses and individuals with top quality, innovative, professional training.
249

Scitech Educational Ltd
Blended learning, learning support, management and customer service resources.
253

Books & packages

ABG Professional Information
The definitive accountancy information source.
76

Audio-Forum – The Language Source
Self-study packs for over 100 languages. Beginners, Intermediate, Advanced. Catalogue.
88

BAB The Business Advisory Bureau Ltd
Publish successful guide to earning a living from independent consultancy.
90

Buckingham Tutors Publishing
Providers of ready to use training materials for trainers.
100

Business Education Publishers
Publishers of academic learning materials in paper and electronic format.
101

The Chartered Institute of Building
The Chartered Institute of Building is a modern professional body with more than 40,000 members. It has a Royal Charter to promote the science and practice of construction for public benefit, and has won recognition from Government, other professional bodies and the industry itself as being the central voice in construction. It provides expertise in all aspects of construction management, giving advice of a legal and technical nature, and sets standards in areas such as education, and health and safety.
In the past year, the Institute has made many valuable contributions to the development and improvement of the construction industry.
These have included the production and implementation of a New Education Framework and a Health and Safety Action Plan, the launch of the Third Edition of Practice for Project Management, our merger with the Architectural and Surveying Institute and numerous research and innovation projects. The CIOB has also recently launched an 'Improving Site Conditions' campaign: 'Change in our Sites', in line with the aims and key issues for the industry that have been identified by the Strategic Forum for Construction.
112

Chartered Institute of Bankers in Scotland
The professional body for the financial services sector.
114

Chrysalis
Management consultancy experienced in organisational development, competence based management development.
117

CiaTraining Ltd
Self teach ECDL training materials guides for computer software applications.
117

Cleaning Industry National Training Organisation
Government accredited employer-led strategic training and education organisation.
119

COTU, Charter House
125

Ellerton Training Services
139

Gower Publishing Ltd
Gower's looseleaf and hardback activity collections come with photocopying rights.
153

The IEE
Your people are your most precious asset – and with the right professional guidance, you can develop their skills and abilities. The result? Enhanced individual performance – plus measurable improvements to your bottom line.
The IEE (Institution of Electrical Engineers) is one of the UK's leaders in management and business training for professionals involved with electrical engineering, IT and electronic engineering. We offer an impressive portfolio of courses for newly qualified and experienced professionals, from careers and business skills through to effective management, negotiating, presentations, marketing – plus a wide range of more technical courses.
With over 130, 000 members worldwide, the IEE is a global organisation representing the interests of IT and electrical engineering professionals - though our courses are equally applicable to other industries and commercial sectors. Most of our programmes are held in London, though we can run them at your premises, for small or large groups.
For more information about how IEE management and business training can bring out the best in your people - and your organisation - call us on 01438 767237 or log on to www.iee.org.uk
162

The Institute of Administrative Management
Established in 1915, the Institute of Administrative Management is the leading Professional Body for both practising and aspiring Administrative Managers.
We can work with you to produce an internationally recognised, in-house qualification, validate your training programmes or provide our training to your employees, in house or through our provider network.

Qualifications
IAM qualifications are targeted at Supervisors, Managers, and those who aspire to these positions. Student members can progress through the Certificate, Diploma and Advanced Diploma, and on to further qualifications (such as the IAM's dedicated degree in Administrative Management) and membership of other professional institutes

168

The Institute of Food Science and Technology (UK)
Professional qualifying body for food scientists and technologists. Educational charity.

170

ISA 2001
Providers & Trainers in Health & Safety Management Systems.

178

i to i
Intensive TEFL training, voluntary teaching placements overseas.

179

John Cole Management Development
Publishes experiential exercises and organises management courses and team building.

184

Keenan Research Limited
Managing change; motivational interviewing; handling stress; assessing risk; psychometric testing.

187

KMA Productions
Quality Induction and safety training packages, editing, VHS/DVD duplication services.

191

Management Learning Resources Ltd
Direct marketing company distributing/producing management training and development materials.

201

Open Mind
5000 learning resources on all topics in all media.

218

Parity Training Ltd
Parity Training delivers bespoke and public scheduled training courses in technology, management and business skills, providing training for over 40,000 delegates a year. Parity's learning consultants increasingly blend traditional training methods with e-learning initiatives to provide integrated learning solutions that ensure return on investment and effective learning outcomes.
With training centres in Antrim, Belfast, Birmingham, Bristol, Edinburgh, Fleet, Leeds, London and Manchester, Parity offers nation-wide in person (classroom based) training and support. Additionally, Parity's managed services offering provides a range of options from simple vendor management to a full outsource training and development service.
Parity's long-term partnerships with leading bodies such as the Information Systems Examination Board, DSDM Consortium, Institute of Management, Outward Bound Trust, Association for Project Management, Microsoft and Lotus Corporation keeps Parity at the forefront of the industry, able to offer an unparalleled range of certified training leading to recognised qualifications. Parity's on-going commitment to delivering effective quality training is reflected in its ISO9001 certification. In 2003 Parity Training was awarded the Institued of IT Training's accolade of Training Company of the Year and Trainer of the Year.
Parity Training is part of Parity Group plc, the international IT consultancy and solutions group with 30 offices in the UK, mainland Europe and the USA. For booking information or course details, call 0800 656 100, email training@parity.net or visit www.parity.net.

224

The Pensions Management Institute
Professional body for those working in pensions and employee benefits.

227

Plain English Campaign
Plain English training - everyday, legal, medical and financial.

232

Retirement Education Services
Mid-life redundancy and retirement in-house or open courses and counselling.

246

Scitech Educational Ltd
Blended learning, learning support, management and customer service resources.

253

Stotts Correspondence College
Distance learning: locksmithing/calligraphy/fitness and nutrition/dressmaking correspondence courses.
265

Sussex Publications
Video/audio learning resources: English, History, Music, Languages. Catalogue.
269

Tony Wheeler Associates
Providers of a wide range of in-house courses and seminars.
273

TTC Training Ltd
NVQ and other training from entry level to management.
279

Competencies

Appleton-Hill
Trainer, assessor, internal verifier of NVQ advice and guidance.
84

British Institute of Non-DestructiveTesting
97

FT Knowledge
FT Knowledge is the world's leading provider of business education.
149

IQdos Ltd
The leading specialists in online performance measurement and development solutions.
177

Open Mind
5000 learning resources on all topics in all media.
218

Parity Training Ltd
Parity Training delivers bespoke and public scheduled training courses in technology, management and business skills, providing training for over 40,000 delegates a year. Parity's learning consultants increasingly blend traditional training methods with e-learning initiatives to provide integrated learning solutions that ensure return on investment and effective learning outcomes.
With training centres in Antrim, Belfast, Birmingham, Bristol, Edinburgh, Fleet, Leeds, London and Manchester, Parity offers nation-wide in person (classroom based) training and support. Additionally, Parity's managed services offering provides a range of options from simple vendor management to a full outsource training and development service.
Parity's long-term partnerships with leading bodies such as the Information Systems Examination Board, DSDM Consortium, Institute of Management, Outward Bound Trust, Association for Project Management, Microsoft and Lotus Corporation keeps Parity at the forefront of the industry, able to offer an unparalleled range of certified training leading to recognised qualifications. Parity's on-going commitment to delivering effective quality training is reflected in its ISO9001 certification. In 2003 Parity Training was awarded the Instituted of IT Training's accolade of Training Company of the Year and Trainer of the Year.
Parity Training is part of Parity Group plc, the international IT consultancy and solutions group with 30 offices in the UK, mainland Europe and the USA.
For booking information or course details, call 0800 656 100, email training@parity.net or visit www.parity.net.
224

Stairway Consultancy Ltd
Customer service and leadership consultancy and tailor-made training courses.
261

Telematica Ltd
E-learning infrastructure products and services including learning & content management systems.
271

Conference venues

Association of British Professional Conference Organisers
ABPCO runs training courses on conferences-industry related topics.
85

British Association of Conference Destinations
BACD offers free assistance in sourcing conference and training venues.
96

Business Development, University of Luton
Diverse range of services and practical training solutions for organisations.
101

The Chartered Institute of Building
The Chartered Institute of Building is a modern professional body with more than 40,000 members. It has a Royal Charter to promote the science and practice of construction for public benefit, and has won recognition from Government, other professional bodies and the industry itself as being the central voice in construction. It provides expertise in all aspects of construction management, giving advice of a legal and technical nature, and sets standards in areas such as education, and health and safety.
In the past year, the Institute has made many valuable contributions to the development and improvement of the construction industry. These have included the production and implementation of a New Education Framework and a Health and Safety Action Plan, the launch of the Third Edition of Practice for Project Management, our merger with the Architectural and Surveying Institute and numerous research and innovation projects. The CIOB has also recently launched an 'Improving Site Conditions' campaign: 'Change in our Sites', in line with the aims and key issues for the industry that have been identified by the Strategic Forum for Construction.
112

Confederation of Tourism, Hotel & Catering Management
Training in hotel, tourism, catering and travel agency management.
123

Conference Search Ltd
Free venue finding service throughout the UK.
123

De Vere Daresbury Park Hotel
Modern 4 star hotel, with a 'Wonderland' location, close to Daresbury Village, birthplace of author Lewis Carroll, famed for the 'Alice' books. Accessibility is second to none being situated at J11, M56, with direct access from M6, 30 minutes drive from Liverpool and Manchester City Centres and airports.
18 meeting room options for up to 300 people, 181 bedrooms and suites for up to 360 guests, Brasserie restaurant and cafe, bars, leisure club and beauty salon, free parking 400 cars, on-site AV technician and business centre.
The hotel offers you quality without compromise and is characterised by superb cuisine, superior service, and an excellent standard of accommodation and state of the art conferencing facilities.
Whatever the occasion, you will be looked after by a friendly, professional team, to ensure your satisfaction is guaranteed.
Call for a range of excellent value residential and day rate packages.
Hospitality Assured Meetings Accreditation & Investor in People. Part of De Vere Group plc.
132

High Trenhouse Management Centre
Exclusive use of exceptional, beautifully located venues for management events.
157

The Institute of Administrative Management
Established in 1915, the Institute of Administrative Management is the leading Professional Body for both practising and aspiring Administrative Managers.
We can work with you to produce an internationally recognised, in-house qualification, validate your training programmes or provide our training to your employees, in house or through our provider network.

Qualifications
IAM qualifications are targeted at Supervisors, Managers, and those who aspire to these positions. Student members can progress through the Certificate, Diploma and Advanced Diploma, and on to further qualifications (such as the IAM's dedicated degree in Administrative Management) and membership of other professional institutes
168

Corporate universities

Courses

ABG Professional Information
The definitive accountancy information source.
76

Anglo-Continental
English language training and consultancy for foreign staff and clients.
82

Brinsbury College
Brinsbury land-based training. The West Sussex College of the countryside.
95

Business Network Ltd
Business consultancy and training. Customer care, TQM, information technology, management.
102

Business Skills Agency
Business skills training: computer, management, sales, marketing, personal development.
103

The Business Training Group
A range of high-quality training to release your potential.
103

Cambridge International College
CIC conducts Diploma Programmes on a wide range of accounting, sales business, management and administration fields, as well as 'support' subjects like Business English & Letter Writing, Communications and Computers, one or more of which are often essential for Members' progress and success in their chosen careers.
All of CIC's Diploma Programmes are designed and written especially for career enhancement and development. The professional Diploma Programmes have proved outstandingly successful in achieving those objectives – as well as the goals and ambitions of the hundreds of thousands of Member who study with CIC.
As appropriate, Diploma Programmes start either from basic principles or with a revision of earlier studies, and then deal comprehensively with the important topics, with emphasis always on the practical application of what is taught.
105

Change Consultancy and Training
CCT specialises in human resources, organisational development and management skills.
111

The Chartered Institute of Building
The Chartered Institute of Building is a modern professional body with more than 40,000 members. It has a Royal Charter to promote the science and practice of construction for public benefit, and has won recognition from Government, other professional bodies and the industry itself as being the central voice in construction. It provides expertise in all aspects of construction management, giving advice of a legal and technical nature, and sets standards in areas such as education, and health and safety.
In the past year, the Institute has made many valuable contributions to the development and improvement of the construction industry. These have included the production and implementation of a New Education Framework and a Health and Safety Action Plan, the launch of the Third Edition of Practice for Project Management, our merger with the Architectural and Surveying Institute and numerous research and innovation projects. The CIOB has also recently launched an 'Improving Site Conditions' campaign: 'Change in our Sites', in line with the aims and key issues for the industry that have been identified by the Strategic Forum for Construction.
112

CIMA Mastercourses
CIMA Master courses, one day management training in management accounting and business management.
117

Computacenter Ltd
Computacenter offer complete IT training solutions delivering real business benefits.
122

Consultancy & Training Centre
Cost effective training providers in management, NVQs, computing, health, safety.
124

New Directions
Facilitating individual, team and organisation development. Profiling, mentoring, influencing skills.
214

School of Postgraduate Medical & Dental Education
Experts in health- providing academic programmes to develop services.
253

Skern Lodge Development Training
Practical programmes using the outdoors; exceptional staff, residential training centre.
255

Stephen M Hall & Associates Ltd
The management consultants that help your managers and business grow.
262

Tregalic (UK) Ltd
NVQ consultancy D32/33 D34/36 training support applications for approved centre.
277

Vetlink Information Services
281

E-learning

act e-learning
Major learning supplier, e-learning consultancy, accreditation services and other training formats.
77

Aris Education Ltd
Aris Education is a leading provider of blended training solutions.
84

Ashridge
An international business school delivering executive education, consulting and research.
85

Cascade Technology Ltd
Development of bespoke e-learning and software.
107

CIMA Mastercourses
CIMA Master courses, one day management training in management accounting and business management.
117

Computacenter Ltd
Computacenter offer complete IT training solutions delivering real business benefits.
122

Easy i Ltd
Developer of innovative and bespoke technology based training programs.
136

Electrovision UK Ltd
500+ stocked products in skills, applications, and professional IT training.
138

Enlightenment Productions
Award-winning multimedia CD-ROM, DVD, e-learning and training material producer.
141

Epic Group plc
E-learning market leader. 18 year trade record in public and private sectors.
141

Excel Communications (HRD) Ltd
Specialists in applying NLP to produce outstanding business results.
145

Huddersfield University Business School (HUBS)
HUBS - a collaborative learning community with a clear vocational emphasis.
160

IQdos Ltd
The leading specialists in online performance measurement and development solutions.
177

i to i
Intensive TEFL training, voluntary teaching placements overseas.
179

Mid & North Wales Training Group LtdT/A Myrick Training Services
Skills training, management training levels 3-5, general consultancy, short courses.
207

Multimedia Marketing.Com
We develop and deliver marketing education and training solutions.
211

Parity Training Ltd
Parity Training delivers bespoke and public scheduled training courses in technology, management and business skills, providing training for over 40,000 delegates a year. Parity's learning consultants increasingly blend traditional training methods with e-learning initiatives to provide integrated learning solutions that ensure return on investment and effective learning outcomes.
With training centres in Antrim, Belfast, Birmingham, Bristol, Edinburgh, Fleet, Leeds, London and Manchester, Parity offers nation-wide in person (classroom based) training and support. Additionally, Parity's managed services offering provides a range of options from simple vendor management to a full outsource training and development service.
Parity's long-term partnerships with leading bodies such as the Information Systems Examination Board, DSDM Consortium, Institute of Management, Outward Bound Trust, Association for Project Management, Microsoft and Lotus Corporation keeps Parity at the forefront of the industry, able to offer an unparalleled range of certified training leading to recognised qualifications. Parity's on-going commitment to delivering effective quality training is reflected in its ISO9001 certification. In 2003 Parity Training was awarded the Instited of IT Training's accolade of Training Company of the Year and Trainer of the Year.
Parity Training is part of Parity Group plc, the international IT consultancy and solutions group with 30 offices in the UK, mainland Europe and the USA.
For booking information or course details, call 0800 656 100, email training@parity.net or visit www.parity.net.
224

Peakdean Interactive
Needs analysis, training design, author training, research and development, evaluation.
226

Peter Dewrance E-Learning Ltd
Television, video, multimedia training, e-lerning design and consultancy services international.
230

PSNTO (Property Services National Training Organisation)
239

The Rapid Results College
RRC specialise in open, distance and e-learning solutions for qualifications.
244

Scitech Educational Ltd
Blended learning, learning support, management and customer service resources.
253

South Nottingham College
Specialists in multi-media, printing, business, computing, management, TUC education, NVQs.
258

Structured Training Ltd
Open and bespoke sales, management and customer service training courses.
267

University of Sunderland
267

Top Performance Communication Consultants
Consultancy and coaching in written communication and advanced presentation techniques.
273

Games, simulation & exercises

Aberdeen Business School
We provide high quality education training and consultancy programmes.
75

Elgood Effective Learning
Engaging materials, management games and business simulaitons to improve performance.
139

Gower Publishing Ltd
Gower's looseleaf and hardback activity collections come with photocopying rights.
153

Hall Marketing
Designer and provider of computer simulations for management training.
154

Management Learning Resources Ltd
Direct marketing company distributing/ producing management training and development materials.
201

Parity Training Ltd
Parity Training delivers bespoke and public scheduled training courses in technology, management and business skills, providing training for over 40,000 delegates a year. Parity's learning consultants increasingly blend traditional training methods with e-learning initiatives to provide integrated learning solutions that ensure return on investment and effective learning outcomes.
With training centres in Antrim, Belfast, Birmingham, Bristol, Edinburgh, Fleet, Leeds, London and Manchester, Parity offers nation-wide in person (classroom based) training and support. Additionally, Parity's managed services offering provides a range of options from simple vendor management to a full outsource training and development service.
Parity's long-term partnerships with leading bodies such as the Information Systems Examination Board, DSDM Consortium, Institute of Management, Outward Bound Trust, Association for Project Management, Microsoft and Lotus Corporation keeps Parity at the forefront of the industry, able to offer an unparalleled range of certified training leading to recognised qualifications. Parity's on-going commitment to delivering effective quality training is reflected in its ISO9001 certification. In 2003 Parity Training was awarded the Instiued of IT Training's accolade of Training Company of the Year and Trainer of the Year.
Parity Training is part of Parity Group plc, the international IT consultancy and solutions group with 30 offices in the UK, mainland Europe and the USA.
For booking information or course details, call 0800 656 100, email training@parity.net or visit www.parity.net.
224

Positive Images
Corporate workshops and individual coaching in image and personal impact.
234

Role Plays for Training
Suppliers of excellent professional role players.
249

Human capital audits

J B Computer Management
JBCM provides HR organisation development programmes for individual and corporate.
182

Mayo Learning International Ltd
Specialists in strategy, talent and career management and HR measurement.
204

Parity Training Ltd
Parity Training delivers bespoke and public scheduled training courses in technology, management and business skills, providing training for over 40,000 delegates a year. Parity's learning consultants increasingly blend traditional training methods with e-learning initiatives to provide integrated learning solutions that ensure return on investment and effective learning outcomes.
With training centres in Antrim, Belfast, Birmingham, Bristol, Edinburgh, Fleet, Leeds, London and Manchester, Parity offers nation-wide in person (classroom based) training and support.
Additionally, Parity's managed services offering provides a range of options from simple vendor management to a full outsource training and development service.
Parity's long-term partnerships with leading bodies such as the Information Systems Examination Board, DSDM Consortium, Institute of Management, Outward Bound Trust, Association for Project Management, Microsoft and Lotus Corporation keeps Parity at the forefront of the industry, able to offer an unparalleled range of certified training leading to recognised qualifications. Parity's on-going commitment to delivering effective quality training is reflected in its ISO9001 certification. In 2003 Parity Training was awarded the Instituted of IT Training's accolade of Training Company of the Year and Trainer of the Year.
Parity Training is part of Parity Group plc, the international IT consultancy and solutions group with 30 offices in the UK, mainland Europe and the USA.
For booking information or course details, call 0800 656 100, email training@parity.net or visit www.parity.net.

224

Performance Consulting Group
The management consultants that help your return on investment grow.

228

Stephen M Hall & Associates Ltd
The management consultants that help your managers and business grow.

262

Needs Analysis

Parity Training Ltd
Parity Training delivers bespoke and public scheduled training courses in technology, management and business skills, providing training for over 40,000 delegates a year. Parity's learning consultants increasingly blend traditional training methods with e-learning initiatives to provide integrated learning solutions that ensure return on investment and effective learning outcomes.
With training centres in Antrim, Belfast, Birmingham, Bristol, Edinburgh, Fleet, Leeds, London and Manchester, Parity offers nation-wide in person (classroom based) training and support.
Additionally, Parity's managed services offering provides a range of options from simple vendor management to a full outsource training and development service.
Parity's long-term partnerships with leading bodies such as the Information Systems Examination Board, DSDM Consortium, Institute of Management, Outward Bound Trust, Association for Project Management, Microsoft and Lotus Corporation keeps Parity at the forefront of the industry, able to offer an unparalleled range of certified training leading to recognised qualifications. Parity's on-going commitment to delivering effective quality training is reflected in its ISO9001 certification. In 2003 Parity Training was awarded the Instituted of IT Training's accolade of Training Company of the Year and Trainer of the Year.
Parity Training is part of Parity Group plc, the international IT consultancy and solutions group with 30 offices in the UK, mainland Europe and the USA.
For booking information or course details, call 0800 656 100, email training@parity.net or visit www.parity.net.

224

Science, Engineering and Manufacturing Technologies Alliance
The sector skills council for stem industries.

253

SkillSoft E M E A
Skillsoft offers e-learning in business and IT skills.

256

Outdoor learning

Abernethy Trust
Personal development, teambuilding and leadership programmes delivered through outdoor projects.
75

Catalyst Training & Development Ltd
Organisational and management development and sales and marketing training.
108

The Outdoor Trust
Successfully proven outdoor based courses tailored to meet client needs.
221

Outward Bound Scotland
Management development, team building and challenge programmes using the outdoors.
221

Pro-Active Learning
Tailored team, management, leadership and personal development courses and events.
236

Rob Kelly & Associates
Developing people in organisations to work effectively in teams.
247

Performance appraisal

CERT Consultancy & Training
Executive, management and project team development and facilitation.
110

The Institute of Administrative Management
Established in 1915, the Institute of Administrative Management is the leading Professional Body for both practising and aspiring Administrative Managers.
We can work with you to produce an internationally recognised, in-house qualification, validate your training programmes or provide our training to your employees, in house or through our provider network.

Qualifications
IAM qualifications are targeted at Supervisors, Managers, and those who aspire to these positions. Student members can progress through the Certificate, Diploma and Advanced Diploma, and on to further qualifications (such as the IAM's dedicated degree in Administrative Management) and membership of other professional institutes
168

Parity Training Ltd
Parity Training delivers bespoke and public scheduled training courses in technology, management and business skills, providing training for over 40,000 delegates a year. Parity's learning consultants increasingly blend traditional training methods with e-learning initiatives to provide integrated learning solutions that ensure return on investment and effective learning outcomes.
With training centres in Antrim, Belfast, Birmingham, Bristol, Edinburgh, Fleet, Leeds, London and Manchester, Parity offers nation-wide in person (classroom based) training and support. Additionally, Parity's managed services offering provides a range of options from simple vendor management to a full outsource training and development service.
Parity's long-term partnerships with leading bodies such as the Information Systems Examination Board, DSDM Consortium, Institute of Management, Outward Bound Trust, Association for Project Management, Microsoft and Lotus Corporation keeps Parity at the forefront of the industry, able to offer an unparalleled range of certified training leading to recognised qualifications. Parity's on-going commitment to delivering effective quality training is reflected in its ISO9001 certification. In 2003 Parity Training was awarded the Instituted of IT Training's accolade of Training Company of the Year and Trainer of the Year.
Parity Training is part of Parity Group plc, the international IT consultancy and solutions group with 30 offices in the UK, mainland Europe and the USA. For booking information or course details, call 0800 656 100, email training@parity.net or visit www.parity.net.
224

Peter Hyde Management Consulting
Facilitation and consultancy skills, change management, TNA, strategy, design, evaluation.
230

Telematica Ltd
E-learning infrastructure products and services including learning & content management systems.
271

Psychometric testing

Aberdeen Business School
We provide high quality education training and consultancy programmes.
75

John Unitt Associates
Career management, counselling, outplacement job search, stress, supervisory, customer care.
185

Livingsuccess.co.uk
Maximixing performance, facilitating change, increasing potential for business and individuals.
198

Organisation & Management Learning (OML) Associates Ltd
Dedicated to improving organisation performance through development of human talent.
220

Parity Training Ltd
Parity Training delivers bespoke and public scheduled training courses in technology, management and business skills, providing training for over 40,000 delegates a year. Parity's learning consultants increasingly blend traditional training methods with e-learning initiatives to provide integrated learning solutions that ensure return on investment and effective learning outcomes.
With training centres in Antrim, Belfast, Birmingham, Bristol, Edinburgh, Fleet, Leeds, London and Manchester, Parity offers nation-wide in person (classroom based) training and support. Additionally, Parity's managed services offering provides a range of options from simple vendor management to a full outsource training and development service.
Parity's long-term partnerships with leading bodies such as the Information Systems Examination Board, DSDM Consortium, Institute of Management, Outward Bound Trust, Association for Project Management, Microsoft and Lotus Corporation keeps Parity at the forefront of the industry, able to offer an unparalleled range of certified training leading to recognised qualifications. Parity's on-going commitment to delivering effective quality training is reflected in its ISO9001 certification. In 2003 Parity Training was awarded the Institued of IT Training's accolade of Training Company of the Year and Trainer of the Year.
Parity Training is part of Parity Group plc, the international IT consultancy and solutions group with 30 offices in the UK, mainland Europe and the USA.
For booking information or course details, call 0800 656 100, email training@parity.net or visit www.parity.net.
224

Training for trainers

Brinsbury College
Brinsbury land-based training. The West Sussex College of the countryside.
95

British Institute of Technology & E-commerce
BITE is developing e-commerce professionals for all sectors of industry.
97

Business Network Ltd
Business consultancy and training.
Customer care, TQM, information technology, management.
102

Cambridge International Study Centre, St Mary's College
Language Training for special purposes available at all levels.
105

Centre for Coaching
Stress management training consultancy with UK coverage.
108

Centre for Stress Management
Stress management training consultancy with UK coverage.
110

CMC Consultants
Facilitation and coaching developing strategic team capability for change leadership.
120

Comtech Associates
HRD, management, training and development, trainer training, organisational performance systems.
122

Consultancy & Training Centre
Cost effective training providers in management, NVQs, computing, health, safety.
124

Cullen Scholefield Group
Innovative consultancy specialising in training trainers and Human Resources people.
128

Developing People Associates
In company management skills development, Trainer training, IIP, Implementation consultancy.
131

Groom House Holdings Ltd
Behavioural training to produce lost for words customer satisfaction.
153

Harris Associates
National innovative training and organisational development company based in Birmingham.
155

Herefordshire College of Technology
HCT provides management, training and professional qualifications.
156

Heriot-Watt University
A research-led technological university with outstanding success in academic-industrial collaboration.
157

The IEE
Your people are your most precious asset – and with the right professional guidance, you can develop their skills and abilities. The result? Enhanced individual performance – plus measurable improvements to your bottom line.
The IEE (Institution of Electrical Engineers) is one of the UK's leaders in management and business training for professionals involved with electrical engineering, IT and electronic engineering. We offer an impressive portfolio of courses for newly qualified and experienced professionals, from careers and business skills through to effective management, negotiating, presentations, marketing – plus a wide range of more technical courses.
With over 130, 000 members worldwide, the IEE is a global organisation representing the interests of IT and electrical engineering professionals - though our courses are equally applicable to other industries and commercial sectors. Most of our programmes are held in London, though we can run them at your premises, for small or large groups.
For more information about how IEE management and business training can bring out the best in your people - and your organisation - call us on 01438 767237 or log on to www.iee.org.uk
162

JD Associates
NVQ Consultancy and Approved Assessment Centre.
182

JHP Training Ltd
Customised highly interactive training developed specifically for targeted business impact.
183

JRTS
Training of trainers, youth, sales, marketing for small companies.
186

KMA Productions
Quality Induction and safety training packages, editing, VHS/DVD duplication services.
191

LD AssociatesTraining Services
Provider of client specific management supervisory and trainer training programmes.
192

The Management Centre
Design and deliver quality training specifically tailored to industry needs.
200

Management Learning Resources Ltd
Direct marketing company distributing/producing management training and development materials.
201

MDA – Management Development Associates
Comprehensive range of in-house management supervisory and staff development programmes.
204

MODAS (Management & Organisation Development Advisory Service)
Human resources; Management development; Interpersonal skills; Training for trainers.
209

New Directions
Facilitating individual, team and organisation development. Profiling, mentoring, influencing skills.
214

The Nottingham Trent University
Range of one day courses including Assertiveness and Team Working.
217

The Oxford Group, Consulting and Training
Provide world-class training and consultancy – deliver solutions and measurable results.
222

Parity Training Ltd
Parity Training delivers bespoke and public scheduled training courses in technology, management and business skills, providing training for over 40,000 delegates a year. Parity's learning consultants increasingly blend traditional training methods with e-learning initiatives to provide integrated learning solutions that ensure return on investment and effective learning outcomes.
With training centres in Antrim, Belfast, Birmingham, Bristol, Edinburgh, Fleet, Leeds, London and Manchester, Parity offers nation-wide in person (classroom based) training and support. Additionally, Parity's managed services offering provides a range of options from simple vendor management to a full outsource training and development service.
Parity's long-term partnerships with leading bodies such as the Information Systems Examination Board, DSDM Consortium, Institute of Management, Outward Bound Trust, Association for Project Management, Microsoft and Lotus Corporation keeps Parity at the forefront of the industry, able to offer an unparalleled range of certified training leading to recognised qualifications. Parity's on-going commitment to delivering effective quality training is reflected in its ISO9001 certification. In 2003 Parity Training was awarded the Instituted of IT Training's accolade of Training Company of the Year and Trainer of the Year.
Parity Training is part of Parity Group plc, the international IT consultancy and solutions group with 30 offices in the UK, mainland Europe and the USA.
For booking information or course details, call 0800 656 100, email training@parity.net or visit www.parity.net.
224

Penny Walker
Learning enabling corporate social responsibility, environmental management and sustainable development.
226

Video

Part 2.7

Qualifications and Standards

Business excellence

Investors in People

ISO 9000

Management certificates

in line with the aims and key issues for the industry that have been identified by the Strategic Forum for Construction.
112

Consultancy & Training Centre
Cost effective training providers in management, NVQs, computing, health, safety.
124

Dearne Valley College
Business management and administration programmes and training including NVQs.
130

Derby College
Education and training provider for various qualifications at all levels.
131

University of East London
UEL offers courses at foundation, undergraduate and postgraduate degree level.
135

Elmwood Business Training
Elmwood Business Training provider of quality training courses and consultancies.
140

Equal Opportunities Consultancy Group
Consultancy and applied research services on equality and diversity issues.
141

Harris Associates
National innovative training and organisational development company based in Birmingham.
155

Herefordshire College of Technology
HCT provides management, training and professional qualifications.
156

Institute of Leadership & Management
Institute of Leadership & Management (ILM) offers membership services together with leadership and management qualifications. ILM is a professional body that supports national objectives to ensure the UK is able to develop leaders and managers of the future, with a particular focus on first line and middle levels. Offering qualifcations for managers and team leaders from Levels 2-5 of the national framework, ILM also supports individual and organisational development through endorsement, awards and learning resources. ILM is a subsidiary of the City & Guilds Group, the UK's largest provider of vocational qualifications.
We provide the following services:
Membership, Vocationally-Related Qualifications, S/NVQs, Management and team leader qualifications, Quality-Assured Awards, Open learning resources from levels 2-5 (Building Success at Level 2, ILM Super Series at Level 3 and The Universal Manager at Level 4/5), CD based assessment materials and management videos (Teams that Work and A Vision for Change).
171

The Institute of Management Specialists (IMS)
Professional membership body providing qualifications by exemption. Distance learning courses.
172

The Institute of Manufacturing
Professional Institute. Qualifications in manufacturing, modem technology and systems.
172

Invest Business Training Solutions
Invest offers training solutions to Hull and East Yorkshire Businesses.
177

Lancaster and Morecambe College
191

Liverpool John Moores University
197

Management and Technology Training
Specialists in HRD, customer service, QA, business skills, H & S, finance.
200

MDA – Management Development Associates
Comprehensive range of in-house management supervisory and staff development programmes.
204

MRA International
The development of organisations and their people.
211

Management diplomas

All of CIC's Diploma Programmes are designed and written especially for career enhancement and development. The professional Diploma Programmes have proved outstandingly successful in achieving those objectives – as well as the goals and ambitions of the hundreds of thousands of Member who study with CIC.
As appropriate, Diploma Programmes start either from basic principles or with a revision of earlier studies, and then deal comprehensively with the important topics, with emphasis always on the practical application of what is taught.

105

Change Consultancy and Training
CCT specialises in human resources, organisational development and management skills.

111

The Chartered Institute of Building
The Chartered Institute of Building is a modern professional body with more than 40,000 members. It has a Royal Charter to promote the science and practice of construction for public benefit, and has won recognition from Government, other professional bodies and the industry itself as being the central voice in construction. It provides expertise in all aspects of construction management, giving advice of a legal and technical nature, and sets standards in areas such as education, and health and safety.
In the past year, the Institute has made many valuable contributions to the development and improvement of the construction industry. These have included the production and implementation of a New Education Framework and a Health and Safety Action Plan, the launch of the Third Edition of Practice for Project Management, our merger with the Architectural and Surveying Institute and numerous research and innovation projects. The CIOB has also recently launched an 'Improving Site Conditions' campaign: 'Change in our Sites', in line with the aims and key issues for the industry that have been identified by the Strategic Forum for Construction.

112

The Chartered Institute of Purchasing & Supply
The leading provider of puchasing and supply chain management courses.

114

COTU, Charter House

125

Dearne Valley College
Business management and administration programmes and training including NVQs.

130

University of East London
UEL offers courses at foundation, undergraduate and postgraduate degree level.

135

European Language & Management Centre
Tailored management, communication and inter-cultural training to improve international effectiveness.

144

FT Knowledge
FT Knowledge is the world's leading provider of business education.

149

Herefordshire College of Technology
HCT provides management, training and professional qualifications.

156

The IEE
Your people are your most precious asset – and with the right professional guidance, you can develop their skills and abilities. The result? Enhanced individual performance – plus measurable improvements to your bottom line.
The IEE (Institution of Electrical Engineers) is one of the UK's leaders in management and business training for professionals involved with electrical engineering, IT and electronic engineering. We offer an impressive portfolio of courses for newly qualified and experienced professionals, from careers and business skills through to effective management, negotiating, presentations, marketing – plus a wide range of more technical courses.
With over 130, 000 members worldwide, the IEE is a global organisation representing the interests of IT and electrical engineering professionals - though our courses are equally applicable to other industries and commercial sectors. Most of our programmes are held in London, though we can run them at your premises, for small or large groups.
For more information about how IEE management and business training can bring out the best in your people - and your organisation - call us on 01438 767237 or log on to www.iee.org.uk

162

MBAs

NVQs

Amethyst Learning & Development
BESPOKE programmes group or individual, via consultancy training or mentoring.
82

Appleton-Hill
Trainer, assessor, internal verifier of NVQ advice and guidance.
84

Bracknell and Wokingham College
Wide range of business training and further education for adults.
94

British Institute of Technology & E-commerce
BITE is developing e-commerce professionals for all sectors of industry.
97

Broadland District Council - Training Services
Provide business and community development through training advice and guidance.
98

Bromley College Business School
Management development with programmes integrating diplomas and certificates with NVQ's.
99

Burnham Management Centre
Organisational and management training development consultancy. NVQs, IIP provision.
100

Business Skills & Services CILT
One-stop shop for all your business language needs.
103

Chamber Business Enterprises Ltd
Management Development Programmes (NVQ L2-L5) and Best Practice Management Benchmarking Service.
111

Change Consultancy and Training
CCT specialises in human resources, organisational development and management skills.
111

The Chartered Institute of Building
The Chartered Institute of Building is a modern professional body with more than 40,000 members. It has a Royal Charter to promote the science and practice of construction for public benefit, and has won recognition from Government, other professional bodies and the industry itself as being the central voice in construction. It provides expertise in all aspects of construction management, giving advice of a legal and technical nature, and sets standards in areas such as education, and health and safety.
In the past year, the Institute has made many valuable contributions to the development and improvement of the construction industry. These have included the production and implementation of a New Education Framework and a Health and Safety Action Plan, the launch of the Third Edition of Practice for Project Management, our merger with the Architectural and Surveying Institute and numerous research and innovation projects. The CIOB has also recently launched an 'Improving Site Conditions' campaign: 'Change in our Sites', in line with the aims and key issues for the industry that have been identified by the Strategic Forum for Construction.
112

Chrysalis
Management consultancy experienced in organisational development, competence based management development.
117

Cleaning Industry National Training Organisation
Government accredited employer-led strategic training and education organisation.
119

Crown College
Crown specialise in information technology, customer services, retail administrative management.
128

Dearne Valley College
Business management and administration programmes and training including NVQs.
130

Further Reading

Our wide range of training and development titles are available direct from Kogan Page or through good booksellers. Best selling titles include:

An A-Z of Training and Development
Michael Potts
£50 Hardback ISBN 0 7494 2563 6 1998
'This 320 page book will provide all the answers.' IT SKILLS
The essential reference resource for anyone involved in training and development. This bumper book provides advice, definitions, contact information and a wealth of detail on all the key topics affecting the world of training.

Accelerating Performance
Sunny Stout Rostron
£19.99 Paperback ISBN 0 7494 3642 5 2002
An inspirational guide which assesses the latest training techniques and explains their uses and impact.

Blended Learning
Kaye Thorne
£15.99 Paperback ISBN 0 7494 3901 7 2002
With blended learning firmly establishing itself in the training world, this excellent resource demonstrates through the use of case studies how the combination of e-learning and mainstream training and staff development techniques can work to achieve better results.

Building a Dynamic Team
Richard Y Chang
£11.99 Paperback ISBN 0 7494 1663 7 1995
This practical guidebook presents a proven, step-by-step, team-building model covering the process in a logical, systematic way.

The Coaching Handbook
Sara Thorpe and Jackie Clifford
£19.99 Paperback ISBN 0 7494 3810 X 2003
This definitive one-stop handbook offers everything you need to know in order benefit from the most popular and successful techniques in training. It offers a highly structured step-by-step approach through the use of case studies and easily accessible practical exercises.

Coaching and Mentoring
Eric Parsloe and Monika Wray
£16.99 Paperback ISBN 0 7494 3118 0 2000
Covering both the theory and practice of coaching and mentoring, this highly readable book demonstrates how important it is to relate theoretical models to specific situations in order to gain real practical benefits. Offering new insights and examples, it clearly demonstrates how recent research suggests that traditional methods need to be adjusted or, in some cases, abandoned in favour of the effective use of coaching and mentoring. This essential book provides a practical toolkit for such change.

The Diversity Training Handbook
Phil Clements and John Jones
£18.99 Paperback ISBN 0 7494 3722 7 2002
This timely new book provides a practical and sensible approach to dealing with the sensitive but vital issue of diversity. Providing clear guidelines, the book provides advice for dealing with a wide variety of issues. With information on designing diversity training and advice on appropriate techniques to help bring about attitudinal change the book offers proven practical advice.

The EQ Edge
Steven Stein and Howard Book
£12.99 Paperback ISBN 0 4947 3602 6 2001
This unique and compelling book offers insights and tools into the world of Emotional Intelligence and how it can improve success in the workplace.

Everything You Ever Needed to Know About Training
Kaye Thorne and David Mackey
Third Edition
£18.99 Paperback ISBN 0 7494 4048 1 2003
This comprehensive jargon-free guide to training covers everything. Ranging from designing, delivering and evaluating training the use (and misuse) of online training this best-seller integrates all aspects of training into a coherent programme. This is an ideal introductory guide for those new to training or wanting to develop their training skills, it also offers valuable advice for trainers on training as a business and going it alone.

The NVQ and GNVQ Assessor Handbook
Ros Ollin and Jenny Tucker
£18.99 Paperback ISBN 0 7494 2143 6 1997
This highly praised and popular book provides all the information, practical advice and background knowledge essential to anyone wishing to obtain the assessor internal verifier or APL (Accreditation of Prior Learning) awards. The user-friendly book offers clear guidelines on how to perform efficiently as an assessor.

Practical Facilitation
Christine Hogan
£19.99 Paperback ISBN 0 7494 3827 4 2003
This new toolkit, which is designed as a companion work to *Understanding Facilitation*, provides users with a range of both traditional techniques and new approaches, offering everything needed to develop and hone facilitation skills.

Solving Skills Shortages
Hilton Catt and Patricia Scudamore
Published in association with the Industrial Society.
£16.99 Paperback ISBN 0 7494 2055 3 1997
How to recruit and retain an excellent skills base.

The Theory and Practice of Training
Roger Buckley and Jim Caple
Fourth Edition
£25.00 Paperback ISBN 0 7494 3199 7 2000
This reliable, well-tested training resource has been updated to encompass not only traditional practices but to also explore the changes seen in training over the past five years. Including new sections on online training, developments in competency, benchmarking, learner attitudes and lifelong learning, this guide offer trainers, managers and IPD students alike an expert overview of the whole training environment.

Training with the Midas Touch
Richard Palmer
£18.99 Paperback ISBN 0 7494 3739 1 2002
Combining a sound theoretical framework with practical content on assessing and developing staff skill base this book provides a structured and practical guide to making the most of the human capital in any type of organisation. Packed with insightful case studies and a toolkit of training techniques this is an excellent resource book.

Understanding the Basics of Return on Investment in Training
Patricia Pulliam Phillips
£15.99 Paperback ISBN 0 7494 1872 9 2002
This expert introduction to a difficult subject demonstrates to staff and trainers the visible and the not-so-obvious benefits of investing in training. Giving detailed worked examples and dispelling significant myths this thought-provoking book will enable organisations to ensure best value for its training spend.

Understanding Facilitation
Christine Hogan
£19.99 Paperback ISBN 0 7494 3826 6 2002
A must-have book that clearly explains the theory and principle behind facilitation. It explores the development of facilitation in management, education, training and it's practice and provides definitions, models and discusses the use of technology, ethics and cross-cultural questions.

PRACTICAL TRAINER SERIES
This user-friendly series provides concise, practical advice on one particular training topic. Each title is presented in an accessible format, with many individual features including summaries, trainers tips, checklists and diagrams.

'Clear, informative, very practically oriented...'
The Training Officer

Analysing Competence
Shirley Fletcher
£16.99 Paperback ISBN 0 7494 2195 9 1997

Competence-based Assessment Techniques
Revised Second Edition
Shirley Fletcher
£16.99 Paperback ISBN 0 7494 3422 8 2000

Designing and Delivering Training for Groups
David Leigh
£16.99 Paperback ISBN 0 7494 2062 6 1996

Designing Competence-based Training
Shirley Fletcher
Second Edition
£16.99 Paperback ISBN 0 7494 2196 7 1997

Effective Feedback Skills
Second Edition
Tim Russell
£16.99 Paperback ISBN 0 7494 2569 5 1998

How to Design and Deliver Equal Opportunities Training
Judith Taylor and Helen Garrett
£16.99 Paperback ISBN 0 7494 0848 0 1993

Managing Training
Sunny Strout Rostron
£16.99 Paperback ISBN 0 7494 0838 3 1992

Training Needs Assessment
Robyn Peterson
Second Edition
£16.99 Paperback ISBN 0 7494 2568 7 1998

Validity Your Training
Tony Newby
£16.99 Paperback ISBN 0 7494 2568 7 1992

Index of Advertisers

Index of Featured Entries